公式 *TOEIC®*
Listening & Reading
問題集

8

一般財団法人 国際ビジネスコミュニケーション協会

ETS, the ETS logo, PROPELL, TOEIC and TOEIC BRIDGE are registered trademarks of
ETS, Princeton, New Jersey, USA, and used in Japan under license.
Portions are copyrighted by ETS and used with permission.

ETS, the ETS logo, PROPELL, TOEIC and TOEIC BRIDGE are registered trademarks of
ETS, Princeton, New Jersey, USA, and used in Japan under license. Portions are copyrighted by ETS and used with permission.

はじめに

本書は『公式 *TOEIC*® Listening & Reading 問題集』シリーズの第8弾です。2016年5月実施の公開テストから加わった新しい出題形式に対応し、実際と同じテスト形式で2回分の問題を掲載しています。*TOEIC*® Listening & Reading Test の受験準備にお使いください。

本シリーズの特長

- 問題は全て、ETSが実際のテストと同じプロセスで制作しています。
- サンプル問題とテスト2回分の問題(200問×2回、計400問)を掲載し、リスニングセクションは *TOEIC*®公式スピーカーによる音声が収録されています。
  - *実際のテストでは、担当スピーカーや発音の種類(どの国の発音か)の割合が変更される場合があります。
- 素点から参考スコア範囲が算出可能です。
- 正解を導くための詳しい解説の他、学習の助けとなる語注「Words & Phrases」(Part 3、4、6、7)や表現紹介のコーナー「Expressions」(Part 6、7)を掲載しています。

付属CD・特典の音声について

- CDは一般的なプレーヤーで再生できます。また、CDの音声をパソコンなどの機器に取り込んで再生することもできます。
- 『公式 *TOEIC*® Listening & Reading 問題集8』の特典として、TEST 1、2のリーディングセクションの以下の音声をダウンロードすることができます。問題に解答した後の学習用教材としてご活用ください。
  - 正解が入った問題音声(Part 5、6)
  - 文書の音声(Part 7)

音声ダウンロードの手順：　　*株式会社 Globee が提供するサービス abceed への会員登録(無料)が必要です。

1. パソコン・スマートフォンで音声ダウンロード用のサイトにアクセスします。
   (右の QR コードまたはブラウザから https://app.abceed.com/audio/iibc-officialprep へ)
2. 表示されたページから、abceed の新規会員登録を行います。既に会員の場合は、ログイン情報を入力して上記1. のサイトへアクセスします。
3. 上記1. のサイトにアクセス後、「公式 *TOEIC*® Listening & Reading 問題集8」の画像をクリックします。クリックすると、教材詳細画面へ遷移します。
4. スマートフォンの場合は、アプリ「abceed」の案内が出ますので、アプリからご利用ください。パソコンの場合は、教材詳細画面の「音声」のアイコンからご利用ください。
   - *音声は何度でもダウンロード・再生ができます。ダウンロードについてのお問い合わせは下記へ
     Eメール:support@globeejphelp.zendesk.com (お問い合わせ窓口の営業日：祝日を除く月〜金曜日)
   - *特典音声は、必ず一度 TEST 1、2 のリーディングセクションの問題に解答した後に、ご利用ください。詳しい使い方は、別冊『解答・解説』p.200 をご参照ください。

本書が、*TOEIC*® Listening & Reading Test の出題形式の理解と受験準備、そして皆さまの英語学習のお役に立つことを願っております。

2021年10月
一般財団法人 国際ビジネスコミュニケーション協会

目　次

＊解答用紙は112ページの後ろに綴じ込まれています。

別冊 『解答・解説』

- 解答・解説で使われている表記の説明
- 参考スコア範囲の算出方法
- 正解一覧
- 解答・解説
- CDトラック・特典音声ファイル　一覧表
- 音声を使った学習例の紹介

TOEIC® Listening & Reading Test について

TOEIC® Listening & Reading Test とは？

   TOEIC® Listening & Reading Test（以下、*TOEIC*® L&R）は、*TOEIC*® Programのテストの一つで、英語における Listening（聞く）と Reading（読む）の力を測定します。結果は合格・不合格ではなく、リスニングセクション5～495点、リーディングセクション5～495点、トータル10～990点のスコアで評価されます。スコアの基準は常に一定であり、 英語能力に変化がない限りスコアも一定に保たれます。知識・教養としての英語ではなく、オフィスや日常生活における英語によるコミュニケーション能力を幅広く測定するテストです。特定の文化を知らないと理解できない表現を排除しているので、誰もが公平に受けることができる「グローバルスタンダード」として活用されています。

問題形式

- リスニングセクション（約45分間・100問）とリーディングセクション（75分間・100問）から成り、約2時間で200問に解答します。
- テストは英文のみで構成されており、英文和訳や和文英訳といった設問はありません。
- マークシート方式の一斉客観テストです。
- リスニングセクションにおける発音は、米国・英国・カナダ・オーストラリアが使われています。

  ＊テスト中、問題用紙への書き込みは一切禁じられています。

リスニングセクション（約45分間）

パート	Part Name	パート名	問題数
1	Photographs	写真描写問題	6
2	Question-Response	応答問題	25
3	Conversations	会話問題	39
4	Talks	説明文問題	30

リーディングセクション（75分間）

パート	Part Name	パート名	問題数
5	Incomplete Sentences	短文穴埋め問題	30
6	Text Completion	長文穴埋め問題	16
7	• Single passages • Multiple passages	1つの文書 複数の文書	29 25

開発・運営団体について

   TOEIC® L&Rは、ETSによって開発・制作されています。ETSは、米国ニュージャージー州プリンストンに拠点を置き、*TOEIC*® ProgramやTOEFL、GRE（大学院入学共通試験）を含む約200のテストプログラムを開発している世界最大の非営利テスト開発機関です。

   日本における*TOEIC*® L&Rを含む*TOEIC*® Programの実施・運営は、一般財団法人 国際ビジネスコミュニケーション協会（IIBC）が行っています。IIBCは、公式教材の出版やグローバル人材育成など、「人と企業の国際化」の推進に貢献するための活動を展開しています。

本書の構成と使い方

本書は、本誌と別冊に分かれています。それぞれの主な内容は以下の通りです。

● 本誌 …… 「サンプル問題」「TEST 1」「TEST 2」「解答用紙」
● 別冊『解答・解説』…… 「参考スコア範囲の算出方法」「正解一覧」「解答・解説」「CDトラック・特典音声ファイル 一覧表」「音声を使った学習例の紹介」

本誌

サンプル問題（29問）[本誌p.8-27] 全パートから合計29問を掲載しています。 CD 1 02-10

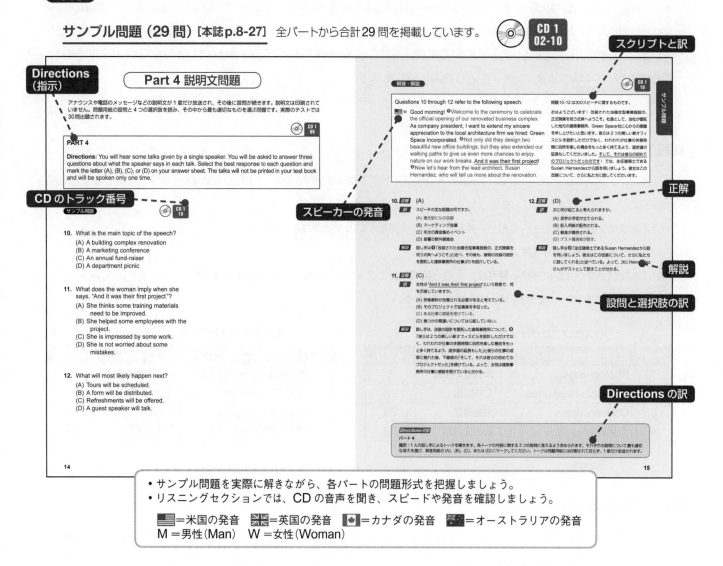

・ サンプル問題を実際に解きながら、各パートの問題形式を把握しましょう。
・ リスニングセクションでは、CDの音声を聞き、スピードや発音を確認しましょう。

🇺🇸=米国の発音　🇬🇧=英国の発音　🇨🇦=カナダの発音　🇦🇺=オーストラリアの発音
M＝男性（Man）　W＝女性（Woman）

TEST 1 [本誌p.29-70] CD 1 11-92　**TEST 2 [本誌p.71-111]** CD 2 01-82

TEST 1、2ともに、実際のテストと同じ、合計200問で構成されています。

リスニングセクション	100問	約45分間
リーディングセクション	100問	75分間

予行演習として時間を計って解答し、時間配分の参考にしたり、伸ばしたい分野や弱点を把握したり、使い方を工夫してみましょう。

別冊『解答・解説』

参考スコア範囲の算出方法 [別冊 p.4]

正解数を基に、参考スコア範囲を算出できます。

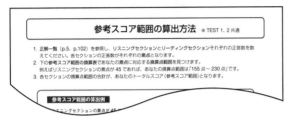

正解一覧 [TEST 1 ➡ 別冊 p.5　TEST 2 ➡ 別冊 p.102]

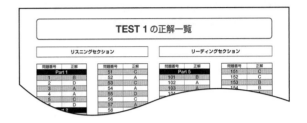

解答・解説 [TEST 1 ➡ 別冊 p.6-101　TEST 2 ➡ 別冊 p.103-197]

表記の説明は、別冊 p.2-3 をご覧ください。

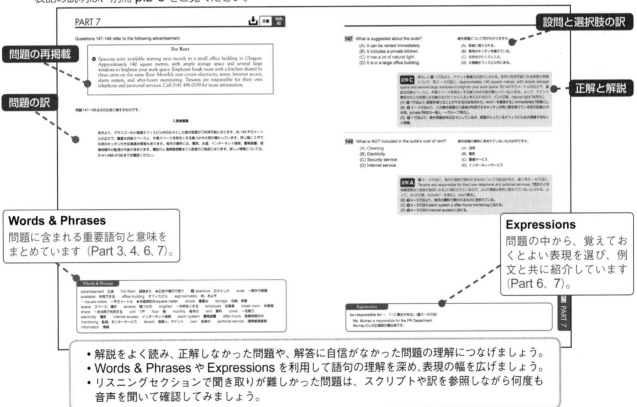

- 解説をよく読み、正解しなかった問題や、解答に自信がなかった問題の理解につなげましょう。
- Words & Phrases や Expressions を利用して語句の理解を深め、表現の幅を広げましょう。
- リスニングセクションで聞き取りが難しかった問題は、スクリプトや訳を参照しながら何度も音声を聞いて確認してみましょう。

CD トラック・特典音声ファイル 一覧表

[別冊 p.198-199]

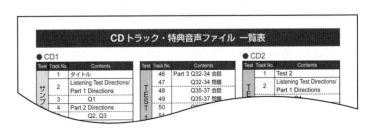

サンプル問題

TOEIC® Listening & Reading Test (以下、TOEIC® L&R) の問題形式を、サンプル問題を使ってご紹介します。サンプル問題は、全部で29問 (リスニングセクション12問、リーディングセクション17問) です。問題の番号は連番になっており、実際のテストの問題番号とは異なります。

TOEIC® L&Rのリスニングセクションは4つ、リーディングセクションは3つのパートに分かれています。問題用紙には、各パートの最初にDirectionsが英文で印刷されています。

Part 1 写真描写問題

1枚の写真について4つの短い説明文が1度だけ放送されます。説明文は印刷されていません。4つのうち写真を最も適切に描写しているものを選ぶ問題です。実際のテストでは6問出題されます。

CD 1 02

LISTENING TEST

In the Listening test, you will be asked to demonstrate how well you understand spoken English. The entire Listening test will last approximately 45 minutes. There are four parts, and directions are given for each part. You must mark your answers on the separate answer sheet. Do not write your answers in your test book.

PART 1

Directions: For each question in this part, you will hear four statements about a picture in your test book. When you hear the statements, you must select the one statement that best describes what you see in the picture. Then find the number of the question on your answer sheet and mark your answer. The statements will not be printed in your test book and will be spoken only one time.

Look at the example item below.

Now listen to the four statements.
(A) They're moving some furniture.
(B) They're entering a meeting room.
(C) They're sitting at a table.
(D) They're cleaning the carpet.

Statement (C), "They're sitting at a table," is the best description of the picture, so you should select answer (C) and mark it on your answer sheet.

Now Part 1 will begin.

＊上記枠内の網掛けの部分は音声のみで、問題用紙には印刷されていません。

1.

解答・解説

1. Look at the picture marked number 1 in your test book.

訳 問題用紙にある問題1の写真を見てください。

M (A) A truck is stopped at a stoplight.
(B) A man is using a gardening tool.
(C) Some people are sitting on the grass.
(D) Some workers are cutting down a tree.

(A) トラックが停止信号で止まっている。
(B) 男性が造園用具を使っている。
(C) 何人かの人々が芝生の上に座っている。
(D) 何人かの作業員が木を切り倒している。

正解 (B)

解説 gardeningは「造園、園芸」、toolは「用具、道具」という意味。

Directionsの訳

リスニングテスト

リスニングテストでは、話されている英語をどのくらいよく理解しているかが問われます。リスニングテストは全体で約45分間です。4つのパートがあり、各パートにおいて指示が与えられます。答えは、別紙の解答用紙にマークしてください。問題用紙に答えを書き込んではいけません。

パート1

指示: このパートの各設問では、問題用紙にある写真について、4つの説明文を聞きます。説明文を聞いて、写真の内容を最も適切に描写しているものを選んでください。そして解答用紙の該当する問題番号にあなたの答えをマークしてください。説明文は問題用紙には印刷されておらず、1度だけ放送されます。

下の例題を見てください。

では4つの説明文を聞きましょう。
(A) 彼らは家具を動かしている。
(B) 彼らは会議室に入ろうとしている。
(C) 彼らはテーブルのところに座っている。
(D) 彼らはカーペットを掃除している。

(C)の文、"They're sitting at a table"(彼らはテーブルのところに座っている)がこの写真を最も適切に描写しているので、(C)を選び、解答用紙にマークします。

ではパート1が始まります。

Part 2 応答問題

1つの質問または発言と、3つの応答がそれぞれ1度だけ放送されます。質問も応答も印刷されていません。質問に対して最も適切な応答を選ぶ問題です。実際のテストでは25問出題されます。

 CD 1 04

PART 2

Directions: You will hear a question or statement and three responses spoken in English. They will not be printed in your test book and will be spoken only one time. Select the best response to the question or statement and mark the letter (A), (B), or (C) on your answer sheet.

Now let us begin with question number 2.

＊上記枠内の網掛けの部分は音声のみで、問題用紙には印刷されていません。

サンプル問題　**CD 1 05**

2. Mark your answer on your answer sheet.
3. Mark your answer on your answer sheet.

解答・解説

2. W Are you taking an international or a domestic flight?

    M (A) I'd prefer a window seat.
        (B) He moved there last year.
        (C) I'm flying internationally.

訳 あなたは国際線の便に乗りますか、それとも国内線の便ですか。

    (A) 私は窓側の席を希望します。
    (B) 彼は昨年、そこへ引っ越しました。
    (C) 私は国際線の飛行機で行きます。

正解 (C)

解説 *A or B?* の形で、国際線と国内線のどちらの便に乗るのかを尋ねているのに対し、「国際線の飛行機で行く」と答えている(C)が正解。

3. M Shouldn't we hire more salespeople?

    W (A) I'm glad they went.
        (B) A higher profit.
        (C) Let's look at the budget.

訳 私たちはもっと販売員を雇った方がいいのではありませんか。

    (A) 私は、彼らが行ってうれしいです。
    (B) より高い利益です。
    (C) 予算を見てみましょう。

正解 (C)

解説 「もっと販売員を雇った方がいいのではないか」という男性の発言に対し、「予算を見てみよう」と雇用の検討を示唆している(C)が正解。

Directionsの訳

パート2

指示：英語による1つの質問または発言と、3つの応答を聞きます。それらは問題用紙には印刷されておらず、1度だけ放送されます。質問または発言に対して最も適切な応答を選び、解答用紙の (A)、(B)、または (C) にマークしてください。

では、問題2から始めましょう。

問題の訳

答えを解答用紙にマークしてください。

Part 3 会話問題

会話が1度だけ放送され、その後に設問が続きます。会話は印刷されていません。問題用紙の設問と4つの選択肢を読み、その中から最も適切なものを選ぶ問題です。実際のテストでは39問出題されます。

 CD 1 06

PART 3

Directions: You will hear some conversations between two or more people. You will be asked to answer three questions about what the speakers say in each conversation. Select the best response to each question and mark the letter (A), (B), (C), or (D) on your answer sheet. The conversations will not be printed in your test book and will be spoken only one time.

サンプル問題 CD 1 07

 CD 1 08

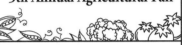

5th Annual Agricultural Fair

Day 1–Vegetables
Day 2–Dairy
Day 3–Flowers
Day 4–Baked goods

4. Which department is the man most likely calling?
   (A) Receiving
   (B) Catering
   (C) Security
   (D) Finance

5. Why does the man apologize?
   (A) He has forgotten his badge.
   (B) His report will be late.
   (C) A meeting location has to be changed.
   (D) A shipment must be delivered after business hours.

6. What does the woman say she will do?
   (A) Arrange additional workspace
   (B) Publish some materials
   (C) Issue a temporary pass
   (D) Ask staff to work late

7. Why do the speakers want to attend the fair?
   (A) To advertise a new business
   (B) To find local food suppliers
   (C) To sell some products
   (D) To participate in a workshop

8. What does the man say he has downloaded?
   (A) An electronic book
   (B) A mobile phone application
   (C) Some photographs
   (D) Some tickets

9. Look at the graphic. Which day do the speakers decide to attend the fair?
   (A) Day 1
   (B) Day 2
   (C) Day 3
   (D) Day 4

11

Questions 4 through 6 refer to the following conversation.　問題4-6 は次の会話に関するものです。

M　Hello. ❶I'm expecting an extra-large load of clothing racks delivered to the store today, and they'll arrive after business hours. Are you the person I should inform about this?

もしもし。今日お店に、洋服ラックの特大の積み荷が配達される予定ですが、それらは営業時間の後に着きます。あなたがこの件についてお知らせすべき方でしょうか。

W　Yes, ❷I'm head of Receiving. But ❸you're supposed to have suppliers make deliveries during business hours.

はい、私が荷受け部門の責任者です。でも、供給業者には、営業時間中に配達してもらうことになっているはずですが。

M　❹I'm sorry, but this is the only time the supplier can deliver them, and we need the racks for a fashion show we're having tomorrow.

申し訳ありません。しかし、これが、供給業者がそれらを配達できる唯一の時間帯で、私たちが明日開催するファッションショーには、そのラックが必要なんです。

W　I understand. ❺I'm not sure which of my staff members is working tonight, but I'll ask one of them to stay late to accept the delivery.

分かりました。今夜うちのスタッフの誰が勤務するのか定かではありませんが、配達物を受け取るために遅くまで残るよう、彼らのうちの1人に頼みます。

---

4. 正解 **(A)**

訳　男性はどの部署に電話をかけていると考えられますか。

(A) 荷受け
(B) ケータリング
(C) 警備
(D) 財務

解説　男性からの電話に応答した女性は❷「私が荷受け部門の責任者だ」と答え、その後も2人は配達物の受け取りについて話をしている。

5. 正解 **(D)**

訳　男性はなぜ謝罪していますか。

(A) 自分のバッジを忘れたから。
(B) 報告書が遅れるから。
(C) 会議の場所が変更されなければならないから。
(D) 荷物が営業時間の後に配達されざるを得ないから。

解説　❶「積み荷が配達される予定だが、それらは営業時間の後に着く」という男性の報告に対し、女性が❸「供給業者には、営業時間中に配達してもらうことになっているはず」と指摘している。それに対して男性は❹で、「申し訳ない」と謝罪後「これが、供給業者がそれらを配達できる唯一の時間帯で、私たちが明日開催するファッションショーには、そのラックが必要だ」と事情を説明している。よって、正解は(D)。

6. 正解 **(D)**

訳　女性は何をすると言っていますか。

(A) 追加の作業スペースを手配する。
(B) 資料を公表する。
(C) 臨時の通行証を発行する。
(D) スタッフに遅くまで勤務するよう頼む。

解説　女性は❺「今夜うちのスタッフの誰が勤務するのか定かではないが、配達物を受け取るために遅くまで残るよう、彼らのうちの1人に頼む」と述べている。stay lateをwork late「遅くまで勤務する」と表した(D)が正解。

Directionsの訳

パート3

指示：2人あるいはそれ以上の人々の会話を聞きます。各会話の内容に関する3つの設問に答えるよう求められます。それぞれの設問について最も適切な答えを選び、解答用紙の (A)、(B)、(C)、または (D) にマークしてください。会話は問題用紙には印刷されておらず、1度だけ放送されます。

Questions 7 through 9 refer to the following conversation and schedule.

問題7-9は次の会話と予定表に関するものです。

🇺🇸 W Pedro, ❶I know we're still looking for local fresh food suppliers for our new restaurant. We should check out the Agricultural Fair next month.

Pedro、私たちはまだ、うちの新しいレストランのために、地元の生鮮食品の供給業者を探しているわよね。来月の農業フェアを見てみるべきだわ。

🇨🇦 M That's a good idea. It's a major event, so many local farmers will be there. ❷I downloaded the fair's mobile phone application. The app has a lot of helpful information, including a schedule. Which day do you think we should go?

それは良い考えだね。大きなイベントだから、多数の地元の農業経営者たちがそこにいるだろう。僕はフェアの携帯電話用アプリをダウンロードしたよ。このアプリには、予定表を含め、役立つ情報がたくさんあるんだ。僕たちはどの日に行くべきだと思う？

🇺🇸 W Well, it looks like they'll have dairy vendors on the second day.

そうね、乳製品の販売業者は2日目にいるみたいね。

🇨🇦 M Hmm, I just contacted a dairy company that might work for us. ❸We really need a vegetable supplier though…

うーん、僕はうちに合いそうな乳製品会社に連絡を取ったばかりなんだ。僕たちには野菜の供給業者はぜひとも必要だけど…。

🇺🇸 W Oh, OK. ❹They have a day for showcasing vegetable farmers. Let's go then.

ああ、分かったわ。野菜農家の出展日があるわ。そのときに行きましょう。

---

7. 正解 **(B)**

訳 なぜ話し手たちはフェアに行きたいと思っていますか。

(A) 新しい店を宣伝するため。
(B) 地元の食品供給業者を見つけるため。
(C) 製品を販売するため。
(D) 講習会に参加するため。

解説 女性は❶「私たちはまだ、うちの新しいレストランのために、地元の生鮮食品の供給業者を探している。来月の農業フェアを見てみるべきだ」と提案し、男性もそれに同意している。よって、(B)が適切。

8. 正解 **(B)**

訳 男性は何をダウンロードしたと言っていますか。

(A) 電子書籍
(B) 携帯電話用アプリ
(C) 数枚の写真
(D) 数枚のチケット

解説 男性は❷「僕はフェアの携帯電話用アプリをダウンロードした」と述べている。

9. 正解 **(A)**

訳 図を見てください。話し手たちはどの日にフェアへ行くことに決めますか。

(A) 1日目
(B) 2日目
(C) 3日目
(D) 4日目

解説 ❸「僕たちには野菜の供給業者がぜひとも必要だ」という男性の発言に対し、女性は❹「野菜農家の出展日がある。そのときに行こう」と提案している。予定表から、野菜農家が集まる日は1日目だと分かる。予定表のbaked goodsはクッキーやパンなどのオーブンで焼いた食品を指す。

図の訳

第5回　年次農業フェア
1日目 — 野菜
2日目 — 乳製品
3日目 — 花
4日目 — パン・焼き菓子

Part 4 説明文問題

アナウンスや電話のメッセージなどの説明文が1度だけ放送され、その後に設問が続きます。説明文は印刷されていません。問題用紙の設問と4つの選択肢を読み、その中から最も適切なものを選ぶ問題です。実際のテストでは30問出題されます。

PART 4

Directions: You will hear some talks given by a single speaker. You will be asked to answer three questions about what the speaker says in each talk. Select the best response to each question and mark the letter (A), (B), (C), or (D) on your answer sheet. The talks will not be printed in your test book and will be spoken only one time.

サンプル問題

10. What is the main topic of the speech?
    (A) A building complex renovation
    (B) A marketing conference
    (C) An annual fund-raiser
    (D) A department picnic

11. What does the woman imply when she says, "And it was their first project"?
    (A) She thinks some training materials need to be improved.
    (B) She helped some employees with the project.
    (C) She is impressed by some work.
    (D) She is not worried about some mistakes.

12. What will most likely happen next?
    (A) Tours will be scheduled.
    (B) A form will be distributed.
    (C) Refreshments will be offered.
    (D) A guest speaker will talk.

Questions 10 through 12 refer to the following speech.

🇺🇸 w Good morning! ❶Welcome to the ceremony to celebrate the official opening of our renovated business complex. As company president, I want to extend my sincere appreciation to the local architecture firm we hired: Green Space Incorporated. ❷Not only did they design two beautiful new office buildings, but they also extended our walking paths to give us even more chances to enjoy nature on our work breaks. And it was their first project! ❸Now let's hear from the lead architect, Susan Hernandez, who will tell us more about the renovation.

問題 10-12 は次のスピーチに関するものです。

おはようございます！ 改装された当複合型事業施設の、正式開業を祝う式典へようこそ。社長として、当社が委託した地元の建築事務所、Green Space 社に心からの感謝を申し上げたいと思います。彼らは 2 つの美しい新オフィスビルを設計しただけでなく、われわれが仕事の休憩時間に自然を楽しむ機会をもっと多く持てるよう、遊歩道の延長もしてくださいました。そして、それは彼らの初めてのプロジェクトだったのです！ では、主任建築士である Susan Hernandez から話を伺いましょう。彼女はこの改装について、さらに私たちに話してくださいます。

10. 正解 **(A)**

訳 スピーチの主な話題は何ですか。

(A) 複合型ビルの改装
(B) マーケティング会議
(C) 年次の資金集めイベント
(D) 部署の野外親睦会

解説 話し手は❶「改装された当複合型事業施設の、正式開業を祝う式典へようこそ」と述べ、その後も、建物の改装の設計を委託した建築事務所の仕事ぶりを紹介している。

11. 正解 **(C)**

訳 女性は "And it was their first project" という発言で、何を示唆していますか。

(A) 研修資料が改善される必要があると考えている。
(B) そのプロジェクトで従業員を手伝った。
(C) ある仕事に感銘を受けている。
(D) 幾つかの間違いについては心配していない。

解説 話し手は、改装の設計を委託した建築事務所について、❷「彼らは 2 つの美しい新オフィスビルを設計しただけでなく、われわれが仕事の休憩時間に自然を楽しむ機会をもっと多く持てるよう、遊歩道の延長もした」と彼らの仕事の成果に触れた後、下線部の「そして、それは彼らの初めてのプロジェクトだった」を続けている。よって、女性は建築事務所の仕事に感銘を受けていると分かる。

12. 正解 **(D)**

訳 次に何が起こると考えられますか。

(A) 見学の予定が立てられる。
(B) 記入用紙が配布される。
(C) 軽食が提供される。
(D) ゲスト講演者が話す。

解説 話し手は❸「主任建築士である Susan Hernandez から話を伺いましょう。彼女はこの改装について、さらに私たちに話してくれる」と述べている。よって、次に Hernandez さんがゲストとして話すことが分かる。

Directions の訳

パート4

指示：1 人の話し手によるトークを聞きます。各トークの内容に関する 3 つの設問に答えるよう求められます。それぞれの設問について最も適切な答えを選び、解答用紙の (A)、(B)、(C)、または (D) にマークしてください。トークは問題用紙には印刷されておらず、1 度だけ放送されます。

ここからはリーディングセクションです。
実際のテストでは、リスニングセクションの終わりに"This is the end of the Listening test. Turn to Part 5 in your test book."(これでリスニングテストは終了です。問題用紙のパート5に進んでください。)というアナウンスがありますので、それが聞こえたらリーディングセクションの解答を始めます。

Part 5 短文穴埋め問題

4つの選択肢の中から最も適切なものを選び、不完全な文を完成させる問題です。実際のテストでは30問出題されます。

READING TEST

In the Reading test, you will read a variety of texts and answer several different types of reading comprehension questions. The entire Reading test will last 75 minutes. There are three parts, and directions are given for each part. You are encouraged to answer as many questions as possible within the time allowed.

You must mark your answers on the separate answer sheet. Do not write your answers in your test book.

PART 5

Directions: A word or phrase is missing in each of the sentences below. Four answer choices are given below each sentence. Select the best answer to complete the sentence. Then mark the letter (A), (B), (C), or (D) on your answer sheet.

サンプル問題

13. Before ------- with the recruiter, applicants should sign in at the personnel department's reception desk.
    (A) meets
    (B) meeting
    (C) to meet
    (D) was met

14. Stefano Linen Company suggests requesting a small fabric ------- before placing your final order.
    (A) bonus
    (B) sample
    (C) feature
    (D) model

13. **正解** **(B)**

訳 採用担当者と会う前に、応募者の方々は人事部の受付で署名して到着を記録してください。

(A) 動詞の三人称単数現在形
(B) 動名詞
(C) to不定詞
(D) 受動態の過去形

解説 選択肢は全て動詞meet「会う」の変化した形。文頭からカンマまでの部分に主語と動詞がないため、Beforeは前置詞と考えられる。前置詞に続く空所には名詞の働きをする語句が入るので、動名詞の (B) meeting が適切である。sign in「署名して到着を記録する」。

14. **正解** **(B)**

訳 Stefanoリネン社は、お客さまが最終的な注文をなさる前に、小さな布地見本をご要望になることをお勧めしています。

(A) 特別手当
(B) 見本
(C) 特徴
(D) 模型

解説 選択肢は全て名詞。空所の後ろは「お客さまが最終的な注文をする前に」という意味。(B) sample「見本」を空所に入れると small fabric sample「小さな布地見本」となり、注文前に要望するものとして適切で、意味が通る。

Directionsの訳

リーディングテスト

リーディングテストでは、さまざまな文章を読んで、読解力を測る何種類かの問題に答えます。リーディングテストは全体で75分間です。3つのパートがあり、各パートにおいて指示が与えられます。制限時間内に、できるだけ多くの設問に答えてください。

答えは、別紙の解答用紙にマークしてください。問題用紙に答えを書き込んではいけません。

パート5

指示：以下の各文において語や句が抜けています。各文の下には選択肢が4つ与えられています。文を完成させるのに最も適切な答えを選びます。そして解答用紙の (A)、(B)、(C)、または (D) にマークしてください。

Part 6 長文穴埋め問題

4つの選択肢の中から最も適切なものを選び、不完全な文書を完成させる問題です。実際のテストでは16問出題されます。

PART 6

Directions: Read the texts that follow. A word, phrase, or sentence is missing in parts of each text. Four answer choices for each question are given below the text. Select the best answer to complete the text. Then mark the letter (A), (B), (C), or (D) on your answer sheet.

サンプル問題

Questions 15-18 refer to the following article.

❶ SAN DIEGO (May 5)—Matino Industries has just bolstered its image with environmentally conscious customers thanks to its ------- to reduce its use of nonrenewable energy to less
   15.
than 20 percent within five years. -------. Best practices guidelines are already being revised
   16.
------- powering down and disconnecting equipment when not in use. In addition, solar-panel
   17.
arrays are slated for installation on-site as early as next year. When weather ------- are clear,
   18.
these panels will offset Matino's reliance on the power grid, as they already do for a growing list of companies.

*❶は解説の中で説明している文書中の段落番号等を示しています。問題用紙には印刷されていません。

---

15. (A) product
    (B) commitment
    (C) contest
    (D) workforce

16. (A) Discounts on all its products have increased Matino's customer base.
    (B) Management predicts that the takeover will result in a net financial gain.
    (C) To achieve this goal, the company will begin by improving its energy efficiency.
    (D) The initial step will involve redesigning the company's logo and slogans.

17. (A) been encouraging
    (B) have encouraged
    (C) encourages
    (D) to encourage

18. (A) conditions
    (B) instructions
    (C) views
    (D) reports

問題 15-18 は次の記事に関するものです。

サンディエゴ（5月5日）——Matino 産業社は、同社の再生不能エネルギーの使用を5年以内に20パーセント未満に削減するという公約のおかげで、環境意識の高い顧客にとっての同社のイメージを強化したところである。*この目標を達成するために同社は、自社のエネルギー効率を改善することから始める予定だ。機器を使用していないときには電源を落として接続を切ることを推奨するために、最良実践ガイドラインがすでに改定されているところである。さらに、早くも来年には、ソーラーパネルの列が構内に設置される予定である。天候条件が晴れのときには、これらのパネルが、増え続ける多くの企業に対してすでにそうしているように、Matino 社の送電網依存を弱めることになる。

*問題 16 の挿入文の訳

15. 正解 **(B)**

訳 (A) 製品
(B) 公約
(C) 競争
(D) 全従業員

解説 ❶の1〜3行目は「Matino 産業社は、同社の--------のおかげで、同社のイメージを強化したところだ」というのが、文の中心の意味。空所の後ろの「同社の再生不能エネルギーの使用を5年以内に20パーセント未満に削減すること」は、空所に入る名詞の内容を示していると考えられるので、文意から (B) commitment「公約」が適切。

16. 正解 **(C)**

訳 (A) 全ての自社製品に対する割引が、Matino 社の顧客基盤を拡大してきた。
(B) 経営陣は、その企業買収は財務上の純利益をもたらすと予測している。
(C) この目標を達成するために同社は、自社のエネルギー効率を改善することから始める予定だ。
(D) 第1段階には、会社のロゴとスローガンを作り直すことが含まれる予定だ。

解説 空所の前の文では、Matino 産業社が同社の再生不能エネルギーの使用を5年以内に20パーセント未満に削減することが述べられている。この内容を this goal で受けて、目標達成のために同社がこれから取り組むことを挙げている (C) が流れとして適切。

17. 正解 **(D)**

訳 (A) 〈be 動詞の過去分詞＋現在分詞〉
(B) 現在完了形
(C) 動詞の三人称単数現在形
(D) to 不定詞

解説 選択肢は全て動詞 encourage「〜を推奨する」が変化した形。空所の前に〈主語＋動詞〉の形があり、and や or などの接続詞もないことから、空所に動詞は入らない。空所には、to 不定詞の (D) to encourage が適切。

18. 正解 **(A)**

訳 (A) 条件
(B) 指示
(C) 見解
(D) 報道

解説 空所を含む文の、文頭からカンマまでは「天候--------が晴れのときには」という意味。these panels 以降では、その際にソーラーパネルがもたらす効果について述べられている。「天候条件が晴れのときには」とすると意味が通るため、(A) conditions「条件」が適切。

Directionsの訳

パート6

指示：以下の文書を読んでください。各文書の中で語や句、または文が部分的に抜けています。文書の下には各設問の選択肢が4つ与えられています。文書を完成させるのに最も適切な答えを選びます。そして解答用紙の (A)、(B)、(C)、または (D) にマークしてください。

19

Part 7 読解問題

いろいろな形式の、1つもしくは複数の文書に関する問題が出題されます。設問と4つの選択肢を読み、その中から最も適切なものを選ぶ問題です。実際のテストでは1つの文書に関する問題が29問、複数の文書に関する問題が25問出題されます。

PART 7

Directions: In this part you will read a selection of texts, such as magazine and newspaper articles, e-mails, and instant messages. Each text or set of texts is followed by several questions. Select the best answer for each question and mark the letter (A), (B), (C), or (D) on your answer sheet.

サンプル問題

Questions 19-20 refer to the following text-message chain.

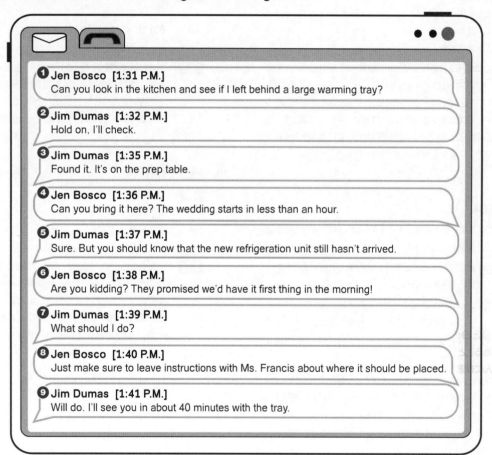

❶ Jen Bosco [1:31 P.M.]
Can you look in the kitchen and see if I left behind a large warming tray?

❷ Jim Dumas [1:32 P.M.]
Hold on, I'll check.

❸ Jim Dumas [1:35 P.M.]
Found it. It's on the prep table.

❹ Jen Bosco [1:36 P.M.]
Can you bring it here? The wedding starts in less than an hour.

❺ Jim Dumas [1:37 P.M.]
Sure. But you should know that the new refrigeration unit still hasn't arrived.

❻ Jen Bosco [1:38 P.M.]
Are you kidding? They promised we'd have it first thing in the morning!

❼ Jim Dumas [1:39 P.M.]
What should I do?

❽ Jen Bosco [1:40 P.M.]
Just make sure to leave instructions with Ms. Francis about where it should be placed.

❾ Jim Dumas [1:41 P.M.]
Will do. I'll see you in about 40 minutes with the tray.

---

19. For whom do the writers most likely work?

(A) A catering company
(B) A home-improvement store
(C) A kitchen-design company
(D) An appliance manufacturer

20. At 1:38 P.M., what does Ms. Bosco most likely mean when she writes, "Are you kidding"?

(A) She thinks Mr. Dumas is exaggerating.
(B) She knew she would have to wait a long time.
(C) She expects the refrigeration unit to arrive soon.
(D) She is upset that a delivery has not been made.

解答・解説

問題19-20は次のテキストメッセージのやり取りに関するものです。

Jen Bosco [午後1時31分]
調理場の中をのぞいて、私が大きな保温トレーを置き忘れたかどうかを確かめてくれるかしら。

Jim Dumas [午後1時32分]
待ってて、確認するよ。

Jim Dumas [午後1時35分]
見つけた。調理台の上にあるよ。

Jen Bosco [午後1時36分]
それをここに持ってきてくれる？ 結婚式が1時間足らずで始まるの。

Jim Dumas [午後1時37分]
もちろん。でも、新しい冷蔵装置がまだ届いていないことを知っておいた方がいいよ。

Jen Bosco [午後1時38分]
冗談でしょう？ 朝一番には私たちにそれを届けてくれると、彼らは約束したのよ。

Jim Dumas [午後1時39分]
僕はどうしたらいい？

Jen Bosco [午後1時40分]
とにかく、どこにそれを置けばいいか、Francisさんに必ず指示を残しておいて。

Jim Dumas [午後1時41分]
そうするよ。約40分後にトレーを持って君に会うね。

---

19. 正解 **(A)**

訳 書き手たちはどこに勤めていると考えられますか。

(A) ケータリング会社
(B) ホームセンター
(C) キッチン設計会社
(D) 電化製品メーカー

解説 ❶と❷のやり取りから、書き手たちの職場には調理場があることが分かる。また❹で、BoscoさんがDumasさんに保温トレーを結婚式の場に持ってくるよう伝えていることから、書き手たちは料理を作り配達を行っていると考えられる。よって、(A)が適切。

20. 正解 **(D)**

訳 午後1時38分にBoscoさんは、"Are you kidding"という発言で、何を意味していると考えられますか。

(A) Dumasさんが誇張していると思っている。
(B) 長い間待たなくてはならないことを知っていた。
(C) 冷蔵装置がもうすぐ届くだろうと見込んでいる。
(D) 配達が行われていないことに動揺している。

解説 Dumasさんが❺「新しい冷蔵装置がまだ届いていないことを知っておいた方がいい」と伝えたのに対して、Boscoさんは「冗談でしょう？」と驚きを示し、「朝一番には私たちにそれを届けてくれると、彼らは約束した」と続けている。つまり、Boscoさんは配達が約束通りに行われていないことに動揺していると考えられる。

Directionsの訳

パート7
指示：このパートでは、雑誌や新聞の記事、Eメールやインスタントメッセージなどのさまざまな文書を読みます。1つの文書または複数の文書のセットにはそれぞれ、幾つかの設問が続いています。各設問について最も適切な答えを選び、解答用紙の (A)、(B)、(C)、または (D) にマークしてください。

Questions 21-24 refer to the following Web page.

http://straubuniversityschoolofmedicine.edu/vendors/rfp0023

❶Straub University School of Medicine is currently seeking a vendor to provide surgical gloves, laboratory coats, and protective goggles. The university requires high-quality, hospital-grade equipment for its students and faculty and is especially interested in providers who currently work with local hospitals and clinics.

❷You can download the complete Request for Proposal (RFP) instructions from our Web site. Below is a summary of the proposal requirements. — [1] —.

• A standard proposal form, which can be downloaded from our Web site
• A general description of the provider and its experience in the industry
• Product descriptions with a complete list of specifications and prices
• Contact information of three current or recent clients who are able to speak to the quality of the provider's products or services

❸If you have any questions about the RFP, please submit them in writing to queries@straub.edu by July 20. — [2] —. Responses to questions will be posted publicly on the Straub University School of Medicine's Web page on August 4.

❹Proposals must be received no later than August 15. — [3] —. All submissions will be thoroughly reviewed, and the winning proposal will be announced on September 10. A contract will be finalized with the strongest candidate that same month, and the agreement will take effect starting October 1. — [4] —.

21. Who are the instructions intended for?

(A) Sellers of medical supplies
(B) Applicants for hospital jobs
(C) Hospital administrators
(D) Medical students

22. What are candidates required to submit?

(A) Questions about the proposal
(B) Professional references
(C) An application fee
(D) Product samples

23. When will candidates learn if they have been selected?

(A) In July
(B) In August
(C) In September
(D) In October

24. In which of the positions marked [1], [2], [3], and [4] does the following sentence best belong?

"All documentation must arrive by this date in a sealed envelope addressed to the School of Medicine's Purchasing Department."

(A) [1]
(B) [2]
(C) [3]
(D) [4]

解答・解説

問題21-24は次のウェブページに関するものです。

http://straubuniversityschoolofmedicine.edu/vendors/rfp0023

Straub 大学医学部は現在、手術用手袋、白衣、保護用ゴーグルを供給してくれる業者を求めています。本学は、学生と教授陣向けの、高品質で病院仕様の備品を必要としており、特に、地元の病院や診療所と現在取引をしている販売会社に関心があります。

本学のウェブサイトから、提案依頼書 (RFP) の指示一式をダウンロードすることができます。以下は提案要件の概略です。

・定型の提案書式。本学のウェブサイトからダウンロード可能
・販売会社の概要および業界における同社の経験
・仕様および価格の全一覧を付した、製品の説明
・販売会社の製品あるいはサービスの質について述べることのできる、現在もしくは最近の顧客３社の連絡先

RFP について何かご質問がございましたら、それらを文書で７月 20 日までに queries@straub.edu 宛てにご提出ください。ご質問に対する回答は、８月４日に Straub 大学医学部のウェブページ上で公開されます。

提案書は８月 15 日必着です。*全ての書類は、封書でこの日付までに医学部の購買部宛てに到着しなければなりません。全ての提出物は入念に検討され、採用された提案書は９月 10 日に発表されます。契約書は最有力候補業者とその同月に最終的な形にされ、契約は10 月１日より発効します。

*問題 24 の挿入文の訳

---

21. **正解** **(A)**

訳 この指示は誰に向けられていますか。

(A) 医療用品の販売会社
(B) 病院の職への応募者
(C) 病院の管理者
(D) 医学生

解説 ❶１〜２行目に「Straub 大学医学部は現在、手術用手袋、白衣、保護用ゴーグルを供給する業者を求めている」とあり、❷では提案要件の概略について、❹では提出期日や選考過程などについて説明されている。よって、この指示は医療用品の販売会社に向けたものだと分かる。

22. **正解** **(B)**

訳 候補者は何を提出することを求められていますか。

(A) 提案書に関する質問
(B) 取引上の照会先
(C) 申込金
(D) 製品の見本

解説 ❷で提案要件の概略として挙げられている箇条書きの4点目に、「販売会社の製品あるいはサービスの質について述べることのできる、現在もしくは最近の顧客３社の連絡先」とある。

23. **正解** **(C)**

訳 候補者はいつ、自分が選出されたかどうかを知りますか。

(A) ７月
(B) ８月
(C) ９月
(D) 10 月

解説 ❹２行目に、the winning proposal will be announced on September 10「採用された提案書は９月 10 日に発表される」とある。

24. **正解** **(C)**

訳 [1]、[2]、[3]、[4] と記載された箇所のうち、次の文が入るのに最もふさわしいのはどれですか。

「全ての書類は、封書でこの日付までに医学部の購買部宛てに到着しなければなりません」

(A) [1]
(B) [2]
(C) [3]
(D) [4]

解説 挿入文は書類の提出方法と宛先を伝えている。(C) [3] に入れると、挿入文中の this date「この日付」が❹１行目の August 15 を指し、提案書の提出期日に続けて提出方法と宛先を伝える自然な流れとなる。

Questions 25-29 refer to the following article, e-mail, and Web page.

❶ (November 6)—The Rudi's store at 47 Kask Highway in Glencoe Park will shut its doors next Saturday, adding another empty building to the local landscape. The shutdown is one of a rash of store closings in the greater Billington area and is a result of two major forces. First, Rudi's has changed its business plan, relying increasingly on online sales. Second, much of the traffic on Kask Highway has been rerouted to the recently completed bypass, resulting in fewer potential customers passing through Billington.

❷ Other Rudi's closings over the past two years include the store at 38 Quail Hill Road, the store at 21 Lowell Boulevard, and the downtown megastore at 59 Claremont Street on the banks of the Corks River. A Rudi's spokesperson stated that no further closures are expected.

To:	nathanpaugh@ioscodesign.com
From:	ccovey@tedesintl.com
Subject:	Tedes Building
Date:	January 25

Dear Mr. Paugh,

❶The preliminary drawings you sent are right on target. I think your proposal to demolish most of the east wall and install floor-to-ceiling windows is terrific. If we were to leave everything as it now is, we would end up with a rather somber interior.

❷Let's keep the current stairway where it is so that people can walk straight through the entrance and up to the second floor meeting rooms. We can configure the remaining area in the center of the first floor as open work space, with the executive offices off to the left side against the west wall. Including a large picture window at the entrance to the fitness center in the back of the first floor space is also a good idea.

❸Please move forward with drawing up draft plans for our board's approval.

Thank you,

Cynthia Covey

http://www.buildingmonthly.com/readersreviews

| HOME | LATEST ISSUE | **READERS' REVIEWS** | ADVERTISERS |

The new Tedes corporate building
Posted by Monty K.

❶ Tedes International has opened its corporate headquarters in a former Rudi's megastore building. In an area with many vacated retail buildings, one is now a workplace for over 400 Tedes employees. Corporations looking for prime real estate should take notice.

❷ The interior design of the Tedes Building is notable for its mixed use of open and closed space. The entrance is open and inviting and leads to a wide staircase up to the second floor, which houses offices for upper management. Large windows installed as one of the exterior walls create a bright atmosphere in the open work space and nearby meeting rooms, while boats glide by on the river right in front of them. On my visit, several employees were exercising on fitness bikes in full view at the rear of the first-floor space.

25. What is the purpose of the article?

(A) To notify readers of recent job openings
(B) To publicize an online sale
(C) To report on a store closing
(D) To alert motorists to changing traffic patterns

26. Who most likely is Mr. Paugh?

(A) An artist
(B) An architect
(C) A real estate agent
(D) A reporter

27. Which former Rudi's location did Tedes International choose for its headquarters?

(A) 47 Kask Highway
(B) 38 Quail Hill Road
(C) 21 Lowell Boulevard
(D) 59 Claremont Street

28. What aspect of the design suggested by Ms. Covey was ultimately rejected?

(A) The replacement of a wall with windows
(B) The layout of the entrance
(C) The inclusion of a fitness center
(D) The location of the offices

29. What is implied by the reviewer?

(A) Tedes International is planning to expand.
(B) Tedes International wants to sell its property.
(C) Vacant buildings have great potential.
(D) Local businesses may experience reduced profits.

問題25-29は次の記事、Eメール、ウェブページに関するものです。

1. 記事

（11月6日）——グレンコーパークのカスク街道47番地にあるRudi's社の店舗は、次の土曜日に扉を閉ざし、その地域の風景にもう1棟空きビルを加えることになる。この閉店は、ビリントン広域圏で頻発する店舗の閉鎖の1つであり、2つの大きな影響力によるものである。第1に、Rudi's社が事業計画を変更し、オンライン販売に一層依存するようになったこと。第2に、カスク街道の交通の大部分が、最近完成した迂回路の方へ流れ、ビリントンを通る潜在顧客が減少する結果となったことだ。

過去2年間のRudi's社の他の閉店には、クウェイルヒル通り38番地の店舗、ローウェル大通り21番地の店舗、そしてコークス川岸のクレアモント通り59番地にあった中心街の超大型店舗が含まれる。Rudi's社の広報担当者は、これ以上の閉店は一切予定されていないと明言した。

2. Eメール

受信者：nathanpaugh@ioscodesign.com
送信者：ccovey@tedesintl.com
件名：　Tedesビル
日付：　1月25日

Paugh様

お送りくださった仮の図面は、まさに期待通りのものです。東側の壁の大半を取り壊し、床から天井までの窓を設置するという貴殿のご提案は素晴らしいと思います。もし何もかも現状のままにしておいたとしたら、最終的にかなり陰気な内装になってしまうでしょう。

今の階段は、そのままの場所で残しましょう。そうすれば人々が入り口をまっすぐ通り抜け、2階の会議室に歩いて上がっていけます。1階の中央にある残りの区域は開放的な作業スペースとし、重役の執務室を左側へ、西の壁際に配置することができます。1階スペースの奥にあるフィットネスセンターへの入り口に大きな一枚ガラスの窓を入れることも良いアイデアです。

当社役員会の承認に向けて、設計図の草案の作成を進めてください。

よろしくお願いいたします。

Cynthia Covey

3. ウェブページ

http://www.buildingmonthly.com/readersreviews

| ホーム | 最新号 | 読者レビュー | 広告主 |

Tedes社の新しいビル
Monty K.投稿

Tedesインターナショナル社は、かつてRudi's社の超大型店舗だった建物に本社を開設した。空き家となった小売店のビルが多数ある地域において、1棟は今や400名超のTedes社の従業員の職場である。優良な不動産を求めている企業は注目すべきである。

Tedesビルの内部設計は、開放的スペースと閉鎖的スペースを取り混ぜて使用していることで注目に値する。入り口は広々として、いざなうようであり、2階に至る広い階段に通じている。2階には、経営上層部のための執務室が入っている。外壁の一部として設置された大型の窓は、開放的な作業スペースと近くの会議室に明るい雰囲気を作り出し、他方で、すぐ目の前にある川をボートが滑るように進む。私の訪問時には、数名の従業員が1階スペースの奥で、よく見える所でフィットネスバイクで運動をしていた。

25. **正解** **(C)**

訳 記事の目的は何ですか。

(A) 読者に最近の求人を知らせること。

(B) オンラインのセールを宣伝すること。

(C) 店舗の閉鎖を報道すること。

(D) 車を運転する人に、交通パターンの変化について注意を喚起すること。

解説 **1**の記事の**❶** 1～3行目に、「グレンコーパークのカスク街道47番地にあるRudi's社の店舗は、次の土曜日に扉を閉ざす」とあり、その後も閉店の要因などが述べられている。よって、記事の目的はRudi's社の店舗の閉鎖を報道することだと分かる。

26. **正解** **(B)**

訳 Paughさんとは誰だと考えられますか。

(A) 芸術家

(B) 建築家

(C) 不動産仲介人

(D) 記者

解説 Paughさんは**2**のEメールの受信者。Eメールの本文では、**❶** 1行目で「お送りくださった仮の図面は、まさに期待通りのものだ」と伝えられ、建物の設計についての話が続いている。さらに、**❸**で「設計図の草案の作成を進めてほしい」と依頼を受けていることから、Paughさんは建築家と考えられる。

27. **正解** **(D)**

訳 Tedesインターナショナル社は、かつてのRudi's社のどの場所を本社に選びましたか。

(A) カスク街道47番地

(B) クウェイルヒル通り38番地

(C) ローウェル大通り21番地

(D) クレアモント通り59番地

解説 **3**のウェブページの**❶** 1～2行目に、「Tedesインターナショナル社は、かつてRudi's社の超大型店舗だった建物に本社を開設した」とある。**1**の記事の**❷** 3～5行目に、閉店したRudi's社の店舗の1つとして、「コークス川岸のクレアモント通り59番地にあった中心街の超大型店舗」が挙げられているので、(D)が正解。

28. **正解** **(D)**

訳 Coveyさんによって示された設計のどの点が、最終的に不採用とされましたか。

(A) 壁を窓で置き換えること

(B) 入り口の配置

(C) フィットネスセンターを含めること

(D) 執務室の位置

解説 Coveyさんは**2**のEメールの送信者。仮の図面を作ったPaughさんに対して、**❷** 2～4行目で「1階の中央にある残りの区域は開放的な作業スペースとし、重役の執務室を左側へ、西の壁際に配置することができる」と述べている。一方、完成したビルの読者レビューを載せた**3**のウェブページには、**❷** 2～3行目に「入り口は広々として、いざなうようであり、2階に至る広い階段に通じている。2階には、経営上層部のための執務室が入っている」とあることから、重役の執務室はCoveyさんが提案した1階ではなく、2階に配置されたと分かる。

29. **正解** **(C)**

訳 レビュー投稿者によって何が示唆されていますか。

(A) Tedesインターナショナル社は拡大する予定である。

(B) Tedesインターナショナル社は同社の不動産を売却したいと思っている。

(C) 空きビルは大きな可能性を持っている。

(D) 地元の企業は減益を経験するかもしれない。

解説 **3**のウェブページの読者レビューの**❶** 1～3行目で、Tedesインターナショナル社がかつてRudi's社の超大型店舗だった建物に本社を開設したことで、空きビル1棟が今や多数の従業員の職場へと変化したことが述べられている。続けて「優良な不動産を求めている企業は注目すべきだ」とあることから、レビュー投稿者は空きビルに大きな可能性があることを示唆していると考えられる。

採点・結果について

$TOEIC^®$ Listening & Reading Test のテスト結果は合格・不合格ではなく、リスニングセクション 5～495 点、リーディングセクション 5～495 点、トータル 10～990 点のスコアで、5 点刻みで表示されます。このスコアは、常に評価基準を一定に保つために統計処理が行われ、英語能力に変化がない限りスコアも一定に保たれる点が大きな特長です。

テスト結果は Official Score Certificate（公式認定証）として、試験日から 30 日以内に発送されます。また、インターネットからお申し込みいただく際、「テスト結果のインターネット表示」で「利用する」を選択すると、試験日から 17 日後にインターネットでスコアを確認することが可能です。（日米の祝日の影響により、遅れる場合がございます。）

Official Score Certificate（公式認定証）のサンプル

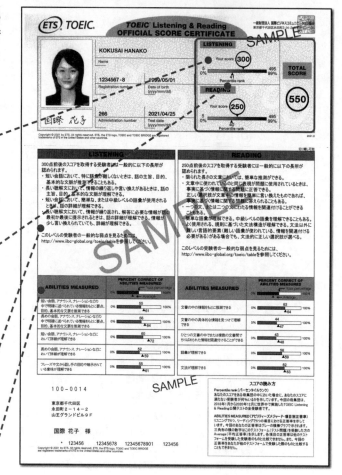

Your Score（スコア）:
今回取得したリスニング、リーディングの各セクションスコアです。右側にトータルスコアが記載されます。

Percentile Rank（パーセンタイルランク）:
あなたが取得したスコアに満たない受験者が全体でどのくらいを占めているかをパーセンテージで示しています。
例えば、リスニングでスコア 300 点、パーセンタイルランクが 41%という場合には、リスニングスコア 300 点未満の受験者が全体の 41%いることを示します。つまり、リスニングスコア 300 点を取得した受験者は上位 59%に位置することになります。

Score Descriptors（スコアディスクリプターズ）:
レベル別評価です。今回取得したスコアをもとに、あなたの英語運用能力上の長所が書かれています。

Abilities Measured（アビリティーズメジャード）:
項目別正答率です。リスニング、リーディングの 5 つの項目における正答率を示しています。

$TOEIC^®$ Listening & Reading 公開テストのお申し込み

IIBC公式サイト https://www.iibc-global.org にてテスト日程、申込方法、注意事項をご確認の上、申込受付期間内にお申し込みください。試験の実施方法などに変更があった場合には IIBC 公式サイト等でご案内いたします。

お問い合わせ

一般財団法人 国際ビジネスコミュニケーション協会　IIBC 試験運営センター
〒 100-0014　東京都千代田区永田町 2-14-2　山王グランドビル
TEL：03-5521-6033（土・日・祝日・年末年始を除く 10:00 ～ 17:00）

TEST 1

＊解答用紙は本誌 p.112 の後ろに綴じ込まれています。

実際のテストでは問題用紙の裏側に、以下のようなテスト全体についての指示が印刷されています。この指示を念頭においてテストに取り組みましょう。

General Directions

This test is designed to measure your English language ability. The test is divided into two sections: Listening and Reading.

You must mark all of your answers on the separate answer sheet. For each question, you should select the best answer from the answer choices given. Then, on your answer sheet, you should find the number of the question and fill in the space that corresponds to the letter of the answer that you have selected. If you decide to change an answer, completely erase your old answer and then mark your new answer.

訳 ### 全体についての指示

このテストはあなたの英語言語能力を測定するよう設計されています。テストはリスニングとリーディングという2つのセクションに分けられています。

答えは全て別紙の解答用紙にマークしてください。それぞれの設問について、与えられた選択肢から最も適切な答えを選びます。そして解答用紙の該当する問題番号に、選択した答えを塗りつぶしてください。答えを修正する場合は、元の答えを完全に消してから新しい答えをマークしてください。

CD 1
12

LISTENING TEST

In the Listening test, you will be asked to demonstrate how well you understand spoken English. The entire Listening test will last approximately 45 minutes. There are four parts, and directions are given for each part. You must mark your answers on the separate answer sheet. Do not write your answers in your test book.

PART 1

Directions: For each question in this part, you will hear four statements about a picture in your test book. When you hear the statements, you must select the one statement that best describes what you see in the picture. Then find the number of the question on your answer sheet and mark your answer. The statements will not be printed in your test book and will be spoken only one time.

Statement (C), "They're sitting at a table," is the best description of the picture, so you should select answer (C) and mark it on your answer sheet.

30

1.

2.

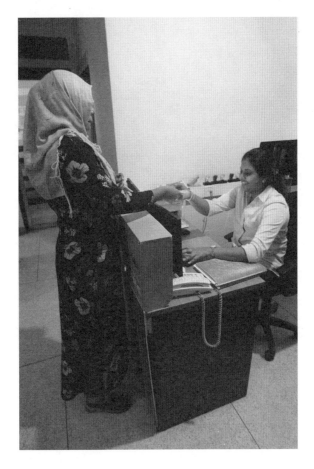

GO ON TO THE NEXT PAGE

3.

4.

5.

6.

GO ON TO THE NEXT PAGE ➤

PART 2

Directions: You will hear a question or statement and three responses spoken in English. They will not be printed in your test book and will be spoken only one time. Select the best response to the question or statement and mark the letter (A), (B), or (C) on your answer sheet.

7. Mark your answer on your answer sheet.

8. Mark your answer on your answer sheet.

9. Mark your answer on your answer sheet.

10. Mark your answer on your answer sheet.

11. Mark your answer on your answer sheet.

12. Mark your answer on your answer sheet.

13. Mark your answer on your answer sheet.

14. Mark your answer on your answer sheet.

15. Mark your answer on your answer sheet.

16. Mark your answer on your answer sheet.

17. Mark your answer on your answer sheet.

18. Mark your answer on your answer sheet.

19. Mark your answer on your answer sheet.

20. Mark your answer on your answer sheet.

21. Mark your answer on your answer sheet.

22. Mark your answer on your answer sheet.

23. Mark your answer on your answer sheet.

24. Mark your answer on your answer sheet.

25. Mark your answer on your answer sheet.

26. Mark your answer on your answer sheet.

27. Mark your answer on your answer sheet.

28. Mark your answer on your answer sheet.

29. Mark your answer on your answer sheet.

30. Mark your answer on your answer sheet.

31. Mark your answer on your answer sheet.

PART 3

Directions: You will hear some conversations between two or more people. You will be asked to answer three questions about what the speakers say in each conversation. Select the best response to each question and mark the letter (A), (B), (C), or (D) on your answer sheet. The conversations will not be printed in your test book and will be spoken only one time.

32. Where does the woman most likely work?
(A) At an airport
(B) At a museum
(C) At a travel agency
(D) At a conference center

33. What benefit does the woman tell the man about?
(A) Free parking
(B) Promotional gifts
(C) Upgraded seating
(D) Invitations to special events

34. What does the woman ask the man to provide?
(A) Some identification
(B) A confirmation number
(C) Employment references
(D) A completed registration form

35. Why is the man at a computer store?
(A) To get technical support
(B) To make a purchase
(C) To get a refund
(D) To apply for a job

36. What does the man ask about?
(A) A shipping cost
(B) A product feature
(C) Customer reviews
(D) Store hours

37. What does the woman suggest the man do?
(A) Sign some papers
(B) Schedule an appointment
(C) Select some merchandise
(D) Save some data

38. Where most likely are the speakers?
(A) At a clothing shop
(B) At an art gallery
(C) At a photography studio
(D) At a stationery store

39. What does the woman give the man?
(A) A poster
(B) A catalog
(C) A gift card
(D) An instruction manual

40. What special offer does the woman mention?
(A) Free shipping
(B) Early entrance
(C) A sales discount
(D) A customer loyalty program

41. What does the company make?
(A) Video games
(B) Mobile phones
(C) Sports equipment
(D) Art supplies

42. What part of a project does the man say is complicated?
(A) Creating a design
(B) Finding investors
(C) Writing some directions
(D) Contacting social media sites

43. What is the next step in a project?
(A) A product will be tested.
(B) A competition will take place.
(C) A sales promotion will begin.
(D) An advertisement will be filmed.

GO ON TO THE NEXT PAGE

44. Where does the woman work?

    (A) At an office complex
    (B) At a community park
    (C) At a sports facility
    (D) At a zoo

45. What is the woman concerned about?

    (A) Installation costs
    (B) Water usage
    (C) Parking capacity
    (D) Ticket sales

46. What does the man suggest the woman do this week?

    (A) Reserve tickets
    (B) Water a garden
    (C) Apply for a loan
    (D) Look at some samples

47. Where does the man most likely work?

    (A) At a manufacturing company
    (B) At a law firm
    (C) At a bank
    (D) At a call center

48. What does the woman ask the man to do?

    (A) Provide a referral
    (B) Process a payment
    (C) Explain a delay
    (D) Review a contract

49. What does the man say he will do next week?

    (A) Conduct interviews
    (B) Attend a conference
    (C) Provide software training
    (D) Redecorate an office

50. Who most likely are the speakers?

    (A) Appliance salespeople
    (B) Bakery employees
    (C) Delivery drivers
    (D) Cooking show hosts

51. What does the woman imply when she says, "The boxes are really big"?

    (A) She thinks the boxes will not fit on a shelf.
    (B) She suspects an order was sent by mistake.
    (C) She cannot do a task on her own.
    (D) She will not need to use more boxes.

52. What will happen next week?

    (A) A wider variety of items will be offered.
    (B) A local competition will be held.
    (C) A new employee will join the team.
    (D) A business will move to a bigger location.

53. Why does the man congratulate the woman?

    (A) She received a promotion.
    (B) She finished a project early.
    (C) She gave a good presentation.
    (D) Her movie won an award.

54. Who does the woman say she received help from?

    (A) An independent consultant
    (B) A department manager
    (C) A sales assistant
    (D) A video editor

55. What does the man think will increase sales?

    (A) Hiring a famous spokesperson
    (B) Providing some promotional pricing
    (C) Publishing a press release
    (D) Focusing on a specific consumer group

56. What industry do the speakers work in?

    (A) Construction
    (B) Software development
    (C) Security
    (D) Equipment supply

57. Why is the woman concerned about hiring more staff?

    (A) It would be too expensive.
    (B) It would require more training.
    (C) The site has too many workers already.
    (D) The site is not big enough.

58. Why does the woman dislike the Borson machines?

    (A) They work too slowly.
    (B) They require too many repairs.
    (C) They take a long time to set up.
    (D) They are not accurate.

---

59. Why are the speakers meeting?

    (A) To discuss an investment opportunity
    (B) To plan a product release event
    (C) To negotiate a shipping agreement
    (D) To revise a product development plan

60. Why does the man say, "I'd imagine people would want to feel the material before purchasing"?

    (A) To suggest sending free samples
    (B) To complain about a purchase
    (C) To express doubt about a business model
    (D) To correct a misunderstanding about a process

61. According to the woman, what rarely happens?

    (A) Deliveries arriving late
    (B) Customers requesting a refund
    (C) Products being unavailable
    (D) Design prototypes being rejected

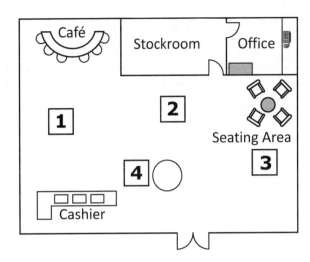

62. What are the speakers discussing?

    (A) Adding a new section of books
    (B) Discounting unpopular books
    (C) Hosting a book-reading event
    (D) Buying a bookshop

63. What concern does the woman express?

    (A) She does not have the necessary information.
    (B) She does not want to exceed a budget.
    (C) She would have to change a work schedule.
    (D) She would have to order more furniture.

64. Look at the graphic. Which location does the man point out?

    (A) Location 1
    (B) Location 2
    (C) Location 3
    (D) Location 4

GO ON TO THE NEXT PAGE

Report on Port Congestion	
Port Location	Wait Time (in Hours)
Tokyo	28
Osaka	53
Nagoya	34
Shimonoseki	58

65. According to the speakers, what are the contents of a shipment?

(A) Books
(B) Clothing
(C) Sports equipment
(D) Construction materials

66. Look at the graphic. Which port do the speakers usually use?

(A) Tokyo
(B) Osaka
(C) Nagoya
(D) Shimonoseki

67. What will the speakers most likely do?

(A) Contact a director
(B) Submit a report
(C) Meet with a client
(D) Change a deadline

20% OFF
10-year warranty
25 cubic feet of storage

Yearly Electricity Use
350 kWh

68. According to the man, what is an advantage of newer refrigerator models?

(A) They keep vegetables fresh longer.
(B) The doors close automatically.
(C) They are available in many colors.
(D) The temperature is adjustable.

69. Which feature does the woman express the most interest in?

(A) Durability
(B) Storage space
(C) Ease of cleaning
(D) Energy efficiency

70. Look at the graphic. Which number will change for next year's model?

(A) 20
(B) 10
(C) 25
(D) 350

PART 4

Directions: You will hear some talks given by a single speaker. You will be asked to answer three questions about what the speaker says in each talk. Select the best response to each question and mark the letter (A), (B), (C), or (D) on your answer sheet. The talks will not be printed in your test book and will be spoken only one time.

TEST 1

71. What caused a delay?

(A) Technical difficulties
(B) Poor weather conditions
(C) Absent staff members
(D) Lost paperwork

72. Why is Ms. Kebede receiving an award?

(A) She published a book.
(B) She led a fund-raising campaign.
(C) She served on the city council.
(D) She developed a useful device.

73. According to the speaker, what is the most important benefit of trees?

(A) They are used in construction.
(B) They provide shade.
(C) They reduce stress.
(D) They protect the soil.

74. Why does the speaker anticipate an increase in business?

(A) A discount will be offered.
(B) A new product will be launched.
(C) Store hours have been extended.
(D) Reviews have been positive.

75. Who are the listeners?

(A) Factory workers
(B) Product designers
(C) Trainers
(D) Technicians

76. What is the company going to add to its meeting rooms?

(A) Microwave ovens
(B) Water dispensers
(C) Wireless connectivity
(D) Teleconferencing equipment

77. Where is the announcement being made?

(A) On an airplane
(B) In a train station
(C) In a hotel
(D) At a department store

78. What must the listeners do to enter a contest?

(A) Make a purchase
(B) Fill out a survey
(C) Download a mobile application
(D) Join a rewards program

79. What will the listeners most likely do next?

(A) Take a photograph
(B) Have a snack
(C) Watch a video
(D) Read a magazine

80. What is the speaker explaining?

(A) How to edit a video
(B) How to reduce electricity costs
(C) How to repair a lamp
(D) How to install a fan

81. According to the speaker, why are the first steps important?

(A) For safety
(B) For efficiency
(C) For cleanliness
(D) For appearance

82. According to the speaker, how can a friend be helpful with a task?

(A) By reading a manual
(B) By reviewing some work
(C) By holding a ladder
(D) By turning the lights off

GO ON TO THE NEXT PAGE

83. What is the speaker's job?

(A) Computer technician
(B) Company executive
(C) Financial consultant
(D) Product developer

84. What has a company recently done?

(A) It moved to another location.
(B) It hired more employees.
(C) It won an award.
(D) It changed its logo.

85. Why does the speaker say, "some computer companies produce mobile phones"?

(A) To correct some information
(B) To make a complaint
(C) To indicate an intention
(D) To provide reassurance

86. Why is the speaker leaving a message?

(A) To congratulate the listener
(B) To complain about a problem
(C) To provide tour information
(D) To schedule a delivery

87. What opportunity does the speaker mention?

(A) Starting a new business
(B) Learning to make some food
(C) Traveling to a new city
(D) Writing a book

88. Why does the speaker say, "but this is one of our best sellers"?

(A) To express surprise
(B) To encourage a quick response
(C) To justify a choice
(D) To ask for some assistance

89. What do the listeners most likely want information about?

(A) Improving public speaking skills
(B) Planning an international trip
(C) Making healthier meals
(D) Starting a small business

90. What does the speaker say about an application process?

(A) It is simple.
(B) It is free.
(C) It requires an interview.
(D) It can be completed online.

91. What will happen next?

(A) A video will be shown.
(B) A guest will speak.
(C) Some refreshments will be served.
(D) Some booklets will be distributed.

92. What special event is the speaker preparing for?

(A) An exhibition opening
(B) A fund-raising banquet
(C) A volunteer orientation
(D) An art auction

93. What does the speaker say about some artwork?

(A) It is covered by insurance.
(B) It will be packaged in two containers.
(C) It will be the focus of the event.
(D) Its delivery has been scheduled.

94. Why does the speaker say, "the software's very complex"?

(A) To recommend training
(B) To request assistance
(C) To suggest a replacement
(D) To explain a delay

Tovin Stove Models	
VX	$118.50
Plus	$94.20
Pro	$182.99
XT	$68.99

TEST 1

95. What does the speaker give to the listeners?

(A) Marketing materials
(B) Product coupons
(C) Business cards
(D) Order forms

96. Look at the graphic. Which model is the speaker discussing?

(A) VX
(B) Plus
(C) Pro
(D) XT

97. What will the speaker demonstrate?

(A) How to pack a stove
(B) How to prepare a meal
(C) How to adjust a setting
(D) How to clean a stove after use

Daily Specials

Monday	Tuesday
Chef's Salad	Fish Sandwich
Wednesday	**Thursday**
Vegetarian Tacos	Grilled Cheese Sandwich

98. What problem is the speaker calling about?

(A) Some equipment is broken.
(B) Some food has spoiled.
(C) A shipment has been delayed.
(D) An employee is not available.

99. Look at the graphic. For which day will the menu be changed?

(A) Monday
(B) Tuesday
(C) Wednesday
(D) Thursday

100. According to the speaker, what does the restaurant plan to do next month?

(A) Expand its dessert menu
(B) Offer a delivery service
(C) Hire another chef
(D) Open an outdoor dining area

This is the end of the Listening test. Turn to Part 5 in your test book.

GO ON TO THE NEXT PAGE

READING TEST

In the Reading test, you will read a variety of texts and answer several different types of reading comprehension questions. The entire Reading test will last 75 minutes. There are three parts, and directions are given for each part. You are encouraged to answer as many questions as possible within the time allowed.

You must mark your answers on the separate answer sheet. Do not write your answers in your test book.

PART 5

Directions: A word or phrase is missing in each of the sentences below. Four answer choices are given below each sentence. Select the best answer to complete the sentence. Then mark the letter (A), (B), (C), or (D) on your answer sheet.

101. Gerardo Lentini will build ------- second clinic in June.

    (A) he
    (B) his
    (C) him
    (D) himself

102. The manufacturer recommends cleaning the natural wood table with a ------- cotton cloth.

    (A) dry
    (B) dryly
    (C) dryness
    (D) to dry

103. If ------- are willing to work on the project this weekend, Ms. Craig will buy everyone lunch.

    (A) employees
    (B) employing
    (C) employments
    (D) employs

104. Analysts ------- significant growth in the robotics industry in the next decade.

    (A) attend
    (B) refer
    (C) think
    (D) predict

105. Please review the ------- schedule and e-mail me right away about any mistakes.

    (A) repeated
    (B) alarmed
    (C) attached
    (D) canceled

106. Niceties Cake Shop added ten more exotic flavors ------- after opening.

    (A) short
    (B) shortest
    (C) shorter
    (D) shortly

107. Mr. Kern has built a shelf in the supply closet ------- all the new materials.

    (A) accommodate
    (B) accommodates
    (C) to accommodate
    (D) is accommodating

108. The neighborhood's newest clothing store will specialize in the sale of ------- wear.

    (A) formal
    (B) quick
    (C) strict
    (D) sudden

109. Office morale ------- after we offered rewards for practical suggestions.

    (A) indicated
    (B) completed
    (C) improved
    (D) controlled

110. At Furnred Finance, ------- encourage associates with different points of view to find common ground.

(A) ourselves
(B) ours
(C) us
(D) we

111. Shipbuilders, Inc., anticipates profits for the second quarter to be ------- 4 and 6 percent.

(A) by
(B) for
(C) upon
(D) between

112. Ovonel Skincare has published ------- testimonials on several social media sites.

(A) consumed
(B) consumer
(C) consume
(D) consuming

113. Saturn Bank is working ------- to resolve technical difficulties with its mobile app and online banking.

(A) quickening
(B) quickened
(C) quickness
(D) quickly

114. The new washing machine has a heavy-duty cycle that is effective in removing the ------- stains.

(A) highest
(B) toughest
(C) uneven
(D) broad

115. Wolff Foods has recently experienced a decrease in ------- for its beef products.

(A) position
(B) approach
(C) force
(D) demand

116. Although construction will begin on Reese-Decker Bridge tomorrow, it should cause ------- traffic problems.

(A) minimal
(B) minimally
(C) minimum
(D) minimize

117. The months of April and May are ------- busy for the workers at Avedis Garden Supply.

(A) readily
(B) accurately
(C) particularly
(D) directly

118. Mr. Kalama will handle the marketing reports ------- Ms. Lewis is away on vacation.

(A) concerning
(B) while
(C) during
(D) just

119. Mr. Nguyen opposes adding a ------- of trail bikes because he thinks it will not be popular with customers.

(A) line
(B) surface
(C) field
(D) front

120. Ms. Nicholas was promoted ------- managing editor of the *Irontown Daily Press*.

(A) of
(B) at
(C) to
(D) on

121. Ms. Chou has ordered the ------- of all the bookcases sold by Bielke Office Furnishings.

(A) narrowly
(B) narrower
(C) narrowest
(D) narrow

122. Failure to pay bills on time ------- result in additional late fees.

(A) when
(B) may
(C) part
(D) itself

123. Financial conditions in the greater Perth region are ------- favorable for economic growth.

(A) privately
(B) centrally
(C) neutrally
(D) currently

GO ON TO THE NEXT PAGE

124. The quarterly data safety report provides ------- for Mardoor Investing's strict security policies.

(A) justify
(B) justifier
(C) justified
(D) justification

125. Sunworth Company's all-in-one shampoos restore natural shine at the same time ------- they condition hair.

(A) even
(B) as
(C) either
(D) like

126. The third box of the shipment, which should have contained the microphones, ------- arrived.

(A) late
(B) rather
(C) never
(D) not

127. The Murnau Company's pepper grinders are ------- durable that the company guarantees them for life.

(A) too
(B) so
(C) such
(D) very

128. The Asawa 4 is ------- any vehicle currently on the market.

(A) unlike
(B) excepting
(C) against
(D) above

129. By the time he signs the lease, Mr. Cooper ------- four months searching for a suitable office space.

(A) will have spent
(B) had spent
(C) to spend
(D) spent

130. ------- I have already been briefed by the product development team, I am fully prepared for my appointment with Mr. Warner.

(A) Until
(B) In spite of
(C) Since
(D) Even though

PART 6

Directions: Read the texts that follow. A word, phrase, or sentence is missing in parts of each text. Four answer choices for each question are given below the text. Select the best answer to complete the text. Then mark the letter (A), (B), (C), or (D) on your answer sheet.

Questions 131-134 refer to the following article.

City Grants Permission for New High-Rise

The city council has approved plans for a new high-rise apartment building on Third Street. The primarily ------- structure will replace a parking area. ------- will include 220 apartments, ranging
131.   132.
from studios to two-bedroom units.

The project was designed by the architecture firm Wagama Clark Reyes. ------- . The Third Street
133.
project will feature a pool, a fitness center, a rooftop terrace, and an underground parking garage. The building will ------- have space for a few retail stores and restaurants at ground level.
134.

131. (A) industrial
     (B) commercial
     (C) residential
     (D) educational

132. (A) It
     (B) One
     (C) They
     (D) Some

133. (A) Downtown is known for its nightlife.
     (B) City traffic is often bumper-to-bumper.
     (C) Many apartment buildings do not allow
         pets.
     (D) The firm previously designed the Vander
         Apartments.

134. (A) instead
     (B) also
     (C) similarly
     (D) otherwise

GO ON TO THE NEXT PAGE

Questions 135-138 refer to the following e-mail.

To: nyoon@velmail.com
From: kbengston@maekerelectric.com
Date: Monday, Oct 1
Subject: RE: Wiring for home projects

Good afternoon Ms. Yoon,

I apologize for taking so long to respond to your e-mail. My team ------- on a big commercial
135.
development project. We just finished it, so I can visit your property sometime next week to see
what electrical work you would like to have done. What is your ------- ? My best times are
136.
Tuesday through Thursday mornings. And in answer to your question, I am not sure how much it
will cost or how long it will take to finish all the wiring. ------- .
137.

To prepare for my visit, could you make a list of the projects you have in mind? We can walk
through the property and discuss the details. ------- , I can give you a price estimate and we can
138.
schedule the work.

Kind regards,

Keith Bengston, Maeker Electric

135. (A) will work
(B) may work
(C) should be working
(D) has been working

136. (A) calculation
(B) availability
(C) career
(D) process

137. (A) You can do these repairs yourself.
(B) I will update the form if you want.
(C) There are a lot of factors to consider.
(D) I am familiar with this contractor.

138. (A) In fact
(B) Then again
(C) After that
(D) For example

Questions 139-142 refer to the following job listing.

Landini Shipping, Inc., is currently seeking hardworking individuals to join our team. Qualified individuals must have a high school diploma and a willingness to work in a fast-paced environment. -------, they must be responsible and follow safety protocols at all times. Open
139.
positions ------- package handlers, general warehouse workers, and warehouse associates. Day
140.
and night shifts are available. -------. No one under 18 years of age will be considered.
141.
------- are available online at www.landinishipping.com.
142.

139. (A) In part
(B) In addition
(C) In other words
(D) In the meantime

140. (A) include
(B) must include
(C) had included
(D) to include

141. (A) Weekend work may be required on occasion.
(B) We will soon be relocating our office.
(C) Please come to our annual company picnic.
(D) Enjoy low shipping rates at all locations.

142. (A) Menus
(B) Tickets
(C) Schedules
(D) Applications

GO ON TO THE NEXT PAGE

Questions 143-146 refer to the following e-mail.

To: Melita Li
From: J. P. Solera
Date: November 21
Subject: Internal Writing Update
Attachment: SOW; Technical specs

Dear Ms. Li,

I would like you ------- the *User's Manual for Brandor Humidifiers*. Attached you will find a slide
     143.
deck with background material. Please give special attention to slides 18 through 27.

------- highlight the main changes we need to incorporate into Section 2 of the manual.
  144.

------- .
  145.

Please get back to me as soon as possible with your estimate of how long the task will take.

We should also discuss changes to your ------- . I would like you to make this task a priority.
                                      146.

Thanks,

Jan Paul Solera

143. (A) to update
     (B) will update
     (C) are updating
     (D) having updated

144. (A) Any
     (B) You
     (C) Both
     (D) These

145. (A) Thank you for notifying us about the
         problem.
     (B) The starting date for the project has
         changed.
     (C) Note that all of the other parts remain
         unchanged.
     (D) It has been a pleasure working with you.

146. (A) office
     (B) code
     (C) uniform
     (D) workload

PART 7

Directions: In this part you will read a selection of texts, such as magazine and newspaper articles, e-mails, and instant messages. Each text or set of texts is followed by several questions. Select the best answer for each question and mark the letter (A), (B), (C), or (D) on your answer sheet.

Questions 147-148 refer to the following coupon.

Clipper Happy

Receive $5 off any haircut.

For first-time customers only.

May not be combined with any other offer.

Valid until April 5 at our Bonnieville location only.

147. At what type of business can the coupon be used?

(A) At a hardware store
(B) At a barbershop
(C) At a restaurant
(D) At a gift shop

148. What is true about the coupon?

(A) It is only for new customers.
(B) It can be used with other offers.
(C) It can be used at any location.
(D) It is valid until the end of April.

GO ON TO THE NEXT PAGE

You are invited to our 50th anniversary celebration.

Harlingen Children's Museum
1321 Danforth Street

Saturday, May 11
8:00 P.M. to 11:00 P.M.

Join us at the Harlingen Children's Museum for a special night of recognition and entertainment as we celebrate a half century of providing stimulating educational experiences for area children and their families. The gala will feature a buffet dinner catered by Café Lyon, a performance by local jazz group Nick and the Exchange, and a video tribute to our many staff members and volunteers.

We are also proud to present renowned author Diana Canul as our keynote speaker. A teacher and longtime supporter of educational causes, Ms. Canul has published over two dozen children's books. Signed copies of her latest release, *Cat Tails*, will be available for purchase in the main lobby.

149. What type of event is being promoted?

(A) An industry conference
(B) A restaurant opening
(C) A museum anniversary
(D) An awards ceremony

150. What will NOT be featured at the event?

(A) A video presentation
(B) A musical performance
(C) A speech
(D) A contest

151. What is indicated about Ms. Canul?

(A) She will be donating some books to the museum.
(B) She will receive an award for her achievements.
(C) She cares greatly about educational matters.
(D) She is a regular customer of Café Lyon.

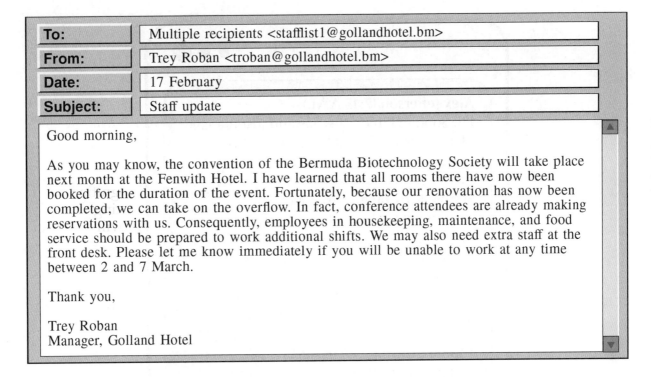

To:	Multiple recipients <stafflist1@gollandhotel.bm>
From:	Trey Roban <troban@gollandhotel.bm>
Date:	17 February
Subject:	Staff update

Good morning,

As you may know, the convention of the Bermuda Biotechnology Society will take place next month at the Fenwith Hotel. I have learned that all rooms there have now been booked for the duration of the event. Fortunately, because our renovation has now been completed, we can take on the overflow. In fact, conference attendees are already making reservations with us. Consequently, employees in housekeeping, maintenance, and food service should be prepared to work additional shifts. We may also need extra staff at the front desk. Please let me know immediately if you will be unable to work at any time between 2 and 7 March.

Thank you,

Trey Roban
Manager, Golland Hotel

152. What is a purpose of the e-mail?

(A) To introduce a new staff member
(B) To confirm a room reservation
(C) To explain the need for additional help
(D) To provide updates on the hotel's expansion

153. What is indicated about the Fenwith Hotel?

(A) It will not be open for a week in March.
(B) It will hold a professional gathering.
(C) It is due to be renovated.
(D) It is interviewing potential employees.

GO ON TO THE NEXT PAGE

Questions 154-155 refer to the following text-message chain.

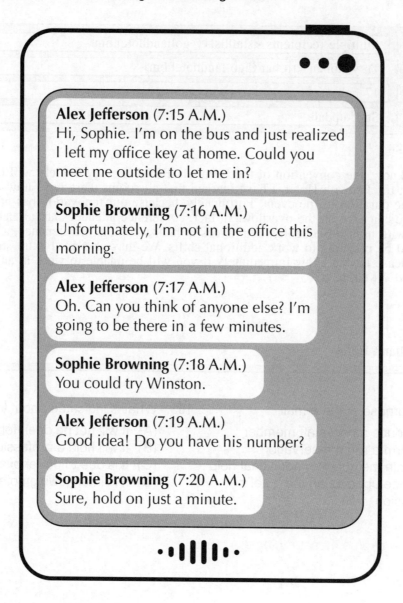

Alex Jefferson (7:15 A.M.)
Hi, Sophie. I'm on the bus and just realized I left my office key at home. Could you meet me outside to let me in?

Sophie Browning (7:16 A.M.)
Unfortunately, I'm not in the office this morning.

Alex Jefferson (7:17 A.M.)
Oh. Can you think of anyone else? I'm going to be there in a few minutes.

Sophie Browning (7:18 A.M.)
You could try Winston.

Alex Jefferson (7:19 A.M.)
Good idea! Do you have his number?

Sophie Browning (7:20 A.M.)
Sure, hold on just a minute.

154. What does Mr. Jefferson ask for help with?

(A) Finishing a project
(B) Getting into a building
(C) Traveling to a meeting
(D) Understanding a bus schedule

155. At 7:18 A.M., what does Ms. Browning most likely mean when she writes, "You could try Winston"?

(A) A coworker might be in the office.
(B) A coworker might give him a ride.
(C) A coworker could make a phone call.
(D) A coworker could give a presentation.

Questions 156-157 refer to the following e-mail.

```
┌─────────────────────────────────────────────────────────────┐
│                          *E-mail*                            │
├─────────────────────────────────────────────────────────────┤
│   To:        Lynn Simmel                                     │
│   From:      Art Moody                                       │
│   Subject:   Repaving                                        │
│   Date:      30 March                                        │
├─────────────────────────────────────────────────────────────┤
```

Dear Ms. Simmel:

I want to check if your company would be able to resurface the asphalt driveway that leads to the corporate headquarters of my company. I was impressed with the work that People's Pavers did on the streets around Rob's Marketplace in downtown Somerville. Our driveway is located on Sycamore Boulevard, the public road that you will soon be repaving during the next phase of your work for the city of Somerville. Our driveway is two lanes wide and just about 400 metres in length. I wonder if you might consider reducing your pricing somewhat since this work would be in such a convenient location.

I look forward to hearing from you.

Sincerely,

Art Moody
Tayco Pharmaceuticals

---

156. What is the purpose of the e-mail?

(A) To accept a cost estimate
(B) To announce some rate changes
(C) To request some measurements
(D) To propose a possible job

157. Where does Ms. Simmel work?

(A) At People's Pavers
(B) At Rob's Marketplace
(C) At Somerville City Hall
(D) At Tayco Pharmaceuticals

GO ON TO THE NEXT PAGE

MEMO

To: All employees at Manoukian Accounting
From: Jared Croce, Office Manager
Date: September 28
Subject: Update

We are now in the process of updating employee work spaces. — [1] —. All of the fixed-height desks and chairs will be replaced with adjustable-height standing desks and active-position chairs.

The new work configurations will allow employees to switch easily from sitting to standing and then back again. — [2] —. Everyone will also receive new energy-efficient desk lamps. — [3] —. Officewide use of these new lamps will allow us to reduce our reliance on overhead ceiling lights, lowering overall energy costs by 10 percent. — [4] —.

158. Why was the memo issued to employees?

(A) To ask them to complete a survey
(B) To alert them to changes in work schedules
(C) To inform them about new office furniture
(D) To provide them with details of changes in management

159. According to the memo, how is Manoukian Accounting planning to save money?

(A) By installing a new heating system
(B) By making less use of ceiling lights
(C) By switching to a low-cost energy supplier
(D) By allowing employees to work from home

160. In which of the positions marked [1], [2], [3], and [4] does the following sentence best belong?

"This flexibility will help employees to remain more active throughout the day."

(A) [1]
(B) [2]
(C) [3]
(D) [4]

TEST 1

```
*E-mail*

To:        All Staff

From:      Jason Saylor

Subject:   Company envelopes

Date:      April 12
```

Dear Team,

Unfortunately, we have run out of Leewood Associates printed envelopes. Until the next batch arrives with our regular office supply order on April 15, please use Leewood Associates return-address labels for any outgoing mail. For brochures about new home listings or our professional property management services, there is no need to include any return address as our current contact information is already printed on all of our promotional materials.

When using return-address labels, please remember to check them carefully since we moved offices only two months ago and some of them still include our former address.

All the best,

Jason Saylor
Executive Assistant

161. According to the e-mail, what will happen on April 15?

(A) A business will move to a new location.
(B) A shipment will arrive.
(C) Mail delivery will be suspended.
(D) A marketing brochure will be printed.

162. What type of business most likely is Leewood Associates?

(A) A real estate agency
(B) A graphic design firm
(C) A shipping company
(D) A stationery store

163. What is the problem with some return-address labels?

(A) They are too small.
(B) They have an error in the company name.
(C) They have the wrong address.
(D) They feature the company's old logo.

GO ON TO THE NEXT PAGE

Glasgow Daily News

News About Town
By Alison Breen

GLASGOW (25 April)—It is taking some time, experimentation, and adjustment, but the robot Angus is here to stay. Angus began his stint at Bread and Greens grocery store on Peterson Street in March.

While Angus is the most advanced robot produced by Cushman Robotics, his adaptation to store life has not gone completely smoothly. For example, during his first days on the job, Angus began quoting to patrons product prices that were largely inaccurate. But this turned out not to be a defect in Angus—someone had accidentally loaded an outdated price list into his memory.

Some customers have enjoyed trying to interact with Angus despite his currently limited abilities. Arif Nothazai is urging both staff and patrons to allow Angus a chance to adjust and learn. Mr. Nothazai explained, "Every new employee needs a training period. I myself have only been here in my supervisory role for less than a year. I needed time to gain familiarity with my new environment. It is the same with Angus."

At the store's bakery reopening last week, Angus told jokes and bantered with customers while offering them samples of fresh-baked goods. Store clerk Andrea Cronin remarked, "Angus has his quirks, but he keeps everyone laughing. He is definitely a valued member of our team."

164. What is the purpose of the article?
(A) To report on local tourism
(B) To discuss a recent change in a store
(C) To outline employee-training techniques
(D) To chronicle the career of a business owner

165. What issue with the robot is mentioned?
(A) It has insufficient memory.
(B) It has upset some staff members.
(C) It has given customers outdated information.
(D) It has defective parts that need to be replaced.

166. Who most likely is Mr. Nothazai?
(A) A mechanical engineer
(B) A shop clerk
(C) A baker
(D) A manager

167. What is suggested about the bakery?
(A) It was closed temporarily.
(B) It will be offering special discounts.
(C) It is hiring more help.
(D) It will soon be selling coffee and tea.

Questions 168-171 refer to the following notice.

> ## Grune Plaza Train Station
> ## Customer Notice
>
> Beginning on Monday, September 30, the Station Enhancement Project will be implemented at the Grune Plaza Train Station. The project is expected to last two months. — [1] —.
>
> During this time, the Forrest Avenue stairway entrance will be closed while the nearby south side hallway undergoes remodeling to accommodate new shops. Please use the alternate entrance on the School Street side to access the waiting area and platforms. For your safety in and around the station, always obey posted signs and do not walk through prohibited areas. — [2] —.
>
> Also, please note that the elevator near the platforms will be shut off after 5:00 P.M. every day for the safety of off-hours construction workers. Passengers requiring an elevator in the evening can use the elevator in the north side hallway, and from there make their way across the indoor bridge to the platforms.
>
> We thank you for your patience as we continue to expand and improve our services based on feedback we have received from our passengers. — [3] —. For more information in English or other languages, please call (221) 555-0101 between the hours of 8:00 A.M. and 9:00 P.M. — [4] —. You may also visit www.gruneplaza.com for the latest updates on the Station Enhancement Project.

168. What is one goal of the project?
(A) To train employees to monitor platforms
(B) To expand the number of waiting areas
(C) To add digital signs to the station
(D) To prepare for more stores

169. What does the notice suggest about Grune Plaza Train Station?
(A) It has only one entrance.
(B) It has several ways to get to the platforms.
(C) It typically closes at 5:00 P.M.
(D) It was built near a famous bridge.

170. According to the notice, who should call the number provided?
(A) People who are interested in customer-service jobs
(B) People who need help accessing the station's Web site
(C) People who want information in a different language
(D) People who want to provide feedback about their experience

171. In which of the positions marked [1], [2], [3], and [4] does the following sentence best belong?

"These spaces will be marked off with yellow tape."
(A) [1]
(B) [2]
(C) [3]
(D) [4]

Questions 172-175 refer to the following online chat discussion.

Kate Blum (9:17 A.M.)
Good morning, everyone. I just wanted to do a quick check to make certain everything is in place for this Saturday's conference.

Ken Miyashiro (9:18 A.M.)
We're all set. And since the conference is sold out, we are going to broadcast it live over the Internet so that people can watch it on their devices.

Yuri Kang (9:19 A.M.)
Is that completely arranged—camera operators, software, viewer access, and so on?

Ken Miyashiro (9:20 A.M.)
Yes. We've hired everyone, and we have the software, so we should be ready. People who want to watch the conference over the Internet still have to register and pay on our Web site, and then they'll get online access to see Tom Akana's keynote address and all the scheduled conference sessions.

Gabriel Lontoc (9:22 A.M.)
It's wonderful that Tom Akana has agreed to speak. It will be interesting to hear how he created Honalo Coffee Roasters and built it into a profitable company.

Kate Blum (9:23 A.M.)
He is pleased to do it. He thinks it could help others who want to start restaurants or food-related businesses. OK. I think that's it. Let's meet again on Wednesday morning.

172. Who most likely is the intended audience for the conference?

(A) Photographers
(B) Software engineers
(C) Technology job candidates
(D) Food industry professionals

173. What is mentioned about the conference?

(A) In-person registration is sold out.
(B) Online access is free.
(C) The date was changed.
(D) The keynote speaker canceled.

174. What does Ms. Kang ask about?

(A) The broadcasting details
(B) The registration forms
(C) The Web site
(D) The hiring process

175. At 9:23 A.M., what does Ms. Blum mean when she writes, "He is pleased to do it"?

(A) Mr. Akana is glad to go out for coffee.
(B) Mr. Akana is happy to give a speech.
(C) Mr. Akana is satisfied with the live-streaming arrangements.
(D) Mr. Akana is delighted with the work arrangements.

TEST 1

GO ON TO THE NEXT PAGE

MEMO

To: All Employees
From: Xinhua Huang, IT Solutions Manager
Date: Wednesday, 18 November
Re: Upcoming Multi-Factor Authentication

Jurong Distribution takes the confidentiality of its communication seriously. This is why we will be implementing multi-factor authentication (MFA). MFA is a two-step process that safeguards corporate information, including data contained in e-mail and other communications.

All Jurong Distribution employees are required to set up MFA for their work e-mail accounts before 1 December. You will receive an e-mail from me tomorrow with instructions.

Once MFA is set up for your company e-mail account, you will be required to enter a six-digit verification code each time you log in to your e-mail account. The code will be sent by text message to your mobile phone. You will have 5 minutes to use it. After this time, the code becomes invalid.

If you still need help or have questions after setting up MFA, please contact it@jurongdistribution.com.sg, and Ms. Laura Smith, an IT specialist, will respond within the next business day. IT support will only be available during the standard business hours of 9 A.M. to 5 P.M.

Thank you,

Xinhua Huang

To:	it@jurongdistribution.com.sg
From:	brettlow@jurongdistribution.com.sg
Date:	Thursday, 19 November, 5:25 P.M.
Subject:	MFA code

Hello,

After I finished setting up MFA, I logged in to my e-mail account and received a code on my mobile phone. However, when I returned to the office after lunch and attempted to enter the code, I received an error message. I am positive I entered the correct code. What should I have done differently? My office line is 6345 0331.

Thank you in advance,

Brett Low

176. Why did Ms. Huang send the memo?

(A) To request contact information
(B) To announce a new company policy
(C) To welcome new employees
(D) To apologize for broken equipment

177. According to the memo, how can employees get additional help?

(A) By calling Ms. Huang directly
(B) By speaking with their supervisor
(C) By contacting the IT department
(D) By attending an instructional session

178. Why was Mr. Low unable to log in to his e-mail account?

(A) He lost his mobile phone.
(B) He used an incorrect password.
(C) He did not enter the verification code in time.
(D) He did not use a valid e-mail address.

179. When most likely will Ms. Smith contact Mr. Low?

(A) On November 19
(B) On November 20
(C) On November 25
(D) On December 1

180. In the e-mail, the word "positive" in paragraph 1, line 3, is closest in meaning to

(A) certain
(B) optimistic
(C) active
(D) helpful

GO ON TO THE NEXT PAGE

Kenfar Packaging
3 Adavale Road
Blue Earth, MN 56013

June 18

Industrial-Tech Farmers Magazine
324 North Valley Road
Phoenixville, PA 19460

Dear Editor,

Mr. Oseed's letter to the editor last month urged that reusable packaging be made available for bulk agricultural products. I am pleased to report that such a product does exist.

My company, Kenfar Packaging, offers high-quality packaging that meets the industry's needs: not only can our products be reused numerous times, but they are made from nearly 50 percent recycled materials as well. This year alone, we project that our company's packaging solutions will prevent over one million kilos of plastics from ending up in landfills.

We offer a wide variety of bag styles, and every one of them effectively secures goods from pests and spillage, both while in transit and while in storage. Kenfar Packaging proudly offers our environmentally friendly products to the farming community.

Sincerely,

Sally Heffentrager
Sally Heffentrager

KENFAR PACKAGING
Environmentally friendly bulk-sized bags

BAG TYPES	SPECIAL FEATURES
Type 1: Large Produce	Wide-mesh fabric for ventilation; suitable for potatoes, onions, and citrus fruits
Type 2: Grains and Seeds	Impermeable liner blocks moisture and prevents product leakage
Type 3: Beans and Nuts	Stackable for efficient use of storage space; suitable for coffee beans and peanuts
Type 4: Animal Feed Pellets	Innovative opening in top of bag allows for rapid filling

Bags can be customized with your logo and information.
See our Web site for further information, quantities, and prices.
www.kenfarpackaging.com

181. What is the purpose of the letter?

(A) To review a popular product
(B) To describe a new storage facility
(C) To respond to a recently published letter
(D) To disagree with a policy change

182. Who most likely is Ms. Heffentrager?

(A) A farmworker
(B) A food-safety expert
(C) A farm-magazine journalist
(D) A packaging-company employee

183. In the letter, the word "project" in paragraph 2, line 3, is closest in meaning to

(A) assign
(B) extend
(C) arrange
(D) estimate

184. What is true about the products listed in the advertisement?

(A) They are less expensive than competitors' products.
(B) They are made from plant-based cloth.
(C) They are manufactured using some recycled materials.
(D) They are recent additions to Kenfar Packaging's product line.

185. What product would likely work best for holding oranges?

(A) Type 1
(B) Type 2
(C) Type 3
(D) Type 4

GO ON TO THE NEXT PAGE

Meet Helpful Hanna, a New Addition to the Modern Home

Helpful Hanna, the Talking Refrigerator, can revolutionize your home. Designed to help organize your life, Hanna uses apps and voice recognition to connect your refrigerator to your phone and to your lifestyle. Available in six stylish colors.

You can ask Hanna to:
- Create a shopping list
- Help plan your meals
- Provide recipes
- Fill your water pitcher
- Display your calendar
  And so much more!

Yohan's Appliances
41 North Franklin Street
Clendenin, West Virginia 25045
(304) 555-0199

Frigation 100 [Model FG-100]	Coolbry 500 [Model CB-500]
• Base model • 22 cubic feet • Excellent reliability and energy ratings • 3 colors in stock • $1,000	• Family, digital hub zone, voice activated • 26 cubic feet • Hot- and cold-water dispenser • Many apps available at additional charge • $2,000 (on sale for $1,800)
Helpful Hanna [Model HRX-276]	**Coolbry 700** [Model CB-700]
• Digital interactive center • 27 cubic feet • Extra-large ice capacity • 2 colors in stock • $3,100	• Digital interactive center • 28 cubic feet • Translator that recognizes and speaks 6 languages • Multilevel lighting • $3,000

Review of Coolbry 500 Refrigerator
May 30

I just returned home from spending two weeks at my daughter's house while she and her husband were away on a business trip. She recently purchased her first smart fridge because she thought it would be helpful to her young family. She likes the novelty of being able to talk to her refrigerator, and I can see that her kids like touching the digital screen. However, I found that the refrigerator doesn't seem to make life easier. It just makes it noisier. Just because the technology exists doesn't mean we need it. For me, a plain old refrigerator that keeps my food cold is more than enough. As long as my refrigerator is reliable, energy saving, and comparatively inexpensive, I'm satisfied. When I buy a new refrigerator in the fall, it will be a simple, old-fashioned model that does not talk back to me. My kitchen is already noisy enough!

—Gertrude Caputo

186. According to the advertisement, what is a feature of Helpful Hanna?

(A) A built-in coffee maker
(B) A hot-water dispenser
(C) A language translator
(D) A meal planner

187. What is suggested about Yohan's Appliances?

(A) It recently opened a store in Clendenin.
(B) It does not have all colors of Helpful Hanna available.
(C) It has multiple locations.
(D) It does not offer discounts on its appliances.

188. How does the Coolbry 700 refrigerator differ from the other refrigerators?

(A) It is more energy efficient.
(B) It offers more apps.
(C) It is larger.
(D) It costs more.

189. What does the review suggest about Ms. Caputo?

(A) She lives with her daughter.
(B) She took a business trip recently.
(C) She was away from home in May.
(D) She has young children.

190. What model refrigerator would Ms. Caputo most likely buy?

(A) FG-100
(B) CB-500
(C) HRX-276
(D) CB-700

GO ON TO THE NEXT PAGE

Questions 191-195 refer to the following e-mails and form.

To:	Bess Sound Systems staff
From:	Hans Loffler
Date:	August 1
Subject:	Bulldogs Basketball Tickets
Attachment:	Group Ticket Form

Get out your Barbosa Bulldogs jerseys! As we have done in recent years, we are planning to coordinate a group ticket purchase for basketball games at Centerway Arena. Once again, the Bulldogs' schedule includes games against teams from around the region, and many games are already sold out. Group tickets are discounted based on the size of the group.

Group Ticket Pricing

8–20 tickets	$20 each
21–50 tickets	$18 each
51–100 tickets	$15 each
101+ tickets	$12 each

Interested employees should complete the attached form by indicating the number of tickets you would like to order. Completed forms must be returned to me by August 10. I will contact the Bulldogs' ticket office by August 15 to reserve tickets for the games. Once we confirm that we can get enough tickets for those games, full payment will be due within two weeks.

Please e-mail me directly if you have any questions.

Hans Loffler

Barbosa Bulldogs Group Tickets

Employee Name: _____

Date	Opponent	Number of Tickets
September 18	Branchfield Parrots	SOLD OUT
September 27	Middletown Rush	
October 1	Tigg Lake Bears	SOLD OUT
October 13	Clarkton Giants	SOLD OUT
November 8	Drake City Comets	

To:	hloffler@besssound.com
From:	jdodson@barbosabulldogs.org
Date:	August 19
Subject:	Re: Barbosa Bulldogs

Dear Mr. Loffler:

Thank you for your inquiry about Barbosa Bulldogs group tickets. I am pleased to hear that the Bess Sound Systems staff is so enthusiastic about our team! To answer your question, yes, we can reserve a block of 120 seats for the Middletown Rush game and 105 for the game against the Drake City Comets. The seats will be in the upper level of the arena. Once you confirm that this plan is acceptable, we can make arrangements for payment and delivery of the tickets.

Regards,

Jorge Dodson

TEST 1

191. In the first e-mail, what does Mr. Loffler suggest about the Barbosa Bulldogs?

(A) Their season begins on August 1.
(B) Their games are popular with fans.
(C) They have moved to a new arena.
(D) They will play fewer games this year.

192. According to the first e-mail, what is true about group tickets?

(A) They are available for groups of eight or more.
(B) They have not been offered in previous years.
(C) They are cheaper before the season begins.
(D) They must be purchased online.

193. In the second e-mail, what does Mr. Dodson tell Mr. Loffler about?

(A) Game times
(B) Ticket prices
(C) Seat locations
(D) A special promotion

194. How much will Bess Sound Systems employees most likely pay for each ticket?

(A) $20
(B) $18
(C) $15
(D) $12

195. When will Bess Sound Systems employees most likely attend a game?

(A) On September 18
(B) On October 1
(C) On October 13
(D) On November 8

GO ON TO THE NEXT PAGE

June 28

Hello, Chelsea Writers board! My name is Thea Fitzgerald. I am leaving my position in one month to take a job in another city, and my team is looking for a candidate to replace me. The opening is for a full-time technology reporter. The reporter would work in-house at one of two locations. The main headquarters is here in New York City, and the satellite office is in Washington, D.C. The team is most interested in candidates who can begin on August 1.

I have worked at Omnitech Review for nearly three years and highly recommend it to writers looking for career growth. This entry-level journalism position is a wonderful way to start your career; it is as rewarding as it is challenging.

I am including a hyperlink to the official job announcement with instructions for applying. Feel free to e-mail me directly with any questions. Though I am not in charge of hiring, I am happy to pass along to my supervisor any applications that stand out. Please act soon; the application deadline is July 15.

Thea Fitzgerald, t.fitzgerald@omnitechreview.com

E-mail

To:	t.fitzgerald@omnitechreview.com
From:	sojinlim@dennisonmail.com
Subject:	Your post
Date:	June 29

Hello, Ms. Fitzgerald,

Thank you for your June 28 post. I am the moderator for this board and a few others. I noticed that the link you mention is actually not included in the post. Would you please edit your post to include the link so readers can access the job announcement?

Also, would it help you if I cross posted this to our hiring board based in Washington, D.C.? Additionally, I am affiliated with the popular Five Boroughs Jobs board and can assist you if you would like to use that board. But unlike with most boards, you need to pay a fee to post a job opening there. If you are interested, let me know.

Sincerely,

So Jin Lim

https://www.omnitechreview.com/open_positions/1256981

Technology Reporter (entry-level)

The technology reporter will be responsible for writing at least two breaking news stories each day. The reporter will also be expected to write additional, longer-form features once a month. These articles will cover broad trends and topics in the industry. For this reason, the reporter will need to be skilled in both research and interviewing.

The reporter will join a growing team responsible for telling bold and original stories that help an audience of technology professionals stay current with industry news and function efficiently and creatively. Expertise in cutting-edge technology is not required; Omnitech Review will train the right person. University degree preferred. Competitive salary is commensurate with experience, and generous benefits are included.

E-mail a cover letter, résumé, and the names of three references (include contact information) to Mr. Kent Xi at k.xi@omnitechreview.com. Reference "Job #1256981" in the subject line of your e-mail.

196. What does Ms. Fitzgerald state about herself?

(A) She is moving soon to Washington, D.C.
(B) She was recently promoted to a supervisory position.
(C) She is leaving her job at Omnitech Review in one month.
(D) She has worked at Omnitech Review for four years.

197. What is most likely true about the Chelsea Writers board?

(A) Posts expire within one week.
(B) Posts are free of charge.
(C) Posts are always revised by a moderator.
(D) Posts often contain conflicting information.

198. What do Ms. Fitzgerald's official work responsibilities at Omnitech Review probably include?

(A) Writing two articles each day
(B) Posting job openings
(C) Conducting training for technology professionals
(D) Corresponding with editors around the world

199. In the e-mail, what does Ms. Lim ask Ms. Fitzgerald to do?

(A) Pay an overdue bill as soon as possible
(B) Add some missing information to her online post
(C) Move her online post to a different board
(D) Decide whether she will become a board moderator

200. According to the Web page, what is a requirement of the technology reporter position?

(A) Attending annual technology conferences
(B) An expert-level understanding of technology issues
(C) An advanced university degree in journalism
(D) The ability to conduct research as needed

Stop! This is the end of the test. If you finish before time is called, you may go back to Parts 5, 6, and 7 and check your work.

NO TEST MATERIAL ON THIS PAGE

TEST 2

LISTENING TEST p.72

READING TEST p.84

＊解答用紙は本誌 p.112 の後ろに綴じ込まれています。

実際のテストでは問題用紙の裏側に、以下のようなテスト全体についての指示が印刷されています。
この指示を念頭においてテストに取り組みましょう。

General Directions

This test is designed to measure your English language ability. The test is divided into two sections: Listening and Reading.

You must mark all of your answers on the separate answer sheet. For each question, you should select the best answer from the answer choices given. Then, on your answer sheet, you should find the number of the question and fill in the space that corresponds to the letter of the answer that you have selected. If you decide to change an answer, completely erase your old answer and then mark your new answer.

訳 ## 全体についての指示

このテストはあなたの英語言語能力を測定するよう設計されています。テストはリスニングとリーディングという2つのセクションに分けられています。

答えは全て別紙の解答用紙にマークしてください。それぞれの設問について、与えられた選択肢から最も適切な答えを選びます。そして解答用紙の該当する問題番号に、選択した答えを塗りつぶしてください。答えを修正する場合は、元の答えを完全に消してから新しい答えをマークしてください。

LISTENING TEST

In the Listening test, you will be asked to demonstrate how well you understand spoken English. The entire Listening test will last approximately 45 minutes. There are four parts, and directions are given for each part. You must mark your answers on the separate answer sheet. Do not write your answers in your test book.

PART 1

Directions: For each question in this part, you will hear four statements about a picture in your test book. When you hear the statements, you must select the one statement that best describes what you see in the picture. Then find the number of the question on your answer sheet and mark your answer. The statements will not be printed in your test book and will be spoken only one time.

Statement (C), "They're sitting at a table," is the best description of the picture, so you should select answer (C) and mark it on your answer sheet.

1.

2.

GO ON TO THE NEXT PAGE

3.

4.

5.

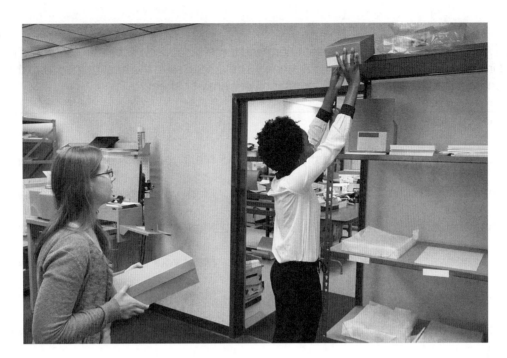

6.

GO ON TO THE NEXT PAGE ➤

PART 2

Directions: You will hear a question or statement and three responses spoken in English. They will not be printed in your test book and will be spoken only one time. Select the best response to the question or statement and mark the letter (A), (B), or (C) on your answer sheet.

7. Mark your answer on your answer sheet.

8. Mark your answer on your answer sheet.

9. Mark your answer on your answer sheet.

10. Mark your answer on your answer sheet.

11. Mark your answer on your answer sheet.

12. Mark your answer on your answer sheet.

13. Mark your answer on your answer sheet.

14. Mark your answer on your answer sheet.

15. Mark your answer on your answer sheet.

16. Mark your answer on your answer sheet.

17. Mark your answer on your answer sheet.

18. Mark your answer on your answer sheet.

19. Mark your answer on your answer sheet.

20. Mark your answer on your answer sheet.

21. Mark your answer on your answer sheet.

22. Mark your answer on your answer sheet.

23. Mark your answer on your answer sheet.

24. Mark your answer on your answer sheet.

25. Mark your answer on your answer sheet.

26. Mark your answer on your answer sheet.

27. Mark your answer on your answer sheet.

28. Mark your answer on your answer sheet.

29. Mark your answer on your answer sheet.

30. Mark your answer on your answer sheet.

31. Mark your answer on your answer sheet.

PART 3

Directions: You will hear some conversations between two or more people. You will be asked to answer three questions about what the speakers say in each conversation. Select the best response to each question and mark the letter (A), (B), (C), or (D) on your answer sheet. The conversations will not be printed in your test book and will be spoken only one time.

32. Where does the man work?
    (A) At a theater
    (B) At a radio station
    (C) At an art gallery
    (D) At a musical instrument shop

33. What does the woman ask the business to do?
    (A) Post some signs
    (B) Sponsor an event
    (C) Mentor some students
    (D) Change a policy

34. Why is the owner currently unavailable?
    (A) He is taking a lunch break.
    (B) He is conducting an interview.
    (C) He is on vacation.
    (D) He is visiting a client.

35. Where does the conversation most likely take place?
    (A) At a café
    (B) At a library
    (C) At an electronics shop
    (D) At a sports arena

36. According to the man, what did the business recently do?
    (A) It opened a second location.
    (B) It released a book.
    (C) It changed a floor plan.
    (D) It finalized a contract.

37. How can the woman win a gift card?
    (A) By posting a photograph
    (B) By completing an online survey
    (C) By attending a special event
    (D) By commenting on a video

38. What field do the speakers most likely work in?
    (A) Hospitality
    (B) Advertising
    (C) Interior design
    (D) Software development

39. What does the man say he did?
    (A) He reserved a car.
    (B) He updated a schedule.
    (C) He created a new logo.
    (D) He paid a registration fee.

40. Why will the speakers need extra time?
    (A) To stop for some food
    (B) To check in at a hotel
    (C) To load some boxes
    (D) To read some directions

41. Why does the woman want to change a meeting time?
    (A) She will be training some employees.
    (B) She is scheduled to attend a lunch.
    (C) She has a doctor's appointment.
    (D) She is finishing a report.

42. What does the man imply when he says, "I can't connect to the Internet"?
    (A) A meeting place is unsuitable.
    (B) He has not read an e-mail.
    (C) A project he is working on is delayed.
    (D) He needs to buy a new computer.

43. What will the woman get for the man?
    (A) A password
    (B) A calendar
    (C) An operator's manual
    (D) A manager's signature

GO ON TO THE NEXT PAGE

TEST 2

44. What does the woman ask for?

(A) An explanation of a policy
(B) A suggestion for a new product
(C) A recommendation for an employee
(D) An update on an assignment

45. What will take place at the end of the month?

(A) A client visit
(B) A marketing meeting
(C) A social media event
(D) A new hire orientation

46. What does the woman want to discuss later?

(A) Speakers for a presentation
(B) Locations for a workshop
(C) Upgrades for equipment
(D) Estimates for a budget

47. What are the speakers most likely preparing for?

(A) A press conference
(B) An industry convention
(C) A team dinner
(D) A news broadcast

48. According to the speakers, why was a project undertaken?

(A) To increase safety
(B) To reduce costs
(C) To improve access to a port
(D) To repair damage to a highway

49. What will the man probably do soon?

(A) Locate a video
(B) Give a talk
(C) Set up some equipment
(D) Pick up a guest speaker

50. What do the men want to do next year?

(A) Expand a business
(B) Host a charity gala
(C) Start an internship program
(D) Attend a trade show

51. What most likely is the woman's job?

(A) Lawyer
(B) Travel agent
(C) Accountant
(D) Computer technician

52. What does the woman need to see?

(A) Some schedules
(B) Product samples
(C) Some data
(D) Security badges

53. What are the speakers discussing?

(A) A company policy
(B) A business merger
(C) Some vacation plans
(D) Some training sessions

54. What does the woman say she did last weekend?

(A) She took a class.
(B) She packed boxes.
(C) She visited a relative.
(D) She prepared a presentation.

55. Why does the man say, "a lot of our coworkers bring a sweater to work"?

(A) To request a favor
(B) To make a suggestion
(C) To disagree with a dress code
(D) To explain a decision

56. Where does the woman most likely work?

    (A) At a farm
    (B) At a supermarket
    (C) At a restaurant
    (D) At a landscaping company

57. Why is the woman unable to fill out a form?

    (A) She is busy with some customers.
    (B) She has lost a vendor's telephone
        number.
    (C) She does not have access to a
        computer.
    (D) She cannot remember a product ID
        number.

58. What does the man agree to do?

    (A) Extend a warranty
    (B) Provide an access code
    (C) Apply a discount
    (D) Send a technician

59. What are the speakers mainly discussing?

    (A) A security-camera network
    (B) A payment system
    (C) A billboard advertisement
    (D) A pedestrian walkway

60. What is the man asked to provide?

    (A) A city map
    (B) Some additional funding
    (C) Some passenger statistics
    (D) Updated transit schedules

61. Why is the man concerned?

    (A) A project is too expensive.
    (B) Some software is unreliable.
    (C) A design is unappealing.
    (D) A deadline might be missed.

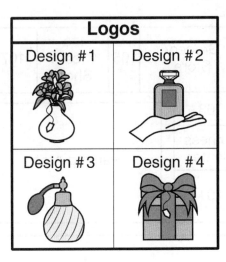

62. What news does the woman share with
    the man?

    (A) Annual revenue has increased.
    (B) An item will be temporarily unavailable.
    (C) A department store will sell their
        product.
    (D) A factory has sent some packaging
        samples.

63. What does the woman suggest doing?

    (A) Filming some commercials
    (B) Ordering shopping bags
    (C) Conducting a survey
    (D) Updating a Web site

64. Look at the graphic. Which logo does the
    woman prefer?

    (A) Design 1
    (B) Design 2
    (C) Design 3
    (D) Design 4

TEST 2

GO ON TO THE NEXT PAGE

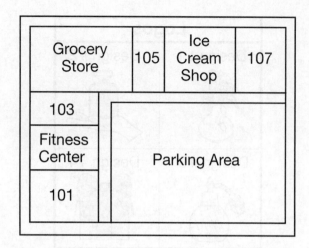

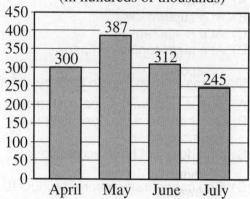

Units Produced per Month
(in hundreds of thousands)

65. What kind of business is the man going to open?

(A) A bakery
(B) A bookstore
(C) A pottery studio
(D) An antique store

66. Look at the graphic. Which unit does the man choose?

(A) Unit 101
(B) Unit 103
(C) Unit 105
(D) Unit 107

67. What will the speakers do next week?

(A) Discuss a contract
(B) Take some pictures
(C) Create a company logo
(D) Meet with an interior decorator

68. What does the woman ask the man about?

(A) A quarterly report
(B) A production schedule
(C) An expense statement
(D) A factory location

69. Look at the graphic. What month is the man referring to?

(A) April
(B) May
(C) June
(D) July

70. Why is the woman optimistic about next year?

(A) A new factory will open.
(B) Demand is expected to increase.
(C) Raw material costs will fall.
(D) A new product will be available.

PART 4

Directions: You will hear some talks given by a single speaker. You will be asked to answer three questions about what the speaker says in each talk. Select the best response to each question and mark the letter (A), (B), (C), or (D) on your answer sheet. The talks will not be printed in your test book and will be spoken only one time.

71. What event will take place on the weekend?

(A) An art fair
(B) A product launch
(C) An award ceremony
(D) An art gallery opening

72. According to the speaker, what is special about Emiko Ito's creations?

(A) They are signed by Ms. Ito.
(B) They are sold entirely online.
(C) They are distributed worldwide.
(D) They are made with recycled materials.

73. What will the speaker most likely do next?

(A) Lead a guided tour
(B) Give a demonstration
(C) Conduct an interview
(D) Announce a prize winner

74. Why was a change made in the company cafeteria?

(A) To reduce food waste
(B) To decrease waiting time
(C) To save energy
(D) To comply with new regulations

75. What action was taken?

(A) Cash registers were upgraded.
(B) Plastic trays were replaced.
(C) Healthier food was made available.
(D) A self-serve area was added.

76. What are the listeners encouraged to do next?

(A) Place an order
(B) Taste some food
(C) Vote on a proposal
(D) Clean up a room

77. What type of product is the speaker discussing?

(A) Automobiles
(B) Headphones
(C) Shoes
(D) Cameras

78. What issue does the speaker mention?

(A) Some padding is uncomfortable.
(B) A budget is limited.
(C) Sound quality needs to be improved.
(D) A shipment has been delayed.

79. Why does the speaker say, "They worked with us on last year's products"?

(A) To request a meeting
(B) To warn the listener
(C) To recommend a supplier
(D) To criticize a decision

80. What will take place on Friday?

(A) A town meeting
(B) A product release
(C) A building inspection
(D) A software update

81. What should the listeners do on Thursday?

(A) Put documents away
(B) Shut down computers
(C) Meet with a supervisor
(D) Sign up for training

82. What will be discussed next week?

(A) Volunteer opportunities
(B) Project expenses
(C) Overseas travel arrangements
(D) Employee schedules

TEST 2

GO ON TO THE NEXT PAGE

83. What subject does the game focus on?

(A) Reading
(B) Science
(C) Math
(D) History

84. What does the speaker say is special about the game?

(A) It is appropriate for families.
(B) It was designed by teachers.
(C) It can be played outdoors.
(D) It is recognized by an educational organization.

85. What does the speaker mean when he says, "this product will be very popular"?

(A) The listeners should act quickly.
(B) A marketing strategy has been successful.
(C) Sales projections were incorrect.
(D) A product line should be expanded.

_____

86. Where is the speech being given?

(A) At a library
(B) At a theater
(C) At a museum
(D) At a convention center

87. What did Gerhard Vogel do last year?

(A) He spoke at a conference.
(B) He wrote an autobiography.
(C) He gave a final performance.
(D) He donated some items.

88. What does the speaker say are available for purchase?

(A) Posters
(B) Books
(C) Tickets
(D) Musical instruments

_____

89. Where does the speaker most likely work?

(A) At a bank
(B) At a pharmacy
(C) At a dental clinic
(D) At an auto repair shop

90. What does the speaker mean when he says, "I hope the rest of your afternoon is free"?

(A) He needs some assistance with a project.
(B) His office is very busy.
(C) A later appointment time would be better.
(D) A procedure might take a long time.

91. What does the speaker say has happened?

(A) A payment has been submitted.
(B) Paperwork has been signed.
(C) Transportation has been scheduled.
(D) Supplies have been ordered.

_____

92. Who are the listeners?

(A) Delivery workers
(B) Automotive mechanics
(C) Professional cyclists
(D) Factory workers

93. What advantage does the speaker mention?

(A) Faster product assembly
(B) Improved workplace safety
(C) Additional storage capacity
(D) Efficient payment processing

94. What does the speaker remind the listeners to do?

(A) Wear their helmets
(B) Submit their time sheets
(C) Collect customer feedback
(D) Use a lock

_____

Airport Departure Board		
Flight	**Destination**	**Gate**
DA3049	Sacramento	1
AA1637	Philadelphia	2
JB2508	San Francisco	3
SW6421	Washington, D.C.	4

Energy Usage	
May	850 kWh
June	900 kWh
July	1,000 kWh
August	1,200 kWh

95. Look at the graphic. Which gate are the listeners waiting at?

(A) Gate 1
(B) Gate 2
(C) Gate 3
(D) Gate 4

96. What is the reason for a delay?

(A) The weather is too windy for takeoff.
(B) Luggage is still being loaded.
(C) The ground crew is fueling the plane.
(D) Repairs are being made.

97. What does the speaker encourage the listeners to do?

(A) Fasten seat belts
(B) Look at a snack menu
(C) Watch in-flight movies
(D) Ask staff for assistance

98. Who most likely is the speaker?

(A) A building inspector
(B) A sales consultant
(C) An apartment landlord
(D) A utility company executive

99. Look at the graphic. Which number is the speaker confused about?

(A) 850 kWh
(B) 900 kWh
(C) 1,000 kWh
(D) 1,200 kWh

100. What does the speaker say he wants to do later this week?

(A) Meet with the listener
(B) Announce a rate change
(C) Repair some equipment
(D) Document some damage

This is the end of the Listening test. Turn to Part 5 in your test book.

TEST 2

GO ON TO THE NEXT PAGE

READING TEST

In the Reading test, you will read a variety of texts and answer several different types of reading comprehension questions. The entire Reading test will last 75 minutes. There are three parts, and directions are given for each part. You are encouraged to answer as many questions as possible within the time allowed.

You must mark your answers on the separate answer sheet. Do not write your answers in your test book.

PART 5

Directions: A word or phrase is missing in each of the sentences below. Four answer choices are given below each sentence. Select the best answer to complete the sentence. Then mark the letter (A), (B), (C), or (D) on your answer sheet.

---

101. It is advisable to assign new tasks ------- to interns during the first month of training.

(A) slow
(B) slowest
(C) slowly
(D) slows

102. Mr. Barton and his team provide services ranging ------- fund-raising to coordinating events.

(A) like
(B) for
(C) from
(D) through

103. Customers who sign up for Garrett Tea Company's mailing list will receive free shipping on ------- next online order.

(A) theirs
(B) them
(C) their
(D) themselves

104. Mr. Iwata likes to be prepared, so he ------- arrives fifteen minutes early to meetings.

(A) very
(B) once
(C) quite
(D) always

105. Ms. Fache is heading a committee that will explore ways to make the province more ------- for small businesses.

(A) afford
(B) affording
(C) affordable
(D) afforded

106. The repair estimate ------- all costs for labor and parts.

(A) prefers
(B) accepts
(C) includes
(D) surrounds

107. The Destven Institute contact is a key ------- of information on energy-related matters.

(A) sourced
(B) source
(C) sources
(D) sourcing

108. East Highlands Adventures now offers guided hikes along several trails that the state ------- opened.

(A) especially
(B) rigidly
(C) recently
(D) intensely

109. Customer complaints that cannot be resolved ------- a call-center representative should be referred to a supervisor.
(A) out
(B) by
(C) and
(D) or

110. ------- filling out the online form, applicants must also upload a résumé.
(A) Furthermore
(B) Except for
(C) As far as
(D) In addition to

111. Allentown Paint Supply relocated ------- downtown office to Trenton Street.
(A) they
(B) ours
(C) yours
(D) its

112. The merchandise will be placed in a storage facility ------- the warehouse roof repairs are completed.
(A) over
(B) past
(C) with
(D) until

113. The Hartsfield Hotel offers ------- contemporary comforts for a building that was constructed a century ago.
(A) impressive
(B) impression
(C) impressed
(D) to impress

114. ------- Mr. Assink placed the order early, it still arrived late.
(A) Equally
(B) Besides
(C) Although
(D) Likewise

115. Due to the lack of -------, the president of Murtha Industries was not informed of the employees' concerns.
(A) communicate
(B) communicative
(C) communicated
(D) communication

116. The board of directors came to the ------- that it was necessary to hire a new CEO.
(A) conclusion
(B) distinction
(C) requirement
(D) statement

117. Claudine Dumay has been Neelon's head of purchasing ------- it opened for business.
(A) ever
(B) before
(C) since
(D) nonetheless

118. Amaford Stationery Store customers are asked to ------- a customer satisfaction survey after shopping.
(A) delegate
(B) rehearse
(C) accompany
(D) complete

119. Argorot Ltd. is working to create a steady supply chain ------- many challenges.
(A) former
(B) despite
(C) about
(D) otherwise

120. The director of North Ridge Library states that giving young children easy ------- to books promotes a love of reading.
(A) access
(B) path
(C) key
(D) way

121. The city council president said that getting the road-improvement bill passed was a significant -------.
(A) achieve
(B) achieves
(C) achieving
(D) achievement

122. ------- the memo, attendance at tomorrow's seminar is mandatory.
(A) According to
(B) Ahead of
(C) Along with
(D) Away from

GO ON TO THE NEXT PAGE

123. Mr. Park ------- missed his flight because of the severe traffic congestion this morning.

   (A) near
   (B) nearly
   (C) nearing
   (D) nearest

124. ------- breakfast is served daily for our club members from 6:00 A.M. to 9:30 A.M.

   (A) Complimentary
   (B) Appreciative
   (C) Favorable
   (D) Courteous

125. The study looks at major competitors in the marketplace and how they ------- themselves.

   (A) different
   (B) difference
   (C) differently
   (D) differentiate

126. Because Mr. Takata will be at the trade show, other marketing team members will ------- be there as well.

   (A) sharply
   (B) longer
   (C) probably
   (D) almost

127. Inxspace Corporation is the region's largest company, employing ------- 4,000 people.

   (A) approximately
   (B) approximate
   (C) approximation
   (D) approximated

128. Rojo Kitchen Products is following its ------- expansion plans by purchasing the Vernick Square Group.

   (A) retired
   (B) ambitious
   (C) hesitant
   (D) automatic

129. Horsham Engineering's accountant Kae Jung-Ho ------- the average yearly cost of company operations.

   (A) determine
   (B) determined
   (C) determining
   (D) determination

130. Making digital copies of files is a smart way to deal with an ------- of important documents.

   (A) abundance
   (B) extension
   (C) accordance
   (D) instance

PART 6

Directions: Read the texts that follow. A word, phrase, or sentence is missing in parts of each text. Four answer choices for each question are given below the text. Select the best answer to complete the text. Then mark the letter (A), (B), (C), or (D) on your answer sheet.

Questions 131-134 refer to the following e-mail.

To: Troy Diallo <diallo.t@bushwickcompany.com>
From: Margery Petersen <petersen.m@bushwickcompany.com>
Date: September 27
Subject: Springford Marketer

Dear Mr. Diallo,

Per your request, I ------- my evaluation of the Springford Marketer application. In my opinion,
                       131.

this would be a ------- purchase for the marketing department. It centralizes all aspects of the
                  132.

production process in one online location. This enables the marketing team leader to

------- the team's workflow on a day-to-day basis. I was particularly impressed by the fact that
133.

Springford Marketer can be used on phones as well as laptops. ------- . However, I am confident
                                                                134.

that the program would ultimately save us time and prove to be cost-effective.

Margery Petersen

TEST 2

131. (A) will complete
     (B) completes
     (C) completing
     (D) have completed

132. (A) trivial
     (B) portable
     (C) useful
     (D) memorable

133. (A) adjust
     (B) remind
     (C) expel
     (D) decline

134. (A) This was our most creative campaign so far.
     (B) The cost is perhaps a little high.
     (C) The reviews have been uniformly positive.
     (D) Our sales increased dramatically afterward.

GO ON TO THE NEXT PAGE

Scherwin-Lloyd Ltd. employees are advised that building maintenance will be conducted starting on 11 July. It is expected to ------- on 14 July. The work will take place only on the second and
135.
third floors of the building and may cause disruptions to staff in the proximity. -------. Workers
136.
with offices on the fourth floor and higher could be ------- affected by the process but should still
137.
plan for possible minor interruptions to their schedules. Please also note that staff will not have

basement access ------- this maintenance process, since that space will be used for storage of
138.
materials.

Please contact the building supervisor at 0149 5285 with any questions or concerns.

135. (A) return
(B) arrive
(C) conclude
(D) increase

136. (A) Those with offices on these floors may request temporary office relocation.
(B) The maintenance crews will work only after all offices close for the day.
(C) The dates of this project have not yet been decided upon.
(D) Disruptions, including noise and dust, have already caused delays.

137. (A) minimum
(B) minimally
(C) minimalize
(D) minimal

138. (A) toward
(B) between
(C) inside
(D) during

Whether for business or relaxation, traveling can ------- you all over the globe. While this can be
                                                     139.
exciting, long flights, for example from New York City to Beijing, can often result in a

phenomenon ------- as jet lag. That is, you may feel extremely tired, due to both the duration of
            140.
the flight and the fact that you crossed multiple time zones.

There are a few ways to fight jet lag so that you can enjoy your trip. First, drink plenty of water.

Hydration is key to feeling good. ------- , skip naps. Napping during the day makes it even more
                                  141.
difficult to fall asleep at the correct time of night. Finally, get some physical exercise, preferably

outdoors. ------- .
          142.

TEST 2

139. (A) teach
     (B) change
     (C) take
     (D) help

140. (A) knows
     (B) known
     (C) knowing
     (D) knowingly

141. (A) Lastly
     (B) Also
     (C) Instead
     (D) Therefore

142. (A) It allows you to adjust more quickly to
         your new environment.
     (B) It increases your ability to be innovative
         and productive.
     (C) It will improve the health and well-being
         of your staff.
     (D) It enables you to manage your travel
         reservations.

GO ON TO THE NEXT PAGE

To: All Tenants
From: Maintenance Team
Date: April 18
Subject: Parking

To all 1520 Elm Street tenants:

We are excited to inform you that next month will see the beginning of ------- updates to the
143.
shared areas of our apartment complex. A complete schedule of updates was posted last month
and is available on the community Web site.

The parking garage ------- for repairs May 15 to 17. ------- . If your car is not removed from the
144.   145.
garage by 8:00 A.M. on May 15, it will be towed at your expense. Temporary ------- are available
146.
at the 1500 Elm Street apartment complex or at the municipal parking lot down the street. The
1520 garage will reopen on May 18. We thank you in advance for your cooperation and
patience.

Sincerely,

Angela Connetti
1520 Elm Street Maintenance Supervisor

---

143. (A) planned
(B) contested
(C) mixed
(D) satisfied

144. (A) has been closed
(B) to close
(C) did close
(D) will be closed

145. (A) The next project involves the installation
of new digital locks on the front doors.
(B) Community members are invited to the
reopening ceremony next weekend.
(C) No vehicles may be parked in the
1520 Elm Street garage during this
time.
(D) There will be more noise outside than
usual due to ongoing work.

146. (A) adjustments
(B) guides
(C) points
(D) spaces

Directions: In this part you will read a selection of texts, such as magazine and newspaper articles, e-mails, and instant messages. Each text or set of texts is followed by several questions. Select the best answer for each question and mark the letter (A), (B), (C), or (D) on your answer sheet.

Questions 147-148 refer to the following advertisement.

For Rent

Spacious suite available starting next month in a small office building in Glasgow. Approximately 140 square metres, with ample storage space and several large windows to brighten your work space. Employee break room with a kitchen shared by three units on the same floor. Monthly rent covers electricity, water, Internet access, alarm system, and after-hours monitoring. Tenants are responsible for their own telephone and janitorial services. Call 0141 496 0199 for more information.

---

147. What is suggested about the suite?

(A) It can be rented immediately.
(B) It includes a private kitchen.
(C) It has a lot of natural light.
(D) It is in a large office building.

148. What is NOT included in the suite's cost of rent?

(A) Cleaning
(B) Electricity
(C) Security service
(D) Internet service

GO ON TO THE NEXT PAGE

Questions 149-150 refer to the following e-mail.

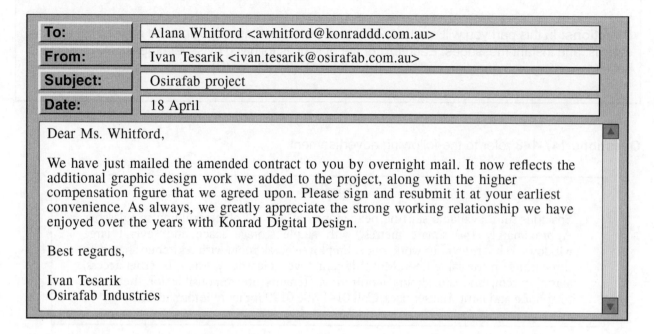

To:	Alana Whitford <awhitford@konraddd.com.au>
From:	Ivan Tesarik <ivan.tesarik@osirafab.com.au>
Subject:	Osirafab project
Date:	18 April

Dear Ms. Whitford,

We have just mailed the amended contract to you by overnight mail. It now reflects the additional graphic design work we added to the project, along with the higher compensation figure that we agreed upon. Please sign and resubmit it at your earliest convenience. As always, we greatly appreciate the strong working relationship we have enjoyed over the years with Konrad Digital Design.

Best regards,

Ivan Tesarik
Osirafab Industries

149. What does Mr. Tesarik indicate in his e-mail?

(A) A new staff member was hired.
(B) An agreement was revised.
(C) A deadline was missed.
(D) Some company policies were updated.

150. What does Mr. Tesarik ask Ms. Whitford to do?

(A) Return a document
(B) Schedule a meeting
(C) Submit a proposal
(D) Change a design

Operating the D343L Drill

The following tips will help you get started using the D343L successfully.

- If necessary, secure the material to be drilled with clamps or a vise.

- Carefully and firmly place the tip of the drill bit exactly on the desired location of the hole to be drilled.

- Start at a slow speed to prevent the drill bit from slipping off the starting point. Begin drilling by lightly pressing the trigger switch.

- Intensify pressure on the trigger to increase to the desired speed once the bit begins to penetrate the material being drilled.

Be careful not to exert too much pressure on the material when using the D343L drill. Doing so may cause the motor of the device to overheat. Overheating the drill's motor may cause premature wear and eventually lead to the failure of the device.

TEST 2

151. What is suggested about the D343L drill?
    (A) It is expensive.
    (B) It is covered under a warranty.
    (C) It is a new model.
    (D) It operates at different speeds.

152. According to the instructions, what might cause the drill to stop working?
    (A) Pressing its trigger too hard when beginning to drill
    (B) Pushing it too hard against a surface being drilled
    (C) Holding it too loosely in place while drilling
    (D) Running it continuously for too long

GO ON TO THE NEXT PAGE

Questions 153-154 refer to the following text-message chain.

Francis Leland (8:22 A.M.)
Hi, Naomi. I'm running late for our department meeting today. Could you help me with a couple of things?

Naomi Jordan (8:24 A.M.)
Sure, Francis. What can I do?

Francis Leland (8:25 A.M.)
I just need you to make 18 copies of a document, the minutes from our last meeting, so that everyone can have one. Also, the caterer is supposed to be arriving at 8:45 A.M. with the food. Could you let him in?

Naomi Jordan (8:27 A.M.)
Of course. And I see a document from Monday, January 11.

Francis Leland (8:28 A.M.)
That's the one.

Naomi Jordan (8:29 A.M.)
OK. I'll head downstairs in a few minutes to meet the caterer and then I can make the copies. Is there anything else?

Francis Leland (8:30 A.M.)
No, nothing else. Thanks for your help!

153. At 8:28 A.M., what does Mr. Leland mean when he writes, "That's the one"?
    (A) He approves of the menu selected for the meeting.
    (B) The meeting location has not changed.
    (C) Ms. Jordan found the right meeting minutes.
    (D) Ms. Jordan should hire the same caterer.

154. What will Ms. Jordan most likely do next?
    (A) Revise a document
    (B) Begin a meeting
    (C) Contact a coworker
    (D) Let the caterer in

Questions 155-157 refer to the following e-mail.

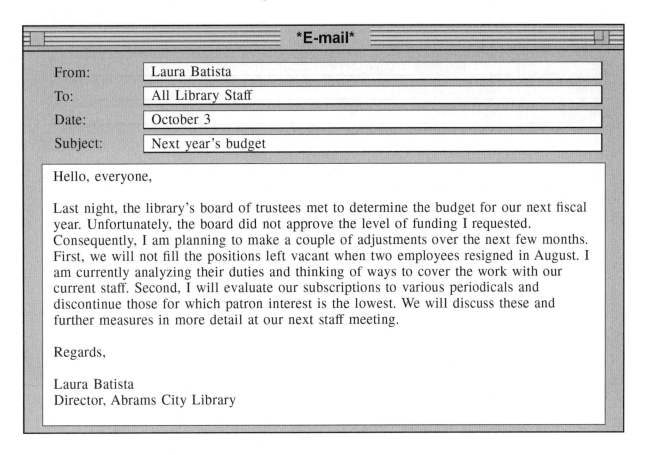

E-mail

From:	Laura Batista
To:	All Library Staff
Date:	October 3
Subject:	Next year's budget

Hello, everyone,

Last night, the library's board of trustees met to determine the budget for our next fiscal year. Unfortunately, the board did not approve the level of funding I requested. Consequently, I am planning to make a couple of adjustments over the next few months. First, we will not fill the positions left vacant when two employees resigned in August. I am currently analyzing their duties and thinking of ways to cover the work with our current staff. Second, I will evaluate our subscriptions to various periodicals and discontinue those for which patron interest is the lowest. We will discuss these and further measures in more detail at our next staff meeting.

Regards,

Laura Batista
Director, Abrams City Library

TEST 2

155. According to the e-mail, what happened earlier in the year?

(A) New board members were chosen.
(B) A building was vacated.
(C) Some employees left their jobs.
(D) Some job requirements changed.

156. The word "duties" in paragraph 1, line 5, is closest in meaning to

(A) taxes
(B) habits
(C) allowances
(D) responsibilities

157. What is suggested about the staff meeting?

(A) It may need to be rescheduled for next month.
(B) It will include a discussion of changes to the budget.
(C) It may be attended by members of the board of trustees.
(D) It will be held in a different location than in the past.

GO ON TO THE NEXT PAGE

Questions 158-160 refer to the following e-mail.

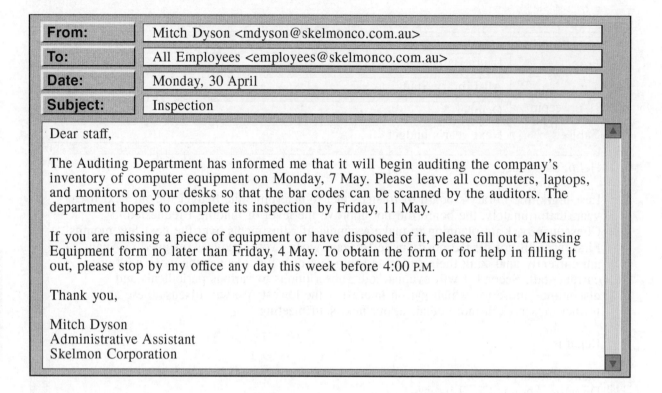

From:	Mitch Dyson <mdyson@skelmonco.com.au>
To:	All Employees <employees@skelmonco.com.au>
Date:	Monday, 30 April
Subject:	Inspection

Dear staff,

The Auditing Department has informed me that it will begin auditing the company's inventory of computer equipment on Monday, 7 May. Please leave all computers, laptops, and monitors on your desks so that the bar codes can be scanned by the auditors. The department hopes to complete its inspection by Friday, 11 May.

If you are missing a piece of equipment or have disposed of it, please fill out a Missing Equipment form no later than Friday, 4 May. To obtain the form or for help in filling it out, please stop by my office any day this week before 4:00 P.M.

Thank you,

Mitch Dyson
Administrative Assistant
Skelmon Corporation

158. What is the purpose of the inspection?

(A) To confirm that all computers are using updated software
(B) To verify the accuracy of the company's inventory list
(C) To determine whether there are any equipment safety violations
(D) To check that employees are using equipment properly

159. When is the inspection expected to end?

(A) On April 30
(B) On May 4
(C) On May 7
(D) On May 11

160. The phrase "fill out" in paragraph 2, line 1, is closest in meaning to

(A) expand
(B) integrate
(C) complete
(D) exchange

Eleanor's Professional Cleaning

Eleanor's has been Forton County's leading professional cleaning service for over 25 years. — [1] —. We customize our services to meet your residential and commercial cleaning needs. For most customers, this includes dusting and polishing furniture, sweeping and vacuuming floors, washing windows, and sanitizing all surfaces. — [2] —.

Our excellent communication and years of experience set Eleanor's Professional Cleaning apart from the rest. — [3] —. In addition, we are proud of our commitment to using only gentle, all-natural products that are free of harsh chemicals and dyes. — [4] —. Call us today at 713-555-0177 to schedule an appointment. Our first visit is free.

---

161. What is stated about Eleanor's Professional Cleaning?

(A) It serves clients in homes and offices.
(B) It uses products supplied by customers.
(C) It provides cost estimates for a small fee.
(D) Its rates are competitive.

162. What does the business NOT typically clean?

(A) Floors
(B) Windows
(C) Dishes
(D) Furniture

163. In which of the positions marked [1], [2], [3], and [4] does the following sentence best belong?

"We also do in-depth cleaning by special arrangement."

(A) [1]
(B) [2]
(C) [3]
(D) [4]

TEST 2

GO ON TO THE NEXT PAGE

```
┌─────────────────────────────────────────────────────────────────┐
│                           CHAT                      —   X         │
├─────────────────────────────────────────────────────────────────┤
│                                                                   │
│   Harry Dreyer [10:00 A.M.] Hello. I'm asking everyone on my     │
│   sales team what they think of the Weiler Cabinet line. I'm      │
│   considering adding it to our inventory.                         │
│                                                                   │
│   Lisa Ritland [10:01 A.M.] They come only in a few standard      │
│   sizes. Customers often request custom-sized dimensions for      │
│   their kitchens.                                                 │
│                                                                   │
│   Susan Yi [10:02 A.M.] That's right. That has been my            │
│   observation.                                                    │
│                                                                   │
│   Anthony Sachs [10:03 A.M.] I like the line in some ways. Their  │
│   products are durable and easy to clean.                         │
│                                                                   │
│   Lisa Ritland [10:04 A.M.] Customers like the galvanized steel   │
│   construction. Some have even had them installed in garages or   │
│   on outdoor porches for storing gardening equipment.             │
│                                                                   │
│   Susan Yi [10:05 A.M.] The Nordness line seems to be a suitable  │
│   product for that purpose too, and it costs less.                │
│                                                                   │
│   Harry Dreyer [10:10 A.M.] Thanks for your input.                │
│                                                                   │
└─────────────────────────────────────────────────────────────────┘
```

164. Who most likely is Mr. Dreyer?

(A) A furniture manufacturer
(B) A sales manager
(C) A cabinet designer
(D) A consumer news reporter

165. At 10:02 A.M., what does Ms. Yi most likely mean when she writes, "That has been my observation"?

(A) She has noticed that many customers have large kitchens.
(B) She feels she is well qualified for her current position.
(C) She has had similar experiences at a previous workplace.
(D) She has found that customers prefer a variety of cabinet sizes.

166. What is indicated about products in the Nordness line?

(A) They are expensive.
(B) They are easy to assemble.
(C) They are available in only one color.
(D) They are appropriate for use outdoors.

167. Which writer mentions the Weiler Cabinet line's construction material?

(A) Mr. Dreyer
(B) Ms. Ritland
(C) Ms. Yi
(D) Mr. Sachs

Questions 168-171 refer to the following e-mail.

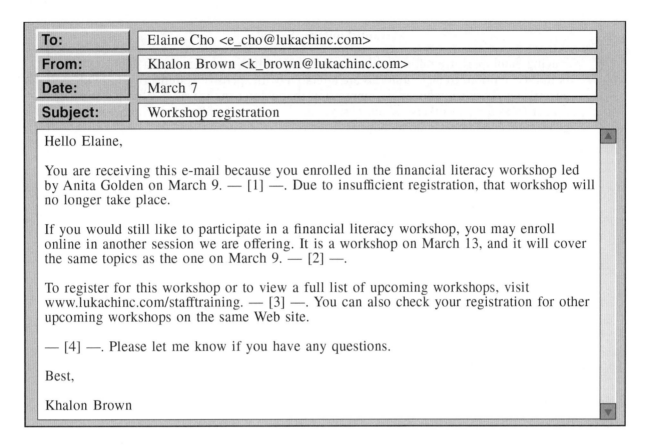

To: Elaine Cho <e_cho@lukachinc.com>

From: Khalon Brown <k_brown@lukachinc.com>

Date: March 7

Subject: Workshop registration

Hello Elaine,

You are receiving this e-mail because you enrolled in the financial literacy workshop led by Anita Golden on March 9. — [1] —. Due to insufficient registration, that workshop will no longer take place.

If you would still like to participate in a financial literacy workshop, you may enroll online in another session we are offering. It is a workshop on March 13, and it will cover the same topics as the one on March 9. — [2] —.

To register for this workshop or to view a full list of upcoming workshops, visit www.lukachinc.com/stafftraining. — [3] —. You can also check your registration for other upcoming workshops on the same Web site.

— [4] —. Please let me know if you have any questions.

Best,

Khalon Brown

---

168. What does the e-mail indicate about the workshop on March 9?

(A) Its location has changed.
(B) It has been canceled.
(C) It is fully booked.
(D) Its content has been updated.

169. What is suggested about Ms. Cho?

(A) She is unable to attend an event on March 13.
(B) She has previously led a workshop.
(C) She works in the same department as Ms. Golden.
(D) She is interested in learning about finance.

170. According to Mr. Brown, what can Ms. Cho do on the Web site?

(A) Make sure she is enrolled in a workshop
(B) Update her contact information
(C) Suggest topics for future workshops
(D) View a list of courses offered in the past

171. In which of the positions marked [1], [2], [3], and [4] does the following sentence best belong?

"It will be held in room 403 from 1:00 P.M. to 2:00 P.M."

(A) [1]
(B) [2]
(C) [3]
(D) [4]

GO ON TO THE NEXT PAGE

Vivanti Uniform Rentals

Having employees in uniforms enhances professionalism and increases a company's brand recognition. In fact, uniforms are a relatively inexpensive yet effective form of advertising. They can convey the impression that a company is well established and that it cares for its workers. When customers observe your uniformed employees, it gives them confidence in doing business with your company.

Our rental system serves businesses that seek a completely managed uniform program. We provide clean and fresh uniforms for your entire staff weekly. We take care of everything, including laundering, making repairs or replacements, and ensuring appropriate sizing.

Contact us to discuss your industry and apparel needs. We offer custom designs and materials for many sectors, including health care, food processing, hospitality, trades, and manufacturing. Let us know the number of uniforms you need. We extend discounts for organizations outfitting 50 or more employees.

Contact a Vivanti Uniform Rentals representative today and receive a quote within two days!

172. What is NOT mentioned as a benefit of having uniformed employees?

(A) It makes employees feel loyal to a company.
(B) It is an inexpensive marketing method.
(C) It raises customers' confidence in a business.
(D) It builds a company's brand recognition.

173. The word "convey" in paragraph 1, line 3, is closest in meaning to

(A) transport
(B) personalize
(C) communicate
(D) resemble

174. How frequently does Vivanti Uniform Rentals deliver items to its clients?

(A) Once a day
(B) Twice a day
(C) Once a week
(D) Once a month

175. According to the advertisement, how can a business receive a discounted rate?

(A) By using a special promotional code
(B) By identifying itself as a manufacturer
(C) By signing a new contract within two days
(D) By ordering a certain number of uniforms

TEST 2

GO ON TO THE NEXT PAGE

Patricia's Clothing

Order number: 12FGE93   **Date of purchase:** 16 April

Quantity	Size	Item No.	Description	Price
1	M	SD2391	Women's trench coat, tan	$100.00
1	M	SS2131	Men's striped sweater, red/white	$70.00
1	L	DS231	Women's crew socks, black 3-pack	$15.00
1	M	LSP23109	Women's long-sleeved blouse, blue	$65.00
1	M	SST210	Men's short-sleeved T-shirt, white	$25.00

	Subtotal	$275.00
	Tax	$41.25
Paid with bank card	Shipping	$0.00
XXXX XXXX XXXX 3457	**Total**	**$316.25**

If you have questions about your order, please contact us at orders@patriciasclothing.co.nz.

Items may be returned within 60 days of purchase by postal mail or at any Patricia's Clothing location in New Zealand. To locate a store, visit www.patriciasclothing.co.nz.

To:	Customer Service <orders@patriciasclothing.co.nz>
From:	Lara Mae Wong <lwong@mymail.co.nz>
Date:	23 April
Subject:	Order 12FGE93

To whom it may concern:

I am writing regarding order 12FGE93, which I placed on 16 April. When I received the parcel, the trench coat was missing. The invoice included in the parcel did show that I paid for this item, and the item was not listed as being on back order when I placed the order. I also checked with my bank and received confirmation that I was charged for the full amount shown on the invoice.

I had been planning to take this coat with me on a trip in just a few days, so please cancel the item and issue a refund.

Lara Mae Wong

176. What information is given on the invoice?

(A) A phone number for customer service
(B) A customer's shipping address
(C) A store's return policy
(D) A list of store locations

177. What does the invoice indicate about Ms. Wong's order?

(A) It included a discounted item.
(B) It was shipped free of charge.
(C) It arrived in two separate boxes.
(D) It consisted of children's clothing.

178. What is the price of the item that Ms. Wong did not receive?

(A) $25.00
(B) $65.00
(C) $70.00
(D) $100.00

179. What did Ms. Wong do before e-mailing customer service?

(A) She contacted her bank.
(B) She visited a nearby store location.
(C) She sent a damaged item back.
(D) She reordered the missing item.

180. What does the e-mail indicate about Ms. Wong?

(A) She frequently places orders with Patricia's Clothing.
(B) She is waiting to receive a new credit card.
(C) She recently changed her e-mail address.
(D) She will be traveling out of town soon.

GO ON TO THE NEXT PAGE ➤

TEST 2

To:	Carlos Redondo
From:	Meg Finley
Date:	March 6
Subject:	Inventory update

Hi Carlos,

Jim Herndon has sent me a list of a number of paperbacks that are selling poorly. Here is what I propose we do to sell some of them.

Memories of a Roadie by Teri Gerrity: It's an insider's perspective on the life of the support team that travels with musicians. Hardesty House Publishing (HHP) will be releasing Ms. Gerrity's new work in October. If we can put displays of *Memories of a Roadie* in the store windows at the same time, we could sell out our stock of 8,439 copies.

African Foundations by James Okuma: We have about 11,000 copies of this book left. It deals with the origins of political thought on the African continent. Given that several African countries will be having presidential elections this year, I suggest we feature Mr. Okuma's book in store displays on world events.

A Considered Point of View by Culp Dillon: This is a biography of the famous economist Judith Dartwell. With a new documentary about her groundbreaking work in economics now available on a popular streaming service, it may be possible to sell half of the 12,850 copies we have in stock.

Meg

To:	Meg Finley
From:	Carlos Redondo
Date:	March 7
Subject:	RE: Inventory update

Hi Meg,

Please give me tip sheets for the three titles. Our sales staff can promote all three when they next call stores. Regarding the displays for *Memories of a Roadie*, I will ask our team to link the release of *She Who Lived* to the timing of HHP's display. I've set a sales target of 10,000 copies; I am hopeful we will sell at least 7,500. Also, I just saw Jim Herndon in the hallway, and he mentioned three other titles with lagging sales: *Pitch Fast*, *Conditional Approval*, and *Middle of Center*. What are your thoughts about those?

Carlos

181. What is the purpose of the first e-mail?

 (A) To recommend an employee for a salary increase
 (B) To suggest that a company publish some new books
 (C) To give details about some books that need to be sold
 (D) To explain the benefits of a partnership with HHP

182. What most likely is Mr. Herndon's role in the company?

 (A) He is the founder of the company.
 (B) He is a new member of the sales staff.
 (C) He heads the marketing department.
 (D) He keeps track of sales and inventory.

183. In the second e-mail, the word "promote" in paragraph 1, line 1, is closest in meaning to

 (A) raise the rank of
 (B) give publicity to
 (C) make an argument for
 (D) increase the amount of

184. In the second e-mail, what is suggested about Mr. Redondo?

 (A) He works for the same company as Mr. Herndon.
 (B) He will reschedule a meeting with Ms. Finley.
 (C) He will be visiting several bookstores.
 (D) He is hiring additional salespeople.

185. What is the title of Ms. Gerrity's new book?

 (A) *She Who Lived*
 (B) *Pitch Fast*
 (C) *Conditional Approval*
 (D) *Middle of Center*

GO ON TO THE NEXT PAGE

Ooltewah Broadcasting Network

The Ooltewah Broadcasting Network (OBN) is proud to be a leader in public programming for the local community. From informative documentaries and investigative local news to high school sports and children's programming, OBN makes it our mission to keep you informed.

We could not do this without the generous support of viewers such as yourself! Here is just some of the quality programming that we are able to offer thanks to the contributions of viewers like you:

* *Greg Travels the World*—Follow our favorite foodie, Greg Romero, as he tries the delicacies of the world in countries like Peru, Morocco, and Japan.

* *Coaching the Game*—Get an inside view of how coaches train and motivate their teams.

* *Mysterious Earth*—Learn about wildlife from diverse climates around the world, such as the elephants that roam the Serengeti and the narwhals that swim in the Arctic waters.

* *The Wonderful Outdoors*—Child-development expert Mary Tisdale takes children on a journey in exploring the nature in their own backyards and parks.

If you have enjoyed our programming, please consider joining our community of supporters. Contributing to OBN has never been easier! Simply visit our Web site at ooltewahbroadcastingnet.org/support for more information.

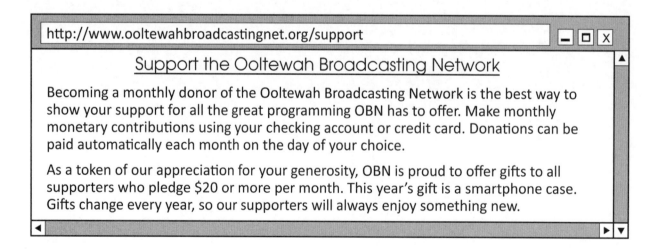

http://www.ooltewahbroadcastingnet.org/support

Support the Ooltewah Broadcasting Network

Becoming a monthly donor of the Ooltewah Broadcasting Network is the best way to show your support for all the great programming OBN has to offer. Make monthly monetary contributions using your checking account or credit card. Donations can be paid automatically each month on the day of your choice.

As a token of our appreciation for your generosity, OBN is proud to offer gifts to all supporters who pledge $20 or more per month. This year's gift is a smartphone case. Gifts change every year, so our supporters will always enjoy something new.

http://www.ooltewahbroadcastingnet.org/support

Become a Supporter

Name	Marco Cerati
Address	4850 Juniper Ln Chattanooga, TN 37422

Contribution Amount

$ 20.00

Payment Source (select one): ☐ Checking Account ■ Credit Card

Payment Details	Account Number	Routing Number	Card Number
			xxxx-xxxx-xxxx-9013

Payment Date: 7th ▲▼

Why are you donating to OBN?
(Your response may be read on our live telethon newscast.)

I love learning about the natural world, and OBN makes that possible. Your wildlife special on animals from around the globe was fantastic! I am happy to support such engaging and informative television programming.

---

186. According to the notice, what is true about Mr. Romero?

(A) He has traveled to many countries.
(B) He coaches a sports team.
(C) He is a nature photographer.
(D) He works with Ms. Tisdale.

187. What does the notice encourage the reader to do?

(A) Contact a news program
(B) Plan an overseas trip
(C) Attend a local event
(D) Go to a Web site

188. What does the Web page indicate about donations?

(A) They can be made in cash.
(B) They can be made automatically each month.
(C) They can be canceled at any time.
(D) They can be set up by sending an e-mail.

189. What is most likely true about Mr. Cerati?

(A) He recently moved to Chattanooga.
(B) He will receive a smartphone case.
(C) He has made donations to OBN for several years.
(D) He was featured on a live television program.

190. What television program did Mr. Cerati enjoy?

(A) *Greg Travels the World*
(B) *Coaching the Game*
(C) *Mysterious Earth*
(D) *The Wonderful Outdoors*

GO ON TO THE NEXT PAGE ➡

TEST 2

YOUTH ARTS FESTIVAL

The annual Leyton Youth Arts Festival features the work of promising artists aged 14 to 24. A panel of experts will critique entries, and the public is invited to exhibitions and live demonstrations at Leyton Town Hall.

Highlights will include the following:

- *Painting Showcase*—April 2 to 4. View original contemporary paintings by young artists.
- *Textile Art*—April 6 to 8. Witness artists create tapestries and more using a variety of weaving techniques. Artists will welcome your questions about their looms and the materials that they use.
- *Sculpture Garden*—April 10 to 12. Walk outside in the town hall's gardens to see classical and modern creations by young sculptors.
- *Furniture Design*—April 14 to 16. See the future of practical household items handcrafted by young designers.
- *Art in an Hour*—April 17. Observe artists as they race to complete a detailed sketch of a model in only 60 minutes. Ask the artists questions as they work—but not too many since they will be very busy!

To see the full brochure, visit our Web site at www.lyafestival.org.

http:// www.lyafestival.org/meet_the_judges

Esme Bacanu writes:

"As a child, there was nothing more fascinating to me than the feel, weight, and color of cloth. Making one's living as an artist is difficult. Having completed almost 100 tapestries in response to commissions from patrons of the art form, I hope I can offer advice and support in my capacity as a judge and mentor to the talented young people who might follow in my footsteps."

To:	publicity@lyafestival.org
From:	sphillips@phillipsfootwear.com
Date:	January 12
Subject:	Brochure

Dear Ms. Marwick,

I would like to place an advertisement for my business on the Web site for this year's youth arts festival. I submitted the online form for a half-page advertisement today but am currently awaiting the finalized image from the ad company. Could you tell me when the final deadline is to submit the finished artwork? Also, I would like to place posters in my shop window to advertise the festival. Do you have any to share?

The Phillips family has supported the arts for generations. My wife and I have been volunteering in arts programs in local schools for years. In addition, we are fans of Esme Bacanu, and so we are very excited to hear that she will be involved with the festival this year!

Kind regards,

Stanley Phillips
Owner, Phillips Footwear

191. What does the advertisement indicate about the youth arts festival?

(A) It will take place at an art studio.
(B) It is being held for the first time.
(C) It will take place every day in April.
(D) It includes reviews by arts specialists.

192. What is the public asked to do during the event of April 17?

(A) Leave the exhibition area after an hour
(B) Limit their interaction with the artists
(C) Vote for their favorite creation
(D) Purchase works of the artists

193. On what dates will Ms. Bacanu most likely work at the festival?

(A) April 2 to April 4
(B) April 6 to April 8
(C) April 10 to April 12
(D) April 14 to April 16

194. Why is Mr. Phillips concerned about a deadline?

(A) He has not been informed about a volunteer position.
(B) He wants more time to print posters.
(C) His advertisement is not finished yet.
(D) He needs to leave town for a business trip.

195. What is true about both Ms. Bacanu and Mr. Phillips?

(A) They work in related lines of business.
(B) They want to support young people in the arts.
(C) They attended Leyton High School together.
(D) They think careers in the arts can be difficult.

GO ON TO THE NEXT PAGE

Questions 196-200 refer to the following Web pages and e-mail.

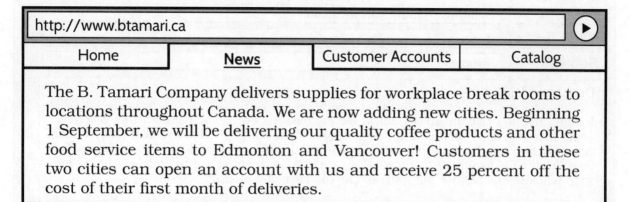

http://www.btamari.ca

| Home | **News** | Customer Accounts | Catalog |

The B. Tamari Company delivers supplies for workplace break rooms to locations throughout Canada. We are now adding new cities. Beginning 1 September, we will be delivering our quality coffee products and other food service items to Edmonton and Vancouver! Customers in these two cities can open an account with us and receive 25 percent off the cost of their first month of deliveries.

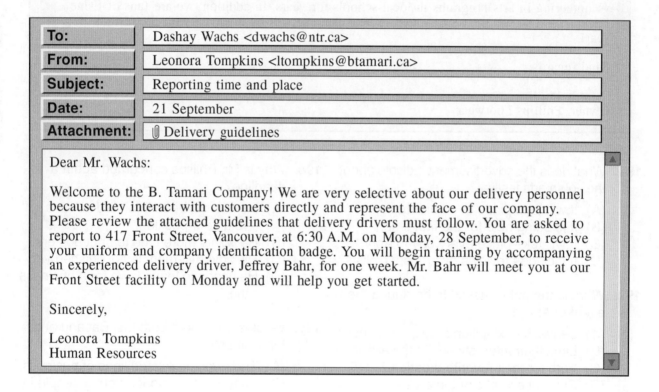

To:	Dashay Wachs <dwachs@ntr.ca>
From:	Leonora Tompkins <ltompkins@btamari.ca>
Subject:	Reporting time and place
Date:	21 September
Attachment:	Delivery guidelines

Dear Mr. Wachs:

Welcome to the B. Tamari Company! We are very selective about our delivery personnel because they interact with customers directly and represent the face of our company. Please review the attached guidelines that delivery drivers must follow. You are asked to report to 417 Front Street, Vancouver, at 6:30 A.M. on Monday, 28 September, to receive your uniform and company identification badge. You will begin training by accompanying an experienced delivery driver, Jeffrey Bahr, for one week. Mr. Bahr will meet you at our Front Street facility on Monday and will help you get started.

Sincerely,

Leonora Tompkins
Human Resources

www.vancouverreviews.ca

It was wonderful to learn that B. Tamari Company was coming to Vancouver—and I have not been disappointed. Every Tuesday morning Mr. Wachs arrives to restock the break room at my workplace. He checks the inventory, examines the coffee machine, and always asks me and another administrative assistant if we need anything else. He is cheerful and efficient. Although our contract will be a bit expensive for my organization, I don't have to think about the break-room supplies at all because everything is well taken care of.

—Ilene Prior
25 October

196. What is the purpose of the first Web page?

(A) To announce new service areas
(B) To explain a break-room policy
(C) To advertise an accounting service
(D) To describe the history of a company

197. What has been sent with the e-mail?

(A) A parking permit
(B) A list of instructions
(C) A building pass
(D) A summary of company benefits

198. What is suggested about Mr. Wachs?

(A) He lives in Edmonton.
(B) He has prior experience as a delivery driver.
(C) He has just received a job promotion.
(D) He will be reporting to a newly opened facility.

199. What is most likely true about Ms. Prior's workplace?

(A) It benefited from a monthlong service discount.
(B) It requested a change in delivery personnel.
(C) Its break room is not used very frequently.
(D) Its offices have just moved to Front Street.

200. What does Ms. Prior indicate in the second Web page?

(A) An order for supplies was incorrect.
(B) Mr. Wachs has made her job easier.
(C) She checks the break-room inventory weekly.
(D) She would prefer a later delivery time.

Stop! This is the end of the test. If you finish before time is called, you may go back to Parts 5, 6, and 7 and check your work.

TEST 2

公式 *TOEIC*® Listening & Reading 問題集 8（音声 CD 2 枚付）

2021 年 10 月 19 日　第 1 版 第 1 刷発行
2022 年 3 月 5 日　第 1 版 第 3 刷発行

著者　　ETS

発行元　一般財団法人 国際ビジネスコミュニケーション協会

〒 100-0014

東京都千代田区永田町 2-14-2

山王グランドビル

電話 (03) 5521-5935

FAX (03) 3581-9801

印刷　　凸版印刷株式会社

乱丁本・落丁本・不良本はお取り換えします。許可なしに転載、複製することを禁じます。
ETS, the ETS logo, PROPELL, TOEIC and TOEIC BRIDGE are registered trademarks of
ETS, Princeton, New Jersey, USA, and used in Japan under license.
Portions are copyrighted by ETS and used with permission.
Printed in Japan
ISBN 978-4-906033-63-8

TEST 1

解 答 用 紙

REGISTRATION No.
受 験 番 号

フリガナ

NAME
氏 名

LISTENING SECTION

Part 1

No.	ANSWER A B C D
1	Ⓐ Ⓑ Ⓒ Ⓓ
2	Ⓐ Ⓑ Ⓒ Ⓓ
3	Ⓐ Ⓑ Ⓒ Ⓓ
4	Ⓐ Ⓑ Ⓒ Ⓓ
5	Ⓐ Ⓑ Ⓒ Ⓓ
6	Ⓐ Ⓑ Ⓒ Ⓓ
7	Ⓐ Ⓑ Ⓒ Ⓓ
8	Ⓐ Ⓑ Ⓒ Ⓓ
9	Ⓐ Ⓑ Ⓒ Ⓓ
10	Ⓐ Ⓑ Ⓒ Ⓓ

Part 2

No.	ANSWER A B C
11	Ⓐ Ⓑ Ⓒ
12	Ⓐ Ⓑ Ⓒ
13	Ⓐ Ⓑ Ⓒ
14	Ⓐ Ⓑ Ⓒ
15	Ⓐ Ⓑ Ⓒ
16	Ⓐ Ⓑ Ⓒ
17	Ⓐ Ⓑ Ⓒ
18	Ⓐ Ⓑ Ⓒ
19	Ⓐ Ⓑ Ⓒ
20	Ⓐ Ⓑ Ⓒ

No.	ANSWER A B C
21	Ⓐ Ⓑ Ⓒ
22	Ⓐ Ⓑ Ⓒ
23	Ⓐ Ⓑ Ⓒ
24	Ⓐ Ⓑ Ⓒ
25	Ⓐ Ⓑ Ⓒ
26	Ⓐ Ⓑ Ⓒ
27	Ⓐ Ⓑ Ⓒ
28	Ⓐ Ⓑ Ⓒ
29	Ⓐ Ⓑ Ⓒ
30	Ⓐ Ⓑ Ⓒ

Part 3

No.	ANSWER A B C D
31	Ⓐ Ⓑ Ⓒ Ⓓ
32	Ⓐ Ⓑ Ⓒ Ⓓ
33	Ⓐ Ⓑ Ⓒ Ⓓ
34	Ⓐ Ⓑ Ⓒ Ⓓ
35	Ⓐ Ⓑ Ⓒ Ⓓ
36	Ⓐ Ⓑ Ⓒ Ⓓ
37	Ⓐ Ⓑ Ⓒ Ⓓ
38	Ⓐ Ⓑ Ⓒ Ⓓ
39	Ⓐ Ⓑ Ⓒ Ⓓ
40	Ⓐ Ⓑ Ⓒ Ⓓ

No.	ANSWER A B C D
41	Ⓐ Ⓑ Ⓒ Ⓓ
42	Ⓐ Ⓑ Ⓒ Ⓓ
43	Ⓐ Ⓑ Ⓒ Ⓓ
44	Ⓐ Ⓑ Ⓒ Ⓓ
45	Ⓐ Ⓑ Ⓒ Ⓓ
46	Ⓐ Ⓑ Ⓒ Ⓓ
47	Ⓐ Ⓑ Ⓒ Ⓓ
48	Ⓐ Ⓑ Ⓒ Ⓓ
49	Ⓐ Ⓑ Ⓒ Ⓓ
50	Ⓐ Ⓑ Ⓒ Ⓓ

No.	ANSWER A B C D
51	Ⓐ Ⓑ Ⓒ Ⓓ
52	Ⓐ Ⓑ Ⓒ Ⓓ
53	Ⓐ Ⓑ Ⓒ Ⓓ
54	Ⓐ Ⓑ Ⓒ Ⓓ
55	Ⓐ Ⓑ Ⓒ Ⓓ
56	Ⓐ Ⓑ Ⓒ Ⓓ
57	Ⓐ Ⓑ Ⓒ Ⓓ
58	Ⓐ Ⓑ Ⓒ Ⓓ
59	Ⓐ Ⓑ Ⓒ Ⓓ
60	Ⓐ Ⓑ Ⓒ Ⓓ

No.	ANSWER A B C D
61	Ⓐ Ⓑ Ⓒ Ⓓ
62	Ⓐ Ⓑ Ⓒ Ⓓ
63	Ⓐ Ⓑ Ⓒ Ⓓ
64	Ⓐ Ⓑ Ⓒ Ⓓ
65	Ⓐ Ⓑ Ⓒ Ⓓ
66	Ⓐ Ⓑ Ⓒ Ⓓ
67	Ⓐ Ⓑ Ⓒ Ⓓ
68	Ⓐ Ⓑ Ⓒ Ⓓ
69	Ⓐ Ⓑ Ⓒ Ⓓ
70	Ⓐ Ⓑ Ⓒ Ⓓ

Part 4

No.	ANSWER A B C D
71	Ⓐ Ⓑ Ⓒ Ⓓ
72	Ⓐ Ⓑ Ⓒ Ⓓ
73	Ⓐ Ⓑ Ⓒ Ⓓ
74	Ⓐ Ⓑ Ⓒ Ⓓ
75	Ⓐ Ⓑ Ⓒ Ⓓ
76	Ⓐ Ⓑ Ⓒ Ⓓ
77	Ⓐ Ⓑ Ⓒ Ⓓ
78	Ⓐ Ⓑ Ⓒ Ⓓ
79	Ⓐ Ⓑ Ⓒ Ⓓ
80	Ⓐ Ⓑ Ⓒ Ⓓ

No.	ANSWER A B C D
81	Ⓐ Ⓑ Ⓒ Ⓓ
82	Ⓐ Ⓑ Ⓒ Ⓓ
83	Ⓐ Ⓑ Ⓒ Ⓓ
84	Ⓐ Ⓑ Ⓒ Ⓓ
85	Ⓐ Ⓑ Ⓒ Ⓓ
86	Ⓐ Ⓑ Ⓒ Ⓓ
87	Ⓐ Ⓑ Ⓒ Ⓓ
88	Ⓐ Ⓑ Ⓒ Ⓓ
89	Ⓐ Ⓑ Ⓒ Ⓓ
90	Ⓐ Ⓑ Ⓒ Ⓓ

No.	ANSWER A B C D
91	Ⓐ Ⓑ Ⓒ Ⓓ
92	Ⓐ Ⓑ Ⓒ Ⓓ
93	Ⓐ Ⓑ Ⓒ Ⓓ
94	Ⓐ Ⓑ Ⓒ Ⓓ
95	Ⓐ Ⓑ Ⓒ Ⓓ
96	Ⓐ Ⓑ Ⓒ Ⓓ
97	Ⓐ Ⓑ Ⓒ Ⓓ
98	Ⓐ Ⓑ Ⓒ Ⓓ
99	Ⓐ Ⓑ Ⓒ Ⓓ
100	Ⓐ Ⓑ Ⓒ Ⓓ

READING SECTION

Part 5

No.	ANSWER A B C D
101	Ⓐ Ⓑ Ⓒ Ⓓ
102	Ⓐ Ⓑ Ⓒ Ⓓ
103	Ⓐ Ⓑ Ⓒ Ⓓ
104	Ⓐ Ⓑ Ⓒ Ⓓ
105	Ⓐ Ⓑ Ⓒ Ⓓ
106	Ⓐ Ⓑ Ⓒ Ⓓ
107	Ⓐ Ⓑ Ⓒ Ⓓ
108	Ⓐ Ⓑ Ⓒ Ⓓ
109	Ⓐ Ⓑ Ⓒ Ⓓ
110	Ⓐ Ⓑ Ⓒ Ⓓ

No.	ANSWER A B C D
111	Ⓐ Ⓑ Ⓒ Ⓓ
112	Ⓐ Ⓑ Ⓒ Ⓓ
113	Ⓐ Ⓑ Ⓒ Ⓓ
114	Ⓐ Ⓑ Ⓒ Ⓓ
115	Ⓐ Ⓑ Ⓒ Ⓓ
116	Ⓐ Ⓑ Ⓒ Ⓓ
117	Ⓐ Ⓑ Ⓒ Ⓓ
118	Ⓐ Ⓑ Ⓒ Ⓓ
119	Ⓐ Ⓑ Ⓒ Ⓓ
120	Ⓐ Ⓑ Ⓒ Ⓓ

Part 6

No.	ANSWER A B C D
121	Ⓐ Ⓑ Ⓒ Ⓓ
122	Ⓐ Ⓑ Ⓒ Ⓓ
123	Ⓐ Ⓑ Ⓒ Ⓓ
124	Ⓐ Ⓑ Ⓒ Ⓓ
125	Ⓐ Ⓑ Ⓒ Ⓓ
126	Ⓐ Ⓑ Ⓒ Ⓓ
127	Ⓐ Ⓑ Ⓒ Ⓓ
128	Ⓐ Ⓑ Ⓒ Ⓓ
129	Ⓐ Ⓑ Ⓒ Ⓓ
130	Ⓐ Ⓑ Ⓒ Ⓓ

No.	ANSWER A B C D
131	Ⓐ Ⓑ Ⓒ Ⓓ
132	Ⓐ Ⓑ Ⓒ Ⓓ
133	Ⓐ Ⓑ Ⓒ Ⓓ
134	Ⓐ Ⓑ Ⓒ Ⓓ
135	Ⓐ Ⓑ Ⓒ Ⓓ
136	Ⓐ Ⓑ Ⓒ Ⓓ
137	Ⓐ Ⓑ Ⓒ Ⓓ
138	Ⓐ Ⓑ Ⓒ Ⓓ
139	Ⓐ Ⓑ Ⓒ Ⓓ
140	Ⓐ Ⓑ Ⓒ Ⓓ

Part 7

No.	ANSWER A B C D
141	Ⓐ Ⓑ Ⓒ Ⓓ
142	Ⓐ Ⓑ Ⓒ Ⓓ
143	Ⓐ Ⓑ Ⓒ Ⓓ
144	Ⓐ Ⓑ Ⓒ Ⓓ
145	Ⓐ Ⓑ Ⓒ Ⓓ
146	Ⓐ Ⓑ Ⓒ Ⓓ
147	Ⓐ Ⓑ Ⓒ Ⓓ
148	Ⓐ Ⓑ Ⓒ Ⓓ
149	Ⓐ Ⓑ Ⓒ Ⓓ
150	Ⓐ Ⓑ Ⓒ Ⓓ

No.	ANSWER A B C D
151	Ⓐ Ⓑ Ⓒ Ⓓ
152	Ⓐ Ⓑ Ⓒ Ⓓ
153	Ⓐ Ⓑ Ⓒ Ⓓ
154	Ⓐ Ⓑ Ⓒ Ⓓ
155	Ⓐ Ⓑ Ⓒ Ⓓ
156	Ⓐ Ⓑ Ⓒ Ⓓ
157	Ⓐ Ⓑ Ⓒ Ⓓ
158	Ⓐ Ⓑ Ⓒ Ⓓ
159	Ⓐ Ⓑ Ⓒ Ⓓ
160	Ⓐ Ⓑ Ⓒ Ⓓ

No.	ANSWER A B C D
161	Ⓐ Ⓑ Ⓒ Ⓓ
162	Ⓐ Ⓑ Ⓒ Ⓓ
163	Ⓐ Ⓑ Ⓒ Ⓓ
164	Ⓐ Ⓑ Ⓒ Ⓓ
165	Ⓐ Ⓑ Ⓒ Ⓓ
166	Ⓐ Ⓑ Ⓒ Ⓓ
167	Ⓐ Ⓑ Ⓒ Ⓓ
168	Ⓐ Ⓑ Ⓒ Ⓓ
169	Ⓐ Ⓑ Ⓒ Ⓓ
170	Ⓐ Ⓑ Ⓒ Ⓓ

No.	ANSWER A B C D
171	Ⓐ Ⓑ Ⓒ Ⓓ
172	Ⓐ Ⓑ Ⓒ Ⓓ
173	Ⓐ Ⓑ Ⓒ Ⓓ
174	Ⓐ Ⓑ Ⓒ Ⓓ
175	Ⓐ Ⓑ Ⓒ Ⓓ
176	Ⓐ Ⓑ Ⓒ Ⓓ
177	Ⓐ Ⓑ Ⓒ Ⓓ
178	Ⓐ Ⓑ Ⓒ Ⓓ
179	Ⓐ Ⓑ Ⓒ Ⓓ
180	Ⓐ Ⓑ Ⓒ Ⓓ

No.	ANSWER A B C D
181	Ⓐ Ⓑ Ⓒ Ⓓ
182	Ⓐ Ⓑ Ⓒ Ⓓ
183	Ⓐ Ⓑ Ⓒ Ⓓ
184	Ⓐ Ⓑ Ⓒ Ⓓ
185	Ⓐ Ⓑ Ⓒ Ⓓ
186	Ⓐ Ⓑ Ⓒ Ⓓ
187	Ⓐ Ⓑ Ⓒ Ⓓ
188	Ⓐ Ⓑ Ⓒ Ⓓ
189	Ⓐ Ⓑ Ⓒ Ⓓ
190	Ⓐ Ⓑ Ⓒ Ⓓ

No.	ANSWER A B C D
191	Ⓐ Ⓑ Ⓒ Ⓓ
192	Ⓐ Ⓑ Ⓒ Ⓓ
193	Ⓐ Ⓑ Ⓒ Ⓓ
194	Ⓐ Ⓑ Ⓒ Ⓓ
195	Ⓐ Ⓑ Ⓒ Ⓓ
196	Ⓐ Ⓑ Ⓒ Ⓓ
197	Ⓐ Ⓑ Ⓒ Ⓓ
198	Ⓐ Ⓑ Ⓒ Ⓓ
199	Ⓐ Ⓑ Ⓒ Ⓓ
200	Ⓐ Ⓑ Ⓒ Ⓓ

TEST 2

解答用紙

REGISTRATION No.
受験番号

フリガナ
NAME
氏名

LISTENING SECTION

Part 1

No.	ANSWER A B C D
1	A B C D
2	A B C D
3	A B C D
4	A B C D
5	A B C D
6	A B C D
7	A B C D
8	A B C D
9	A B C D
10	A B C D

Part 2

No.	ANSWER A B C	No.	ANSWER A B C
11	A B C	21	A B C
12	A B C	22	A B C
13	A B C	23	A B C
14	A B C	24	A B C
15	A B C	25	A B C
16	A B C	26	A B C
17	A B C	27	A B C
18	A B C	28	A B C
19	A B C	29	A B C
20	A B C	30	A B C

Part 3

No.	ANSWER A B C D	No.	ANSWER A B C D
31	A B C D	41	A B C D
32	A B C D	42	A B C D
33	A B C D	43	A B C D
34	A B C D	44	A B C D
35	A B C D	45	A B C D
36	A B C D	46	A B C D
37	A B C D	47	A B C D
38	A B C D	48	A B C D
39	A B C D	49	A B C D
40	A B C D	50	A B C D

Part 4

No.	ANSWER A B C D	No.	ANSWER A B C D	No.	ANSWER A B C D	No.	ANSWER A B C D	No.	ANSWER A B C D
51	A B C D	61	A B C D	71	A B C D	81	A B C D	91	A B C D
52	A B C D	62	A B C D	72	A B C D	82	A B C D	92	A B C D
53	A B C D	63	A B C D	73	A B C D	83	A B C D	93	A B C D
54	A B C D	64	A B C D	74	A B C D	84	A B C D	94	A B C D
55	A B C D	65	A B C D	75	A B C D	85	A B C D	95	A B C D
56	A B C D	66	A B C D	76	A B C D	86	A B C D	96	A B C D
57	A B C D	67	A B C D	77	A B C D	87	A B C D	97	A B C D
58	A B C D	68	A B C D	78	A B C D	88	A B C D	98	A B C D
59	A B C D	69	A B C D	79	A B C D	89	A B C D	99	A B C D
60	A B C D	70	A B C D	80	A B C D	90	A B C D	100	A B C D

READING SECTION

Part 5

No.	ANSWER A B C D	No.	ANSWER A B C D
101	A B C D	111	A B C D
102	A B C D	112	A B C D
103	A B C D	113	A B C D
104	A B C D	114	A B C D
105	A B C D	115	A B C D
106	A B C D	116	A B C D
107	A B C D	117	A B C D
108	A B C D	118	A B C D
109	A B C D	119	A B C D
110	A B C D	120	A B C D

Part 6

No.	ANSWER A B C D
121	A B C D
122	A B C D
123	A B C D
124	A B C D
125	A B C D
126	A B C D
127	A B C D
128	A B C D
129	A B C D
130	A B C D

Part 7

No.	ANSWER A B C D	No.	ANSWER A B C D	No.	ANSWER A B C D	No.	ANSWER A B C D	No.	ANSWER A B C D
131	A B C D	141	A B C D	151	A B C D	161	A B C D	171	A B C D
132	A B C D	142	A B C D	152	A B C D	162	A B C D	172	A B C D
133	A B C D	143	A B C D	153	A B C D	163	A B C D	173	A B C D
134	A B C D	144	A B C D	154	A B C D	164	A B C D	174	A B C D
135	A B C D	145	A B C D	155	A B C D	165	A B C D	175	A B C D
136	A B C D	146	A B C D	156	A B C D	166	A B C D	176	A B C D
137	A B C D	147	A B C D	157	A B C D	167	A B C D	177	A B C D
138	A B C D	148	A B C D	158	A B C D	168	A B C D	178	A B C D
139	A B C D	149	A B C D	159	A B C D	169	A B C D	179	A B C D
140	A B C D	150	A B C D	160	A B C D	170	A B C D	180	A B C D

No.	ANSWER A B C D
181	A B C D
182	A B C D
183	A B C D
184	A B C D
185	A B C D
186	A B C D
187	A B C D
188	A B C D
189	A B C D
190	A B C D
191	A B C D
192	A B C D
193	A B C D
194	A B C D
195	A B C D
196	A B C D
197	A B C D
198	A B C D
199	A B C D
200	A B C D

公式 *TOEIC*® Listening & Reading 問題集

問題集

8

別冊 『解答・解説』

一般財団法人 国際ビジネスコミュニケーション協会

ETS, the ETS logo, PROPELL, TOEIC and TOEIC BRIDGE are registered trademarks of
ETS, Princeton, New Jersey, USA, and used in Japan under license.
Portions are copyrighted by ETS and used with permission.

ETS TOEIC®

OFFICIAL TEST
PREPARATION
AND LEARNING

目　次

解答・解説で使われている表記の説明

● **CD のトラック番号（Part 1 ～ 4）**

会話の音声が CD 1 のトラック番号 50 に、
問題の音声が CD 1 のトラック番号 51 に入っていることを示しています。

● **スクリプトの前の記号（Part 1 ～ 4）**

🇺🇸 = 米国の発音
🇬🇧 = 英国の発音
🇨🇦 = カナダの発音
🇦🇺 = オーストラリアの発音

M = 男性（Man）
W = 女性（Woman）

● **スクリプト中の ❶ ❷ 等の番号（Part 3、4）**

解説の中で説明している箇所を示しています。

🔘 | 会話 **CD 1 50** | 問題 **CD 1 51**

Questions 38 through 40 refer to the following conversation.

🇦🇺 M ❶I'm here to pick up the photographs your studio took of me and my family last month. The last name is Park.

🇺🇸 W OK, ❷let me go find them in the back room. ❸While you're waiting, here's a catalog that shows other items we can put photographs on, like T-shirts, calendars, or mugs.

🇦🇺 M That's a great idea. I see there are lots of items to choose from.

🇺🇸 W Yes, and ❹we have a special offer this month. ❺We'll ship anything you purchase free of charge.

問題38-40は次の会話に関するものです。

こちらのスタジオで先月撮っていただいた、私と家族の写真を受け取りに来ました。名字はParkです。

かしこまりました。奥の部屋にそれらを探しに行ってまいります。お待ちになっている間、Tシャツやカレンダー、マグカップといった、当店が写真をプリントできる他の商品が載っているカタログをどうぞ。

それはいい考えですね。選べる商品がたくさん載っていますね。

はい、それから、当店は今月特別サービスを提供しています。ご購入の品をいずれも無料で発送いたします。

---

38 Where most likely are the speakers?
(A) At a clothing shop
(B) At an art gallery
(C) At a photography studio
(D) At a stationery store

話し手たちはどこにいると考えられますか。
(A) 衣料品店
(B) 画廊
(C) 写真スタジオ
(D) 文房具店

正解 C 男性は❶で写真を受け取りに来た旨を女性に伝え、名字を名乗っている。それに対し、女性は❷で、奥の部屋にそれらを探しに行ってくると言っているので、話し手たちは写真スタジオにいると考えられる。

(A) (D) 女性はTシャツとカレンダーに言及しているが、それらは、店が写真をプリント可能な商品の例として紹介しているだけ。
(A) clothing「衣料品」。
(B) art gallery「画廊、美術館」。
(D) stationery「文房具」。

---

39 What does the woman give the man?

男性の写真を探しに行ってくると述べた

● **色の区別**

青字：正答に関する解説や語句の意味
黒字：誤答に関する解説や語句の意味

● 特典音声ファイルの番号（Part 5 〜 7）

「109-111」は特典音声のファイル番号を示しています。ダウンロード
音声ファイルのタイトル名に、「特典 109」、「特典 110」、「特典 111」
と表示されています。

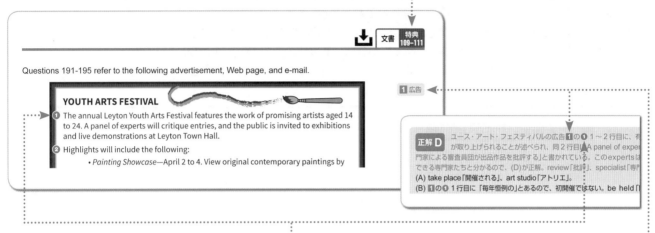

● 文書中の ❶❷ 等の番号（Part 6、7）

解説の中で説明している文書中の段落番号
等を示しています。解説文中の段落番号に
続く行数は、英文中の各段落の何行目かを
表しています。

● 文書を示す ❶ ❷ 等の番号（Part 7）

解説の中で説明している文書を示しています。

● Words & Phrases（Part 3、4、6、7）

会話やトーク、文書などに含まれる重要な語句と意味を紹介しています。Part 6、7 では、上記に示した ❶ ❷ や ❶❷
の番号により、本文で使われている場所が参照できます。

● Expressions（Part 6、7）

文書の中から、知っておくと
便利な表現を例文とともに紹
介しています。覚えて使える
ようになると、大変便利です。

Expressions

in addition 「さらに、その上」（❸の❷2行目）
It will cost a lot of money to carry out the plan. In addition, there are many technical problems to be solved.
その計画を実行するには多くのお金がかかるでしょう。さらに、解決すべき多くの技術的な問題があります。

＊『公式 *TOEIC*® Listening & Reading 問題集 8』の特典として、ダウンロード音声の中には、TEST 1、2 のリーディングセクションの以
下の音声が入っています。音声ダウンロードの手順は本誌 p. 3 をご参照ください。
・正解が入った問題音声（Part 5、6）
・文書の音声（Part 7）

参考スコア範囲の算出方法 ※ TEST 1、2 共通

1. 正解一覧（p.5、p.102）を参照し、リスニングセクションとリーディングセクションそれぞれの正答数を数えてください。各セクションの正答数がそれぞれの素点となります。
2. 下の参考スコア範囲の換算表であなたの素点に対応する換算点範囲を見つけます。
   例えばリスニングセクションの素点が 45 であれば、あなたの換算点範囲は「160 点～230 点」です。
3. 各セクションの換算点範囲の合計が、あなたのトータルスコア（参考スコア範囲）となります。

参考スコア範囲の算出例

リスニングセクションの素点が 45 で、リーディングセクションの素点が 64 だった場合、
トータルスコアは①と②の合計である③ 415—570 の間ということになります。

	素点	換算点範囲	
リスニングセクション	45	160 — 230	①
リーディングセクション	64	255 — 340	②
トータルスコア（参考スコア範囲）		415 — 570	③（①＋②）

参考スコア範囲の換算表

リスニングセクション		リーディングセクション	
素点	換算点範囲	素点	換算点範囲
96 — 100	475 — 495	96 — 100	460 — 495
91 — 95	435 — 495	91 — 95	425 — 490
86 — 90	405 — 470	86 — 90	400 — 465
81 — 85	370 — 450	81 — 85	375 — 440
76 — 80	345 — 420	76 — 80	340 — 415
71 — 75	320 — 390	71 — 75	310 — 390
66 — 70	290 — 360	66 — 70	285 — 370
61 — 65	265 — 335	61 — 65 【算出例②】	255 — 340
56 — 60	240 — 310	56 — 60	230 — 310
51 — 55	215 — 280	51 — 55	200 — 275
46 — 50	190 — 255	46 — 50	170 — 245
41 — 45 【算出例①】	160 — 230	41 — 45	140 — 215
36 — 40	130 — 205	36 — 40	115 — 180
31 — 35	105 — 175	31 — 35	95 — 150
26 — 30	85 — 145	26 — 30	75 — 120
21 — 25	60 — 115	21 — 25	60 — 95
16 — 20	30 — 90	16 — 20	45 — 75
11 — 15	5 — 70	11 — 15	30 — 55
6 — 10	5 — 60	6 — 10	10 — 40
1 — 5	5 — 50	1 — 5	5 — 30
0	5 — 35	0	5 — 15

TEST 1 の正解一覧

リスニングセクション

問題番号	正解
Part 1	
1	B
2	D
3	A
4	A
5	C
6	D
Part 2	
7	A
8	B
9	B
10	C
11	C
12	C
13	A
14	A
15	B
16	C
17	C
18	B
19	B
20	A
21	A
22	A
23	A
24	C
25	B
26	C
27	B
28	B
29	A
30	B
31	C
Part 3	
32	B
33	D
34	A
35	A
36	A
37	D
38	C
39	B
40	A
41	A
42	C
43	A
44	C
45	B
46	D
47	B
48	A
49	B
50	B

問題番号	正解
51	C
52	A
53	C
54	A
55	D
56	C
57	A
58	A
59	A
60	C
61	B
62	A
63	A
64	B
65	D
66	B
67	A
68	B
69	D
70	C
Part 4	
71	A
72	B
73	C
74	B
75	C
76	D
77	A
78	D
79	B
80	D
81	A
82	C
83	B
84	C
85	C
86	C
87	B
88	B
89	D
90	A
91	B
92	A
93	D
94	D
95	A
96	D
97	A
98	C
99	B
100	D

リーディングセクション

問題番号	正解
Part 5	
101	B
102	A
103	A
104	D
105	C
106	D
107	C
108	A
109	C
110	D
111	D
112	B
113	D
114	B
115	D
116	A
117	C
118	B
119	A
120	C
121	C
122	B
123	D
124	D
125	B
126	C
127	B
128	A
129	A
130	C
Part 6	
131	C
132	A
133	D
134	B
135	D
136	B
137	C
138	C
139	B
140	A
141	A
142	D
143	A
144	D
145	C
146	D
Part 7	
147	B
148	A
149	C
150	D

問題番号	正解
151	C
152	C
153	B
154	B
155	A
156	D
157	A
158	C
159	B
160	B
161	B
162	A
163	C
164	B
165	C
166	D
167	A
168	D
169	B
170	C
171	B
172	D
173	A
174	A
175	B
176	B
177	C
178	C
179	B
180	A
181	C
182	D
183	D
184	C
185	A
186	D
187	B
188	C
189	C
190	A
191	B
192	A
193	C
194	D
195	D
196	C
197	B
198	A
199	B
200	D

PART 1

1

2

3

---

1 🇦🇺 M

(A) A table lamp is turned on.
(B) Some beverages are on display.
(C) Some picture frames are in a box.
(D) A rug is rolled up in a corner.

(A) 電気スタンドの明かりがついている。
(B) 飲み物が陳列してある。
(C) 額縁が箱の中にある。
(D) 敷物が隅に巻かれてある。

正解 B 店内の商品棚に複数の飲料品が陳列してある。beverage「飲み物」、on display「陳列して」。
(A) 天井灯はあるが、table lamp「電気スタンド」は見つからない。turn on ～「～（明かりなど）をつける」。
(C) picture frame「（絵画用の）額縁」が複数、壁に掛かっているが、箱に入ってはいない。
(D) rug「敷物」は写っているが、丸く巻かれた状態で隅に置かれてはいない。roll up ～「～を巻く」、corner「隅」。

---

2 🇬🇧 W

(A) One of the women is holding a file folder.
(B) One of the women is talking on the telephone.
(C) One of the women is adjusting the height of a chair.
(D) One of the women is standing in front of a desk.

(A) 女性の1人はファイルフォルダーを手に持っている。
(B) 女性の1人は電話で話をしている。
(C) 女性の1人は椅子の高さを調節している。
(D) 女性の1人は机の前に立っている。

正解 D 左側にいる女性が机の前に立っている。in front of ～「～の前に」。
(A) hold「～を手に持っている」、file folder「ファイルフォルダー、書類挟み」。
(B) 電話は写っているが、受話器は置かれた状態である。talk on the telephone「電話で話をする」。
(C) 右側の女性は椅子に座っているが、その高さを調節してはいない。adjust「～を調節する」、height「高さ」。

---

3 🇺🇸 W

(A) Some loaves of bread are piled on a counter.
(B) One of the men is placing food in a refrigerator.
(C) One of the men is putting on an apron.
(D) Some food is being handed to a customer.

(A) パンが調理台の上に積み重ねられている。
(B) 男性の1人は食べ物を冷蔵庫の中に入れているところである。
(C) 男性の1人はエプロンを身に着けているところである。
(D) 食べ物が顧客に手渡されているところである。

正解 A counter「調理台」の上に複数のパンが積み重ねられている。loavesはloaf「（パンなどの）1塊」の複数形。pile「～を積み重ねる」。
(B) refrigerator「冷蔵庫」に食べ物を入れている男性は写っていない。place「～を置く」。
(C) 男性の1人はapron「エプロン」を着用しているが、それを身に着けている最中ではない。put on ～「～を身に着ける」。
(D) hand「～を手渡す」、customer「顧客」。

4

5

6

---

4 🇦🇺 M

(A) The man is entering a waiting area.
(B) The man is holding a door open.
(C) One of the women is looking at a monitor.
(D) One of the women is reaching for a bag on the floor.

(A) 男性は待合エリアに入っていくところである。
(B) 男性はドアを押さえて開けたままにしている。
(C) 女性の1人はモニターを見ている。
(D) 女性の1人は床の上のバッグを取ろうと手を伸ばしている。

正解 A 男性がドアから待合スペースのような場所に入って来ている。enter「～に入る」、waiting area「待合エリア、待合所」。
(B) ドアは開いているが、男性はそれを押さえてはいない。hold ～ …「～を…のままにしておく」。
(C) monitor「モニター、ディスプレー」はあるが、女性たちは2人とも、それを見てはいない。
(D) バッグは床に置かれてはいない。reach for ～「～を取ろうと手を伸ばす」、floor「床」。

---

5 🇺🇸 W

(A) A worker is replacing some windowpanes.
(B) A worker is operating a polishing machine.
(C) Some items have been stacked on a cart.
(D) A hose has been wrapped around a wheel.

(A) 作業員が窓ガラスを交換している。
(B) 作業員が研磨機を操作している。
(C) 物が台車の上に積み重ねられている。
(D) ホースが車輪に巻き付けられている。

正解 C 台車の上に複数の物が積み重ねられた状態で置かれている。〈have[has] been＋過去分詞〉で「～された状態である」という意味。stack「～を積み重ねる」、cart「台車」。
(A) replace「～を交換する」、windowpane「窓ガラス」。
(B) polishing machine「研磨機」。
(D) hose「ホース」は写っているが、wheel「車輪」に巻き付けられてはいない。wrap ～ around …「～を…に巻き付ける」。

---

6 🇨🇦 M

(A) The woman is locking up her bicycle.
(B) The woman is strolling down a garden path.
(C) A picnic basket has been unpacked on the grass.
(D) Some tents have been set up in a park.

(A) 女性は自分の自転車に鍵を掛けているところである。
(B) 女性は庭の小道を散歩している。
(C) ピクニック用のかごの中身が芝生の上に広げられている。
(D) 公園にテントが張られている。

正解 D 公園のような場所の奥に複数のテントが張られている。tent「テント」、set up ～「～を設置する」。
(A) 女性は自転車のそばに立っているが、施錠しているところではない。lock up ～「～を施錠する」。
(B) stroll down ～「～を散歩する」、path「小道」。
(C) picnic basket「ピクニック用のかご」、unpack「～を開いて中身を取り出す」、grass「芝生」。

PART 2

7 🇦🇺 M　Which floor has the largest conference room?

🇺🇸 W　(A) The seventh floor.
　　　 (B) We installed new telephones.
　　　 (C) The janitor cleans the floors.

どの階に最も広い会議室がありますか。

(A) 7階です。
(B) 私たちは新しい電話機を設置しました。
(C) 用務員が床を掃除します。

> **正解 A**　Which 〜?で最も広い会議室がどの階
> にあるか尋ねているのに対し、具体的
> な階を伝えている(A)が正解。floor「階、床」、
> conference room「会議室」。
> (B) 電話機については尋ねられていない。install「〜
> を設置する」、telephone「電話機」。
> (C) 質問にあるfloorが含まれるが、応答になってい
> ない。janitor「用務員、管理人」。

---

8 🇨🇦 M　How often does the train stop here?

🇦🇺 M　(A) A round-trip ticket.
　　　 (B) Every half hour.
　　　 (C) Only two miles.

電車はどのくらいの頻度でここに止まりますか。

(A) 往復切符です。
(B) 30分おきです。
(C) わずか2マイルです。

> **正解 B**　How often 〜?で電車がどのくらいの
> 頻度でこの場所に止まるか尋ねている
> のに対し、「30分おきだ」と一定の間隔で停車するこ
> とを伝えている(B)が正解。
> (A) 切符の種類は尋ねられていない。round-trip「往
> 復の」。
> (C) 距離は尋ねられていない。mile「マイル（約1.6
> キロメートル）」。

---

9 🇦🇺 M　Haven't you heard back from the project manager?

🇬🇧 W　(A) The back of the room.
　　　 (B) No, not yet.
　　　 (C) Can I see a menu?

プロジェクトマネージャーから返事をもらっていないのですか。

(A) 部屋の奥です。
(B) もらっていません、まだです。
(C) メニューを見ることはできますか。

> **正解 B**　否定疑問文で、「プロジェクトマネージ
> ャーから返事をもらっていないのか」と
> 確認しているのに対し、Noと答え、まだ返事を受け
> 取っていないことを伝えている(B)が正解。hear
> back from 〜「〜から返事をもらう」。
> (A) 質問にあるbackが含まれるが、ここでは名詞
> 「奥」の意味。
> (C) menu「メニュー」。

---

10 🇺🇸 W　Does the furniture store offer free shipping?

🇨🇦 M　(A) One table and four chairs.
　　　 (B) A retail business.
　　　 (C) Yes, it does.

その家具店は無料配送を提供していますか。

(A) テーブル1脚と椅子4脚です。
(B) 小売業です。
(C) はい、しています。

> **正解 C**　家具店が無料配送を提供しているか尋
> ねているのに対し、Yesと肯定し、店が
> 無料配送サービスを提供していることを伝えている
> (C)が正解。itは質問にあるthe furniture storeを
> 指す。furniture「家具」、free「無料の」、shipping「配
> 送」。
> (A) 質問にあるfurnitureと関連するtableやchairs
> が含まれるが、応答になっていない。
> (B) retail「小売り」。

---

11 🇦🇺 M　What do you think of using this cover photo on our Web site?

🇺🇸 W　(A) I can cover your shift.
　　　 (B) In the file folder.
　　　 (C) Sure, that looks great.

当社のウェブサイト上でこのカバー写真を使うのはどうですか。

(A) 私はあなたのシフトの代わりを務めることができます。
(B) ファイルフォルダーの中です。
(C) いいですね、とてもすてきに見えます。

> **正解 C**　ウェブサイト上で使うカバー写真につい
> て意見を求めているのに対し、「とても
> すてきに見える」と肯定的な評価を述べている(C)が
> 正解。cover「カバー、表紙」、photo「写真」。
> (A) 質問にあるcoverが含まれるが、ここでは動詞
> で用いられている。cover one's shift「〜のシフト
> の代わりを務める」。
> (B) file folder「ファイルフォルダー」。

12 🇬🇧 W Do you like the red logo or the blue logo?

🇨🇦 M (A) Some colorful flowers.
(B) The designer didn't think so.
(C) Can we do yellow instead?

あなたは赤色のロゴが好きですか、それとも青色のロゴが好きですか。

(A) 幾つかの色鮮やかな花です。
(B) デザイナーはそうは考えませんでした。
(C) 代わりに黄色にすることはできますか。

正解 C *A or B?*の形で、赤色のロゴと青色のロゴのどちらが好きか尋ねている。これに対し、「代わりに黄色にすることはできるか」と別の色のロゴを提案している(C)が正解。logo「ロゴ」。instead「その代わりに」。
(A) colorful「色鮮やかな」。
(B) デザイナーの意見は尋ねられていない。designer「デザイナー、設計者」。

13 🇦🇺 M You've been to this warehouse before, haven't you?

🇬🇧 W (A) No, I haven't.
(B) Bin number four.
(C) The house at the corner.

あなたは以前に、この倉庫に来たことがありますよね?

(A) いいえ、ありません。
(B) 容器番号4です。
(C) 角にある住宅です。

正解 A 肯定文の文末に ～, haven't you?を付けて「～ですよね」と、以前倉庫に来たことがあるか確認している。これに対し、Noと否定し、倉庫を訪れた経験がないことを伝えている(A)が正解。warehouse「倉庫」。
(B) 質問にあるbeforeと似た音のfourに注意。bin「容器、大箱」。
(C) 質問にあるwarehouseと似た音のhouseに注意。corner「角」。

14 🇨🇦 M Why haven't the tables been set for dinner service?

🇺🇸 W (A) Because we're short on staff.
(B) The seasonal menu is great.
(C) Yes, at five o'clock.

テーブルはなぜ、ディナー提供の用意がされていないのですか。

(A) 私たちはスタッフ不足なのです。
(B) 季節限定メニューは素晴らしいですね。
(C) はい、5時に。

正解 A Why ～?で、テーブル上に食器類の用意がされていない理由を尋ねている。これに対し、Because ～を用いて、「私たちはスタッフ不足なので」と、理由が人手不足であることを説明している(A)が正解。set「～（食卓）の用意をする」、dinner service「ディナーの提供」。be short on ～「～が不足している」、staff「スタッフ、従業員」。
(B) メニューについては尋ねられていない。seasonal「季節的な」。
(C) 理由を尋ねられているので、Yes/Noでは応答にならない。また、時刻も尋ねられていない。

15 🇺🇸 W Would you like to speak to a customer service representative?

🇦🇺 M (A) The keynote speech.
(B) Thanks, I'd love to.
(C) I already saw that movie.

顧客サービス担当者とお話しなさりたいですか。

(A) 基調演説です。
(B) ありがとう、ぜひそうしたいです。
(C) 私はすでにその映画を見ました。

正解 B Would you like to do ～?「～したいですか」は、丁寧に相手の意向を尋ねる表現。顧客サービス担当者と話したいかと尋ねているのに対し、お礼を述べ、「ぜひそうしたい」と伝えている(B)が正解。I'dはI wouldの短縮形。I would love to do「ぜひ～したい」。ここではtoの後に質問にあるspeak以降が省略されている。customer「顧客」、representative「担当者」。
(A) 質問にあるspeakと関連するspeechが含まれるが、応答になっていない。keynote speech「基調演説」。

16 🇬🇧 W I thought the tickets to the show were sold out.

🇨🇦 M (A) Twenty dollars, I think.
(B) The nominations were just announced.
(C) One of my friends had an extra.

そのショーのチケットは売り切れだと思っていました。
(A) 20ドルだと思います。
(B) 候補作品はちょうど発表されたところです。
(C) 私の友人の1人が1枚余分を持っていたのです。

正解 **C**　「そのショーのチケットは売り切れだと思っていた」という発言に対し、「私の友人の1人が1枚余分を持っていた」と述べ、その余分なチケットでショーを見られることを示唆している(C)が正解。show「ショー、見せ物」、be sold out「売り切れている」。extra「余分のもの」。
(A) 料金は尋ねられていない。
(B) 発言にあるshowと関連するnomination「推薦された人・物、推薦」が含まれるが、応答になっていない。announce「〜を発表する」。

17 🇦🇺 M Can I get fifteen meters of the fabric on display?

🇺🇸 W (A) The parking meter is paid.
(B) Not too far.
(C) Sure, do you want the same color?

飾ってある布を15メートル頂けますか。
(A) パーキングメーターは支払い済みです。
(B) それほど遠くありません。
(C) もちろんです、同じ色をご希望ですか。

正解 **C**　Can I get 〜?で、飾ってある布を15メートル注文しているのに対し、Sureと応答してから、同じ色を希望するか聞き返している(C)が正解。meter「メートル」、fabric「布」、on display「陳列して」。
(A) 質問にあるmetersと似た音が含まれるparking meter「パーキングメーター(駐車料金計)」があるが、応答になっていない。pay「〜に代金を支払う」。
(B) 距離は尋ねられていない。

18 🇬🇧 W Who needs to sign the budget approval form?

🇨🇦 M (A) Let's hang the sign here.
(B) I just sent it to Noriko.
(C) Thirty thousand euros.

誰が予算承認書に署名する必要がありますか。
(A) ここに看板を掛けましょう。
(B) ちょうどそれをNorikoに送ったところです。
(C) 3万ユーロです。

正解 **B**　Who 〜?で誰が予算承認書に署名する必要があるか尋ねているのに対し、「ちょうどそれをNorikoに送ったところだ」と答えて、署名すべき人物を示唆している(B)が正解。itは質問にあるthe budget approval formを指す。sign「〜に署名する」、budget「予算」、approval「承認」、form「書式、フォーム」。
(A) 質問にあるsignが含まれるが、ここでは名詞「看板」の意味で用いられており、応答になっていない。hang「〜を掛ける」。
(C) 金額は尋ねられていない。euro「ユーロ」。

19 🇬🇧 W Where are the cleaning supplies kept?

🇺🇸 W (A) A mop and a broom.
(B) I'll be happy to show you.
(C) Every two weeks.

清掃用品はどこに保管されていますか。
(A) モップとほうきです。
(B) 喜んであなたをご案内しますよ。
(C) 2週間おきです。

正解 **B**　Where 〜?で清掃用品がどこに保管されているか尋ねているのに対し、場所を答える代わりに保管場所への案内を申し出ている(B)が正解。cleaning supplies「清掃用品」。be happy to do「喜んで〜する」、show「〜を案内する」。
(A) 質問にある清掃用品のmop「モップ」やbroom「ほうき」が含まれるが、何が保管されているかは尋ねられていない。
(C) 頻度は尋ねられていない。

20 🇦🇺 M Aren't you afraid the shipment may be delayed at customs?

🇬🇧 W (A) No, I've done all the paperwork.
　　　 (B) Please set it down in the corner.
　　　 (C) He has a custom-made guitar.

出荷物が税関で遅延するかもしれないと心配ではないのですか。
(A) 心配していません、私は全ての書類事務を済ませましたから。
(B) それを隅に下ろしてください。
(C) 彼は特注のギターを持っています。

正解 A　否定疑問文で、「出荷物の税関での遅延が心配ではないのか」と確認しているのに対し、Noと答え、遅れを危惧していない理由を述べている(A)が正解。be afraid (that) ～「～ではないかと心配する」、shipment「出荷物」、delay「～を遅延させる」、customs「税関」。paperwork「書類事務」。
(B) itが出荷物を指すとしても、置く場所は尋ねられていない。set down ～「～を下に置く」。
(C) custom-made「あつらえの」。

---

21 🇨🇦 M When is my article going to be published?

🇺🇸 W (A) Your editor's out of town this week.
　　　 (B) Yes, that illustration works.
　　　 (C) Because they finished earlier than expected.

私の記事はいつ掲載される予定ですか。
(A) あなたの担当編集者は今週、町から離れているのです。
(B) はい、その挿絵は効果的です。
(C) 彼らは予想していたよりも早く終わったからです。

正解 A　When ～?で自分の記事がいつ掲載されるか尋ねている。これに対し、「あなたの担当編集者は今週、町から離れている」と述べ、記事の担当者が不在のため、掲載時期について回答できないことを示唆している(A)が正解。article「記事」、publish「～を掲載する、～を出版する」。editor「編集者」、out of town「町から離れて」。
(B) 時期を尋ねられているので、Yes/Noでは応答にならない。illustration「挿絵」、work「効果がある」。
(C) expect「～を予想する」。

---

22 🇺🇸 W Do you want to leave now?

🇦🇺 M (A) I haven't eaten my dessert yet.
　　　 (B) It's great seeing you again.
　　　 (C) I live there now.

もう出発したいですか。
(A) 私はまだ自分のデザートを食べていません。
(B) またあなたに会えてうれしいです。
(C) 私は今、そこに住んでいます。

正解 A　「もう出発したいか」と希望を尋ねているのに対し、「私はまだ自分のデザートを食べていない」と、今すぐに出発したくはないことを示唆している(A)が正解。
(B) 希望を尋ねられているのに対し、相手との再会を喜んでいると伝える内容は応答にならない。
(C) 質問にあるleaveと似た音の動詞liveに注意。

---

23 🇺🇸 W Sally handles the payroll, doesn't she?

🇨🇦 M (A) That's right, she does.
　　　 (B) Yes, everything's discounted this week.
　　　 (C) Congratulations on the promotion!

Sallyが給料支払い業務を担当しているのですよね?
(A) その通りです、彼女が担当しています。
(B) はい、今週は全ての物が割引になっています。
(C) 昇進おめでとうございます!

正解 A　肯定文の文末に ～, doesn't she?を付けて「～ですよね」と、Sallyが給料支払い業務を担当しているか確認している。これに対し、That's right「その通りだ」と肯定し、さらにshe does (= she handles the payroll)と付け加えている(A)が正解。handle「～を担当する」、payroll「給料支払い業務」。
(B) everything'sはeverything isの略。discount「～を割り引いて売る」。
(C) Congratulations on ～「～おめでとう」、promotion「昇進」。

24 M Why is this office closed today?

W (A) At the management conference.
(B) When the new director arrives.
(C) There's some repair work going on.

このオフィスはなぜ、今日閉まっているのですか。
(A) 経営会議においてです。
(B) 新しい担当責任者が到着する際です。
(C) 修理作業が行われているのです。

正解 **C** Why ～?でオフィスが今日閉まっているのはなぜか尋ねているのに対し、「修理作業が行われている」からだと、その理由を伝えている(C)が正解。repair「修理」、go on「(状況などが)続く」。
(A) 場所は尋ねられていない。management「経営」、conference「会議」。
(B) 時は尋ねられていない。director「担当責任者」。

---

25 W Shouldn't the machines on the factory floor be cleaned?

M (A) No, I haven't seen him.
(B) Definitely — I'll put in a request now.
(C) Actually, it's on Main Street.

工場内の作業現場にある機械は掃除した方がいいのではありませんか。
(A) いいえ、私は彼に会っていません。
(B) 確かに——今すぐ要請を出します。
(C) 実は、それは大通りにあります。

正解 **B** 否定疑問文で、「工場内の作業現場にある機械は掃除した方がいいのではないか」と確認しているのに対し、Definitely「確かに」と強く肯定してから、「今すぐ要請を出す」と掃除を依頼する意思を伝えている(B)が正解。machine「機械」、factory floor「(工場内の)作業現場」。put in ～「～(要求や書類など)を提出する」、request「要請」。
(A) himが誰を指すか不明。
(C) itがfactoryを指すとしても、場所に関する発言は応答にならない。

---

26 M Where should we advertise for more volunteers?

W (A) Because I used to work there.
(B) Every Thursday at noon.
(C) The positions have all been filled.

どこに追加ボランティア募集の広告を出せばいいですか。
(A) 私はかつて、そこで働いていたからです。
(B) 毎週木曜日の正午です。
(C) その枠は全て埋まっています。

正解 **C** Where ～?で追加ボランティア募集の広告をどこに出すべきか尋ねているのに対し、ボランティア枠が全て埋まっている状況を述べ、追加で募集をかける必要がないことを示唆している(C)が正解。advertise「(求人などの)広告を出す」、volunteer「ボランティア」。position「職、地位」、fill「～を埋める」。
(A) 理由は尋ねられていない。used to do「かつて～していた」。
(B) 曜日や時間帯は尋ねられていない。

---

27 M The workshop participants are arriving in 30 minutes.

M (A) It was a great seminar.
(B) I'll put out the name cards.
(C) Yes, I work at an auto shop.

講習会の参加者は30分後に到着します。
(A) それは素晴らしいセミナーでした。
(B) 名札を出しておきます。
(C) はい、私は自動車店で働いています。

正解 **B** 講習会の参加者の到着時刻が迫っていることを知らせる発言に対し、「名札を出しておく」と、事前に名札を用意する意思を伝えている(B)が正解。workshop「講習会」、participant「参加者」、arrive「到着する」。put out ～「～を使えるように出しておく」、name card「名札」。
(A) Itがworkshopを指すとしても、過去の感想は応答にならない。seminar「セミナー」。
(C) 質問にあるworkshopには「作業場」の意味もあるが、勤務先は尋ねられていない。auto「自動車」。

TEST1 PART 2

28 🇬🇧 W Could you make some changes to the building plans?

🇨🇦 M (A) No, I didn't go there.
(B) All right, but I need to log on to my computer first.
(C) I bought a new car.

建物の設計図に幾つかの変更を加えていただけますか。
(A) いいえ、私はそこへ行きませんでした。
(B) 分かりました、でも私はまず、自分のコンピューターにログオンする必要があります。
(C) 私は新しい車を買いました。

正解 B　Could you ～?で建物の設計図に変更を加えることを依頼しているのに対し、All right「分かった」と了承しながらも、その前にまず、自分がコンピューターにログオンしなければならないと説明している(B)が正解。make a change「変更を加える」、plans「設計図」。log on to ～「～にログオンする、～にログインする」。
(A) thereがどこを指すか不明。
(C) 車については言及がない。

29 🇺🇸 W How often are the storage tanks inspected?

🇦🇺 M (A) You can check the records.
(B) There's a fuel station nearby.
(C) No, the inspector has left.

貯蔵タンクはどのくらいの頻度で点検されますか。
(A) あなたは記録を調べることができますよ。
(B) 近くに燃料補給所があります。
(C) いいえ、検査官は出発しました。

正解 A　How often ～?で貯蔵タンクが点検される頻度を尋ねているのに対し、頻度を答える代わりに、「あなたは記録を調べることができる」と述べ、それを確認できる記録があることを伝えている(A)が正解。storage「貯蔵」、tank「タンク」、inspect「～を点検する」。record「記録」。
(B) 質問にあるtanksと関連するfuelが含まれるが、応答になっていない。fuel station「燃料補給所」、nearby「近くに」。
(C) 質問にあるinspectedと関連するinspector「検査官」が含まれるが、応答になっていない。

30 🇨🇦 M Would you like to sit outside on the patio or inside?

🇺🇸 W (A) No, tomorrow at noon.
(B) It's quite windy this morning.
(C) Two glasses of water, please.

屋外のテラス席にお座りになりたいですか、それとも屋内にお座りになりたいですか。
(A) いいえ、明日の正午です。
(B) 今朝はかなり風が強いですね。
(C) 水を2杯、お願いします。

正解 B　A or B?の形で、屋外のテラス席と屋内の席のどちらを希望しているか尋ねている。これに対し、「今朝はかなり風が強い」と述べ、強風なのでテラス席ではなく屋内の席を希望することを暗に伝えている(B)が正解。outside「屋外に」、patio「(食事用の)テラス」、inside「屋内に」。quite「かなり」、windy「風が強い」。
(A) 日や時間帯は尋ねられていない。
(C) 注文内容は尋ねられていない。

31 🇬🇧 W Who's going to the post office today?

🇨🇦 M (A) In yesterday's delivery.
(B) Whenever she can.
(C) Do you have mail to send?

誰が今日、郵便局に行くことになっていますか。
(A) 昨日の配達物の中です。
(B) 彼女が行けるときならいつでも。
(C) 送る郵便物があるのですか。

正解 C　Who ～?で誰が今日郵便局に行くことになっているか尋ねている。これに対し、今日の担当者を答える代わりに、発送する郵便物があるのかと聞き返している(C)が正解。post office「郵便局」。mail「郵便物」。
(A) delivery「配達物、配達」。
(B) sheが誰を指すか不明。

PART 3

Questions 32 through 34 refer to the following conversation.

問題32-34は次の会話に関するものです。

M Hello. ❶I'm considering buying an annual membership to this art museum. Can you tell me about the benefits that members receive?

こんにちは。こちらの美術館の年間会員資格を購入しようかと思っています。会員が受けられる特典について私に教えてもらえますか。

W Sure. ❷Members receive benefits such as invitations for early admission to new exhibits and lectures by local artists.

もちろんです。会員さまは、新しい展覧会や地元芸術家による講演会への先行入場招待などの特典を受けることができます。

M Oh, that sounds good. I'm a student at Westmont University. ❸Is there a special rate for students?

ああ、それはいいですね。私はWestmont大学の学生です。学生向けの特別料金はありますか。

W Yes, ❹students receive ten percent off a regular membership. ❺I'll just need to see your student ID.

はい、学生の方々は通常の会員価格からの10パーセント引きを受けることができます。学生証を拝見するだけで済みます。

---

32 Where does the woman most likely work?

(A) At an airport
(B) At a museum
(C) At a travel agency
(D) At a conference center

女性はどこで働いていると考えられますか。

(A) 空港
(B) 美術館
(C) 旅行代理店
(D) 会議場

正解 B 男性は❶で、美術館の年間会員資格を購入したいと伝え、その会員特典についての情報を女性に求めている。それに対し女性は快諾して❷で、特典について具体的に説明しているので、美術館で働いていると考えられる。museum「美術館、博物館」。
(A) airport「空港」。
(C) travel agency「旅行代理店」。
(D) conference center「会議場」。

33 What benefit does the woman tell the man about?

(A) Free parking
(B) Promotional gifts
(C) Upgraded seating
(D) Invitations to special events

女性はどんな特典について男性に伝えていますか。

(A) 無料駐車
(B) 販促ギフト
(C) 座席のアップグレード
(D) 特別なイベントへの招待

正解 D 美術館の会員特典についての情報を求める男性に対し、女性は❷「会員は、新しい展覧会や地元芸術家による講演会への先行入場招待などの特典を受けられる」と説明している。new exhibits and lectures by local artistsをspecial eventsと表している(D)が正解。
(A) free「無料の」、parking「駐車（すること）」。
(B) promotional「販売促進の」、gift「贈り物」。
(C) upgrade「～をアップグレードする」、seating「座席」。

34 What does the woman ask the man to provide?

(A) Some identification
(B) A confirmation number
(C) Employment references
(D) A completed registration form

女性は男性に何を提供するよう求めていますか。

(A) 身元証明書
(B) 確認番号
(C) 雇用照会先
(D) 記入済みの登録用紙

正解 A ❸で、学生向けの料金があるか尋ねる男性に対し、女性は❹で学生割引について説明した後、❺「あなたの学生証を見る必要があるだけだ」と、男性に学生証の提示を求めている。student IDをidentificationと表している(A)が正解。provide「～を提供する」。
(B) confirmation「確認」。
(C) employment「雇用」、reference「信用照会先」。
(D) complete「～に全て記入する」、registration「登録」、form「用紙」。

Words & Phrases

consider *doing* ～することを検討する　annual 1年間の　membership 会員資格
art museum 美術館　benefit 特典　member 会員　receive ～を受ける　such as ～ ～などの、～のような
invitation 招待、招待状　early 早期の　admission 入場許可　exhibit 展覧会　lecture 講演　local 地元の
artist 芸術家　sound ～に聞こえる　special 特別な　rate 料金　off ～から割り引いて　regular 通常の
student ID 学生証　★IDはidentification「身元証明書」の略

Questions 35 through 37 refer to the following conversation.

W Hello, what brings you to Altu Computers today?

M Hi, ①I bought this laptop here just last month. But ②the image on the screen is fuzzy.

W It's probably a hardware issue. ③We may have to ship it to our repair facility.

M Oh! ④How much extra would that cost?

W Well, since you bought it recently, repair and shipping will be covered under the manufacturer's warranty. But ⑤you should back up your data first.

M ⑥I do have some important documents in my files.

W I wouldn't risk losing those. ⑦Why don't you take a few minutes to back them up now?

問題35-37は次の会話に関するものです。

こんにちは、本日はどのようなご用件でAltuコンピューター店にいらっしゃいましたか。

こんにちは、私はちょうど先月、こちらでこのノートパソコンを購入しました。でも、画面の画像が不鮮明なのです。

それはおそらくハードウエアの問題でしょう。当店の修理施設にそれを送る必要があるかもしれません。

ああ！それには幾ら追加料金がかかるでしょうか。

そうですね、お客さまはそれを最近ご購入なさったので、修理と配送はメーカー保証の対象となるでしょう。しかし、まずご自分のデータをバックアップした方がいいですよ。

私のファイルの中には確かに大事な文書が入っています。

私なら、それらを失うリスクは冒したくありません。数分お時間を取って、今からそれらをバックアップしてはいかがでしょうか。

TEST1 PART 3

35 Why is the man at a computer store?

(A) To get technical support
(B) To make a purchase
(C) To get a refund
(D) To apply for a job

男性はなぜコンピューター店にいるのですか。

(A) 技術的なサポートを得るため
(B) 買い物をするため
(C) 払い戻しを受けるため
(D) 職に応募するため

正解 A コンピューター店への来店目的を尋ねられた男性は、①で、同店で購入したノートパソコンに言及し、続けて②「画面の画像が不鮮明だ」とその問題点を伝えている。よって、男性は不具合が生じている購入製品に対する技術的なサポートを得るために来店していると判断できる。technical「技術的な」、support「サポート、支援」。
(B) make a purchase「買い物をする」。
(C) refund「払い戻し」。
(D) apply for ～「～に応募する」、job「職」。

36 What does the man ask about?

(A) A shipping cost
(B) A product feature
(C) Customer reviews
(D) Store hours

男性は何について尋ねていますか。

(A) 配送料
(B) 製品の特徴
(C) 顧客レビュー
(D) 店の営業時間

正解 A ③で、不具合が生じている男性のノートパソコンを修理施設に送る必要があるかもしれないと述べる女性に対し、男性は④「それには幾ら追加料金がかかるか」と尋ねている。それに対して女性は修理費と配送料はメーカー保証の対象となると答え、それらの追加料金はかからないことを示唆している。
(B) product「製品」、feature「特徴」。
(C) customer「顧客」、review「レビュー、批評」。
(D) hours「営業時間」。

37 What does the woman suggest the man do?

(A) Sign some papers
(B) Schedule an appointment
(C) Select some merchandise
(D) Save some data

女性は男性に何をすることを提案していますか。

(A) 書類に署名する
(B) 予約を入れる
(C) 商品を選択する
(D) データを保存する

正解 D 男性のパソコンを修理施設に送る必要性を伝えた女性は、⑤「まずあなたのデータをバックアップした方がいい」と男性に勧めている。⑥でファイルには大事な文書が入っていると言う男性に、女性は⑦で、即座のバックアップを提案している。back upをsave「～を保存する」で言い換えている(D)が正解。
(A) sign「～に署名する」、papers「書類」。
(B) schedule「～を予定に入れる」、appointment「予約」。
(C) select「～を選択する」、merchandise「商品」。

Words & Phrases
What brings you to ～ 何の用件で～へ来たのか　laptop ノートパソコン　image 画像　fuzzy 不鮮明な　probably おそらく　hardware ハードウエア機器　issue 問題　ship ～を送る　repair 修理　facility 施設　extra 追加料金　cost ～（費用）がかかる　recently 最近　shipping 配送(料)　cover ～を補償する、～を賄う　warranty 保証　manufacturer メーカー、製造業者　back up ～ ～をバックアップする　important 大事な　document 文書　risk ～の危険を冒す　lose ～を失う

Questions 38 through 40 refer to the following conversation.

M ❶I'm here to pick up the photographs your studio took of me and my family last month. **The last name is Park.**

W OK, ❷let me go find them in the back room. ❸While you're waiting, here's a catalog that shows other items we can put photographs on, like T-shirts, calendars, or mugs.

M That's a great idea. I see there are lots of items to choose from.

W Yes, and ❹we have a special offer this month. ❺We'll ship anything you purchase free of charge.

問題38-40は次の会話に関するものです。

こちらのスタジオで先月撮っていただいた、私と家族の写真を受け取りに来ました。名字はParkです。

かしこまりました、奥の部屋にそれらを探しに行ってまいります。お待ちになっている間、Tシャツやカレンダー、マグカップといった、当店が写真をプリントできる他の商品が載っているカタログをどうぞ。

それはいい考えですね。選べる商品がたくさん載っていますね。

はい、それから、当店は今月特別サービスを提供しています。ご購入の品をいずれも無料で発送いたします。

38 Where most likely are the speakers?

(A) At a clothing shop
(B) At an art gallery
(C) At a photography studio
(D) At a stationery store

話し手たちはどこにいると考えられますか。

(A) 衣料品店
(B) 画廊
(C) 写真スタジオ
(D) 文房具店

正解 C 男性は❶で写真を受け取りに来た旨を女性に伝え、名字を名乗っている。それに対し、女性は❷で、奥の部屋にそれらを探しに行ってくると言っているので、話し手たちは写真スタジオにいると考えられる。
(A) (D) 女性はTシャツとカレンダーに言及しているが、それらは、店が写真をプリント可能な商品の例として紹介しているだけ。
(A) clothing「衣料品」。
(B) art gallery「画廊、美術館」。
(D) stationery「文房具」。

39 What does the woman give the man?

(A) A poster
(B) A catalog
(C) A gift card
(D) An instruction manual

女性は男性に何を差し出していますか。

(A) ポスター
(B) カタログ
(C) ギフトカード
(D) 取扱説明書

正解 B 男性の写真を探しに行ってくると述べた女性は、続けて❸「待っている間、Tシャツやカレンダー、マグカップといった、当店が写真をプリントできる他の商品が載っているカタログをどうぞ」と、男性に店のカタログを差し出し、見るよう勧めている。
(A) poster「ポスター」。
(C) gift card「ギフトカード（お金の代わりに利用可能な金券）」。
(D) instruction manual「取扱説明書」。

40 What special offer does the woman mention?

(A) Free shipping
(B) Early entrance
(C) A sales discount
(D) A customer loyalty program

女性はどんな特別サービスについて述べていますか。

(A) 無料配送
(B) 先行入場
(C) 販売額の割引
(D) お得意さまプログラム

正解 A 女性は❹「当店は今月特別サービスを提供している」と言ってから、❺で、購入品をどれも無料で顧客に発送していると述べている。free「無料の」、shipping「配送（料）」。
(B) entrance「入場、入る権利」。
(C) sales「販売額」、discount「割引」。
(D) customer「顧客」、loyalty program「お得意さまプログラム（顧客をつなぎとめるためのポイントカードなどの制度）」。

Words & Phrases
pick up ~ ～を受け取る　take a photograph 写真を撮る　studio スタジオ
last name 名字　back 奥の　while ～する間　here's ~ はい～をどうぞ　★here is ～の短縮形　catalog カタログ
item 商品　T-shirt Tシャツ　calendar カレンダー　mug マグカップ　choose ~ from … …から～を選ぶ
offer サービス、提供　ship ～を発送する　purchase ～を購入する　free of charge 無料で

Questions 41 through 43 refer to the following conversation with three speakers.

🇺🇸 W Maria and Jerome, ❶could you give me an update on how our new video game is coming along?

🇬🇧 W Sure. ❷I'm done updating all of the digital graphics.

🇨🇦 M And ❸I'm working on writing the instructions for how to play the game. ❹They're rather complicated, but I'll finish by the end of the week.

🇺🇸 W Excellent. ❺It sounds like we're almost ready to field-test the game. ❻We'll need to get feedback from the gaming community.

問題 41-43 は 3 人の話し手による次の会話に関するものです。

Maria、Jerome、当社の新しいテレビゲームの進捗に関する最新情報を教えてもらえますか。

はい。私は、全てのデジタルグラフィックの更新が終わっています。

そして私は、ゲームのプレイ方法についての説明書の執筆に取り組んでいるところです。それはかなり複雑ですが、週末までに終えるつもりです。

素晴らしい。ゲームを実地試験する準備がほぼ整っているようですね。私たちはゲームコミュニティーから意見をもらう必要があるでしょう。

---

41 What does the company make?

(A) Video games
(B) Mobile phones
(C) Sports equipment
(D) Art supplies

会社は何を作っていますか。

(A) テレビゲーム
(B) 携帯電話
(C) スポーツ用具
(D) 美術用品

正解 A　1 人目の女性は❶で、自社の新しいテレビゲームの進捗を尋ねている。それに対し、2 人目の女性は❷「私は、全てのデジタルグラフィックの更新が終わっている」と答え、男性は❸「私は、ゲームのプレイ方法についての説明書の執筆に取り組んでいる」と、テレビゲーム制作の進捗状況を報告しているので、(A) が正解。
(C) equipment「用具、機器」。
(D) art supplies「美術用品」。

42 What part of a project does the man say is complicated?

(A) Creating a design
(B) Finding investors
(C) Writing some directions
(D) Contacting social media sites

男性は計画のどの部分が複雑だと言っていますか。

(A) デザインを考案すること
(B) 出資者を見つけること
(C) 説明書を書くこと
(D) ソーシャルメディアのサイトと連絡を取ること

正解 C　テレビゲーム制作の進捗を尋ねられた男性は❸で、説明書の執筆に取り組んでいると報告した後、❹「それはかなり複雑だ」と述べている。They は the instructions を指しているので、(C) が正解。part「部分」。directions「説明書」。
(A) create「～を考案する」、design「デザイン」。
(B) investor「出資者」。
(D) contact「～と連絡を取る」、social media「ソーシャルメディア」、site「サイト」。

43 What is the next step in a project?

(A) A product will be tested.
(B) A competition will take place.
(C) A sales promotion will begin.
(D) An advertisement will be filmed.

計画の次の段階は何ですか。

(A) 製品がテストされる。
(B) 大会が開催される。
(C) 販売促進活動が始まる。
(D) 広告が撮影される。

正解 A　制作中のテレビゲームの進捗を聞いた 1 人目の女性は、❺「ゲームを実地試験する準備がほぼ整っているようだ」と述べた後、❻でゲームコミュニティーから意見を得る必要性に言及している。よって、計画の次の段階は、制作中の製品の実地試験をすることだと判断できる。step「段階」。product「製品」、test「～をテストする」。
(B) competition「競技会」、take place「開催される」。
(C) sales promotion「販売促進活動」。
(D) advertisement「広告」、film「～を撮影する」。

Words & Phrases

update 〈名詞で〉最新情報、〈動詞で〉～を更新する　video game テレビゲーム
come along うまく進む　digital graphics デジタルグラフィックス ★コンピューターなどを使って生成されるデジタル画像
work on doing ～することに取り組む　instructions 取扱説明書　rather かなり　complicated 複雑な
excellent 素晴らしい　be ready to do ～する準備が整っている
field-test ～を実地試験する ★製品の性能などを、実際に使用する場所や状況で試すこと　feedback 意見、評価
gaming ゲーム(の)　community コミュニティー、(共通の趣味などを持つ)集団

Questions 44 through 46 refer to the following conversation.

M Jones Sod Company. How may I help you?

W Hi. ❶This is Dolores Garcia, the facilities manager at West Town Stadium. ❷We're looking into replacing the artificial turf on our playing field with natural grass. But ❸we're concerned about how much water it'll require. ❹Especially during the months when there isn't much rain.

M There are a number of drought-resistant grasses on the market now for facilities like yours— ❺Bermuda and St. Augustine grasses in particular can tolerate long dormant seasons. We have patches growing out here in our nursery. ❻Can you come by and take a look sometime this week?

問題44-46は次の会話に関するものです。

Jones芝生社です。どのようなご用件でしょうか。

こんにちは。こちらは、West Townスタジアムの設備管理者のDolores Garciaです。運動場の人工芝を天然芝に張り替えることを検討しています。でも、私たちは、その場合にどのくらいの量の水が必要になるか心配しています。特に、あまり雨が降らない数カ月の間です。

最近は、お客さまの所のような施設に適した、乾燥に強い芝が幾つか市場に出ています——とりわけバミューダ芝とセントオーガスティン芝は、長い休眠期も耐えられます。当社がこちらの養苗場で育てているものがございます。今週中のどこかで立ち寄ってご覧になることはできますか。

44 Where does the woman work?

(A) At an office complex
(B) At a community park
(C) At a sports facility
(D) At a zoo

女性はどこで働いていますか。
(A) オフィス複合施設
(B) 地域の公園
(C) スポーツ施設
(D) 動物園

正解C 用件を尋ねる男性に対し、女性は❶「こちらは、West Townスタジアムの設備管理者のDolores Garciaだ」と、自分の勤め先と名前を伝えている。女性は続けて❷で、運動場の人工芝を天然芝に張り替えることを検討中だと伝えているので、(C)が正解。
(A) complex「複合施設、総合ビル」。
(B) community「地域社会」。

45 What is the woman concerned about?

(A) Installation costs
(B) Water usage
(C) Parking capacity
(D) Ticket sales

女性は何について心配していますか。
(A) 設置費
(B) 水の使用量
(C) 駐車可能な台数
(D) チケットの販売

正解B 施設の人工芝を天然芝に張り替えることを検討していると伝えた女性は、❸「私たちは、その場合にどのくらいの量の水が必要になるか心配している」と懸念点に言及し、❹で、特に降雨量が少ない数カ月の間が心配だと補足している。usage「使用(量)」。
(A) installation「設置」、costs「経費、コスト」。
(C) parking「駐車」、capacity「収容能力」。

46 What does the man suggest the woman do this week?

(A) Reserve tickets
(B) Water a garden
(C) Apply for a loan
(D) Look at some samples

男性は、女性に今週何をすることを勧めていますか。
(A) チケットを予約する
(B) 庭に水をやる
(C) 融資を申し込む
(D) サンプルを見る

正解D 男性は❺で、バミューダ芝やセントオーガスティン芝という、乾燥に耐性のある芝に言及し、その芝を自社の養苗場で育てていることを伝えている。その後、❻「今週中のどこかで立ち寄って見てもらうことはできるか」と女性に尋ねているので、男性は女性に、その芝の実物を見に来るよう勧めていると判断できる。(D)ではpatchesをsamples「サンプル、見本」と言い換えている。
(B) water「~に水をやる」。
(C) apply for ~「~を申し込む」、loan「融資」。

Words & Phrases
sod 芝生　facility 施設、設備　look into doing ~することを検討する
replace ~ with … ~を…と交換する　artificial 人工の　turf 芝、芝土　playing field 運動場　grass 芝
be concerned about ~ ~について心配している　require ~を必要とする　especially 特に
a number of ~ 幾つかの~　drought-resistant 渇水に強い　★-resistantは「~に耐性のある」という意味
in particular とりわけ　tolerate ~に耐える　dormant season 休眠期　★夏季や冬季の発育休止の期間
patch 小地面(に栽培された作物)　grow 育つ　nursery 養苗場　come by 立ち寄る　take a look 見る

Questions 47 through 49 refer to the following conversation.

🇨🇦 M Hello, this is Mustafa Hamam, returning your call.

🇺🇸 W Thanks for getting back to me, Mustafa. ❶You helped me with the legal work to set up my furniture store. ❷Now I'd like to hire an accountant to take over the finances for the business, but I'm not sure how to select one.

🇨🇦 M Oh, ❸I'm often asked to make these kinds of professional connections for my clients. ❹I'll prepare a list of names and send it to you later today.

🇺🇸 W Excellent.

🇨🇦 M One thing though, ❺I'll be away at a conference next week. But ❻if you should have any questions while I'm away, one of the other lawyers can assist you.

🇺🇸 W OK, thanks.

問題47-49は次の会話に関するものです。

もしもし、こちらはMustafa Hamamで、折り返しお電話しています。

折り返しご連絡いただきありがとうございます、Mustafa。あなたは、私が家具店を立ち上げるための法務を手伝ってくださいましたね。私は今、店の財務を引き受けてくれる会計士を雇用したいと思っているのですが、その選び方が分かりません。

ああ、私はよく、自分の顧客のためにこういった専門職の人脈作りを頼まれるんです。名前のリストを用意して、本日後ほどあなたに送ります。

とても助かります。

ですが1点、私は来週、会議で不在になります。しかし、万が一、私が不在の間に何かご質問があれば、他の弁護士のいずれかがあなたの力になれます。

分かりました、ありがとうございます。

---

47 Where does the man most likely work?

(A) At a manufacturing company
(B) At a law firm
(C) At a bank
(D) At a call center

男性はどこで働いていると考えられますか。

(A) 製造会社
(B) 法律事務所
(C) 銀行
(D) コールセンター

正解 **B** 女性は、折り返しの連絡に対して男性にお礼を伝えた後、❶「あなたは、私が家具店を立ち上げるための法務を手伝ってくれた」と述べているので、男性は法律に関する業務を行っていると考えられる。law firm「法律事務所」。
(A) manufacturing「製造(の)」。
(D) call center「コールセンター(客からの注文や問い合わせなどに電話対応する部門や施設)」。

---

48 What does the woman ask the man to do?

(A) Provide a referral
(B) Process a payment
(C) Explain a delay
(D) Review a contract

女性は男性に何をするよう求めていますか。

(A) 紹介する
(B) 支払いを処理する
(C) 遅延の理由を説明する
(D) 契約書を精査する

正解 **A** ❷で、会計士を雇用したいが、その選び方が分からないと述べる女性に対し、男性は❸で、顧客にこういった専門職の人脈作りをよく頼まれると言った後、❹「名前のリストを用意して、本日後ほどあなたに送る」と伝えている。よって、女性は男性に会計士の紹介を求めていると判断できる。provide「~を提供する」、referral「紹介」。
(B) process「~を処理する」、payment「支払い」。
(C) explain「~の理由を説明する」、delay「遅延」。
(D) review「~を精査する」、contract「契約書」。

---

49 What does the man say he will do next week?

(A) Conduct interviews
(B) Attend a conference
(C) Provide software training
(D) Redecorate an office

男性は来週に何をすると言っていますか。

(A) 面接を行う
(B) 会議に出席する
(C) ソフトウエアの研修を提供する
(D) オフィスを改装する

正解 **B** 男性は❺「私は来週、会議で不在になる」と女性に知らせ、❻で、不在中は他の弁護士のいずれかが女性の力になると伝えている。会議で不在になることをattend a conferenceと表している(B)が正解。attend「~に出席する」。
(A) conduct「~を行う」、interview「面接」。
(C) training「研修」。
(D) redecorate「~を改装する」。

Words & Phrases

return one's call ~に折り返し電話する　　get back to ~ ~に折り返し連絡する
legal 法律に関する　　set up ~ ~(店など)を立ち上げる　　hire ~を雇用する　　accountant 会計士
take over ~ ~を引き受ける、~を引き継ぐ　　finances 財務状態　　business 店、企業　　sure 確信して
professional 専門職の　　connection つながり、関係　　client 顧客　　prepare ~を用意する　　though でも
away 不在で　　conference 会議　　should do 〈if節で〉万が一~するなら　　lawyer 弁護士　　assist ~を手伝う

Questions 50 through 52 refer to the following conversation.

W ❶Chef Pierre, there are several boxes stacked near the back door—I took a look inside and they're full of new pans and bowls.

M Yes, ❷I ordered new cooking equipment, and it arrived late yesterday. I'd actually like to use the pans to bake this morning's bread. ❸Could you bring the boxes into the kitchen?

W The boxes are really big.

M Ah, right. ❹Let's get the cart and load them together, then.

W I noticed some pans that are specially shaped. ❺Are you planning to sell some additional types of baked goods?

M Yes, ❻starting next week, we'll be offering a bigger selection.

問題50-52は次の会話に関するものです。

Pierreシェフ、裏口のそばに幾つかの箱が積み重なっています――中を見てみたところ、新しい焼き型とボウルがぎっしり詰まっています。

はい、私が新しい調理器具を注文して、それが昨日遅くに到着したのです。実は、今日の午前のパンを焼くのにその焼き型を使いたいと思っています。箱を厨房内へ動かしてもらえますか。

箱はとても大きいですよ。

ああ、そうですね。それなら、台車を取ってきて、一緒にそれらを載せましょう。

私は、特殊な形をした幾つかの焼き型に気が付きました。別の種類の焼き菓子を販売しようとしているのですか。

はい、来週から、より多くの品ぞろえを提供する予定です。

50 Who most likely are the speakers?

(A) Appliance salespeople
(B) Bakery employees
(C) Delivery drivers
(D) Cooking show hosts

話し手たちは誰だと考えられますか。
(A) 電化製品の販売員
(B) パン屋の従業員
(C) 配達運転手
(D) 料理番組の司会者

正解 B ❶で、裏口の箱に新しい焼き型とボウルが詰まっている、とシェフの男性に知らせる女性に対し、男性は❷で、それは注文した調理器具が届いたものであり、今日の午前のパンを焼くのに使いたいと伝えている。よって、2人はパン屋の従業員だと考えられる。employee「従業員」。
(A) appliance「電化製品」、salespeople「販売員」。
(C) delivery「配達」、driver「運転手」。
(D) show「番組」、host「(番組の)司会者」。

51 What does the woman imply when she says, "The boxes are really big"?

(A) She thinks the boxes will not fit on a shelf.
(B) She suspects an order was sent by mistake.
(C) She cannot do a task on her own.
(D) She will not need to use more boxes.

女性は "The boxes are really big" という発言で、何を示唆していますか。
(A) 彼女は箱が棚にうまく収まらないだろうと考えている。
(B) 彼女は注文品が誤って送られたのではないかと思っている。
(C) 彼女は独力で作業をすることができない。
(D) 彼女はこれ以上多くの箱を使う必要がないだろう。

正解 C 下線部の発言は、男性が女性に❸で、箱を厨房内へ動かすよう頼んだことに対するもの。女性の下線部の発言を受けて男性は、箱を動かすのが大変そうだと気付き、❹「それなら、台車を取ってきて、一緒にそれらを載せよう」と、台車を使って2人で箱を動かすことを提案している。よって、女性は、自分だけでは箱を厨房内へ移せないことを示唆していると判断できる。
(A) fit「うまく収まる」、shelf「棚」。
(B) suspect (that) ～「～ではないかと思う」、order「注文品」、by mistake「誤って」。

52 What will happen next week?

(A) A wider variety of items will be offered.
(B) A local competition will be held.
(C) A new employee will join the team.
(D) A business will move to a bigger location.

来週に何が起こりますか。
(A) より幅広い種類の商品が提供される。
(B) 地元のコンテストが開催される。
(C) 新しい従業員がチームに加わる。
(D) 店がより広い場所へと移転する。

正解 A 女性が❺で、別の種類の焼き菓子を販売するつもりか尋ねると、男性は肯定した後、❻「来週から、より多くの品ぞろえを提供する予定だ」と店の今後の計画を知らせている。a wide variety of ～「さまざまな～、多種多様な～」、item「商品」。
(B) competition「コンテスト」、hold「～を開催する」。
(D) business「店、企業」、location「場所」。

Words & Phrases

several 幾つかの　stack ～を積み重ねる　back door 裏口　inside 内部に　be full of ～ ～でいっぱいである　pan 焼き型　bowl ボウル　equipment 器具　actually 実は　cart 台車　load ～を載せる　notice ～に気が付く　specially 特別に　shape ～を形作る　plan to *do* ～するつもりである　additional 追加の　baked goods パン、焼き菓子　offer ～を提供する　selection 品ぞろえ、選択

Questions 53 through 55 refer to the following conversation.

M Megumi, ❶I wanted to congratulate you on your successful presentation to the managers this morning. We think the marketing strategy you presented is well suited to our new video streaming service.

W Thank you. ❷The consultant we hired last month actually helped me quite a bit. ❸His market research showed exactly which age groups would be most interested in the movies and TV shows that we're going to offer.

M ❹I was especially interested in the data about spending and viewing patterns of consumers in their thirties. ❺We should make a special effort to target them. That should increase our sales.

問題53-55は次の会話に関するものです。

Megumi、今朝の成功に終わった経営陣へのあなたのプレゼンテーションのことで、お祝いを言いたいと思っていました。私たちは、あなたが提示したマーケティング戦略が当社の新しい動画ストリーミングサービスによく適していると思います。

ありがとうございます。実は、先月雇ったコンサルタントがかなり力になってくれました。彼の市場調査はまさに、どの年齢層が当社が提供する予定の映画やテレビ番組に最も関心を持ちそうかを示していたのです。

私は特に、30代の消費者の消費パターンと視聴パターンに関するデータに関心を持ちました。私たちは彼らをターゲットにする特別な工夫をするべきです。そうすれば、当社の売上高は伸びるはずです。

53 Why does the man congratulate the woman?

(A) She received a promotion.
(B) She finished a project early.
(C) She gave a good presentation.
(D) Her movie won an award.

男性はなぜ、女性に祝いの言葉を述べているのですか。

(A) 彼女は昇進した。
(B) 彼女はプロジェクトを早く終えた。
(C) 彼女は良いプレゼンテーションをした。
(D) 彼女の映画は賞を獲得した。

正解 C 男性は❶「今朝の成功に終わった経営陣へのあなたのプレゼンテーションのことで、祝いを言いたいと思っていた」と女性に祝辞を述べている。your successful presentationをa good presentationと表している(C)が正解。give a presentation「プレゼンテーションをする」。
(A) receive「～を得る」、promotion「昇進」。
(D) win「～を獲得する」、award「賞」。

54 Who does the woman say she received help from?

(A) An independent consultant
(B) A department manager
(C) A sales assistant
(D) A video editor

女性は、自分が誰の助けを借りたと言っていますか。

(A) 独立のコンサルタント
(B) 部長
(C) 店員
(D) 動画編集者

正解 A 女性は自分のプレゼンについて、❷「実は、先月雇ったコンサルタントがかなり力になってくれた」と述べてから、❸で、プレゼンの成功に寄与した外部コンサルタントの市場調査内容を詳しく説明している。社外のコンサルタントをan independent consultantと表している(A)が正解。independent「独立した」。
(B) department「部署」。
(C) sales assistant「店員」。
(D) editor「編集者」。

55 What does the man think will increase sales?

(A) Hiring a famous spokesperson
(B) Providing some promotional pricing
(C) Publishing a press release
(D) Focusing on a specific consumer group

男性は、何が売上高を伸ばすと考えていますか。

(A) 有名な広報担当者を雇うこと
(B) 販売促進用の価格設定を用意すること
(C) プレスリリースを発表すること
(D) 特定の消費者グループに焦点を当てること

正解 D ❹で、30代の消費者に関するデータに注目していると述べた男性は、❺で「彼らをターゲットにする特別な工夫をすることで、当社の売上高は伸びるはずだ」と主張している。focus on ～「～に焦点を当てる」、specific「特定の」。
(A) spokesperson「広報担当者」。
(B) provide「～を提供する」、promotional「販売促進の」、pricing「価格設定」。
(C) publish「～を発表する」、press release「プレスリリース、報道用文書」。

Words & Phrases
congratulate ～ on … …のことで～を祝う　successful 成功した　manager 経営者　marketing マーケティング、市場取引　strategy 戦略　present ～を提示する　suited 適した　streaming ストリーミング　★インターネット上で映像などを受信しながら再生する方式　consultant コンサルタント、顧問　quite a bit かなり　market research 市場調査　exactly まさしく、正確に　age group 年齢層　be interested in ～ ～に関心がある　offer ～を提供する　especially 特に　spending 消費、支出　viewing 視聴　pattern パターン　consumer 消費者　in one's thirties 30代の　make an effort to do ～するよう努力する　target ～を対象とする　increase ～を増やす　sales 売上高

TEST 1 PART 3

Questions 56 through 58 refer to the following conversation with three speakers.

🇦🇺 M Nadia, Omar— ❶I'd like us to talk about access to the Skyline Towers construction site. ❷As the security contractors for this project, we'll be in charge of checking badges for all personnel. **That's a lot of work.**

🇨🇦 M ❸We could always hire more guards for each site entrance.

🇬🇧 W ❹The temp agencies are charging too much these days. We don't have the budget for that.

🇨🇦 M Well, why don't we rent badge-reading machines then. Remember we used the Borson readers for that summer festival?

🇬🇧 W ❺The Borson machines were terrible—they were so slow, people had to wait in line.

🇦🇺 M I like the idea of using an automated system though. Maybe we can try another brand.

問題56-58は3人の話し手による次の会話に関するものです。

Nadia、Omar——皆で、Skylineタワーズの建設現場へのアクセスについて話し合いたいと思っています。この計画の警備請負業者として、当社は全ての人員のバッジ確認を担当することになります。これはかなり手間のかかる作業です。

いつでも、各現場への入り口の警備員をもっと雇ってもいいのではありませんか。

人材派遣会社はこのところ、かなり多くの料金を請求しています。私たちにはそのための予算はありません。

そうですね、それならバッジ読み取り機をレンタルしてはどうでしょうか。例の夏祭りで当社がBorson社の読み取り機を使用したことは覚えていますよね？

Borson社の機械は最悪でした——あれは非常に遅かったので、人々は列になって待たなければなりませんでした。

でも、自動システムを使用するという考えは良いと思います。別の製品を試してみてもいいかもしれませんね。

56 What industry do the speakers work in?

(A) Construction
(B) Software development
(C) Security
(D) Equipment supply

話し手たちはどんな業界で働いていますか。

(A) 建設
(B) ソフトウエア開発
(C) 警備
(D) 機器供給

正解 C　1人目の男性は❶で、建設現場へのアクセスについて話し合いたいと述べた後、❷「この計画の警備請負業者として、当社は全ての人員のバッジ確認を担当することになる」と自社の役割を確認している。よって、話し手たちは警備業界で働いていると考えられる。
(A) 話し手たちの会社は建設現場の警備担当であって、彼らが建設業界で働いているのではない。
(B) development「開発」。
(D) equipment「機器」、supply「供給」。

57 Why is the woman concerned about hiring more staff?

(A) It would be too expensive.
(B) It would require more training.
(C) The site has too many workers already.
(D) The site is not big enough.

女性はなぜ、追加のスタッフの雇用について心配しているのですか。

(A) 費用がかかり過ぎるだろう。
(B) もっと研修が必要になるだろう。
(C) 現場にはすでにあまりにも多くの作業者がいる。
(D) 現場が十分に広くない。

正解 A　❸で、追加の警備員の雇用を提案する2人目の男性に対し、女性は❹「人材派遣会社は最近、かなり多くの料金を請求している」と述べてから、自分たちにはそのための予算はないと、追加人材に充てる予算の不足を伝えている。be concerned about ～「～について心配している」、staff「スタッフ、従業員」。expensive「費用のかかる」。
(B) require「～を必要とする」、training「研修」。

58 Why does the woman dislike the Borson machines?

(A) They work too slowly.
(B) They require too many repairs.
(C) They take a long time to set up.
(D) They are not accurate.

女性はなぜBorson社の機械を気に入らないのですか。

(A) 動作が遅過ぎる。
(B) あまりに多くの修理作業を必要とする。
(C) セッティングするのに長い時間がかかる。
(D) 正確ではない。

正解 A　女性はBorson社の機械について、❺「Borson社の機械は最悪だった——あれは非常に遅かったので、人々は列になって待つ必要があった」と、気に入らない理由を伝えている。dislike「～を嫌う」。slowly「ゆっくりと」。
(B) repairs「修理作業」。
(C) 時間がかかるのはバッジの読み取りであり、そのセッティングではない。set up ～「～を設定する」。
(D) accurate「正確な」。

Words & Phrases
access アクセス、入る権利　construction 建設　site 現場　security 警備、セキュリティー　contractor 請負業者　in charge of ～ ～を担当して　badge バッジ、名札　personnel 人員、職員　guard 警備員　temp agency 人材派遣会社　charge ～(料金)を請求する　rent ～をレンタルする　terrible 最悪な、ひどい　in line 列になって　automated 自動の　though でも

Questions 59 through 61 refer to the following conversation.

🇺🇸 W ❶Thanks for meeting with me, Mr. Chung.

🇨🇦 M Sure. ❷I'm always looking for companies to invest in.

🇺🇸 W ❸My company designs and manufactures high-quality bedding, like sheets and blankets. ❹What makes our products unique is that they're only sold online. Quality linens aren't cheap, so we keep prices low by selling directly to customers.

🇨🇦 M Hmm. I'd imagine people would want to feel the material before purchasing.

🇺🇸 W ❺That's why we offer a 30-day trial period. If customers aren't satisfied, they can return any item for a full refund. ❻But it's rare that that happens.

🇨🇦 M How rare?

🇺🇸 W Well, in three years, we've only had to process eighteen returns.

問題59-61は次の会話に関するものです。

お会いいただきありがとうございます、Chungさん。

こちらこそ。私は常々、投資先となる企業を探しています。

私の会社はシーツや毛布といった、高品質な寝具の設計と製造を行っています。当社製品を比類のないものにしているのは、それらがオンラインでのみ販売されているという点です。上質なリネンは安価ではないので、当社は顧客に直接販売することで価格を低く抑えているのです。

うーん。人々は購入前に生地に触ってみることを望むのではないかと思うのですが。

だからこそ、当社は30日間のお試し期間を提供しているのです。顧客は満足できなければ、どの商品も返品して全額返金を受けられます。でも、そのようなことが起こるのはまれです。

どのくらいまれなのですか。

そうですね、3年間で、当社はわずか18件の返品を処理する必要があっただけです。

59 Why are the speakers meeting?

(A) To discuss an investment opportunity
(B) To plan a product release event
(C) To negotiate a shipping agreement
(D) To revise a product development plan

話し手たちはなぜ会合しているのですか。

(A) 投資機会について話し合うため
(B) 製品の発売イベントを計画するため
(C) 配送契約を取り決めるため
(D) 製品開発計画を見直すため

正解 A ❶で、会合のお礼を述べる女性に対し、男性は❷「私は常々、投資先となる企業を探している」と伝えている。女性は❸・❹で、自社製品や販売方法を詳しく説明しているので、投資について話し合うために会合していると考えられる。investment「投資」、opportunity「機会」。
(B) plan「～を計画する」、release「発売」。
(C) negotiate「～を取り決める」、shipping「配送」、agreement「契約」。
(D) revise「～を見直す、～を改訂する」。

60 Why does the man say, "I'd imagine people would want to feel the material before purchasing"?

(A) To suggest sending free samples
(B) To complain about a purchase
(C) To express doubt about a business model
(D) To correct a misunderstanding about a process

男性はなぜ "I'd imagine people would want to feel the material before purchasing" と言っていますか。

(A) 無料の試供品を送ることを提案するため
(B) 購入品について不平を言うため
(C) ビジネスモデルについての疑念を示すため
(D) 手順についての誤解を正すため

正解 C ❹で、製品をオンラインでのみ販売していると述べる女性に対し、男性は下線部の発言で、顧客目線からの疑問を投げ掛けている。それを受け、女性は❺でその疑念を払拭しようとしているので、男性は下線部の発言で、オンラインのみという販売方法に疑念を示していると判断できる。express「～を示す」、doubt「疑念」。
(A) sample「試供品」。
(B) complain about ～「～について不平を言う」。
(D) correct「～を正す」、misunderstanding「誤解」、process「手順、工程」。

61 According to the woman, what rarely happens?

(A) Deliveries arriving late
(B) Customers requesting a refund
(C) Products being unavailable
(D) Design prototypes being rejected

女性によると、何がめったに起こりませんか。

(A) 配達物が遅れて到着すること
(B) 顧客が返金を要請すること
(C) 製品が在庫のない状態になること
(D) デザインの試作品が却下されること

正解 B 女性は❺で、顧客は商品のお試し期間中に全額返金を受けられる返品が可能だと説明し、続けて❻「でも、そのようなことが起こるのはまれだ」と、顧客が返金を要求する頻度の低さを強調している。according to ～「～によると」、rarely「めったに～ない」。request「～を要請する」。
(C) unavailable「入手できない」。
(D) design「デザイン」、prototype「試作品」、reject「～を拒否する」。

Words & Phrases

look for ～　～を探す　　invest in ～　～に投資する　　manufacture　～を製造する
high-quality　高品質な　　bedding　寝具　　unique　類いまれな　　quality　上質な　　linen　リネン、布製品　　cheap　安価な
imagine (that) ～　～と推察する　　feel　～に触ってみる　　material　生地　　trial period　お試し期間　　satisfied　満足した
return　〈動詞で〉～を返す、〈名詞で〉返品　　full refund　全額返金　　rare　まれな　　process　～を処理する

23

Questions 62 through 64 refer to the following conversation and floor plan.

問題62-64は次の会話とフロアプランに関するものです。

W Wataru, since there aren't any customers in the shop, it's a good time to talk. ❶You mentioned you had an idea to diversify our selection?

Wataru、店内にお客さんが1人もいないので、話をするのに良いタイミングです。あなたは、当店の品ぞろえを拡充するアイデアがあると言っていましたよね?

M Sure. So… ❷what about adding a section of books written by people who've lived around here? I've read several novels by local authors, and they're great.

はい。ええと…この近辺に暮らしたことのある人々によって書かれた本のコーナーを加えるのはどうでしょうか。私は地元の作家の小説を何冊か読んだことがありますが、素晴らしいですよ。

W ❸I like that idea, but I'm afraid I'm not familiar with any local authors or their work. ❹Could you select the books?

その考えは良いと思いますが、残念ながら私は地元の作家やその作品には詳しくありません。あなたが本を選んでくれますか。

M Sure, I'd be happy to. And I was thinking… ❺we could display them on the shelf next to the stockroom door. That one's only half full.

もちろんです、喜んでやりますよ。それで、考えていたのですが…私たちは倉庫のドアのすぐそばにある棚に、それらを陳列することができるでしょう。あの棚は半分しか埋まっていませんから。

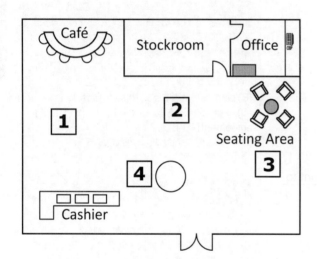

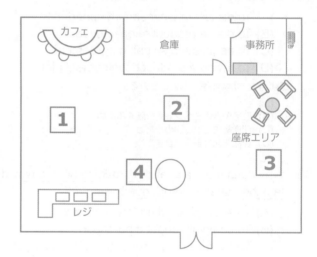

62 What are the speakers discussing?

(A) Adding a new section of books
(B) Discounting unpopular books
(C) Hosting a book-reading event
(D) Buying a bookshop

話し手たちは何について話し合っていますか。

(A) 本の新コーナーを加えること
(B) 不人気の本を値引きすること
(C) 読書イベントを催すこと
(D) 本屋を買収すること

正解 A	女性は、話をするのに良い機会だと述べてから、❶で、男性が以前、店の品ぞろえを拡充するアイデアがあると言っていたことについて確認している。男性はそれを肯定した後、❷「この近辺に暮らしたことのある人々によって書かれた本のコーナーを加えるのはどうか」と、本の新コーナーを加えること提案している。 (B) discount「～を値引きする」、unpopular「不人気の」。 (C) host「～を主催する」、book-reading「読書の」。 (D) buy「～を買収する」、bookshop「本屋」。

63 What concern does the woman express?

(A) She does not have the necessary information.
(B) She does not want to exceed a budget.
(C) She would have to change a work schedule.
(D) She would have to order more furniture.

女性はどんな懸念を示していますか。

(A) 彼女は必要な情報を持っていない。
(B) 彼女は予算を超過したくない。
(C) 彼女は仕事のスケジュールを変更する必要があるだろう。
(D) 彼女はもっと家具を注文する必要があるだろう。

正解 A	地元の作家によって書かれた本のコーナーを加えることを提案する男性に対し、女性は❸「その考えは良いと思うが、残念ながら私は地元の作家やその作品には詳しくない」と懸念を示し、続けて❹で、本の選定を男性に頼んでいる。地元の作家やその作品に詳しくないことをdoes not have the necessary informationと表している(A)が正解。concern「懸念」、express「～を示す」。necessary「必要な」。 (B) exceed「～を超過する」、budget「予算」。 (D) order「～を注文する」、furniture「家具」。

64 Look at the graphic. Which location does the man point out?

(A) Location 1
(B) Location 2
(C) Location 3
(D) Location 4

図を見てください。男性はどの位置を指し示していますか。

(A) 位置1
(B) 位置2
(C) 位置3
(D) 位置4

正解 B	男性は、新コーナー用の本の選定を喜んですると述べてから、❺「私たちは倉庫のドアのすぐそばにある棚に、それらを陳列することができるだろう」と、選んだ本を並べる位置を女性に提案している。図を見ると、倉庫のドアのすぐそばに数字の2が記載されている。よって、(B) Location 2が正解。location「位置」、point out ～「～を指し示す」。

Words & Phrases

floor plan　フロアプラン、店内レイアウト　　mention (that) ～　～と述べる　diversify　～に変化を持たせる、～を多様化する

selection　品ぞろえ　add　～を追加する　section　コーナー、区画　several　数個の　novel　小説　local　地元の

author　作家　I'm afraid (that) ～　残念ながら～　★言いにくいことなどを伝える際に前置きで使う表現

be familiar with ～　～に精通している　work　作品　select　～を選ぶ

I'd be happy to *do*　喜んで～します　★I'd はI wouldの短縮形　display　～を陳列する　shelf　棚

next to ～　～のすぐそばに、～の隣に　stockroom　保管倉庫　full　満杯の

フロアプラン　café　カフェ　seating　座席　area　エリア、区域　cashier　レジ係

Questions 65 through 67 refer to the following conversation and report.

問題65-67は次の会話と報告書に関するものです。

🏴󠁧󠁢󠁥󠁮󠁧󠁿 w Alonso, ❶do you have an update on the status of the WoodWorks LLC shipment from Australia? ❷We need to deliver their timber and building materials by October tenth. Are we going to meet the deadline?

Alonso、オーストラリアからのWoodWorks社の貨物の状況に関する最新情報は把握していますか。私たちは同社の木材と建材を10月10日までに届ける必要があります。期限には間に合いそうですか。

🇦🇺 M I think so, ❸but we probably shouldn't ship that timber to the port we typically use. ❹The average wait time at the port is 53 hours. It's too long.

そう思いますが、私たちはおそらく、当社が普段利用している港にその木材を送るべきではないでしょう。同港での平均待機時間は53時間です。それだと長過ぎます。

🏴󠁧󠁢󠁥󠁮󠁧󠁿 w Well, ❺that was last week. So, ❻before we make any changes, we should follow up with the port authority director.

ですが、それは先週の話ですね。だから、変更する前に、私たちは港湾局の責任者に最新情報を確認した方がいいでしょう。

Report on Port Congestion	
Port Location	Wait Time (in Hours)
Tokyo	28
Osaka	53
Nagoya	34
Shimonoseki	58

港の混雑状況に関する報告書	
港の場所	待機時間 (時間)
東京	28
大阪	53
名古屋	34
下関	58

65 According to the speakers, what are the contents of a shipment?

(A) Books
(B) Clothing
(C) Sports equipment
(D) Construction materials

話し手たちによると、貨物の中身は何ですか。

(A) 本
(B) 衣料品
(C) スポーツ用具
(D) 建設資材

正解 D 女性は❶で、オーストラリア発の貨物の状況に関する最新情報を把握しているか男性に尋ねた後、❷「私たちは同社の木材と建材を10月10日までに届ける必要がある」と配達期限を伝えている。以降でも、その木材を送る港について話しているので、話し手たちは貨物の到着を待っているところであり、その中身は建設資材だと判断できる。contents「中身」。construction「建設」、material「材料」。
(B) clothing「衣料品」。
(C) equipment「用具」。

66 Look at the graphic. Which port do the speakers usually use?

(A) Tokyo
(B) Osaka
(C) Nagoya
(D) Shimonoseki

図を見てください。話し手たちは通常、どの港を利用していますか。

(A) 東京
(B) 大阪
(C) 名古屋
(D) 下関

正解 B 男性は、配達期限に間に合うだろうと伝えてから、❸「しかし、私たちはおそらく、当社が普段利用している港にその木材を送るべきではない」と言い、続けて❹「同港での平均待機時間は53時間だ」とその理由を述べている。図を見ると、待機時間が53時間なのは大阪の港なので、(B)が正解。

67 What will the speakers most likely do?

(A) Contact a director
(B) Submit a report
(C) Meet with a client
(D) Change a deadline

話し手たちは何をすると考えられますか。

(A) 責任者に連絡する
(B) 報告書を提出する
(C) 顧客と会う
(D) 最終期限を変更する

正解 A 自社が普段利用している港の待機時間が長いために、そこに木材を送るべきではないと述べる男性に対し、女性は❺で、その考えの根拠となっている情報が先週のものだと伝えている。続けて❻「変更する前に、私たちは港湾局の責任者に最新情報を確認すべきだ」と提案しているので、(A)が正解。contact「〜に連絡する」。
(B) submit「〜を提出する」。
(C) client「顧客」。
(D) 期限への言及はあるが、それに間に合うかどうかが話題に上っているだけ。

Words & Phrases

update 最新情報　　status 状況　　LLC 有限責任会社　★Limited Liability Company の略　　shipment 輸送貨物、積荷

deliver 〜を届ける　　timber 木材　　building material 建設材料　　meet 〜（要件など）を満たす

deadline 最終期限、締め切り　　probably おそらく　　ship 〜を輸送する　　port 港　　typically 通常

average 平均的な　　wait 待機　　make a change 変更する　　follow up with 〜 〜に追って確認する

authority 権限、当局、官庁　　director 責任者、管理者

報告書 congestion 混雑状況　　location 場所

Questions 68 through 70 refer to the following conversation and sign.

問題68-70は次の会話と表示に関するものです。

M Welcome to Thompson Bay Electronics. Can I help you find something?

Thompson Bay電子機器店へようこそ。何かお探しでしょうか。

W Yes. ❶I heard you have a good selection of refrigerators.

はい。こちらのお店は冷蔵庫を豊富に取りそろえていると聞きました。

M We do! Any specific features you'd like? ❷With these newer models, if you forget to close the doors, they'll just close themselves. ❸Is that something you'd be interested in?

その通りです！お求めの具体的な機能は何かございますか？これらの新型モデルなら、ドアを閉め忘れても勝手に閉まります。そのようなものにご関心をお持ちでしょうか。

W ❹Actually, I'd like one that's more efficient. ❺My current refrigerator is old—it uses a lot of energy, and I'm trying to lower my bills.

実は、もっと効率の良いものが欲しいと思っています。私が現在使っている冷蔵庫は古いのです——それはたくさんのエネルギーを消費するので、請求額を減らそうとしているところでして。

M OK. Well, ❻this one has been popular. This model actually has the highest efficiency rating. But ❼the manufacturer is replacing it soon with next year's model. It'll have a little more storage space inside.

なるほど。そうですね、この製品は人気がありますよ。実際、このモデルはエネルギー効率で最高の評価を受けています。しかし、メーカーはもうすぐ、これを来年のモデルと入れ替える予定です。そちらは、内部の収納スペースがもう少し広くなります。

20% OFF

10-year warranty
25 cubic feet of storage

Yearly Electricity Use
350 kWh

20パーセント引き

10年保証
容量25立方フィート

年間電気使用量
350キロワット時

68 According to the man, what is an advantage of newer refrigerator models?

    (A) They keep vegetables fresh longer.
    (B) The doors close automatically.
    (C) They are available in many colors.
    (D) The temperature is adjustable.

男性によると、何が新型モデルの冷蔵庫の強みですか。

    (A) それらは野菜をより長く新鮮な状態に保つ。
    (B) ドアが自動的に閉まる。
    (C) それらは多くの色の選択肢がある。
    (D) 温度が調節可能である。

正解 B ❶で、男性の店の豊富な冷蔵庫の取りそろえについて聞いたと伝える女性に対し、男性は、❷「これらの新型モデルなら、ドアを閉め忘れても勝手に閉まる」と、新型の冷蔵庫を特徴を交えて紹介している。they'll just close themselves をautomatically「自動的に」を用いて言い換えている(B)が正解。advantage「強み」。
(A) keep 〜 … 「〜を…の状態に保つ」、fresh「新鮮な」。
(C) available「入手可能な、求めに応じられる」。
(D) temperature「温度」、adjustable「調節可能な」。

69 Which feature does the woman express the most interest in?

    (A) Durability
    (B) Storage space
    (C) Ease of cleaning
    (D) Energy efficiency

女性はどんな特徴に最大の関心を示していますか。

    (A) 耐久性
    (B) 収納スペース
    (C) 掃除のしやすさ
    (D) エネルギー効率

正解 D ❸で、ドアが自動で閉まる冷蔵庫に関心があるか尋ねる男性に対し、女性は❹「実は、もっと効率の良いものが欲しいと思っている」と述べ、続けて❺で、現在使用中の冷蔵庫は多くのエネルギーを消費するため、電気代を減らそうとしていることを伝えている。よって、女性はエネルギー効率に最も関心を示していると判断できる。express「〜を示す」、interest「関心」。
(A) durability「耐久性」。
(B) 男性は、次モデルで収納スペースが広くなる冷蔵庫を紹介しているが、女性は収納スペースには言及していない。
(C) ease「容易さ」。

70 Look at the graphic. Which number will change for next year's model?

    (A) 20
    (B) 10
    (C) 25
    (D) 350

図を見てください。来年のモデルではどの数値が変わりますか。

    (A) 20
    (B) 10
    (C) 25
    (D) 350

正解 C 男性は❻で、エネルギー効率で最高評価を受けている冷蔵庫を紹介し、続けて❼「メーカーはもうすぐ、これを来年のモデルと入れ替える予定だ。そちらは、内部の収納スペースがもう少し広くなる」と来年のモデルについて述べている。図は現行モデルの割引率と性能を表示していると考えられ、3行目に「容量25立方フィート」とあるので、来年のモデルではこの容量数値が増えると判断できる。よって、(C)が正解。
(A) 割引率の数値。
(B) 保証年数の数値。
(D) 消費電力量の数値。電気代削減が女性の望みだが、来年モデルでの改善は述べられていない。

Words & Phrases

sign 表示	electronics 電子機器	selection 品ぞろえ	refrigerator 冷蔵庫	specific 具体的な、特定の

feature 機能、特徴   model モデル、型   forget to *do* 〜し忘れる   be interested in 〜 〜に関心がある

efficient 効率の良い   current 現在の   energy エネルギー   lower 〜を下げる   bill 請求書   efficiency 効率

rating 評価   manufacturer メーカー、製造業者   replace 〜 with … 〜を…と交換する   storage 容量、収納

space スペース、空間   inside 内部に

表示 off 割り引いて   warranty 保証、保証書   〜 cubic feet 〜立方フィート ★体積の単位   yearly 1年の

electricity 電気   use 使用(量)   kWh キロワット時 ★kilowatt-hour(s)の略。1時間当たりの消費電力量を示す

Questions 71 through 73 refer to the following introduction.

🇦🇺 M

Good evening. ❶I apologize for the delay. ❷We were having some problems with the microphone. ❸It's my pleasure to present this year's Community Excellence Award to Mary Kebede. ❹Ms. Kebede's tireless fund-raising made it possible to purchase 5,000 trees to plant throughout our city. Trees are essential because they improve air quality and cool the environment. But ❺most importantly, studies have shown that they reduce the symptoms of stress in city residents. So, on behalf of the community, thank you, Ms. Kebede.

問題71-73は次の紹介に関するものです。

こんばんは。遅延についておわび申し上げます。マイクに問題が生じていました。今年の地域優秀賞をMary Kebedeさんに贈呈できることを喜ばしく思います。Kebedeさんのたゆみない資金集めにより、5,000本の木を購入して当市全域に植えることが可能となりました。木は、大気質を改善し環境を涼しくするので必要不可欠な存在です。しかし、最も重要なことには、それらは市民のストレス症状を軽減するということが研究によって示されています。そのため、当地域社会を代表し、お礼申し上げます、Kebedeさん。

---

71 What caused a delay?

(A) Technical difficulties
(B) Poor weather conditions
(C) Absent staff members
(D) Lost paperwork

何が遅れを引き起こしましたか。

(A) 技術的問題
(B) 悪い気象条件
(C) スタッフの不在
(D) 必要書類の紛失

正解 A　話し手は❶で、遅延に対して謝罪をした後、❷「マイクに問題が生じていた」と遅れの原因を説明している。そのことをtechnical difficultiesと表している(A)が正解。cause「～を引き起こす」。technical「技術的な」、difficulty「問題」。
(B) poor「悪い」、weather conditions「気象条件」。
(C) absent「不在の」、staff「スタッフ」。
(D) lost「紛失した」、paperwork「必要書類」。

---

72 Why is Ms. Kebede receiving an award?

(A) She published a book.
(B) She led a fund-raising campaign.
(C) She served on the city council.
(D) She developed a useful device.

Kebedeさんはなぜ賞を受賞しているのですか。

(A) 彼女は本を出版した。
(B) 彼女は資金集めの運動を主導した。
(C) 彼女は市議会の一員として働いた。
(D) 彼女は有用な装置を開発した。

正解 B　話し手は❸で、今年の地域優秀賞をMary Kebedeに贈呈できることを喜ばしく思うと述べた後、❹「Kebedeさんのたゆみない資金集めが、5,000本の木を購入して当市全域に植えることを可能にした」と市への貢献内容を紹介しているので(B)が正解。receive「～を受け取る」。lead「～を主導する」、campaign「運動」。
(C) serve on ～「～の一員として働く」、city council「市議会」。
(D) develop「～を開発する」、useful「有用な」、device「装置」。

---

73 According to the speaker, what is the most important benefit of trees?

(A) They are used in construction.
(B) They provide shade.
(C) They reduce stress.
(D) They protect the soil.

話し手によると、木の最も重要な恩恵は何ですか。

(A) それらは建設作業で使用される。
(B) それらは日陰を提供する。
(C) それらはストレスを減らす。
(D) それらは土壌を保全する。

正解 C　話し手は、木が大気質の改善と環境の冷却に寄与することに言及してから、❺「最も重要なことには、それらは市民のストレス症状を軽減するということが研究によって示されている」と、木がもたらす最も重要な恩恵を強調している。benefit「恩恵、メリット」。
(A) construction「建設作業」。
(B) provide「～を提供する」、shade「日陰」。
(D) protect「～を保護する」、soil「土壌」。

Words & Phrases

introduction 紹介　apologize for ～ ～をわびる　delay 遅れ　pleasure 喜び　present ～を贈呈する　community 地域社会　excellence 優秀　award 賞　tireless たゆみない、不断の　fund-raising 資金集め(の)　make it possible to do ～することを可能にする　purchase ～を購入する　plant ～を植える　throughout ～の至る所に　essential 必要不可欠な　improve ～を改善する　air quality 大気質　cool ～を涼しくする　environment 環境　most importantly 最も重要なことには　study 研究　reduce ～を減らす　symptom 症状　resident 住民　on behalf of ～ ～を代表して

Questions 74 through 76 refer to the following excerpt from a meeting.

問題74-76は次の会議の抜粋に関するものです。

🇺🇸 W

As you know, ❶next month we're releasing our first electric car, and we're likely to see a sharp increase in customer interest. ❷That's why every one of our dealerships is hiring new sales associates this week, and you'll need to train them. Well, I have some good news for you: ❸we're having state-of-the-art teleconferencing equipment installed in our meeting rooms. From now on, you will no longer need to travel around the country to do your job!

ご存じのように、来月当社は初の電気自動車を発売する予定で、顧客の関心の急増が予想されます。それゆえ、当社の販売代理店の全店舗で今週新しい販売員を雇用する予定で、皆さんは彼らを研修する必要があります。ところで、皆さんに良いお知らせがあります。当社の会議室に最新鋭のテレビ会議用機器が設置される予定です。今後は、皆さんは職務を遂行するために国中を移動して回る必要がもうなくなります！

74 Why does the speaker anticipate an increase in business?

    (A) A discount will be offered.
    (B) A new product will be launched.
    (C) Store hours have been extended.
    (D) Reviews have been positive.

話し手はなぜ、取引の増加を予期しているのですか。

    (A) 割引が提供される予定である。
    (B) 新製品が売り出される予定である。
    (C) 店舗の営業時間が延びた。
    (D) レビューが肯定的な内容である。

正解 **B** 話し手は、❶「来月当社は初の電気自動車を発売する予定で、顧客の関心の急増が予想される」と新製品発売による、取引増加の見込みを伝えている。we're releasing our first electric car を a new product will be launched と表している (B) が正解。anticipate「～を予期する」、business「取引、売買」。launch「～を売り出す」。
(A) discount「割引」、offer「～を提供する」。
(C) 販売代理店に言及しているが、store hours「店の営業時間」に触れてはいない。extend「～を延ばす」。
(D) review「レビュー、批評」、positive「肯定的な」。

75 Who are the listeners?

    (A) Factory workers
    (B) Product designers
    (C) Trainers
    (D) Technicians

聞き手は誰ですか。

    (A) 工場労働者
    (B) 製品設計者
    (C) 研修の指導者
    (D) 技術者

正解 **C** 話し手は、新製品発売により顧客の関心が急増するという予想を述べてから、❷「それゆえ、当社の販売代理店の全店舗で今週新しい販売員を雇用する予定で、皆さんは彼らを研修する必要がある」と伝えている。よって、聞き手は販売員の研修を行う指導者だと考えられる。trainer「研修の指導者、トレーナー」。
(A) factory「工場」。
(B) designer「設計者」。
(D) technician「技術者」。

76 What is the company going to add to its meeting rooms?

    (A) Microwave ovens
    (B) Water dispensers
    (C) Wireless connectivity
    (D) Teleconferencing equipment

会社は会議室に何を追加する予定ですか。

    (A) 電子レンジ
    (B) ウォーターサーバー
    (C) 無線接続環境
    (D) テレビ会議用機器

正解 **D** 話し手は、新しい販売員の研修を行う聞き手に対し、朗報があると言った後、❸「当社の会議室に最新鋭のテレビ会議用機器が設置される予定だ」と知らせている。add ～ to …「～を…に追加する」。
(A) microwave oven「電子レンジ」。
(B) dispenser「ディスペンサー（必要な量だけ取り出せる装置）」。
(C) wireless「無線の」、connectivity「接続性」。

Words & Phrases
excerpt 抜粋　　release ～を発売する　　electric car 電気自動車　　be likely to do ～しそうである、～する可能性が高い　　sharp 急激な　　increase 増大、増加　　customer 顧客　　interest 関心　　dealership 販売代理店　　hire ～を雇用する　　sales associate 販売員　　train ～を研修する　　news 知らせ　　state-of-the-art 最新鋭の　　teleconferencing テレビ会議(の)　　equipment 機器　　install ～を設置する　　from now on これからは　　no longer ～ もはや～ない　　travel around ～ ～中を移動して回る　　do one's job 職務を遂行する

Questions 77 through 79 refer to the following announcement.

問題77-79は次のお知らせに関するものです。

🇬🇧 W

❶We hope you're enjoying your flight with Light Speed Airlines this morning. If I can have your attention for one moment, I'd like to tell you about a special promotion we're offering. ❷This month only, when you sign up for our Light Speed Airlines rewards program, you'll be entered into a contest to win two round-trip tickets to Paris! Enrolling in the rewards program is a very simple process, and the brochure in your seat-back pocket explains how to do it. And ❸now, flight attendants will be coming around with a selection of snacks.

皆さまがこの午前中、Light Speed航空の空の旅をお楽しみいただいていることを願っています。少しお時間を頂戴できましたら、当社が提供中の特別キャンペーンについてお知らせしたく存じます。今月中に限り、当Light Speed航空のリワードプログラムにお申し込みいただきますと、パリ行きの往復航空券2枚を獲得できるコンテストにご参加いただけます! リワードプログラムへのお申し込みはとても簡単な手順で、お座席前部の背もたれのポケット内にあるパンフレットにその方法が説明されています。さて、今から、客室乗務員がよりすぐりの軽食を持って順に回ります。

77 Where is the announcement being made?

(A) On an airplane
(B) In a train station
(C) In a hotel
(D) At a department store

お知らせはどこで行われていますか。
(A) 機内
(B) 鉄道駅構内
(C) ホテル内
(D) 百貨店内

正解 **A** 話し手は❶「皆さんがこの午前中、Light Speed航空の空の旅を楽しんでくれていることを願っている」と述べているので、お知らせは現在飛行中の機内乗客に向けたものだと判断できる。また❸で、今から客室乗務員が軽食を持って回ると伝えていることからも分かる。airplane「飛行機」。
(D) department store「百貨店」。

78 What must the listeners do to enter a contest?

(A) Make a purchase
(B) Fill out a survey
(C) Download a mobile application
(D) Join a rewards program

聞き手はコンテストに参加するために何をする必要がありますか。
(A) 買い物をする
(B) 調査票に記入する
(C) 携帯機器用アプリをダウンロードする
(D) リワードプログラムに加入する

正解 **D** 話し手は、提供中のキャンペーンに言及してから、❷「今月中に限り、当Light Speed航空のリワードプログラムに申し込むと、パリ行きの往復航空券2枚を獲得できるコンテストに参加できる」とコンテストの参加方法を伝えている。プログラムに参加することをsign up for ~の代わりにjoinで表した(D)が正解。enter「~に参加する」。
(A) make a purchase「買い物をする」。
(B) fill out ~「~に記入する」、survey「調査(票)」。
(C) download「~をダウンロードする」、mobile application「携帯機器用アプリ」。

79 What will the listeners most likely do next?

(A) Take a photograph
(B) Have a snack
(C) Watch a video
(D) Read a magazine

聞き手は次に何をすると考えられますか。
(A) 写真を撮る
(B) 軽食を食べる
(C) 動画を見る
(D) 雑誌を読む

正解 **B** 話し手は、提供中のキャンペーンについて一通り説明し終えた後、❸「今から、客室乗務員がよりすぐりの軽食を持って順に回る」と聞き手に知らせている。よって、聞き手は次に配られた軽食を食べると考えられる。
(A) take a photograph「写真を撮る」。
(C) video「動画」。
(D) 話し手はプログラムへの申し込み方法が載っているパンフレットに言及しているが、雑誌については述べていない。magazine「雑誌」。

Words & Phrases

announcement お知らせ　flight （飛行機の）便、フライト　airline 航空会社　★社名は通例複数形
attention 注目　for one moment 少しの間　promotion （販売促進の）キャンペーン　offer ～を提供する
sign up for ～ ～に申し込む　rewards program リワードプログラム　★継続利用した顧客に特典を提供する施策
be entered into ～ ～に参加する　win ～を獲得する　round-trip 往復の　enroll in ～ ～に申し込む　simple 簡単な
brochure パンフレット　seat-back 前部座席の背面(の)　flight attendant 客室乗務員　come around 順に回る
selection 選ばれた物、精選品　snack 軽食

Questions 80 through 82 refer to the following instructions.

🇨🇦 M

❶Welcome to this instructional video. **❷**Many subscribers to my channel have asked about installing ceiling fans, so I thought I'd help. **❸**Your first steps are to shut off the electricity in the room, put on protective eye covering, and make sure you have a sturdy ladder. **❹**These are essential for your safety. Once the electricity is off, hold the base of the fan to the ceiling and draw a circle around it with a pencil. Then, **❺**cut along the circle with a drywall saw. **❻**The saw will shake quite strongly so I suggest asking a friend to hold the ladder while you do it.

問題80-82は次の説明に関するものです。

本教則動画へようこそ。大勢の私のチャンネル登録者がシーリングファンの設置について尋ねているので、手助けできればと思いました。最初の手順は、室内の電気を止め、保護用ゴーグルを着用し、必ず頑丈なはしごを用意することです。これらはあなたの安全にとって必要不可欠です。電気が止まったら、ファンの基底部を天井に押し付けて、鉛筆でその周りに円を描きます。次に、乾式壁用のこぎりでその円に沿って切ります。のこぎりはかなり激しく揺れるので、その作業を行っている間は友人に頼んで、はしごを支えてもらうことをお勧めします。

---

80 What is the speaker explaining?

(A) How to edit a video
(B) How to reduce electricity costs
(C) How to repair a lamp
(D) How to install a fan

話し手は何について説明していますか。

(A) 動画を編集する方法
(B) 電気代を減らす方法
(C) 電気スタンドを修理する方法
(D) ファンを設置する方法

正解 D 話し手は❶で、この教則動画へようこそと聞き手を歓迎してから、❷「大勢の私のチャンネル登録者がシーリングファンの設置について尋ねているので、手助けできればと思った」と動画を公開した動機を述べている。❸以降でファンの設置方法について詳しく説明しているので、(D)が正解。
(A) edit「〜を編集する」。
(B) reduce「〜を減らす」、costs「経費」。
(C) repair「〜を修理する」、lamp「電気スタンド」。

---

81 According to the speaker, why are the first steps important?

(A) For safety
(B) For efficiency
(C) For cleanliness
(D) For appearance

話し手によると、最初の手順はなぜ重要なのですか。

(A) 安全のために
(B) 効率のために
(C) 清潔さのために
(D) 見た目のために

正解 A 話し手はファンの設置について、❸「最初の手順は、室内の電気を止め、保護用ゴーグルを着用し、必ず頑丈なはしごを用意することだ」と、最初にすべき3点を説明している。その直後に❹「これらはあなたの安全にとって必要不可欠だ」と、最初の手順の重要性を強調しているので、(A)が正解。
(B) efficiency「効率」。
(C) cleanliness「清潔さ」。
(D) appearance「見た目、外観」。

---

82 According to the speaker, how can a friend be helpful with a task?

(A) By reading a manual
(B) By reviewing some work
(C) By holding a ladder
(D) By turning the lights off

話し手によると、友人はどのように作業の助けとなることができますか。

(A) マニュアルを読むことによって
(B) 作業を見直すことによって
(C) はしごを支えることによって
(D) 照明を消すことによって

正解 C 話し手は❺で、鉛筆で描いた円に沿って天井をのこぎりで切るように言った後、❻「のこぎりはかなり激しく揺れるので、その作業を行っている間は友人に頼んで、はしごを支えてもらうことを勧める」と推奨している。helpful「助けとなる」、task「作業」。
(A) manual「マニュアル、手引書」。
(B) review「〜を見直す」。
(D) turn off 〜「〜（電気など）を消す」、light「照明」。

Words & Phrases

instructions 説明、指示　instructional 教育の　subscriber （チャンネルなどの）登録者、定期購読者　install 〜を設置する　ceiling 天井　fan 扇風機、ファン　shut off 〜 〜（電気供給など）を止める　electricity 電気　put on 〜 〜を着用する　protective 保護用の　eye covering ゴーグル　make sure (that) 〜 必ず〜ようにする　sturdy 頑丈な　ladder はしご　essential 必要不可欠な　off 止まって、切れて　hold 〜 to … 〜を…(位置)に保つ　base 基底部　draw 〜を描く　circle 円　along 〜に沿って　drywall saw 乾式壁用のこぎり　shake 揺れる　suggest *doing* 〜することを提案する

TEST 1　PART 4

Questions 83 through 85 refer to the following excerpt from a meeting.

問題83-85は次の会議の抜粋に関するものです。

🇬🇧 W

❶As your company president, I'm inspired by your commitment to our team. ❷I'm happy to announce that our computer company has won the award for Tech Company of the Year by our city's leading technology magazine. **What a great accomplishment!** ❸Management feels it is time to expand our product line. **As you know, some computer companies produce mobile phones.** Now, I'd like to open the floor to your questions. Would anyone like to go first?

皆さんの会社の社長として、私はチームへの皆さんの献身に鼓舞されています。わがコンピューター会社が当市有数のテクノロジー雑誌で年間最優秀テクノロジー企業の賞を獲得したことをお知らせできるのをうれしく思います。なんと素晴らしい業績なのでしょうか! 経営陣は、当社の製品ラインを拡大すべき時期だと考えています。ご存じの通り、何社かのコンピューター企業は携帯電話を製造していますね。さて、皆さんからの質問を受け付けたいと思います。最初にしたい人はいますか。

83 What is the speaker's job?

(A) Computer technician
(B) Company executive
(C) Financial consultant
(D) Product developer

話し手の職業は何ですか。

(A) コンピューター技術者
(B) 会社の重役
(C) 財務顧問
(D) 製品開発者

正解 **B** 話し手は、❶「皆さんの会社の社長として、私はチームへの皆さんの献身に鼓舞される」と聞き手である従業員の貢献をたたえている。company presidentをcompany executiveと言い換えている(B)が正解。executive「重役」。
(A) technician「技術者」。
(C) financial consultant「財務顧問、ファイナンシャルアドバイザー」。
(D) developer「開発者」。

84 What has a company recently done?

(A) It moved to another location.
(B) It hired more employees.
(C) It won an award.
(D) It changed its logo.

会社は最近、何をしましたか。

(A) 別の場所へ移転した。
(B) 従業員をさらに雇用した。
(C) 賞を獲得した。
(D) 自社のロゴを変更した。

正解 **C** 話し手は聞き手の貢献をたたえた後、❷「私たちのコンピューター会社が当市有数のテクノロジー雑誌で年間最優秀テクノロジー企業の賞を獲得したことを知らせられるのはうれしい」と、会社が賞を受賞したことを発表している。
(A) location「場所、所在地」。
(B) hire「~を雇用する」、employee「従業員」。
(D) logo「ロゴ」。

85 Why does the speaker say, "some computer companies produce mobile phones"?

(A) To correct some information
(B) To make a complaint
(C) To indicate an intention
(D) To provide reassurance

話し手はなぜ "some computer companies produce mobile phones" と言っていますか。

(A) 情報を訂正するため
(B) 苦情を言うため
(C) 意向を示すため
(D) 安心感を与えるため

正解 **C** 話し手は❸で、製品ラインを拡大すべき時期だという経営陣の考えに言及した後、知っての通りと前置きをしてから、「何社かのコンピューター企業は携帯電話を製造している」と他社の例を挙げて下線部の発言をしている。よって、話し手はこの発言で、今後は携帯電話などの他製品の製造をしていくという会社の意向を示していると判断できる。indicate「~を示す」、intention「意向」。
(A) correct「~を訂正する」。
(B) complaint「苦情」。
(D) provide「~を与える」、reassurance「安心感」。

Words & Phrases

president 社長　inspire ~を鼓舞する　commitment 献身、貢献
be happy to *do* 喜んで~する　announce (that) ~ ~と発表する　win ~を獲得する　award 賞
tech テクノロジー、科学技術　★technologyの略　~ of the year 年間最優秀の~　leading 一流の、トップの
magazine 雑誌　accomplishment 業績　management 経営陣　expand ~を拡大する　product line 製品ライン
produce ~を製造する　mobile phone 携帯電話　open the floor to questions 質問を受け付ける

Questions 86 through 88 refer to the following telephone message.

問題86-88は次の電話のメッセージに関するものです。

🇨🇦 M

Hello, ❶this is Robert from Shanghai Food Tours. ❷I'm returning your call regarding one of our popular tasting tours. Ahh… ❸you requested additional information about the evening dim sum tour. That tour visits several downtown eateries. And ❹at the tour's final stop, you'll learn how to make dumplings from a renowned local chef. So… ❺I'll need a credit card number in order to complete your reservation. ❻I can hold a spot for you for a day or two, but this is one of our best sellers.

もしもし、こちらは上海料理ツアー社のRobertです。当社の人気味覚ツアーの件で折り返しお電話しています。えーと…お客さまは、夜の点心ツアーに関する追加の情報をお求めになりましたね。そのツアーでは、繁華街にある数軒の料理店を訪れます。そして、ツアーで最後に立ち寄る場所では、地元の有名シェフからギョーザの作り方を学ぶ予定です。それで…ご予約を完了するにはクレジットカード番号が必要になります。一両日の間、お客さまのために枠を取っておくことができます、しかし、こちらは当社で最も人気のあるものの一つです。

86 Why is the speaker leaving a message?

(A) To congratulate the listener
(B) To complain about a problem
(C) To provide tour information
(D) To schedule a delivery

話し手はなぜメッセージを残しているのですか。

(A) 聞き手を祝うため
(B) 問題について苦情を言うため
(C) ツアーの情報を提供するため
(D) 配達の予定を組むため

正解 C 話し手は❶で、上海料理ツアー社のRobertだと名乗り、❷「当社の人気味覚ツアーの件で折り返し電話している」と電話の目的を述べている。そして❸で、聞き手が特定のツアーに関する追加の情報を求めていたことを確認し、以降ではそのツアーの詳しい情報を提供しているので、(C)が正解。provide「～を提供する」。
(A) congratulate「～を祝う」。
(B) complain about ～「～について苦情を言う」。
(D) schedule「～の予定を組む」、delivery「配達」。

87 What opportunity does the speaker mention?

(A) Starting a new business
(B) Learning to make some food
(C) Traveling to a new city
(D) Writing a book

話し手はどんな機会について述べていますか。

(A) 新事業を始めること
(B) 料理の作り方を学ぶこと
(C) 新しい都市に旅行すること
(D) 本を書くこと

正解 B 話し手は、夜の点心ツアーでは繁華街にある数軒の料理店を訪れると説明した後、❹「ツアーで最後に立ち寄る場所では、地元の有名シェフからギョーザの作り方を学ぶ予定だ」と、ツアー内容について補足している。そのことをlearning to make some foodと表している(B)が正解。opportunity「機会」、mention「～について述べる」。learn to do「～の仕方を学ぶ」。
(C) 話し手はツアーの立ち寄り先として繁華街に言及しているが、新しい都市だとは述べていない。

88 Why does the speaker say, "but this is one of our best sellers"?

(A) To express surprise
(B) To encourage a quick response
(C) To justify a choice
(D) To ask for some assistance

話し手はなぜ "but this is one of our best sellers" と言っていますか。

(A) 驚きを表すため
(B) 素早い返答を促すため
(C) 選択を正当化するため
(D) 支援を求めるため

正解 B 話し手は❺で、ツアーの予約完了にはクレジットカード番号が必要であると伝え、❻で、聞き手のために一両日間その枠を押さえておくことができると申し出ている。その直後に、下線部の発言でツアーの人気の高さを強調しているので、話し手は、このツアーが人気のため、極力早く返答するよう促していると判断できる。encourage「～を促す」、quick「素早い」、response「返答」。
(A) express「～を表す」、surprise「驚き」。
(C) justify「～を正当化する」、choice「選択」。
(D) ask for ～「～を求める」、assistance「支援」。

TEST1 PART 4

Words & Phrases
return one's call ～に折り返し電話する　regarding ～に関して　taste ～を味わう
additional 追加の　dim sum 点心 ★中華料理の軽食　several 幾つかの、複数の　downtown 繁華街の
eatery 料理店　stop 立ち寄り先　dumpling ギョーザ、蒸し団子　renowned 有名な　in order to do ～するために
complete ～を完了する　reservation 予約　hold ～を確保する　spot 枠、場所
best seller 特によく売れる商品、ベストセラー

Questions 89 through 91 refer to the following talk.

🇦🇺 M

Thanks for coming to this business workshop. ❶An important part of starting a business is financing, and a microloan is a great way to do that. A microloan is basically a small bank loan—usually up to 50,000 dollars—designed specifically for people who are starting a small business. ❷These loans are popular because the application process is straightforward. ❸It only requires completing one form and submitting three documents. OK. ❹I've invited a special guest today, Gertrude Lee. ❺She's here to give an overview of the application process for a microloan. ❻Gertrude?

本ビジネス講習会へお越しいただきありがとうございます。事業立ち上げの重要な点の1つは資金調達で、小口融資はそれをするのに最適な方法です。小口融資とは基本的に銀行の少額融資のことです——一般的には最大5万ドルまでで——特に小規模事業を立ち上げる方々を対象としたものです。これらの融資は、申し込み手続きが簡単なので人気があります。必要なのは、1枚の用紙に記入することと3通の書類を提出することだけです。さて。本日は特別ゲスト、Gertrude Leeをお招きしています。彼女には、小口融資に必要な申し込み手続きの概要を説明してもらうためにここへお越しいただいています。Gertrude?

89 What do the listeners most likely want information about?

(A) Improving public speaking skills
(B) Planning an international trip
(C) Making healthier meals
(D) Starting a small business

聞き手は何についての情報を求めていると考えられますか。

(A) 人前で話すスキルを向上させること
(B) 海外旅行を計画すること
(C) より健康的な食事を作ること
(D) 小規模事業を立ち上げること

正解 D 話し手は、ビジネス講習会への出席に対するお礼を述べた後、❶「事業立ち上げの重要な点の1つは資金調達で、小口融資はそれをするのに最適な方法だ」と伝え、以降ではその小口融資について説明している。よって、講習会の出席者である聞き手は、事業立ち上げについての情報を求めていると考えられる。
(A) improve「～を向上させる」、public speaking「人前で話をすること、講演」、skill「技能、スキル」。
(B) plan「～を計画する」、international「国際的な」。
(C) healthy「健康的な」、meal「食事」。

90 What does the speaker say about an application process?

(A) It is simple.
(B) It is free.
(C) It requires an interview.
(D) It can be completed online.

話し手は申し込み手続きについて何と言っていますか。

(A) 簡単である。
(B) 無料である。
(C) 面接を必要とする。
(D) オンラインで完了可能である。

正解 A 話し手は、資金調達に最適な方法である小口融資について、❷「これらの融資は、申し込み手続きが簡単なので人気がある」と述べた後、❸「必要なのは、1枚の用紙に記入することと3通の書類を提出することだけだ」と、申し込み手続きの簡便さを強調している。straightforwardをsimpleと言い換えている(A)が正解。
(C) require「～を必要とする」、interview「面接」。
(D) complete「～を完了する」、online「オンラインで」。

91 What will happen next?

(A) A video will be shown.
(B) A guest will speak.
(C) Some refreshments will be served.
(D) Some booklets will be distributed.

次に何が起こりますか。

(A) 動画が上映される。
(B) ゲストが話をする。
(C) 軽食が出される。
(D) 小冊子が配られる。

正解 B 話し手は、❹「本日は特別ゲスト、Gertrude Leeを招いている」と講習会のゲストに言及し、❺で、小口融資に必要な申し込み手続きの概要を説明するという彼女の役割を説明している。その直後に❻で、彼女の名を呼んでいるので、次にはゲストであるGertrudeという人物が話をすると判断できる。
(A) video「動画」、show「～を上映する」。
(C) refreshments「軽食」、serve「～(飲食物)を出す」。
(D) booklet「小冊子」、distribute「～を配る」。

Words & Phrases

business ビジネス、事業　workshop 講習会　financing 資金調達　microloan 小口融資　basically 基本的に　loan 融資　up to ~ 最大～まで　designed for ~ ～のために作られた　specifically 特に　application 申し込み　process 手続き　straightforward 簡単な　require ～を必要とする　complete ～に全て記入する　form 用紙、書式　submit ～を提出する　document 書類　invite ～を招く　overview 概要

Questions 92 through 94 refer to the following telephone message.

問題92-94は次の電話のメッセージに関するものです。

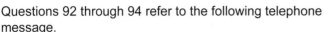 W

Hi, Julie. ❶Preparations are going well for the museum's special exhibit starting next week. ❷I just got an e-mail from the Covingdale Gallery about the painting they're loaning us—delivery has been scheduled for three P.M. today. ❸As for the second project, we continue to take inventory of our collection using the new software. ❹I know the inventory was scheduled to be completed this month, but as we've discussed before, the software's very complex. ❺I'll keep you informed on progress as we go on.

こんにちは、Julie。来週から始まる美術館特別展に向けた準備は順調に進んでいます。私はちょうどCovingdale画廊から、先方が当館に貸し出してくれる予定の絵画についてのEメールを受け取ったところです——引き渡しは今日の午後3時に設定されました。2つ目のプロジェクトに関しては、私たちは引き続き、新しいソフトウエアを使って当館所蔵品の目録を作ります。目録が今月中に完成する予定だったということは承知しています、でも以前話し合ったように、このソフトウエアは非常に複雑です。進捗について逐次お知らせします。

92 What special event is the speaker preparing for?
(A) An exhibition opening
(B) A fund-raising banquet
(C) A volunteer orientation
(D) An art auction

話し手はどんな特別なイベントに向けて準備していますか。
(A) 展覧会の開幕
(B) 資金集めの宴会
(C) ボランティア向けの説明会
(D) 美術品の競売

正解 A 話し手は❶「来週から始まる美術館特別展に向けた準備は順調に進んでいる」と進捗を報告した後、❷で、貸し出しを受ける絵画の引き渡し予定時刻を伝えている。よって、来週から始まる特別展をan exhibition openingと表している(A)が正解。prepare for ～「～に向けて準備する」。exhibition「展覧会」、opening「開幕」。
(B) fund-raising「資金集めの」、banquet「宴会」。
(C) volunteer「ボランティア」、orientation「説明会」。
(D) art「美術品」、auction「競売、オークション」。

93 What does the speaker say about some artwork?
(A) It is covered by insurance.
(B) It will be packaged in two containers.
(C) It will be the focus of the event.
(D) Its delivery has been scheduled.

話し手はある美術品について何と言っていますか。
(A) それは保険で補償される。
(B) それは2つの容器に荷詰めされる予定である。
(C) それはイベントの目玉となる予定である。
(D) その引き渡しの日時が設定された。

正解 D 話し手は、❷「私はちょうどCovingdale画廊から、先方が当館に貸し出してくれる予定の絵画についてのEメールを受け取ったところだ——引き渡しは今日の午後3時に設定された」と、美術品の引き渡し予定日時を伝えている。artwork「美術品」。
(A) cover「～を補償する」、insurance「保険」。
(B) package ～ in …「～を…(容器など)に詰める」、container「容器、(輸送用)コンテナ」。
(C) focus「(注目などの)的、中心」。

94 Why does the speaker say, "the software's very complex"?
(A) To recommend training
(B) To request assistance
(C) To suggest a replacement
(D) To explain a delay

話し手はなぜ "the software's very complex" と言っていますか。
(A) 研修を推奨するため
(B) 支援を要請するため
(C) 代替物を提案するため
(D) 遅延の理由を説明するため

正解 D 話し手は❸で、新しいソフトウエアを使用して所蔵品目録を作る作業を続けると伝えた後、❹「目録が今月中に完成する予定だったということは分かっている」と述べている。その直後に「でも」と続け、下線部の発言でソフトウエアの複雑さを強調し、❺で進捗を逐次知らせると言っている。よって、話し手は、目録作成作業が予定よりも遅れている理由を説明するために下線部の発言をしていると判断できる。explain「～の理由を説明する」、delay「遅延」。
(A) recommend「～を推奨する」、training「研修」。
(C) replacement「代替物、代替者」。

Words & Phrases
preparation 準備 exhibit 展示 gallery 画廊、美術館 painting 絵画 loan ～ … ～に…を貸し出す delivery 引き渡し、配達 be scheduled for ～ ～に予定されている as for ～ ～に関しては continue to do ～し続ける take inventory of ～ ～の目録を作る collection 所蔵品 complete ～を完成させる discuss ～について話し合う complex 複雑な keep ～ informed ～に最新情報を逐次提供する progress 進捗 go on 進む

Questions 95 through 97 refer to the following talk and price list.

問題95-97は次の話と価格表に関するものです。

M

Thanks for inviting me to come to your camping store to demonstrate Tovin's newest portable, lightweight stove. ❶I'll begin by handing you these brochures to look over later. ❷They describe this revolutionary new cooking device in detail, which should help you decide whether to stock it in your store. ❸The best part is, since this particular model is a scaled-down version of one of our larger models, you pay a fraction of the price—just 68 dollars and 99 cents. ❹Now, let me show you just how easy it is to fold it and stick it in my backpack.

Tovin社の最新型携帯用軽量コンロの実演のために、こちらのキャンプ用品店に私をお招きくださりありがとうございます。後ほど目を通していただけるよう、これらのパンフレットを皆さまにお渡しすることから始めます。そこにはこの革命的な調理器具の新製品について詳しい説明があるので、皆さまのお店にそれを仕入れるべきかどうか判断するのに役立つはずです。最良の点は、このモデルが当社のある大型モデルの小型版なので、お支払いもその価格のごく一部だということです——たったの68ドル99セントです。さて、いかに簡単にそれを折りたたんで私のリュックに差し込むことができるかを皆さまに実演させてください。

Tovin Stove Models	
VX	$118.50
Plus	$94.20
Pro	$182.99
XT	$68.99

Tovin社製コンロ 製品モデル	
VX	118ドル50セント
Plus	94ドル20セント
Pro	182ドル99セント
XT	68ドル99セント

95 What does the speaker give to the listeners?

(A) Marketing materials
(B) Product coupons
(C) Business cards
(D) Order forms

話し手は聞き手に何を渡していますか。

(A) 販促資料
(B) 商品クーポン
(C) 名刺
(D) 注文用紙

正解 A 話し手は、最新製品の実演のために聞き手のキャンプ用品店に招いてくれたことに謝意を述べた後、❶で、パンフレットを渡すことから始めると伝えている。そして、パンフレットの内容について、❷「そこにはこの革命的な調理器具の新製品について詳しい説明があるので、あなたたちの店にそれを仕入れるべきかどうか判断するのに役立つはずだ」と補足している。brochuresを marketing materialsと表している(A)が正解。marketing「販売促進活動」、material「資料」。
(B) coupon「クーポン」。
(C) business card「名刺」。
(D) order「注文」、form「用紙」。

96 Look at the graphic. Which model is the speaker discussing?

(A) VX
(B) Plus
(C) Pro
(D) XT

図を見てください。話し手はどのモデルについて話していますか。

(A) VX
(B) Plus
(C) Pro
(D) XT

正解 D 話し手は、最新製品について、❸「最良の点は、このモデルが当社のある大型モデルの小型版なので、支払いもその価格のごく一部だということだ——たった68ドル99セントだ」と、製品の最大の売りである価格の安さを強調している。図を見ると、価格が68ドル99セントのモデルは最下行にあるXTなので、(D)が正解。
(A) (B) (C) いずれも価格表に掲載されているが、価格が68ドル99セントではないので、不適切。

97 What will the speaker demonstrate?

(A) How to pack a stove
(B) How to prepare a meal
(C) How to adjust a setting
(D) How to clean a stove after use

話し手は何を実演しますか。

(A) コンロを荷物に入れる方法
(B) 食事を作る方法
(C) 設定を調節する方法
(D) 使用後のコンロを掃除する方法

正解 A 話し手は❸で、最新型の携帯用軽量コンロが持つ最大の売りを説明してから、❹「さて、いかに簡単にそれを折りたたんで私のリュックに差し込むことができるかをあなたたちに実演させてください」と述べている。itは最新製品のコンロを指しているので、(A)が正解。pack「～を荷造りする」。
(B) prepare「～(食事)を作る」。
(C) adjust「～を調節する」、setting「設定」。
(D) clean「～を掃除する」、use「使用」。

Words & Phrases

invite ～を招待する　camping store キャンプ用品店　demonstrate ～(商品)を実演して見せる　portable 携帯用の

lightweight 軽量の　stove (料理用の)コンロ、レンジ　begin by doing ～することから始める　hand ～ … ～に…を渡す

brochure パンフレット　look over ～ ～にざっと目を通す　describe ～を説明する　revolutionary 革命的な

device 器具、装置　in detail 詳しく　help ～ do ～が…するのを手伝う

decide whether to do ～すべきかどうかを決める　stock ～(商品)を仕入れる、～を在庫として持つ　this particular 特にこの

scaled-down (規模などが)縮小された　version 版、バージョン　fraction ほんの少し　cent セント ★通貨の単位

show ～ … ～に…かをやって見せる　fold ～を折りたたむ　stick ～ in … ～を…に差し込む　backpack リュックサック

Questions 98 through 100 refer to the following telephone message and menu.

🇺🇸 W

Hi, Ernesto. It's Leslie calling from the restaurant with a couple of updates. First, ❶we have a problem with food deliveries. ❷Our supplier for seafood has delayed the shipment of fish until next week, so we'll have to offer something else instead of the fish sandwich. ❸Let me know what you'd like to substitute, and I'll change the menu for that day. Also, ❹I was thinking about the outdoor dining area we plan to open next month; I have some sketches to show you for the table arrangements out there.

問題 98-100 は次の電話のメッセージとメニューに関するものです。

こんにちは、Ernesto。こちらはLeslieで、レストランから電話していますが、最新情報が2つあります。まず、食品の配達に問題が生じています。当店の水産物の仕入れ先が来週まで魚の出荷を先延ばししたので、私たちは魚のサンドイッチの代わりに何か別のものを提供しなければなりません。何を代わりにしたらよいと思うか教えてください、私がその曜日のメニューを変更しますので。それから、当店が来月開設を計画している屋外の食事エリアについて考えていました。屋外のテーブル配置の略図があるので、あなたに見せたいと思います。

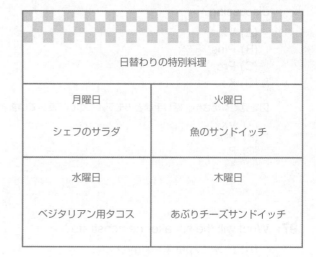

Daily Specials	
Monday Chef's Salad	**Tuesday** Fish Sandwich
Wednesday Vegetarian Tacos	**Thursday** Grilled Cheese Sandwich

日替わりの特別料理	
月曜日 シェフのサラダ	火曜日 魚のサンドイッチ
水曜日 ベジタリアン用タコス	木曜日 あぶりチーズサンドイッチ

98 What problem is the speaker calling about?

(A) Some equipment is broken.
(B) Some food has spoiled.
(C) A shipment has been delayed.
(D) An employee is not available.

話し手はどんな問題について電話していますか。

(A) 機器が故障している。
(B) 食品が傷んでいる。
(C) 出荷が遅れている。
(D) 従業員の都合がつかない。

正解 C 話し手は、聞き手に知らせるべき最新情報の1つについて、❶「食品の配達に問題が生じている」と述べた後、❷で、店の水産物の仕入れ先が来週まで魚の出荷を先延ばししたために、メニューを一部変更する必要があると伝えている。(our supplier) has delayed the shipmentを受動態で表している(C)が正解。
(A) equipment「機器」、broken「故障した」。
(B) 話し手は食品の配達の遅れに言及しているが、食品の傷みについては述べていない。spoil「(食べ物などが)腐る」。
(D) employee「従業員」、available「都合がつく」。

99 Look at the graphic. For which day will the menu be changed?

(A) Monday
(B) Tuesday
(C) Wednesday
(D) Thursday

図を見てください。どの曜日のメニューが変更されますか。

(A) 月曜日
(B) 火曜日
(C) 水曜日
(D) 木曜日

正解 B 話し手は、水産物の配達に問題が生じたと伝えた後、❷で、魚のサンドイッチの代わりに別の料理を提供する必要性に言及している。そして、❸「何を代わりにしたらよいと思うか教えてください、私がその曜日のメニューを変更するので」と言っている。図を見ると、見出しには「日替わりの特別料理」とあり、魚のサンドイッチが提供されているのは火曜日なので、(B)が正解。

100 According to the speaker, what does the restaurant plan to do next month?

(A) Expand its dessert menu
(B) Offer a delivery service
(C) Hire another chef
(D) Open an outdoor dining area

話し手によると、レストランは来月に何をする計画ですか。

(A) デザートメニューを拡充する
(B) 配達サービスを提供する
(C) 別のシェフを雇う
(D) 屋外の食事エリアを開設する

正解 D 話し手は自分たちのレストランに生じている問題とその対応策に言及した後、❹「当店が来月開設を計画している屋外の食事エリアについて考えていた」と述べている。よって、(D)が正解。
(A) expand「～を拡大する」、dessert「デザート」。
(C) hire「～を雇う」。

Words & Phrases

| a couple of ～ | 2つの～、幾つかの～ | update | 最新情報 | delivery | 配達 | supplier | 仕入れ先、供給業者 |

seafood　水産物、魚介類　　delay　～を遅らせる　　shipment　出荷、出荷品　　offer　～を提供する

something else　何か他のもの　　instead of ～　～の代わりに　　substitute　～を代わりにする　　outdoor　屋外の

dining　食事　　plan to *do*　～する計画である　　sketch　略図、スケッチ　　arrangement　配置　　out there　あそこに

メニュー　daily　日々の　　special　特別料理　　vegetarian　ベジタリアンの、菜食主義(者)の

taco　タコス　★具をトルティーヤに挟んだメキシコ料理　　grilled　あぶった、焼いた　　cheese　チーズ

101 Gerardo Lentini will build ------- second clinic in June.

    (A) he
    (B) his
    (C) him
    (D) himself

Gerardo Lentiniは6月に、彼の2つ目の診療所を建てる予定です。

    (A) 彼は
    (B) 彼の
    (C) 彼を
    (D) 彼自身

> **正解 B** 選択肢は全て三人称単数の人称代名詞。空所の前に他動詞 buildがあり、後ろにはsecond clinic「2つ目の診療所」が続いている。これを修飾してbuildの目的語となる名詞句を作る所有格の (B) his「彼の」が適切。clinic「診療所」。
> (A) 主格。(C) 目的格。(D) 再帰代名詞。

---

102 The manufacturer recommends cleaning the natural wood table with a ------- cotton cloth.

    (A) dry
    (B) dryly
    (C) dryness
    (D) to dry

製造業者はその天然木のテーブルを、乾いた木綿の布で拭くことを推奨しています。

    (A) 乾いた
    (B) 冷淡に
    (C) 乾燥状態
    (D) 乾かすための

> **正解 A** 空所の前に冠詞aがあり、後ろに名詞句cotton cloth「木綿の布」が続いているので、空所には名詞句を修飾する語が入る。形容詞の(A) dry「乾いた」が適切。manufacturer「製造業者、メーカー」、recommend *doing*「〜することを勧める」、natural wood「天然木」、cotton「木綿、コットン」、cloth「布」。
> (B) 副詞。(C) 名詞。(D) 動詞「〜を乾かす」のto不定詞。

---

103 If ------- are willing to work on the project this weekend, Ms. Craig will buy everyone lunch.

    (A) employees
    (B) employing
    (C) employments
    (D) employs

もし従業員たちが今週末そのプロジェクトの仕事をしてくれるなら、Craigさんは全員にランチをおごるつもりです。

    (A) 従業員たち
    (B) 雇用すること
    (C) 職
    (D) 〜を雇用する

> **正解 A** 主節はカンマの後ろで、「Craigさんは全員にランチをおごるつもりだ」。カンマまでのIf節が、その条件となる。If節には主語がないので、空所に(A) employees「従業員たち」を入れると、「もし従業員たちが今週末そのプロジェクトの仕事をしてくれるなら」となり、意味が通る。be willing to *do*「（相手の意をくんで）快く〜する、〜するのをいとわない」、work on 〜「〜の仕事をする、〜に取り組む」、project「プロジェクト」、buy 〜 …「〜に…をおごる」。
> (B) employ「〜を雇用する」の動名詞。後ろが複数形に続くareなので不適切。また、適した文意にならない。
> (C) 名詞だが、適した文意にならない。
> (D) employの三人称単数現在形。

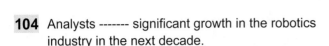

104 Analysts ------- significant growth in the robotics industry in the next decade.

(A) attend
(B) refer
(C) think
(D) predict

アナリストたちは、今後10年間のロボット工学産業における顕著な成長を予測しています。

(A) ～に出席する
(B) ～を参照させる
(C) ～と考える
(D) ～を予測する

正解 D 最も自然な文になる動詞を選ぶ。空所の後ろは、「今後10年間のロボット工学産業における顕著な成長」を表している。(D) predict「～を予測する」を入れると、アナリストたちが今後10年間の顕著な成長を予測していることになり、意味が通る。analyst「アナリスト、評論家」、significant「顕著な」、growth「成長、発展」、robotics「ロボット工学、ロボティクス」、industry「産業」、decade「10年間」。

105 Please review the ------- schedule and e-mail me right away about any mistakes.

(A) repeated
(B) alarmed
(C) attached
(D) canceled

添付の予定表を確認して、どんなことでも誤りがあれば、直ちに私にメールしてください。

(A) 繰り返された
(B) 警告された
(C) 添付された
(D) 取り消された

正解 C Pleaseで始まる命令文で、review「～を見直す、～を精査する」とe-mail「～にEメールを送る」の2つのことを求めている。空所の前に冠詞the、後ろに名詞schedule「予定表」が続いているので、空所にはscheduleを修飾する語が入る。(C) attached「添付された」を入れると、メールに添付の予定表を検討の上、問題があれば返信してほしいという意味になり、適切。right away「直ちに」、any ～「いかなる～でも」。

106 Niceties Cake Shop added ten more exotic flavors ------- after opening.

(A) short
(B) shortest
(C) shorter
(D) shortly

Nicetiesケーキ店は、開業後間もなく、さらに10種類のエキゾチックな風味を追加しました。

(A) 短い
(B) 最も短い
(C) より短い
(D) すぐに

正解 D 空所に何も入れなくても文として成立するので、空所には修飾語が入ると考えられる。空所の後ろのafter opening「開業後に」を修飾する副詞の(D) shortly「すぐに、間もなく」を入れると、開業後間もなく、新しい風味の商品をラインアップに追加したことになり、意味が通る。add「～を追加する」、exotic「エキゾチックな、魅惑的で珍しい」、flavor「風味、フレーバー」。
(A)(B)(C) 形容詞の原級、最上級、比較級。shortは副詞として使われることもあるが、「～の後間もなく」の意味でshort after ～とは言わない。

107 Mr. Kern has built a shelf in the supply closet ------- all the new materials.

    (A) accommodate
    (B) accommodates
    (C) to accommodate
    (D) is accommodating

Kernさんは備品保管室の中に、全ての新しい資材を収納する棚を作りました。

    ＊選択肢の訳は省略

正解 C 動詞accommodate「～を収納する、～に対応する」の適切な形を選ぶ。空所の前までは「Kernさんは備品保管室の中に棚を作った」という意味で、文として完結しているので、空所以降の部分は修飾語句と考えられる。to不定詞の(C) to accommodateを入れると、空所以降が「全ての新しい資材を収納するための」と、a shelfを修飾する不定詞となり、適切。shelf「棚」、supply closet「備品保管室」、materials「資材、材料」。
(A) 原形。(B) 三人称単数現在形。(D) 現在進行形。

108 The neighborhood's newest clothing store will specialize in the sale of ------- wear.

    (A) formal
    (B) quick
    (C) strict
    (D) sudden

その地域の一番新しい衣料品店は、フォーマルウエアの販売を専門にする予定です。

    (A) フォーマルな
    (B) 素早い
    (C) 厳しい
    (D) 突然の

正解 A 選択肢は全て形容詞の働きを持つ語。新しい衣料品店の専門ジャンルを伝える内容の文に最も適したものを選ぶ。(A) formalを入れると、formal wear「フォーマルウエア」という衣料品分野を専門に販売することになり、意味が通る。neighborhood「地域、地区」、clothing store「洋品店、服屋」、specialize in ～「～を専門にする、～に特化する」、sale「販売」。
(B) (C) (D) 適した文意にならない。

109 Office morale ------- after we offered rewards for practical suggestions.

    (A) indicated
    (B) completed
    (C) improved
    (D) controlled

有用な提案に対して報奨金を支払うと私たちが言って以降、職場の士気は向上しました。

    (A) ～を指し示した
    (B) ～を完了した
    (C) 向上した
    (D) ～を制御した

正解 C 選択肢は全て動詞の過去形。空所の後ろは、「私たちが有用な提案に対して報奨金を支払うと言った後」という意味。報奨金を払うと言った後にOffice morale「職場の士気」に起こったこととして適した意味になるのは、(C) improved「向上した」。improveは他動詞としても使えるが、ここでは自動詞。office「職場、事務所」、morale「士気」、offer ～ for …「…に対して～を支払うと言う」、reward「報奨(金)」、practical「有用な」、suggestion「提案」。

110 At Furnred Finance, ------- encourage associates with different points of view to find common ground.

    (A) ourselves

    (B) ours

    (C) us

    (D) we

Furnredファイナンス社では、異なる観点を持つ同僚たちが共通点を見いだすように奨励しています。

    (A) 私たち自身

    (B) 私たちのもの

    (C) 私たちを

    (D) 私たちは

正解 D 選択肢は全て一人称複数の人称代名詞。空所直後のencourageが述語動詞で、主語に相当する語がないので、空所には主格の(D) weが適切。encourage 〜 to do「〜に…するよう奨励する」、associate「同僚、仕事仲間」、point of view「観点、視点」、common ground「共通点、一致点、共通基盤」。
(A) 再帰代名詞。(B) 所有代名詞。(C) 目的格。

---

111 Shipbuilders, Inc., anticipates profits for the second quarter to be ------- 4 and 6 percent.

    (A) by

    (B) for

    (C) upon

    (D) between

Shipbuilders社は、第2四半期の利益を4〜6パーセントの間になると予想しています。

    (A) 〜による

    (B) 〜のための

    (C) 〜の上に

    (D) 〜の間に

正解 D 選択肢は全て前置詞の働きを持つ語。文頭から空所までは「Shipbuilders社は、第2四半期の利益を…になると予想している」という意味。空所の後ろに4 and 6 percentがあるので、(D) betweenを入れてbetween A and B「AからBの間に」の形にすると適した文意になる。anticipate「〜を予想する」、profit「利益」、quarter「四半期」。

---

112 Ovonel Skincare has published ------- testimonials on several social media sites.

    (A) consumed

    (B) consumer

    (C) consume

    (D) consuming

Ovonelスキンケア社は幾つかのソーシャルメディアサイトに、消費者の声を掲載しました。

    (A) 消費された

    (B) 消費者

    (C) 〜を消費する

    (D) 消費している

正解 B 選択肢は動詞consume「〜を消費する」と、その変化した形や派生語。空所直後のtestimonialsと共に、述語動詞has publishedの目的語となる名詞句を作る(B) consumer「消費者」が適切。consumer testimonialで、「お客さまの声、実際に使用した人の感想」という意味になる。publish「〜を掲載する」、testimonial「証言、証明書」、social media site「ソーシャルメディアサイト」。
(A) (D) 形容詞の働きがあるが、testimonialsを修飾しても適した文意にならない。(C) 動詞の原形。

113 Saturn Bank is working ------- to resolve technical difficulties with its mobile app and online banking.

(A) quickening
(B) quickened
(C) quickness
(D) quickly

Saturn銀行は、携帯アプリとインターネット・バンキングの技術的障害を解決するため、早急に作業しています。

(A) 速めている
(B) 速められた
(C) 素早さ
(D) 早急に

正解 D 空所に何も入れなくても文として成り立つので、修飾語が入ると考えられる。副詞の(D) quickly「早急に」を入れると、述語動詞is working「作業している、取り組んでいる」を修飾する形となり、意味が通る。resolve「～を解決する」、technical「技術的な」、difficulties「障害、問題点」、mobile app「携帯電話用アプリ（appはapplicationの略）」、online banking「インターネット・バンキング」。
(A) (B) quicken「～を速める」の現在分詞、過去分詞。workingまでを副詞的に修飾しているとしても、適した文意にならない。(C) 名詞。

114 The new washing machine has a heavy-duty cycle that is effective in removing the ------- stains.

(A) highest
(B) toughest
(C) uneven
(D) broad

その新しい洗濯機は、最も頑固な汚れを取り除くのに効果的な、パワフル・コースを搭載しています。

(A) 最も高い
(B) 最も頑固な
(C) 不均等な
(D) 幅広い

正解 B 選択肢は全て形容詞の働きを持つ語。新しい洗濯機の機能の説明に適した語を選ぶ。heavy-dutyは「強力な、頑丈な」。cycleはここでは洗濯機の「洗い、すすぎ、脱水などの一連の動作」を表しており、heavy-duty cycleで「パワフル・コース」といった意味になる。that以降はa heavy-duty cycleを修飾する関係代名詞節で「------- 汚れを取り除くのに効果的な」という意味。(B) toughest「最も頑固な」を入れると適した文意になる。washing machine「洗濯機」、effective in *doing*「～するのに効果的な」、remove「～を取り除く」、stain「汚れ、しみ」。

115 Wolff Foods has recently experienced a decrease in ------- for its beef products.

(A) position
(B) approach
(C) force
(D) demand

Wolff食品社は最近、自社の牛肉製品に対する需要の減少を経験しました。

(A) 位置
(B) 接近
(C) 力
(D) 需要

正解 D 選択肢は全て名詞の働きを持つ語。a decrease in ------- は「-------の減少」、空所直後のfor its beef productsは「その（Wolff食品社の）牛肉製品に対する」という意味。食品会社が最近、減少を経験したこととして適切なのは、(D) demand「需要」。experience「～を経験する」、product「製品」。
(A) (B) (C) 適した文意にならない。

116 Although construction will begin on Reese-Decker Bridge tomorrow, it should cause ------- traffic problems.

(A) minimal
(B) minimally
(C) minimum
(D) minimize

Reese-Decker橋での建設工事が明日始まりますが、それは最小限の交通問題しか引き起こさないはずです。

(A) 最小限の
(B) 最小限に
(C) 最小限
(D) ～を最小限にする

正解 A　カンマまでは、「Reese-Decker橋での建設工事が明日始まるが」という意味で、カンマの後ろの節の主語itは建設工事を指す。空所には、traffic problemsを修飾して名詞句を作り、全体で述語動詞should causeの目的語となる形容詞の(A) minimal「最小限の」が適切。minimal traffic problemsで「最小限の交通問題」を表す。although「～だが」、construction「建設工事」、cause「～を引き起こす」。
(C) 名詞または形容詞。形容詞としては通常、取り得る範囲があらかじめ限定されている場合（最低限必要な卒業単位など）に使われるので、ここでは不適切。

117 The months of April and May are ------- busy for the workers at Avedis Garden Supply.

(A) readily
(B) accurately
(C) particularly
(D) directly

Avedis園芸用品社の従業員たちにとって、4月と5月はとりわけ忙しい月です。

(A) 容易に
(B) 正確に
(C) とりわけ
(D) 直接

正解 C　選択肢は全て副詞。空所を含むforまでの部分は、「4月と5月は-------忙しい月だ」という意味。12カ月の中で4月と5月を取り上げて述べているので、(C) particularly「とりわけ、特に」を入れると園芸用品社の繁忙期を説明する適した文意になる。busy for ～「～にとって忙しい」。
(A) (B) (D) 適した文意にならない。

118 Mr. Kalama will handle the marketing reports ------- Ms. Lewis is away on vacation.

(A) concerning
(B) while
(C) during
(D) just

Lewisさんが休暇で不在の間は、Kalamaさんがマーケティング報告書を担当します。

(A) ～に関して
(B) ～する間
(C) ～の間
(D) ちょうど

正解 B　空所の前後は共に〈主語＋動詞〉という節の形なので、空所には2つの節をつなぐ接続詞が入る。選択肢中で唯一の接続詞である(B) while「～する間」が意味の上でも適切。handle「～を担当する、～を取り扱う」、marketing report「マーケティング報告書、マーケティング・レポート」、away「不在の」、on vacation「休暇中で」。
(A) (C) 前置詞。〈主語＋動詞〉の形は続かない。
(D) 副詞。2つの節をつなぐことはできない。

TEST1 PART 5

119 Mr. Nguyen opposes adding a ------- of trail bikes because he thinks it will not be popular with customers.

(A) line
(B) surface
(C) field
(D) front

Nguyenさんは、顧客に人気が出ないだろうと考えているので、トレイルバイクの商品ラインを追加することに反対しています。

(A) 商品ライン
(B) 表面
(C) 分野
(D) 前面

正解 **A** 　選択肢は全て名詞の働きを持つ語。文頭からbikesまでの主節は、「Nguyenさんは、トレイルバイクの-------を追加することに反対している」という意味。(A) lineには「商品ライン（あるカテゴリーに属する一連の商品群）」の意味があり、これを入れるとbecause以降の従属節でitが新商品のラインを指すことになり、自然な文になる。oppose *doing*「～することに反対する」、add「～を追加する」、trail bike「トレイルバイク（悪路用の頑丈な自転車）」、be popular with ～「～に人気がある」、customer「顧客」。

---

120 Ms. Nicholas was promoted ------- managing editor of the *Irontown Daily Press*.

(A) of
(B) at
(C) to
(D) on

Nicholasさんは、『Irontown日刊新聞』の編集長に昇進しました。

(A) ～の
(B) ～で
(C) ～に
(D) ～の上の

正解 **C** 　選択肢は全て前置詞の働きを持つ語。promote ～ to …「～を…に昇進させる」を受動態にした、～ be promoted to …「～は…に昇進する」の形になるように (C) toを入れると、Ms. Nicholas was promoted to managing editorが「Nicholasさんは編集長に昇進した」という適した意味になる。managing editor「編集長」、daily press「日刊紙」。

---

121 Ms. Chou has ordered the ------- of all the bookcases sold by Bielke Office Furnishings.

(A) narrowly
(B) narrower
(C) narrowest
(D) narrow

Chouさんは、Bielkeオフィス家具社で販売されている全ての書棚の中で、最も幅の狭いものを注文しました。

(A) 狭く
(B) より幅の狭い
(C) 最も幅の狭い
(D) 幅の狭い

正解 **C** 　選択肢は形容詞narrow「幅の狭い」と、その変化した形や派生語。空所の前に定冠詞のtheがあり、後ろにof all the bookcasesという、名詞を限定する表現が続いている。〈the+形容詞の最上級+of all the+複数名詞〉で、「全ての…の中で最も～なもの」という意味になるので、最上級の (C) narrowestが適切。〈the+形容詞〉は、「～なもの」を表す名詞として用いられる。order「～を注文する」、bookcase「書棚、本棚」、furnishing「備え付け家具」。
(A) 副詞。(B) 形容詞の比較級。(D) 形容詞の原級。

122 Failure to pay bills on time ------- result in additional late fees.

(A) when
(B) may
(C) part
(D) itself

期限内の支払いの不履行は、追加の延滞料という結果をもたらす可能性があります。

(A) ～するとき
(B) ～する可能性がある
(C) 部分
(D) それ自身

> **正解 B** Failure to pay bills on timeで「期限内に支払いをしないこと」の意味。これが文の主語で、result in ～「～という結果になる」が述語動詞になると考えられる。主語が三人称単数なので、助動詞の(B) may「～する可能性がある、～かもしれない」を入れると、resultが助動詞に続く動詞の原形となり、適切。failure to do「～の不履行、～をしないこと」、pay a bill「支払いをする、勘定を払う」、on time「時間通りに、遅れずに」、additional「追加の」、late fee「延滞料」。

123 Financial conditions in the greater Perth region are ------- favorable for economic growth.

(A) privately
(B) centrally
(C) neutrally
(D) currently

パース市とその近郊を含む地域の経済状況は、現在のところ、経済成長に好ましい状況です。

(A) 内密に
(B) 中心に
(C) 中立的に
(D) 現在のところ

> **正解 D** 選択肢は全て副詞。空所の後ろの形容詞句favorable for economic growth「経済成長に好ましい」を修飾するのに適切な語を選ぶ。(D) currently「現在のところ」を入れると、この地域の今の経済状況を述べていることになり、意味が通る。financial conditions「経済状況、財政状態」、greater「(都市が)近郊を含めた」、region「地域」、favorable for ～「～にとって好都合な」、growth「成長、発展」。

124 The quarterly data safety report provides ------- for Mardoor Investing's strict security policies.

(A) justify
(B) justifier
(C) justified
(D) justification

データの安全性に関する四半期報告書は、Mardoor投資会社の厳格なセキュリティー方針に正当性の根拠を与えています。

(A) ～を正当化する
(B) 正当化するもの
(C) 正当化された
(D) 正当性の根拠

> **正解 D** 文の主語はThe quarterly data safety reportで、述語動詞はprovides。報告書が、for以降で示されているMardoor投資会社の厳格なセキュリティー方針に与えるものとして適切なのは、名詞の(D) justification「正当性の根拠、正当化」。quarterly「四半期の」、safety「安全(性)」、report「報告書」、provide ～ for …「…に～を与える」、strict「厳格な、厳しい」、security「セキュリティー(に関する)、安全確保」、policy「方針、ポリシー」。
> (A) 動詞justify「～を正当化する」の原形、(C) 過去分詞。どちらも動詞providesの目的語にならない。
> (B) 名詞だが、ここでは適した文意にならない。

TEST1 PART 5

49

125 Sunworth Company's all-in-one shampoos restore natural shine at the same time ------- they condition hair.

(A) even
(B) as
(C) either
(D) like

Sunworth社のオールインワン・シャンプーは、髪の状態を整えるのと同時に、自然な輝きを取り戻します。

(A) 〜さえ
(B) 〜と同じく
(C) 〜のどちらか
(D) 〜のように

正解 B　空所の前後は〈主語＋動詞〉という節の形で、「Sunworth社のオールインワン・シャンプーは自然な輝きを取り戻す」と「それらは髪の状態を整える」を意味している。空所に (B) as を入れると、2つを at the same time as 〜「〜と同時に」という接続詞句でつなぐことになり、意味が通る。all-in-one shampoo「オールインワン・シャンプー、リンスイン・シャンプー」、restore「〜を取り戻す」、shine「輝き」、condition「〜の状態を整える」。

126 The third box of the shipment, which should have contained the microphones, ------- arrived.

(A) late
(B) rather
(C) never
(D) not

積み荷の3つ目の箱は、マイクが入っていたはずでしたが、結局届きませんでした。

(A) 遅れて
(B) 幾分
(C) 決して〜ない
(D) 〜ない

正解 C　主節の主語は The third box of the shipment「積み荷の3つ目の箱」で、カンマで挟まれた関係代名詞節は The third box に説明を加えている。述語動詞 arrived「届いた」を修飾するのに適切なのは、副詞の (C) never。「3つ目の箱は結局届かなかった」という意味になる。shipment「積み荷、発送品」、should have *done*「〜するはずだった」、contain「〜が入っている、〜を含む」、microphone「マイク」。
(A) arrived late「遅れて届いた」なら可。(B) 意味が通らない。
(D) did not arrive「届かなかった」なら可。

127 The Murnau Company's pepper grinders are ------- durable that the company guarantees them for life.

(A) too
(B) so
(C) such
(D) very

Murnau社のペッパーミルは非常に耐久性が高いので、同社はそれらを永久保証しています。

(A) あまりにも
(B) 非常に
(C) そんな
(D) 非常に

正解 B　that で始まる節は、「その会社（Murnau社）はそれら（同社のペッパーミル）を永久保証している」という意味。so 〜 that …の形で「非常に〜なので…」を表す (B) so を空所に入れると、非常に高い耐久性があるために、永久保証が可能であるという説明になり、意味が通る。pepper grinder「ペッパーミル、こしょうひき」、durable「耐久性のある」、guarantee「〜を保証する」、for life「永久に」。
(C) such 〜 that …で「非常に〜なので…」の意味となるが、such の後ろには名詞、または〈形容詞＋名詞〉の形が続く。

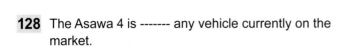

128 The Asawa 4 is ------- any vehicle currently on the market.

　(A) unlike
　(B) excepting
　(C) against
　(D) above

Asawa 4 は現在市販されている、いかなる乗り物とも似ていません。

　(A) 〜に似ていない
　(B) 〜を除いて
　(C) 〜に反対して
　(D) 〜の上の

> **正解 A** 選択肢は全て前置詞の働きを持つ語。(A) unlike「〜に似ていない、〜と違って」を入れると、「Asawa 4 (という名前の乗り物)は現在市販されている、いかなる乗り物とも似ていない」となり、意味が通る。vehicle「乗り物、自動車」、currently「現在」、on the market「市販されて、売りに出されて」。

129 By the time he signs the lease, Mr. Cooper ------- four months searching for a suitable office space.

　(A) will have spent
　(B) had spent
　(C) to spend
　(D) spent

賃貸借契約書にサインする時までに、Cooperさんは満足のいく事務所スペースを探して4カ月間を費やしたことになるでしょう。

　＊選択肢の訳は省略

> **正解 A** Mr. Cooper以降が主節なので、空所には述語動詞が入る。カンマまでのBy the time he signs the lease「彼が賃貸借契約書にサインする時までに」は、時を表す副詞節であり、現在形だが内容は未来のある時までの状況・動作を表している。よって、主節の述語動詞には、未来完了形の(A) will have spentが適切。spend 〜 *doing* で「…するのに〜 (時間) を費やす」の意味になる。by the time 〜「〜する時までに」、lease「賃貸借契約 (書)」、search for 〜「〜を探す」、suitable「満足のいく、適した」、office space「事務所スペース」。

130 ------- I have already been briefed by the product development team, I am fully prepared for my appointment with Mr. Warner.

　(A) Until
　(B) In spite of
　(C) Since
　(D) Even though

私はすでに製品開発チームから手短な説明を受けましたので、Warnerさんとの面会のための準備は十分にできています。

　(A) 〜まで
　(B) 〜にもかかわらず
　(C) 〜なので
　(D) 〜にもかかわらず

> **正解 C** 文頭からカンマまでは、「私はすでに製品開発チームから手短な説明を受けた」、カンマの後ろは「私はWarnerさんとの面会のための準備が十分にできている」という意味。2つの節があり、文脈から前半が後半の理由となっていると考えられるので、理由を表す接続詞の(C) Since「〜なので」が適切。brief「〜に手短に説明する、〜にブリーフィングを行う」、product development「製品開発」、be prepared for 〜「〜の準備ができている」、fully「十分に、完全に」、appointment「面会、アポイントメント」。
> (A) 接続詞の働きがあるが、適した文意にならない。
> (B) 前置詞句。〈主語＋動詞〉の形は続かない。
> (D) 接続詞句だが、適した文意にならない。

TEST1 PART 5

Questions 131-134 refer to the following article.

City Grants Permission for New High-Rise

❶ The city council has approved plans for a new high-rise apartment building on Third Street. The primarily ------- structure will replace a parking area. ------- will include 220 apartments, ranging
131.   132.
from studios to two-bedroom units.

❷ The project was designed by the architecture firm Wagama Clark Reyes. ------- . The Third Street
133.
project will feature a pool, a fitness center, a rooftop terrace, and an underground parking
garage. The building will ------- have space for a few retail stores and restaurants at ground level.
134.

問題131-134は次の記事に関するものです。

市が新たな高層ビルを認可

市議会は、三番通りの新しい高層マンション計画を承認した。その主として住宅用となる建造物は、駐車場の後に建てられることになる。それには、ワンルームから寝室2つの住戸まで、220戸が入る予定だ。

このプロジェクトは建築会社のWagama Clark Reyes社によって設計された。*同社は以前、Vanderマンションの設計をした。この三番通りのプロジェクトは、プール、フィットネスセンター、屋上テラス、地下駐車場が特色となる予定だ。この建物には、1階に数軒の小売店およびレストラン用スペースもできる予定だ。

*問題133の挿入文の訳

Words & Phrases

grant ～を与える、～を認める   permission 認可、許可   high-rise 〈名詞で〉高層ビル、〈形容詞で〉高層の
❶ council 議会、評議会   approve ～を承認する   apartment building マンション、集合住宅   primarily 主として
structure 建造物   replace ～に取って代わる   parking area 駐車場   include ～を含む
apartment 住戸 ★マンションなどの一戸分の区画を指す   studio ワンルームの住戸
two-bedroom unit 寝室が2つの住戸(2DK、2LDKなど)   ❷ project プロジェクト、事業計画
design ～の設計をする、～のデザインをする   architecture 建築   firm 会社
feature ～を特色として持っている、～を目玉にする   fitness center フィットネスセンター   rooftop 屋上
terrace テラス   underground 地下の   parking garage 駐車場   a few 幾つかの、少しの   retail store 小売店
ground level 1階

Expressions

range from A to B 「AからBに及ぶ」(❶2～3行目)
We have rooms, ranging from $200 to $650.
200ドルから650ドルまでの部屋があります。

131
(A) industrial
(B) commercial
(C) residential
(D) educational

(A) 産業の
(B) 商業の
(C) 住宅用の
(D) 教育の

正解 C 選択肢は全て形容詞の働きを持つ語。空所を含む文は、主語に当たるstructure「建造物」が前文のa new high-rise apartment building「新しい高層マンション」を受けており、「その主として------建造物は、駐車場の後に建てられることになる」と述べている。また、この文をさらに補足説明していると考えられる直後の文にも、「ワンルームから寝室2つの住戸まで、220戸が入る」とある。従って、この建造物は主として住宅用だと考えられるので、(C) residential「住宅用の」が適切。

132
(A) It
(B) One
(C) They
(D) Some

(A) それ
(B) 1つのもの
(C) それら
(D) 幾つかのもの

正解 A ❶1行目では、高層マンション計画について伝えている。問題132の空所を含む文の文頭からカンマまでは「------は220の住戸を含む」という意味。述語動詞はwill includeで220 apartmentsはその目的語となるが、この文には主語がないので、空所には主語として220の住戸を持つものが入る。直前の問題131の空所を含む文ではstructure「建造物」について述べており、問題132の文ではこの建造物について補足している。よって、前述のthe structureという単数形を受けて主語となることができる(A) Itが適切。
(B) 代名詞だとしても、特定のものを受けることはできないので不適切。

133
(A) Downtown is known for its nightlife.
(B) City traffic is often bumper-to-bumper.
(C) Many apartment buildings do not allow pets.
(D) The firm previously designed the Vander Apartments.

(A) 繁華街は、夜の娯楽で知られている。
(B) 市の交通はしばしば、渋滞している。
(C) 多くのマンションが、ペットを許可していない。
(D) 同社は以前、Vanderマンションの設計をした。

正解 D 空所の直前の文で、この高層マンションのプロジェクトの設計をしたのがWagama Clark Reyes社という建築会社であることが述べられている。空所の文の後ろでは、このプロジェクトの特色となる施設や、1階に小売店やレストランが入居するスペースができることが説明されている。空所には、この会社が過去に設計した建築物を紹介する(D)を入れると、流れとして自然。previously「以前に」、apartments「マンション・アパートの建物全体（＝apartment building）」。
(A) downtown「繁華街」、nightlife「夜の娯楽」。
(B) bumper-to-bumper「渋滞の、車が数珠つなぎの」。
(C) allow「～を許可する」。

134
(A) instead
(B) also
(C) similarly
(D) otherwise

(A) その代わりに
(B) ～もまた
(C) 同様に
(D) さもなければ

正解 B 選択肢は全て副詞の働きを持つ語。空所を含む文は、「この建物は------1階に数軒の小売店とレストランのスペースを持つ予定だ」という意味。直前の文で、このプロジェクトで設置が予定されている施設について言及しており、空所を含む文でも建物に入居予定の施設について続けて述べているので、(B) also「～もまた」が適切。
(A) (C) (D) 前の文と、話の内容が論理的につながらない。

Questions 135-138 refer to the following e-mail.

To: nyoon@velmail.com
From: kbengston@maekerelectric.com
Date: Monday, Oct 1
Subject: RE: Wiring for home projects

Good afternoon Ms. Yoon,

❶ I apologize for taking so long to respond to your e-mail. My team ------- on a big commercial
    135.
development project. We just finished it, so I can visit your property sometime next week to see

what electrical work you would like to have done. What is your -------? My best times are
                                                                 136.
Tuesday through Thursday mornings. And in answer to your question, I am not sure how much it

will cost or how long it will take to finish all the wiring. -------.
                                                            137.

❷ To prepare for my visit, could you make a list of the projects you have in mind? We can walk

through the property and discuss the details. -------, I can give you a price estimate and we can
                                              138.
schedule the work.

Kind regards,

Keith Bengston, Maeker Electric

問題135-138は次のEメールに関するものです。

受信者：nyoon@velmail.com
送信者：kbengston@maekerelectric.com
日付：10月1日（月曜日）
件名：RE：ご自宅の電気配線工事計画

こんにちは、Yoonさん

あなたのEメールにお返事するのに大変長くかかってしまったことをおわび申し上げます。私のチームはずっと、大きな商業開発案件に携わっておりました。それがちょうど終了しましたので、私は来週のどこかで、あなたがどんな電気工事の施工をご要望なのかを確かめるために、お宅を訪問することが可能です。ご都合の良い日時はいつですか。私が一番都合が良いのは火曜日から木曜日の午前中です。それから、ご質問にお答えしますと、全ての配線を終えるのにどのくらいの費用と時間がかかるのかについては、はっきりとご返答いたしかねます。*考慮すべき要素がたくさんあります。

私の訪問前の準備として、お考えになっている計画のリストをご作成いただけますか。ご一緒にお宅を見て回って、詳細について話し合えると思います。その後で、料金の見積もりをお出しすることができますし、私たちは作業のスケジュールを組むことができます。

敬具

Keith Bengston、Maekerエレクトリック社

*問題137の挿入文の訳

Expressions

have ～ in mind 「～を考えている、～を考慮している」（❷1行目）

The designer wants to show us what she has in mind for our company's lobby.
デザイナーは、当社のロビーのために考えていることを私たちに見せたがっています。

135
(A) will work
(B) may work
(C) should be working
(D) has been working

(A) 働くだろう
(B) 働くかもしれない
(C) 働いているはずだ
(D) ずっと働いてきている

正解 **D** 　送信者は冒頭で、YoonさんのEメールに対する返信に時間がかかったことを謝罪し、空所を含む文の直後でWe just finished it, so I can visit your property sometime next week「それがちょうど終了したので、私は来週のどこかで、お宅を訪問することが可能だ」と述べている。空所に現在完了進行形の(D) has been workingを入れると、空所を含む文が「私のチームはずっと、大きな商業開発案件に携わってきた」という意味になり、返信が遅くなった理由として文脈に合う。また、来週からはYoonさんの依頼に対応が可能だと伝える内容が続くことになり、流れとしても自然。
(A) (B) (C) いずれも、今まで返信ができず、来週から依頼に対応できるようになった理由を説明するのに不適切。

136
(A) calculation
(B) availability
(C) career
(D) process

(A) 計算
(B) 都合の良い日時
(C) 職歴
(D) 手順

正解 **B** 　空所を含む文の直前で、「私は来週のどこかで、あなたがどんな電気工事の施工をご要望なのかを確かめるために、お宅を訪問することができる」と述べており、直後の文では、自分にとって都合の良い日時を伝えている。よって、空所を含む文は事前訪問の約束をするために相手の都合を尋ねていると考えられる。(B) availability「都合の良い日時、都合がつくこと」が適切。
(A) (C) (D) いずれも文脈に適した文意にならない。

137
(A) You can do these repairs yourself.
(B) I will update the form if you want.
(C) There are a lot of factors to consider.
(D) I am familiar with this contractor.

(A) あなたはこの修理作業をご自身でできます。
(B) ご希望ならば、私はその書式を更新いたします。
(C) 考慮すべき要素がたくさんあります。
(D) 私はこの請負業者をよく知っています。

正解 **C** 　❶1行目より、このEメールはYoonさんからのEメールに対する返信だと分かる。空所直前の文に、「質問に答えると、全ての配線を終えるのにどのくらいの費用と時間がかかるのかについては、私は確信がない」と述べられていることから、YoonさんはEメールで費用と工期を問い合わせていたと考えられる。(C)を入れると、今の段階では費用や工期の見積もりが出せないという前文の説明の理由となって、自然な流れになる。factor「要素」、consider「～を考慮する」。
(A) repairs「修理作業」。
(B) update「～を更新する、～を最新のものにする」、form「書式、フォーム」。
(D) be familiar with ～「～をよく知っている」、contractor「請負業者、契約会社」。

138
(A) In fact
(B) Then again
(C) After that
(D) For example

(A) 実際
(B) しかしまた
(C) その後で
(D) 例えば

正解 **C** 　❶4～5行目では、考慮すべき要素が多いため、費用や工期の見積もりが出せない旨を述べているが、空所を含む文で「私はあなたに料金の見積もりを出すことができ、私たちは作業のスケジュールを組むことができる」と締めくくっている。また、空所の直前では、「私たちはお宅を見て回って、詳細について話し合うことができる」と述べているので、(C) After that「その後で」を入れると、家を見て詳細を話し合った後なら見積もりを出せるということになり、文脈に合う。
(A) (B) (D) 前後の話の内容が論理的につながらない。

Words & Phrases

wiring 電気配線工事　　project 計画、案件　　❶ apologize for ～ ～についてわびる　　take ～(時間)がかかる
respond to ～ ～に返答する、～に答える　　commercial 商業の　　development 開発　　property 所有地、建物
sometime いつか　　see ～を知る　　electrical 電気の　　work 作業、仕事　　would like to *do* ～したい
have ～ *done* ～を…してもらう　　～ through … ～から…まで　　in answer to ～ ～に答えて
be sure (that) ～ ～であることを確信している　　cost ～(費用)がかかる　　❷ prepare for ～ ～の準備をする、～に備える
list リスト、一覧表　　walk through ～ ～を見て回る、～を(端から端まで)通って歩く　　discuss ～について話し合う
details 詳細　　estimate 見積もり　　schedule ～のスケジュールを組む　　electric 電気

Questions 139-142 refer to the following job listing.

❶Landini Shipping, Inc., is currently seeking hardworking individuals to join our team. Qualified individuals must have a high school diploma and a willingness to work in a fast-paced environment. ------- , they must be responsible and follow safety protocols at all times. Open
139.
positions ------- package handlers, general warehouse workers, and warehouse associates. Day
140.
and night shifts are available. ------- . No one under 18 years of age will be considered.
141.
------- are available online at www.landinishipping.com.
142.

問題139-142は次の求人情報に関するものです。

Landini運送社は現在、チームに加わっていただける勤勉な方を求めています。必須条件は、高校卒業の資格と、活気ある環境下で働く意欲です。さらに、責任感があり、いかなる時でも安全手順に従っていただく必要があります。求人中の職種には、荷物取扱者、倉庫一般職員、および倉庫作業員があります。昼間シフト・夜間シフト共に空いています。*時折、週末の勤務を求められる可能性があります。18歳未満の方は選考対象になりません。応募用紙はwww.landinishipping.comにて、オンラインで入手できます。

*問題141の挿入文の訳

Words & Phrases

job listing　求人情報、求人案内　　❶ ~, Inc.　～社　★incorporatedの略　　currently　現在　　seek　～を求める、～を探す
hardworking　勤勉な　　individual　人、個人　　join　～に加わる　　qualified　資格のある　　diploma　卒業証書、学位
willingness　意欲　　fast-paced　ペースの速い、活気のある　　environment　環境　　responsible　責任感のある
follow　～に従う　　safety protocol　安全手順、安全プロトコル　　open　（職・地位が）空いている　　position　職、ポジション
package　荷物、貨物　　handler　取扱者　　general　一般の　　warehouse　倉庫　　worker　従業員、作業員
associate　従業員、仕事仲間　　day shift　昼間シフト、昼間勤務　　night shift　夜間シフト、夜間勤務
available　空きがある、入手可能な　　consider　～を考慮する　　online　オンラインで、インターネット上で

Expressions

at all times　「いかなる時でも、常に」（❶3行目）
Participants must wear life jackets at all times during the whale-watching tour.
ホエールウォッチング・ツアーの間、参加者は常に救命胴衣を着用していなければなりません。

139

(A) In part
(B) In addition
(C) In other words
(D) In the meantime

(A) ある程度
(B) さらに
(C) 言い換えれば
(D) 一方では

正解 B 選択肢は全て副詞の働きを持つ前置詞句。空所の直前の文で、応募資格者の条件として、高校卒業の資格と、活気ある環境下で働く意欲が挙げられている。空所の後ろでも、「責任感があり、いかなる時でも安全手順に従う必要がある」と、資格者の条件が付け加えられているので、(B) In addition「さらに」を入れると、文脈に合う。
(A) (C) (D) いずれも文脈に合わない。

140

(A) include
(B) must include
(C) had included
(D) to include

＊選択肢の訳は省略

正解 A 動詞include「〜を含む」の適切な形を選ぶ。空所直前のOpen positions「求人中の職種」が主語、直後のpackage handlers, general warehouse workers, and warehouse associates「荷物取扱者、倉庫一般職員、および倉庫作業員」が、目的語で、空所に入るのはこの文の述語動詞と考えられる。スタッフを募集しているのは現在の話なので、現在形の (A) include が適切。
(B) must「〜しなければならない」。文脈に合わない。
(C) 過去完了形。文脈に合わない。
(D) to不定詞。述語動詞にならない。

141

(A) Weekend work may be required on occasion.
(B) We will soon be relocating our office.
(C) Please come to our annual company picnic.
(D) Enjoy low shipping rates at all locations.

(A) 時折、週末の勤務を求められる可能性があります。
(B) 当社は近いうちに、事務所を移転することになっています。
(C) 毎年恒例の当社のピクニックに来てください。
(D) 全ての場所で、安い配送料金をご活用ください。

正解 A 空所直前の文ではDay and night shifts are available.「昼間シフト・夜間シフト共に空いている」と、募集職位の勤務時間帯に言及している。空所に(A)を入れると、勤務時間に関わる情報を付け加える形になり、流れとして自然。weekend「週末」、require「〜を求める、〜を必要とする」、on occasion「時折、たまに」。
(B) relocate「〜を移転させる」。
(C) annual「毎年の」、picnic「ピクニック」。
(D) enjoy「〜を享受する、〜の恩恵を受ける」、shipping「配送、輸送」、rate「料金」、location「場所」。

142

(A) Menus
(B) Tickets
(C) Schedules
(D) Applications

(A) メニュー
(B) チケット
(C) 予定表
(D) 応募用紙

正解 D この文書はjob listing「求人情報、求人案内」であり、応募資格者の条件、職種、勤務条件などが書かれている。(D) Applications「応募用紙」を入れると、空所を含む文が「応募用紙は、www.landinishipping.comにて、オンラインで入手できる」となり、応募方法についての言及で締めくくる形となって、求人情報として文脈に合う。
(A) (B) (C) いずれも文脈に合わない。

Questions 143-146 refer to the following e-mail.

To: Melita Li
From: J. P. Solera
Date: November 21
Subject: Internal Writing Update
Attachment: SOW; Technical specs

Dear Ms. Li,

❶ I would like you ------- the *User's Manual for Brandor Humidifiers*. Attached you will find a slide
143.
deck with background material. Please give special attention to slides 18 through 27.

------- highlight the main changes we need to incorporate into Section 2 of the manual.
144.

------- .
145.

❷ Please get back to me as soon as possible with your estimate of how long the task will take.

We should also discuss changes to your ------- . I would like you to make this task a priority.
146.

Thanks,

Jan Paul Solera

問題143-146は次のEメールに関するものです。

受信者：Melita Li
送信者：J. P. Solera
日付：11月21日
件名：文章作成業務更新の社内連絡
添付ファイル：作業指示書、技術仕様書

Liさん

あなたに『Brandor加湿器の使用者向け説明書』の改訂をお願いしたいと思っています。参考資料とスライド一式を添付します。18番から27番のスライドに、特に注意を払ってください。これらは説明書のセクション2に組み入れる必要のある主要な変更点を強調しています。*他の部分は全て変更なしのままである点に注意してください。

この仕事の所要時間についてのあなたの見積もりを、できるだけ早く私に返信してください。あなたの作業量の変更についても、私たちは話し合うべきだと思っています。あなたにはこの仕事を優先してもらいたいと考えています。

よろしくお願いします。

Jan Paul Solera

*問題145の挿入文の訳

Expressions

give attention to ～ 「～に注意を払う」（❶ 2行目）
The committee gave no attention to the matter.
委員会は、その件には何の注意も払いませんでした。

143
(A) to update
(B) will update
(C) are updating
(D) having updated

＊選択肢の訳は省略

正解 **A** 動詞update「〜を更新する」の適切な形を選ぶ。空所の前にI would like youとあるので、would like 〜 to *do*「〜に…してほしい、〜が…することを望む」の形になるように、(A) to updateを入れるのが適切。空所を含む文が「あなたに『Brandor加湿器の使用者向け説明書』の改訂をしてほしい」となり、文脈にも合う。
(B) 未来形。
(C) 現在進行形。
(D) 完了形のing形。

144
(A) Any
(B) You
(C) Both
(D) These

(A) どんな〜でも
(B) あなたは
(C) 両方とも
(D) これらは

正解 **D** 空所を含む文は、「-------は説明書のセクション2に組み入れる必要のある主要な変更点を強調している」という意味で、空所が文の主語になっている。また、空所の直前にPlease give special attention to slides 18 through 27.とある。空所に(D) These「これらは」を入れると、Theseが前文のslides 18 through 27を指し、この文が前文の指示の理由を伝えていることになるので、これが適切。

145
(A) Thank you for notifying us about the problem.
(B) The starting date for the project has changed.
(C) Note that all of the other parts remain unchanged.
(D) It has been a pleasure working with you.

(A) その問題について私たちにお知らせいただき、ありがとうございます。
(B) そのプロジェクトの開始日は変更されました。
(C) 他の部分は全て変更なしのままである点に注意してください。
(D) あなたとお仕事ができて良かったです。

正解 **C** ❶1〜3行目で、このメールの差出人であるSoleraさんはLiさんに、使用者向け説明書の改訂を依頼し、その作業時に参照すべき添付ファイルについて説明している。それに続く空所に(C)を入れると、資料を参照する際の注意点を付け加えていることになり、依頼のメールとして自然な流れになる。note that 〜「〜ということに注意する」、remain「〜のままである」、unchanged「変化していない、元のままの」。
(A) notify 〜 about …「〜に…を知らせる」。
(B) starting date「開始日」。
(D) pleasure「喜び」。

146
(A) office
(B) code
(C) uniform
(D) workload

(A) 職場
(B) 規則
(C) 制服
(D) 作業量

正解 **D** 空所を含む文は、「あなたの-------の変更についても、私たちは話し合うべきだと思う」という意味。空所を含む文の直前では、今頼んでいる新しい仕事の所要時間の見積もりをLiさんに依頼している。空所に(D) workload「作業量」を入れると、この依頼によりLiさんの仕事量が増えることについて、Soleraさんが話し合う考えを示している内容になり、文脈に合う。
(A) (B) (C) いずれも文脈に合わない。

Words & Phrases

internal 社内の、内部の　　writing 文章作成、執筆　　update 改訂、更新　　attachment 添付ファイル、添付書類
SOW 作業指示書 ★Statement of Workの略　　technical specs 技術仕様書 ★specsはspecificationsの略
❶ user's manual 使用者向け説明書　　humidifier 加湿器
Attached you will find 〜　　〜を添付します ★Eメール文でよく使われる表現　　slide deck スライド一式
background material 参考資料、背景説明資料　　highlight 〜を強調する、〜を目立たせる　　main 主要な、主な
change 変更、変更点　　incorporate 〜 into … 〜を…に組み入れる　　❷ get back to 〜 〜に返信する、〜に改めて連絡する
estimate 見積もり、概算　　task 仕事、作業　　take 〜(時間)がかかる　　discuss 〜について話し合う
make 〜 … 〜を…にする　　priority 優先事項

Questions 147-148 refer to the following coupon.

Clipper Happy

❶ **Receive $5 off any haircut.**

❷ For first-time customers only.

❸ May not be combined with any other offer.

❹ Valid until April 5 at our Bonnieville location only.

問題 147-148 は次のクーポンに関するものです。

Clipper Happy

どんなヘアカットでも 5 ドルの割引をお受けになれます。

初めてのお客さま限定。

他の割引との併用不可。

ボニービル店限定、4 月 5 日まで有効。

Words & Phrases

coupon　クーポン　　clipper　切る道具、切る人　　❶ receive　〜を受ける　　off　〜から割引して　　haircut　ヘアカット
❷ first-time　初めての　　customer　顧客　　❸ offer　割引、サービス　　❹ valid　有効な　　location　店舗、所在地

147 At what type of business can the coupon be used?

(A) At a hardware store
(B) At a barbershop
(C) At a restaurant
(D) At a gift shop

クーポンはどのような店で使用可能ですか。

(A) 工具店
(B) 理髪店
(C) レストラン
(D) 土産物店

> 正解 **B** 見出しにClipper Happyとあり、❶にReceive $5 off any haircut.「どんなヘアカットでも5ドルの割引を受けられる」と割引の内容が示されていることから、このクーポンは、Clipper Happyという名の理髪店で使用可能だと分かる。(B)が正解。business「店」。barbershop「理髪店」。
> (A) hardware「(刃物、家庭用金物などの)金属製品」。
> (D) gift shop「土産物店、ギフトショップ」。

---

148 What is true about the coupon?

(A) It is only for new customers.
(B) It can be used with other offers.
(C) It can be used at any location.
(D) It is valid until the end of April.

クーポンについて何が正しいですか。

(A) それは新規顧客のみを対象としている。
(B) それは他の割引と併用可能である。
(C) それはどの店舗でも使用可能である。
(D) それは4月末まで有効である。

> 正解 **A** ❷にFor first-time customers only.「初めての客限定」とクーポンの対象者が記されている。first-time customersをnew customersと表している(A)が正解。true「正しい、真実の」。
> (B) ❸より、他の割引との併用は不可。
> (C) ❹に、ボニービル店のみで有効とあり、他の店舗での使用は不可。
> (D) ❹に、有効期限は4月5日までとある。

Expressions

combine ～ with … 「～を…と組み合わせる」(❸)

Ken Garcia's music combines jazz with classical music.
Ken Garciaの音楽は、ジャズとクラシック音楽を組み合わせたものです。

Questions 149-151 refer to the following invitation.

You are invited to our 50th anniversary celebration.

Harlingen Children's Museum
1321 Danforth Street

Saturday, May 11
8:00 P.M. to 11:00 P.M.

❶ Join us at the Harlingen Children's Museum for a special night of recognition and entertainment as we celebrate a half century of providing stimulating educational experiences for area children and their families. The gala will feature a buffet dinner catered by Café Lyon, a performance by local jazz group Nick and the Exchange, and a video tribute to our many staff members and volunteers.

❷ We are also proud to present renowned author Diana Canul as our keynote speaker. A teacher and longtime supporter of educational causes, Ms. Canul has published over two dozen children's books. Signed copies of her latest release, *Cat Tails*, will be available for purchase in the main lobby.

問題149-151は次の招待状に関するものです。

当館の50周年祝賀会にご招待いたします。
Harlingen 子ども博物館
ダンフォース通り1321番地

5月11日、土曜日
午後8時から午後11時まで

当Harlingen子ども博物館で、半世紀にわたって地域の子どもたちとそのご家族に刺激的でためになる体験をご提供してきたことを記念する、表彰とエンターテインメントの特別な一夜にご参加ください。祝賀会は、Café Lyon提供のビュッフェ形式の夕食、地元のジャズグループNick and the Exchangeによる演奏、多数の職員とボランティアの方々にささげる動画を目玉とする予定です。

また、高名な作家Diana Canulを基調講演者としてご紹介できることを光栄に思います。教員であり、教育運動の長年の支援者でもあるCanulさんは、これまでに児童書を25冊以上、出版しています。彼女の最新作である『猫のしっぽ』のサイン本は、メインロビーにてご購入いただけます。

Words & Phrases

invitation　招待状　　invite ~ to …　~を…に招待する　　anniversary　記念日、記念行事　　celebration　祝賀会
museum　博物館　❶ join　~に加わる　　recognition　表彰　　entertainment　エンターテインメント、娯楽
celebrate　~を記念する、~を祝う　　century　100年間　　provide ~ for …　…に~を提供する　　stimulating　刺激的な
educational　教育的な、有益な　　experience　体験　　area　地域　　gala　祝賀会、特別な催し　　feature　~を目玉とする
buffet　ビュッフェ、セルフサービス式の食事　　cater　~(料理)を提供する　　performance　演奏　　local　地元の
tribute　ささげ物、賛辞　　volunteer　ボランティア　❷ present　~を正式に紹介する　　renowned　高名な　　author　作家
keynote speaker　基調講演者　　longtime　長年の　　supporter　支援者　　cause　運動、大義　　publish　~を出版する
dozen　1ダースの、10余りの　　sign　~に署名する　　copy　1冊　　latest　最新の　　release　新刊本
available　利用可能な　　purchase　購入　　main　主要な　　lobby　ロビー、玄関ホール

Expressions

be proud to *do* 「~することを光栄に思う、~できてうれしく思う」(❷1行目)
I am proud to announce that our cosmetics company received the Company of the Year Award.
私たちの化粧品会社が年間最優秀企業賞を受賞したことを喜んでお知らせします。

149 What type of event is being promoted?

(A) An industry conference
(B) A restaurant opening
(C) A museum anniversary
(D) An awards ceremony

どのようなイベントが告知されていますか。

(A) 業界の協議会
(B) レストランの開店イベント
(C) 博物館の記念行事
(D) 授賞式

正解 C 見出しの一番上にYou are invited to our 50th anniversary celebration.「当館の50周年祝賀会に招待する」とあり、そのすぐ下にHarlingen Children's Museum「Harlingen子ども博物館」と記載されている。また、❶1～3行目で、「当Harlingen子ども博物館で、半世紀にわたって地域の子どもたちとその家族に刺激的でためになる体験を提供してきたことを記念する、表彰とエンターテインメントの特別な一夜に参加してください」と告知されているので、博物館の50周年記念行事への招待状だと分かる。(C)が正解。promote「～を宣伝する」。
(A) industry「業界、産業」、conference「協議会、会議」。
(B) opening「開店祝い」。
(D) 見出しと❶1～3行目より、イベントの目的は博物館の50年間の功績をたたえることであり、賞を授与することではない。award「賞」、ceremony「式典」。

150 What will NOT be featured at the event?

(A) A video presentation
(B) A musical performance
(C) A speech
(D) A contest

イベントの目玉とされていないものは何ですか。

(A) 動画上映
(B) 演奏
(C) 講演
(D) コンテスト

正解 D ❶3～6行目で祝賀会の目玉3つをA, B, and Cの形で列挙している。そこには、a performance by local jazz group「地元のジャズグループによる演奏」と、a video tribute to our many staff members and volunteers「多数の職員とボランティアの人々にささげる動画」とあるので、(A)の動画上映と(B)の演奏はどちらも目玉。また、❷1～2行目で、We are also proud to present renowned author Diana Canul as our keynote speaker.「また、高名な作家Diana Canulを基調講演者として紹介できることを光栄に思う」と述べられているので、(C)の講演も目玉だと分かる。(D)のコンテストには言及がないので、(D)が正解。contest「コンテスト、競技会」。
(A) presentation「上映、発表」。(B) musical performance「演奏」。

151 What is indicated about Ms. Canul?

(A) She will be donating some books to the museum.
(B) She will receive an award for her achievements.
(C) She cares greatly about educational matters.
(D) She is a regular customer of Café Lyon.

Canulさんについて何が示されていますか。

(A) 彼女は博物館に本を寄贈することになっている。
(B) 彼女はその功績に対して賞を受賞する予定である。
(C) 彼女は教育問題に非常に関心がある。
(D) 彼女はCafé Lyonの常連客である。

正解 C 祝賀会の基調講演者のDiana Canulさんについては、❷2～3行目にA teacher and longtime supporter of educational causes, Ms. Canul has published over two dozen children's books.「教員であり、教育運動の長年の支援者でもあるCanulさんは、これまでに児童書を25冊以上、出版している」と紹介がある。よって、Canulさんは教育問題への関心が非常に高いと判断できるので、(C)が正解。care about ～「～に関心がある」、greatly「非常に」、matter「問題、事柄」。
(A) donate「～を寄付する」。
(B) achievement「功績」。
(D) Café Lyonについては、❶3～6行目で祝賀会当日に食事を提供する店として挙げられているのみで、Canulさんが常連客という言及はない。regular customer「常連客」。

Questions 152-153 refer to the following e-mail.

To:	Multiple recipients <stafflist1@gollandhotel.bm>
From:	Trey Roban <troban@gollandhotel.bm>
Date:	17 February
Subject:	Staff update

Good morning,

① As you may know, the convention of the Bermuda Biotechnology Society will take place next month at the Fenwith Hotel. I have learned that all rooms there have now been booked for the duration of the event. Fortunately, because our renovation has now been completed, we can take on the overflow. In fact, conference attendees are already making reservations with us. Consequently, employees in housekeeping, maintenance, and food service should be prepared to work additional shifts. We may also need extra staff at the front desk. Please let me know immediately if you will be unable to work at any time between 2 and 7 March.

Thank you,

Trey Roban
Manager, Golland Hotel

問題152-153は次のEメールに関するものです。

受信者：複数の受信者 <stafflist1@gollandhotel.bm>
送信者：Trey Roban <troban@gollandhotel.bm>
日付：2月17日
件名：従業員への最新情報

おはようございます。

ご存じかもしれませんが、Bermuda生物工学会の協議会が来月Fenwithホテルで開催されます。この催しの期間中について、同ホテルは全室がすでに予約済みであると聞き及んでいます。幸運なことに、当ホテルの改修はもう完了しているので、そのあふれた宿泊客を受け入れることができます。実際、協議会参加者がすでに当ホテルに予約を入れてきています。従って、清掃部門、保守管理部門、料飲部門の従業員は追加のシフト勤務に備える必要があります。フロントにも増員が必要かもしれません。3月2日から7日の間のいずれかの時間帯に勤務することができない場合、すぐに私に知らせてください。

よろしくお願いします。

Trey Roban
Gollandホテル支配人

Words & Phrases

multiple 多数の　　recipient 受取人　　update 最新情報　　**①** convention 協議会、代表者会議
biotechnology 生物工学、バイオテクノロジー　　society （共通の目的や関心などによる）会、協会　　take place 開催される
book ～を予約する　　event 催し、イベント　　fortunately 幸運なことに　　renovation 改修　　complete ～を完了する
take on ～ ～（人）を迎え入れる、～を引き受ける　　overflow あふれ出るもの、過剰　　in fact 実際
conference 協議会、会議　　attendee 参加者　　make a reservation 予約をする　　consequently 従って、その結果
employee 従業員　　housekeeping （ホテルの）清掃部門　　maintenance 保守管理　　food service 料飲部門
be prepared to do ～する用意ができている　　additional 追加の　　shift シフト、交替勤務時間　　extra 臨時の、追加の
front desk （ホテルの）フロント、受付　　immediately すぐに、即座に　　be unable to do ～することができない
manager 支配人、マネージャー

152 What is a purpose of the e-mail?

    (A) To introduce a new staff member
    (B) To confirm a room reservation
    (C) To explain the need for additional help
    (D) To provide updates on the hotel's expansion

Eメールの一つの目的は何ですか。

    (A) 新しい従業員を紹介すること
    (B) 部屋の予約を確認すること
    (C) 追加の助力の必要性を説明すること
    (D) ホテルの拡張に関する最新情報を提供すること

正解 C このEメールは❶の最下行の送信者の肩書から、Gollandホテル支配人であるRobanさんからのものと分かる。Robanさんは、同1～5行目で、協議会の期間中、会場となる別のホテルがすでに予約で満室のため、協議会の参加者からの予約がGollandホテルに入っている現状を伝えている。そして、続く同5～6行目で、Consequently, employees ...... should be prepared to work additional shifts. 「従って、従業員は追加のシフト勤務に備える必要がある」と述べている。よって、Eメールの一つの目的は、追加勤務の必要性を従業員に説明することだと判断できるので、(C)が正解。
(A) introduce「～を紹介する」。
(B) confirm「～を確認する」。
(D) ❶3～4行目で、自分たちのホテルの改修完了に言及があるが、Robanさんはそれを宿泊客の受け入れが可能な理由として述べているのであって、改修の最新情報を伝えることが目的ではない。provide「～を提供する」、expansion「拡張」。

---

153 What is indicated about the Fenwith Hotel?

    (A) It will not be open for a week in March.
    (B) It will hold a professional gathering.
    (C) It is due to be renovated.
    (D) It is interviewing potential employees.

Fenwithホテルについて何が示されていますか。

    (A) 3月中に1週間、営業しない予定である。
    (B) 専門家の集まりを開催する予定である。
    (C) 改修されることになっている。
    (D) 従業員候補者と面接を実施することになっている。

正解 B ❶1～2行目に、the convention of the Bermuda Biotechnology Society will take place next month at the Fenwith Hotel「Bermuda生物工学会の協議会が来月Fenwithホテルで開催される」とあるので、その協議会をa professional gatheringと表している(B)が正解。hold「～を開催する」、professional「専門家の」、gathering「集まり」。
(A) ❶7～8行目に、3月中の特定の期間への言及があるが、Gollandホテル支配人のRobanさんが従業員に対し、勤務の都合がつかない時間帯があれば知らせるように伝えている期間。
(C) ❶3～4行目から、Gollandホテルの改修は完了していると分かるが、Fenwithホテルの改修予定には言及がない。be due to do「～することになっている」、renovate「～を改修する」。
(D) ❶6～7行目に、Gollandホテルのフロントでの増員に言及はあるが、Fenwithホテルでの面接の実施には触れていない。interview「～と面接をする」、potential「潜在的な、可能性のある」。

Expressions

for the duration of ～ 「～の間ずっと」(❶3行目)

Please turn off your mobile devices for the duration of the movie.
映画上映中は携帯機器の電源をお切りください。

Questions 154-155 refer to the following text-message chain.

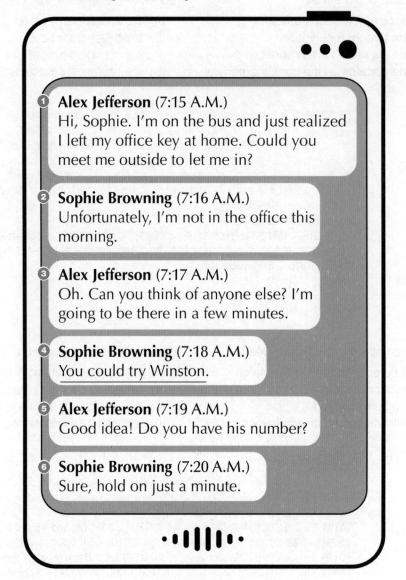

① **Alex Jefferson** (7:15 A.M.)
Hi, Sophie. I'm on the bus and just realized I left my office key at home. Could you meet me outside to let me in?

② **Sophie Browning** (7:16 A.M.)
Unfortunately, I'm not in the office this morning.

③ **Alex Jefferson** (7:17 A.M.)
Oh. Can you think of anyone else? I'm going to be there in a few minutes.

④ **Sophie Browning** (7:18 A.M.)
You could try Winston.

⑤ **Alex Jefferson** (7:19 A.M.)
Good idea! Do you have his number?

⑥ **Sophie Browning** (7:20 A.M.)
Sure, hold on just a minute.

問題154-155は次のテキストメッセージのやりとりに関するものです。

Alex Jefferson (午前7時15分)	こんにちは、Sophie。僕はバスに乗車中で、オフィスの鍵を家に置き忘れたことにたった今気が付いたんです。外で僕と待ち合わせて中に入れてもらえますか。
Sophie Browning (午前7時16分)	あいにく、私は今朝はオフィスにいないのです。
Alex Jefferson (午前7時17分)	ああ。他に誰か思い付きますか。あと数分で着きそうなんです。
Sophie Browning (午前7時18分)	Winstonに当たってみるといいかもしれないですよ。
Alex Jefferson (午前7時19分)	名案です！彼の番号は分かりますか。
Sophie Browning (午前7時20分)	はい、そのままちょっと待っていてください。

154 What does Mr. Jefferson ask for help with?

    (A) Finishing a project
    (B) Getting into a building
    (C) Traveling to a meeting
    (D) Understanding a bus schedule

Jeffersonさんは何に関する手助けを求めていますか。

    (A) プロジェクトを仕上げること
    (B) 建物に入ること
    (C) 会議に行くこと
    (D) バスの時刻表を把握すること

> **正解 B** Jeffersonさんは❶で、オフィスの鍵を家に置き忘れたことに気が付いたと伝えた後、Could you meet me outside to let me in?「外で僕と待ち合わせて中に入れてもらえるか」とBrowningさんに手助けを求めている。よって、(B)が正解。ask for ～「～を求める」。get into ～「～の中へ入る」。
> (A) finish「～を仕上げる」、project「プロジェクト、計画」。
> (C) travel to ～「～へ行く」。
> (D) ❶で、Jeffersonさんはバスに乗車中だと伝えているが、schedule「時刻表」には言及していない。

155 At 7:18 A.M., what does Ms. Browning most likely mean when she writes, "You could try Winston"?

    (A) A coworker might be in the office.
    (B) A coworker might give him a ride.
    (C) A coworker could make a phone call.
    (D) A coworker could give a presentation.

午前7時18分に、Browningさんは "You could try Winston" という発言で、何を意味していると考えられますか。

    (A) 同僚がオフィスにいるかもしれない。
    (B) 同僚が彼を車に乗せてくれるかもしれない。
    (C) 同僚が電話をかけられるかもしれない。
    (D) 同僚がプレゼンテーションができるかもしれない。

> **正解 A** Jeffersonさんは外で待ち合わせをしてオフィスの中に入れてくれるよう頼んでいるが、Browningさんは❷で、自分が今朝オフィスにいないことを伝えている。それに対し、Jeffersonさんは❸で、Can you think of anyone else?「他に誰か思い付くか」と尋ねており、下線部の発言はそれに応答するもの。続く❺では、JeffersonさんはWinstonさんという人物の電話番号をBrowningさんに尋ねているので、Browningさんは下線部の発言で、Winstonさんならオフィスにいる可能性があるため、代わりにWinstonさんに頼んでみることを提案していると判断できる。よって、(A)が正解。選択肢は、2人と同じオフィスで働くWinstonさんのことをa coworker「同僚」と表している。
> (B) give ～ a ride「～を車に乗せる」。
> (C) ❺・❻より、Winstonさんから電話があるのではなく、JeffersonさんがWinstonさんに電話をかけると考えられる。make a phone call「電話をする」。
> (D) give a presentation「プレゼンテーションをする」。

Words & Phrases

❶ on the bus　バスに乗車中で　　realize (that) ～　～ということに気が付く　　leave　～を置き忘れる　　office key　オフィスの鍵　at home　家に　　outside　外で　　let ～ in　～を中に入れる　❷ unfortunately　あいにく、残念ながら　❸ else　他に　in a few minutes　数分後に、すぐに　❹ try　～に当たってみる、～を試す　❺ number　(電話などの)番号　❻ hold on　待つ、電話を切らずにおく　　just a minute　ちょっと待って

Expressions

think of ～　「～を思い付く、～を考え出す」(❸)

Can you think of any ideas for a short promotional video that appeals to the younger generation?
あなたは、若い世代の心に訴える短い宣伝用動画のアイデアを何か考えることができますか。

Questions 156-157 refer to the following e-mail.

E-mail

To:	Lynn Simmel
From:	Art Moody
Subject:	Repaving
Date:	30 March

Dear Ms. Simmel:

❶ I want to check if your company would be able to resurface the asphalt driveway that leads to the corporate headquarters of my company. I was impressed with the work that People's Pavers did on the streets around Rob's Marketplace in downtown Somerville. Our driveway is located on Sycamore Boulevard, the public road that you will soon be repaving during the next phase of your work for the city of Somerville. Our driveway is two lanes wide and just about 400 metres in length. I wonder if you might consider reducing your pricing somewhat since this work would be in such a convenient location.

❷ I look forward to hearing from you.

Sincerely,

Art Moody
Tayco Pharmaceuticals

問題156-157は次のEメールに関するものです。

受信者：Lynn Simmel
送信者：Art Moody
件名：再舗装
日付：3月30日

Simmel様

貴社に、弊社の本社ビルに通じるアスファルトの私道を再舗装していただけないかご相談したいと考えています。私は、People's Pavers社が担当されたサマービル市中心部のRob'sショッピングセンター周辺の街路のお仕事ぶりに感銘を受けました。弊社の私道は、貴社がサマービル市向け工事の次の段階で間もなく再舗装を行う公道、シカモア大通りに接しています。弊社私道は2車線の道路幅で、長さは400メートルほどです。この作業は非常に便利な場所で行われるので、幾らか代金の値下げをご検討いただけないだろうかと思っております。

ご連絡を心待ちにしております。

敬具

Art Moody
Tayco製薬会社

156 What is the purpose of the e-mail?

    (A) To accept a cost estimate
    (B) To announce some rate changes
    (C) To request some measurements
    (D) To propose a possible job

Eメールの目的は何ですか。

    (A) 費用見積りを受諾すること
    (B) 規定料金の変更を知らせること
    (C) 測量を依頼すること
    (D) 可能性のある仕事を打診すること

正解 D　Eメールの送信者のMoodyさんは❶1～2行目で、「あなたの会社に、弊社の本社ビルに通じるアスファルトの私道を再舗装してもらえないか相談したい」と受信者のSimmelさんに依頼している。さらに同2～3行目で、People's Pavers社が過去に担当した仕事に感銘を受けた、と仕事の打診の理由を伝えている。よって、(D)が正解。propose「～を提案する」、possible「可能性のある、見込みのある」。
(A) accept「～を受諾する」、cost「費用」、estimate「見積もり」。
(B) announce「～を知らせる」、rate「規定料金」。
(C) ❶1～2行目より、Moodyさんが依頼している作業は私道の再舗装であって、測量ではない。request「～を依頼する」、measurement「測量」。

---

157 Where does Ms. Simmel work?

    (A) At People's Pavers
    (B) At Rob's Marketplace
    (C) At Somerville City Hall
    (D) At Tayco Pharmaceuticals

Simmelさんはどこで働いていますか。

    (A) People's Pavers社
    (B) Rob'sショッピングセンター
    (C) サマービル市役所
    (D) Tayco製薬会社

正解 A　Moodyさんは❶1～2行目で、私道の再舗装工事をSimmelさんの会社に依頼し、続く同2～3行目で、I was impressed with the work that People's Pavers did on the streets around Rob's Marketplace in downtown Somerville.「私は、People's Pavers社が担当したサマービル市中心部のRob'sショッピングセンター周辺の街路の仕事ぶりに感銘を受けた」とPeople's Pavers社による作業を称賛している。このことから、People's Pavers社とは道路の舗装関連作業を行う会社であり、SimmelさんはPeople's Pavers社に勤務していると判断できる。
(B) ❶2～3行目より、People's Pavers社が作業を行った場所。
(C) city hall「市役所」。
(D) Eメール末尾の署名欄より、Moodyさんの勤め先。

Words & Phrases

repave　～を再舗装する　❶ check if ～　～かどうか確かめる　be able to *do*　～することができる
resurface　～を再舗装する　asphalt　アスファルト　driveway　私道　★公道から建物などに通じる車道
lead to ～　(道などが)～に通じる　corporate　会社の　headquarters　本社、本部
be impressed with ～　～に感銘を受ける　work　工事、作業　paver　舗装工、舗装機械　marketplace　市場、広場
downtown　中心部の　be located　位置している　～ Boulevard　～大通り　★道路名　public road　公道
phase　段階　lane　車線　～ wide　幅が～の　just about　だいたい、ほぼ　metre　メートル　★米国表記はmeter
～ in length　長さ～の　I wonder if ～　～していただけないでしょうか　★丁寧な依頼などを表す　reduce　～を減らす
pricing　価格設定　somewhat　幾分　convenient　好都合な　location　場所
❷ look forward to *doing*　～することを心待ちにする　pharmaceuticals　製薬会社

Expressions

consider *doing*　「～することを検討する」(❶6～7行目)
I am considering running a small business in downtown Hakata.
私は、博多中心部で小さな店を経営することを検討しています。

Questions 158-160 refer to the following memo.

MEMO

To: All employees at Manoukian Accounting
From: Jared Croce, Office Manager
Date: September 28
Subject: Update

❶ We are now in the process of updating employee work spaces. — [1] —. All of the fixed-height desks and chairs will be replaced with adjustable-height standing desks and active-position chairs.

❷ The new work configurations will allow employees to switch easily from sitting to standing and then back again. — [2] —. Everyone will also receive new energy-efficient desk lamps. — [3] —. Officewide use of these new lamps will allow us to reduce our reliance on overhead ceiling lights, lowering overall energy costs by 10 percent. — [4] —.

問題158-160は次のメモに関するものです。

メモ

宛先：Manoukian会計事務所員各位
差出人：Jared Croce、総務責任者
日付：9月28日
件名：最新情報

現在、従業員の作業スペースを刷新中です。高さが固定された机と椅子は全て、高さ調節可能なスタンディングデスクおよびアクティブポジションチェアと交換されます。

この新しい職場環境により、従業員の皆さんは座って立ち上がってまた座るという切り替えが楽にできるようになります。*この柔軟性は、従業員の皆さんが終日、より活動的な状態でいるのに役立つでしょう。また、皆さん全員にエネルギー効率の優れた新しい卓上電気スタンドが支給されます。この新しい電気スタンドをオフィス全体で使用することで、当社は頭上の天井照明への依存度を減らし、光熱費全体を10パーセント下げることが可能になります。

*問題160の挿入文の訳

Words & Phrases

employee 従業員　accounting 会計　update 〈名詞で〉最新情報、〈動詞で〉〜を最新のものにする
❶ space スペース、場所　fixed-height 高さが固定された　replace 〜 with … 〜を…と交換する
adjustable-height 高さ調節可能な　standing desk スタンディングデスク ★立ったまま作業可能な机
active-position chair アクティブポジションチェア ★その時々に合わせて姿勢を保てる設計の可変式の椅子
❷ configuration 状況、(各部分の)配置　allow 〜 to do 〜が…するのを可能にする、〜に…するのを許可する
switch from 〜 to … 〜から…へ切り替える　easily 楽に、容易に　energy-efficient エネルギー効率の優れた
lamp 電気スタンド　officewide オフィス全体の　use 使用　reduce 〜を減らす　reliance 依存
overhead 頭上の　ceiling 天井　light 照明　lower 〜を下げる　overall 全体の　energy costs 光熱費

70

158 Why was the memo issued to employees?

(A) To ask them to complete a survey
(B) To alert them to changes in work schedules
(C) To inform them about new office furniture
(D) To provide them with details of changes in management

メモはなぜ従業員に出されたのですか。

(A) 彼らに調査票への記入を依頼するため
(B) 彼らに仕事の予定変更に対する注意喚起をするため
(C) 彼らに新しいオフィス家具について知らせるため
(D) 彼らに経営陣の交替についての詳細情報を提供するため

正解 C ❶1行目で、従業員の作業スペースを刷新中だと述べており、続く同1〜3行目では、高さ調節可能な机と椅子への交換予定を伝えている。❷では、交換によるメリットおよび新しい卓上電気スタンドの支給について説明しているので、このメモは、従業員に新しいオフィス家具について知らせるためのものだと分かる。新しい机、椅子、電気スタンドをnew office furnitureと表している(C)が正解。issue「〜を出す、〜を発行する」。inform 〜 about … 「〜に…について知らせる」、furniture「家具」。
(A) complete「〜に全て記入する」、survey「調査票、調査」。
(B) alert 〜 to … 「〜に…に対して注意喚起する」。
(D) provide 〜 with … 「〜に…を提供する」、details「詳細情報」、management「経営陣」。

159 According to the memo, how is Manoukian Accounting planning to save money?

(A) By installing a new heating system
(B) By making less use of ceiling lights
(C) By switching to a low-cost energy supplier
(D) By allowing employees to work from home

メモによると、Manoukian会計事務所はどのようにして経費を節約する計画ですか。

(A) 新しい暖房装置を設置することによって
(B) 天井照明の使用を減らすことによって
(C) 低コストのエネルギー供給業者に切り替えることによって
(D) 従業員に在宅勤務を許可することによって

正解 B ❷3〜5行目に、Manoukian会計事務所の全従業員が受け取る卓上電気スタンドについて、Officewide use of these new lamps will allow us to reduce our reliance on overhead ceiling lights, lowering overall energy costs by 10 percent.「この新しい電気スタンドをオフィス全体で使用することで、当社は頭上の天井照明への依存度を減らし、光熱費全体を10パーセント下げることが可能になる」とある。よって、同事務所は天井照明の使用を削減することで光熱費を節約しようとしていると分かるので、(B)が正解。plan to do「〜することを計画する」、save「〜を節約する」。make use of 〜「〜を使う」。
(A) install「〜を設置する」、heating「暖房」、system「装置」。
(C) low-cost「低コストの」、supplier「供給業者」。
(D) work from home「在宅勤務をする」。

160 In which of the positions marked [1], [2], [3], and [4] does the following sentence best belong?

"This flexibility will help employees to remain more active throughout the day."

(A) [1]   (C) [3]
(B) [2]   (D) [4]

[1]、[2]、[3]、[4]と記載された箇所のうち、次の文が入るのに最もふさわしいのはどれですか。

「この柔軟性は、従業員の皆さんが終日、より活動的な状態でいるのに役立つでしょう」

正解 B 挿入文では、This flexibility「この柔軟性」のメリットについて説明されている。❶1〜3行目では、オフィス内の机と椅子を高機能なものに交換すると述べられ、続く❷1〜2行目では、The new work configurations will allow employees to switch easily from sitting to standing and then back again.「この新しい職場環境により、従業員の皆さんは座って立ち上がってまた座るという切り替えが楽にできるようになる」と説明されている。この直後の(B)[2]に挿入文を入れると、This flexibilityが着席・起立動作の切り替えが容易になる柔軟性を指し、前文の補足説明になる。flexibility「柔軟性」、help 〜 to do「〜が…するのに役立つ」、remain「〜のままである」、active「活動的な」、throughout the day「終日」。

Expressions

in the process of 〜 「〜の最中で」(❶1行目)

Jeff's Bistro is currently in the process of being renovated.
Jeff'sビストロは現在、改装中です。

Questions 161-163 refer to the following e-mail.

E-mail

To:	All Staff
From:	Jason Saylor
Subject:	Company envelopes
Date:	April 12

Dear Team,

❶ Unfortunately, we have run out of Leewood Associates printed envelopes. Until the next batch arrives with our regular office supply order on April 15, please use Leewood Associates return-address labels for any outgoing mail. For brochures about new home listings or our professional property management services, there is no need to include any return address as our current contact information is already printed on all of our promotional materials.

❷ When using return-address labels, please remember to check them carefully since we moved offices only two months ago and some of them still include our former address.

All the best,

Jason Saylor
Executive Assistant

問題161-163は次のEメールに関するものです。

受信者：従業員各位
送信者：Jason Saylor
件名：社用封筒
日付：4月12日

皆さん

あいにく、Leewood Associatesの社名が印字された封筒を切らしています。オフィス用品の定期注文で4月15日に次回分が届くまで、社外宛ての全郵便物には、Leewood Associatesの差出人住所ラベルを使用してください。新規住宅物件一覧や当社の不動産管理専門業務に関するパンフレットについては、販促資料の全てにすでに当社の最新の連絡先情報が印字されているため、差出人住所を入れる必要はありません。

差出人住所ラベルを使用する際は、それらを入念に確認するようにしてください、というのも、当社はつい2カ月前にオフィスを移転したばかりで、一部のラベルにはまだ以前の住所が載っているからです。

よろしくお願いします。

Jason Saylor
役員補佐

Words & Phrases

envelope 封筒　❶ unfortunately あいにく、残念ながら　associate 共同経営者、同僚　batch （封筒などの）1束、1度分　arrive 到着する　regular 定期的な　office supply オフィス用品　return-address 差出人住所の、返信用宛名の　label ラベル　outgoing 発信用の、出て行く　mail 郵便物　brochure パンフレット　listing 一覧表　professional 専門の　property management 不動産管理　service 業務　include ～を含める　current 最新の、現在の　contact information 連絡先情報　promotional 販売促進用の　material 資料　❷ remember to do 忘れずに～する　carefully 入念に　move ～を移転する　former 以前の　all the best よろしく　★親しい人へのEメールなどの結びの言葉　executive 役員、重役　assistant 補佐

161 According to the e-mail, what will happen on April 15?

   (A) A business will move to a new location.
   (B) A shipment will arrive.
   (C) Mail delivery will be suspended.
   (D) A marketing brochure will be printed.

Eメールによると、4月15日に何が起こりますか。

   (A) 会社が新しい場所に移転する。
   (B) 荷物が届く。
   (C) 郵便配達が一時停止される。
   (D) 販促用パンフレットが印刷される。

> **正解 B** ❶ 1～3行目に、「オフィス用品の定期注文で4月15日に次回分が届くまで、社外宛ての全郵便物には、Leewood Associatesの差出人住所ラベルを使用してください」とある。よって、4月15日には注文したオフィス用品が会社に届くと分かるので、(B)が正解。shipment「荷物、出荷品」。
> (A) business「会社」、location「場所、所在地」。
> (C) delivery「配達」、suspend「～を一時停止する」。
> (D) ❶ 3～6行目にパンフレットや販促資料への言及があるが、販促用パンフレットが印刷されるという記述はない。marketing「販促用の、マーケティングの」。

162 What type of business most likely is Leewood Associates?

   (A) A real estate agency
   (B) A graphic design firm
   (C) A shipping company
   (D) A stationery store

Leewood Associatesはどのような事業者だと考えられますか。

   (A) 不動産業者
   (B) グラフィックデザイン事務所
   (C) 運送会社
   (D) 文房具店

> **正解 A** Eメールの送信者であるSaylorさんは、全従業員宛てのEメールの❶ 1～3行目で、社外宛て郵便物にはLeewood Associatesの差出人住所ラベルを使用するよう伝えた後、同3～6行目で、For brochures about new home listings or our professional property management services, there is no need to include any return address「新規住宅物件一覧や当社の不動産管理専門業務に関するパンフレットについては、差出人住所を入れる必要はない」と述べている。よって、Leewood Associatesは不動産業者だと考えられる。real estate agency「不動産業者」。
> (B) graphic design「グラフィックデザイン」、firm「事務所、会社」。
> (C) shipping「運送」。
> (D) stationery「文房具」。

163 What is the problem with some return-address labels?

   (A) They are too small.
   (B) They have an error in the company name.
   (C) They have the wrong address.
   (D) They feature the company's old logo.

一部の差出人住所ラベルにはどのような問題がありますか。

   (A) 小さ過ぎる。
   (B) 会社名が間違っている。
   (C) 間違った住所が書かれている。
   (D) 会社の古いロゴが使われている。

> **正解 C** Saylorさんは❷ 1～2行目で、When using return-address labels, please remember to check them carefully「差出人住所ラベルを使用する際は、それらを入念に確認するようにしてください」とラベルの確認を促し、続けてその理由を since we moved offices only two months ago and some of them still include our former address「当社はつい2カ月前にオフィスを移転したばかりで、一部のラベルにはまだ以前の住所が載っているから」と述べている。つまり、差出人住所ラベルの中には移転前の住所を記載したものがあると分かるので、(C)が正解。
> (B) error「間違い」。
> (D) feature「～を特色とする」。

Expressions

run out of ~ 「～を切らす」（❶ 1行目）
I heard that Pinnacle's Drugstore has run out of toilet paper.
Pinnacle's薬局はトイレットペーパーの在庫を切らしていると聞きました。

Questions 164-167 refer to the following article.

Glasgow Daily News

News About Town
By Alison Breen

❶ GLASGOW (25 April)—It is taking some time, experimentation, and adjustment, but the robot Angus is here to stay. Angus began his stint at Bread and Greens grocery store on Peterson Street in March.

❷ While Angus is the most advanced robot produced by Cushman Robotics, his adaptation to store life has not gone completely smoothly. For example, during his first days on the job, Angus began quoting to patrons product prices that were largely inaccurate. But this turned out not to be a defect in Angus—someone had accidentally loaded an outdated price list into his memory.

❸ Some customers have enjoyed trying to interact with Angus despite his currently limited abilities. Arif Nothazai is urging both staff and patrons to allow Angus a chance to adjust and learn. Mr. Nothazai explained, "Every new employee needs a training period. I myself have only been here in my supervisory role for less than a year. I needed time to gain familiarity with my new environment. It is the same with Angus."

❹ At the store's bakery reopening last week, Angus told jokes and bantered with customers while offering them samples of fresh-baked goods. Store clerk Andrea Cronin remarked, "Angus has his quirks, but he keeps everyone laughing. He is definitely a valued member of our team."

問題164-167は次の記事に関するものです。

グラスゴー・デイリーニュース
町のニュース
Alison Breen 記

グラスゴー(4月25日)——まだ時間、実験、そして調整が必要だが、ロボットのAngusは町に定着している。Angusは3月に、ピーターソン通りのBread and Greens食料雑貨店で勤務を開始した。

Angusは Cushman Robotics社で製造されている最も先進的なロボットだが、店の生活への適応は順風満帆にはいっていない。例えば勤務開始当初、Angusは製品価格を常連客に伝え始めたが、その大部分が不正確だった。しかし、これは結局、Angusの欠陥ではないことが明らかとなった——誰かが誤って古い価格表を彼のメモリに読み込んでいたのだ。

彼の現在の限られた能力にもかかわらず、Angusとの交流の試みを楽しんでいる顧客もいる。Arif Nothazaiは従業員にも常連客にも、適応と学習の機会をAngusに与えるよう強く訴えている。「どんな新しい従業員も研修期間が必要です。私自身、ここで監督職を務めてまだ1年もたっていません。私も自分の新しい環境に慣れるのに時間が必要でした。Angusにとっても、それは同じです」とNothazaiさんは説明した。

先週再開した同店のパン売り場では、Angusは顧客に焼きたての商品の試食品を差し出しながら、冗談を言ったり、彼らと軽口を交わし合ったりした。店員のAndrea Croninは、「Angusには変わっているところもありますが、皆を何度も笑わせてくれます。彼は間違いなく当店チームの大切なメンバーです」と述べた。

Words & Phrases

❶ take ～を必要とする　experimentation 実験　adjustment 調整、適応　here to stay 定着して、普及して　stint 勤め、割り当てられた仕事　grocery store 食料雑貨店　❷ advanced 先進的な　produce ～を製造する　robotics ロボット工学　adaptation 適応　go smoothly 順調に進む　completely 完全に　quote ~ to … …に～(値段)を伝える　patron 常連客　largely 大部分は、主として　inaccurate 不正確な　turn out (to be) ～ 結局～であることが分かる　defect in ～ ～の欠陥　accidentally 誤って　load ~ into … …に～(データなど)を読み込む　outdated (情報が)古くて正しくない　price list 価格表　memory メモリ、記憶装置　❸ try to do ～しようとする　interact with ～ ～と交流する　despite ～にもかかわらず　currently 現在は　limited 限られた　ability 能力　urge ~ to do ～に…するよう強く訴える　allow ~ … ～に…(時間や金)を与える　adjust 適応する　explain ～と説明する　period 期間　supervisory 監督の　role 職務、役割　less than ～ ～未満　gain ～(経験など)を増す、～を獲得する　familiarity よく知っていること　environment 環境　❹ reopen 再開する　joke 冗談　banter with ～ ～と軽口をたたき合う　offer ~ … ～に…を差し出す　sample 試食品　fresh-baked 焼きたての　goods 商品　clerk 店員　remark ～と述べる　quirk 変な癖　definitely 間違いなく　valued 大切な

164 What is the purpose of the article?

(A) To report on local tourism
(B) To discuss a recent change in a store
(C) To outline employee-training techniques
(D) To chronicle the career of a business owner

記事の目的は何ですか。

(A) 地元の観光業について報道すること
(B) 店における最近の変化を考察すること
(C) 従業員研修技術の概要を説明すること
(D) 事業主の経歴を時系列に沿って記録すること

正解 B 4月25日付けの記事の❶1～3行目に、ロボットのAngusが町に定着していることが述べられ、続く同3～5行目に、Angus began his stint at Bread and Greens grocery store on Peterson Street in March.「Angusは3月に、ピーターソン通りのBread and Greens食料雑貨店で勤務を開始した」とある。以降には、Angusおよび同ロボット導入後のBread and Greens食料雑貨店の状況が紹介されているので、(B)が正解。discuss「～を考察する」、recent「最近の」。

(A) report on ～「～について報道する」、local「地元の」、tourism「観光業」。
(C) ❸6～7行目に、新規従業員の研修期間の必要性に言及があるが、その内容や技術については述べられていない。outline「～の概要を説明する」、employee-training「従業員研修の」、technique「専門技術」。
(D) chronicle「～を年代順に記録する」、career「経歴」、business owner「事業主」。

165 What issue with the robot is mentioned?

(A) It has insufficient memory.
(B) It has upset some staff members.
(C) It has given customers outdated information.
(D) It has defective parts that need to be replaced.

ロボットに関するどんな問題が述べられていますか。

(A) メモリが不十分である。
(B) 一部の従業員を困らせたことがある。
(C) 顧客に古い情報を与えたことがある。
(D) 交換の必要がある欠陥部品が搭載されている。

正解 C ロボットのAngusが店の仕事に円滑に適応できなかった例として、❷4～7行目に「勤務開始当初、Angusは製品価格を常連客に伝え始めたが、その大部分が不正確だった」とあり、同8～10行目で、その原因について、someone had accidentally loaded an outdated price list into his

memory「誰かが誤って古い価格表を彼のメモリに読み込んでいた」と説明されている。よって、(C)が正解。issue「問題」。
(A) insufficient「十分でない」。
(B) upset「～を困らせる」。
(D) defective「欠陥のある」、replace「～を交換する」。

166 Who most likely is Mr. Nothazai?

(A) A mechanical engineer
(B) A shop clerk
(C) A baker
(D) A manager

Nothazaiさんとは誰だと考えられますか。

(A) 機械技師
(B) 店員
(C) パン職人
(D) 管理者

正解 D ❸3～5行目で、Arif Nothazaiさんが、Bread and Greens食料雑貨店の従業員と常連客に対して、適応と学習の機会をAngusに与えるよう強く訴えていることが述べられている。そして、Nothazaiさんが語った内容を示している同7～9行目に、I myself have only been here in my supervisory role for less than a year.「私自身、ここで監督職

を務めてまだ1年もたっていない」とあることから、Nothazaiさんとは、Bread and Greens食料雑貨店の店員を監督する立場にある人物だと考えられるので、(D)が正解。manager「管理者、責任者」。
(A) mechanical engineer「機械技師」。
(C) baker「パン職人」。

167 What is suggested about the bakery?

(A) It was closed temporarily.
(B) It will be offering special discounts.
(C) It is hiring more help.
(D) It will soon be selling coffee and tea.

パン売り場について何が分かりますか。

(A) 一時的に閉鎖していた。
(B) 特別割引を提供する予定である。
(C) 追加の従業員を雇用するところである。
(D) 間もなくコーヒーと紅茶を販売する予定である。

正解 A ❹1～4行目に、Bread and Greens食料雑貨店について、At the store's bakery reopening last week「先週再開した同店のパン売り場では」とあるので、店のパン売り場は先週まで一時的に閉鎖していたと判断できる。(A)が正解。

closed「閉鎖して、休業して」、temporarily「一時的に」。
(B) offer「～を提供する」、discount「割引」。
(C) hire「～を雇う」、help「(手助けのために雇用される)従業員」。

Questions 168-171 refer to the following notice.

Grune Plaza Train Station
Customer Notice

① Beginning on Monday, September 30, the Station Enhancement Project will be implemented at the Grune Plaza Train Station. The project is expected to last two months. — [1] —.

② During this time, the Forrest Avenue stairway entrance will be closed while the nearby south side hallway undergoes remodeling to accommodate new shops. Please use the alternate entrance on the School Street side to access the waiting area and platforms. For your safety in and around the station, always obey posted signs and do not walk through prohibited areas. — [2] —.

③ Also, please note that the elevator near the platforms will be shut off after 5:00 P.M. every day for the safety of off-hours construction workers. Passengers requiring an elevator in the evening can use the elevator in the north side hallway, and from there make their way across the indoor bridge to the platforms.

④ We thank you for your patience as we continue to expand and improve our services based on feedback we have received from our passengers. — [3] —. For more information in English or other languages, please call (221) 555-0101 between the hours of 8:00 A.M. and 9:00 P.M. — [4] —. You may also visit www.gruneplaza.com for the latest updates on the Station Enhancement Project.

問題 168-171 は次のお知らせに関するものです。

Grune Plaza 鉄道駅
利用客の皆さまへのお知らせ

9月30日月曜日より、当Grune Plaza鉄道駅では駅舎改良計画が実施されます。本計画は2カ月間続く見通しです。

この期間中、フォレスト大通りの階段入り口は閉鎖され、その近くの南側通路は新店舗を収容できるように改築されます。待合所やプラットホームに行くには、学校通り側にある別の入り口をご利用ください。駅の構内および周辺における皆さまの安全のため、常に掲示標識を守り、立入禁止区域を通らないでください。＊これらの場所は黄色のテープで区切られます。

また、すいている時間帯の工事作業員の安全のため、プラットホーム近くのエレベーターが毎日午後5時以降は停止されることにご注意ください。夜間にエレベーターを必要とする乗客の皆さまは、北側通路のエレベーターを利用し、そこから構内歩道橋を渡ってプラットホームへと進むことができます。

当駅が乗客の皆さまから頂いたご意見に基づいてサービスの拡大と改良を継続するに当たり、皆さまのご理解に感謝いたします。英語または他言語での詳しい情報については午前8時から午後9時の時間帯に、(221)555-0101までお電話ください。また、駅舎改良計画に関する最新情報は www.gruneplaza.com にてご覧いただけます。

＊問題171の挿入文の訳

Words & Phrases

notice お知らせ　plaza ショッピングセンター、広場　❶ enhancement 向上　project 計画
implement ～を実施する　be expected to *do* ～する見通しである　last 続く　❷ ～ Avenue ～大通り
stairway 階段　entrance 入り口　nearby 近くの　south 南　side 側　hallway 通路
undergo ～を受ける、～を経る　remodeling 改築　accommodate ～を収容する　alternate 別の、代わりの
access ～に入る　waiting area 待合所　platform (駅の)プラットホーム　safety 安全性　obey ～を守る、～に従う
post ～を掲示する　sign 標識　walk through ～ ～を通り抜ける　prohibit ～を禁止する
❸ note that ～ ～ということに注意する　shut off ～ ～(機械などの運転)を止める
off-hours すいている時間の、勤務時間外の　construction 工事　passenger 乗客　require ～を必要とする
north 北　make *one's* way to ～ ～へ進む　across ～を渡って　indoor 屋内の　bridge 歩道橋、橋
❹ patience 忍耐　continue to *do* ～し続ける　expand ～を拡大する　improve ～を向上させる
based on ～ ～に基づいて　feedback 意見　language 言語　latest 最新の　update 最新情報

168 What is one goal of the project?

(A) To train employees to monitor platforms
(B) To expand the number of waiting areas
(C) To add digital signs to the station
(D) To prepare for more stores

計画の一つの目標は何ですか。

(A) プラットホームの監視ができるよう従業員を研修すること
(B) 待合所の数を増やすこと
(C) 電子掲示板を駅に増設すること
(D) 店舗増設に備えること

正解 D	見出しと❶1～2行目より、Grune Plaza鉄道駅の利用者向けにthe Station Enhancement Project「駅舎改良計画」の実施を知らせる文書だと分かる。その計画の内容について、❷1～2行目に、「フォレスト大通りの階段入り口は閉鎖され、その近くの南側通路は新店舗を収容できるよう改築される」とあるので、計画の一つの目標は、複数の新たな店舗の増	設だと判断できる。そのことをTo prepare for more storesと表している(D)が正解。goal「目標」。prepare for ～「～に備える」。 (A) train「～を研修する」、monitor「～を監視する」。 (C) add ～ to …「～を…に追加する」。

169 What does the notice suggest about Grune Plaza Train Station?

(A) It has only one entrance.
(B) It has several ways to get to the platforms.
(C) It typically closes at 5:00 P.M.
(D) It was built near a famous bridge.

お知らせは、Grune Plaza鉄道駅について何を示唆していますか。

(A) 同駅は入り口が1つしかない。
(B) 同駅はプラットホームに行き着く方法が幾つかある。
(C) 同駅は通常、午後5時に閉まる。
(D) 同駅は有名な橋の近くに建てられた。

正解 B	❷1～2行目で、Grune Plaza鉄道駅改築中のフォレスト大通りの階段入り口の閉鎖を伝えた後、続く同2～3行目で、「待合所やプラットホームに行くには、学校通り側にある別の入り口を利用してください」と呼び掛けている。また、❸1～2行目で、プラットホーム近くのエレベーターが午後5時以降は停止されると知らせ、続く同2～4行目で、「北側通路	のエレベーターを利用し、そこから構内歩道橋を渡ってプラットホームへと進むことができる」と別の方法を案内しているので、同駅にはプラットホームへ至る方法が複数あることが分かる。(B)が正解。get to ～「～に到達する」。 (C) typically「通常」。

170 According to the notice, who should call the number provided?

(A) People who are interested in customer-service jobs
(B) People who need help accessing the station's Web site
(C) People who want information in a different language
(D) People who want to provide feedback about their experience

お知らせによると、提示された電話番号に電話すべきなのは誰ですか。

(A) 顧客サービスの職に関心のある人々
(B) 駅のウェブサイトにアクセスする上で手助けを必要とする人々
(C) 異なる言語での情報を望む人々
(D) 自分の経験について意見提供することを望む人々

正解 C	❹2～3行目に、「英語または他言語での詳しい情報については、(221)555-0101まで電話してください」とあるので、(C)が正解。provide「～を提示する」。	(D) ❹1～2行目に、乗客の意見に基づくサービス拡充に言及があるが、そのために電話番号を提示しているとは述べていない。experience「経験」。

171 In which of the positions marked [1], [2], [3], and [4] does the following sentence best belong?

"These spaces will be marked off with yellow tape."

(A) [1]   (C) [3]
(B) [2]   (D) [4]

[1]、[2]、[3]、[4]と記載された箇所のうち、次の文が入るのに最もふさわしいのはどれですか。

「これらの場所は黄色のテープで区切られます」

正解 B	挿入文にあるThese spaces「これらの場所」に注目する。❷4～5行目に、For your safety in and around the station, always obey posted signs and do not walk through prohibited areas.「駅の構内および周辺における皆さんの安全のため、常に掲示標識を守り、立入禁止区域を通らないでください」とある。この直後の(B)[2]に挿入文を入れると、挿入文中のThese spacesがprohibited areasを指し、立入禁止区域は黄色のテープで区切られると知らせる内容が続くことになる。space「場所、スペース」、mark off ～「～(場所)を区切る」、tape「テープ」。

Questions 172-175 refer to the following online chat discussion.

Kate Blum (9:17 A.M.)
Good morning, everyone. I just wanted to do a quick check to make certain everything is in place for this Saturday's conference.

Ken Miyashiro (9:18 A.M.)
We're all set. And since the conference is sold out, we are going to broadcast it live over the Internet so that people can watch it on their devices.

Yuri Kang (9:19 A.M.)
Is that completely arranged—camera operators, software, viewer access, and so on?

Ken Miyashiro (9:20 A.M.)
Yes. We've hired everyone, and we have the software, so we should be ready. People who want to watch the conference over the Internet still have to register and pay on our Web site, and then they'll get online access to see Tom Akana's keynote address and all the scheduled conference sessions.

Gabriel Lontoc (9:22 A.M.)
It's wonderful that Tom Akana has agreed to speak. It will be interesting to hear how he created Honalo Coffee Roasters and built it into a profitable company.

Kate Blum (9:23 A.M.)
He is pleased to do it. He thinks it could help others who want to start restaurants or food-related businesses. OK. I think that's it. Let's meet again on Wednesday morning.

問題172-175は次のオンラインチャットの話し合いに関するものです。

Kate Blum（午前9時17分）
おはようございます、皆さん。今度の土曜日の協議会に向けて全て準備が整っているようにするために、手短に確認したいと思いまして。

Ken Miyashiro（午前9時18分）
私たちは準備万端です。それから協議会は完売なので、人々が自分の機器で見られるようにインターネット上で生配信をする予定です。

Yuri Kang（午前9時19分）
それは完全に手配済みですか——撮影スタッフ、ソフトウエア、視聴者の参加方法なども。

Ken Miyashiro（午前9時20分）
はい。私たちは全員を雇いましたし、ソフトウエアも用意してあるので、準備はできているはずです。インターネット上で協議会の視聴を希望する人々は当社ウェブサイトで登録と支払いをする必要はありますが、そうすれば、彼らはTom Akana氏の基調講演や予定されている協議会の全セッションにオンラインでアクセスできるようになります。

Gabriel Lontoc（午前9時22分）
Tom Akana氏が講演することに応じてくれたのは素晴らしいですね。彼がどうやってHonalo Coffee Roasters社を創立し、それを高収益企業に築き上げたのかを聞くのは興味深いものでしょう。

Kate Blum（午前9時23分）
彼は喜んでそれをやってくれます。彼は、それがレストランや食品関連事業の立ち上げを望む人々の助けになるだろうと考えています。さて。以上だと思います。水曜日の午前中にまた集まりましょう。

172 Who most likely is the intended audience for the conference?

(A) Photographers
(B) Software engineers
(C) Technology job candidates
(D) Food industry professionals

誰が協議会の参加対象者だと考えられますか。

(A) 写真家
(B) ソフトウエア開発者
(C) 技術職の求職者
(D) 食品業界のプロ

正解 D ❺より、今度の協議会で講演するTom Akana氏は、Honalo Coffee Roasters社を創立し、それを高収益企業に築き上げたことが分かる。さらに❻で、Tom Akana氏が自分の講演について、it could help others who want to start restaurants or food-related businesses「それがレストランや食品関連事業の立ち上げを望む人々の助けになるだろう」と考えていることが述べられている。よって、話し手たちが準備している協議会の参加対象者は、食品業界に携わる人々だと判断できるので、(D)が正解。intended「意図された」、audience「聴衆、視聴者」。industry「業界」、professional「プロ、専門家」。
(A) photographer「写真家」。
(B) software engineer「ソフトウエア開発者」。
(C) technology「技術」、candidate「志望者」。

---

173 What is mentioned about the conference?

(A) In-person registration is sold out.
(B) Online access is free.
(C) The date was changed.
(D) The keynote speaker canceled.

協議会について何が述べられていますか。

(A) 会場参加の登録枠が売り切れている。
(B) オンラインアクセスが無料である。
(C) 日程が変更された。
(D) 基調講演者がキャンセルした。

正解 A Miyashiroさんは❷で、since the conference is sold out, we are going to broadcast it live over the Internet「協議会は完売なので、インターネット上で生配信をする予定だ」と述べ、❹では、People who want to watch the conference over the Internet still have to register and pay on our Web site「インターネット上で協議会の視聴を希望する人々は当社ウェブサイトで登録と支払いをする必要はある」と補足説明している。よって、協議会への参加には事前登録が必要であり、会場に行って直接参加できる登録枠はすでに売り切れてしまっていると分かるので、そのことをIn-person registration is sold out.と表している(A)が正解。in-person「直接の」。
(B) ❹に協議会のインターネット視聴者はウェブサイトで支払いが必要とあるので、協議会へのオンラインアクセスは有料。
(D) ❹～❻で基調講演者に言及があるが、キャンセルについては述べられていない。

Words & Phrases

❶ quick 手短な　in place 準備が整って　conference 協議会、会議　❷ all set 準備が完了して sold out 売り切れで　broadcast ～を放送する　live 生で、ライブで　over the Internet インターネット上で device 機器　❸ completely 完全に　arrange ～を手配する　camera operator 撮影スタッフ software ソフトウエア　viewer 視聴者　access 利用する方法、アクセス　～, and so on ～など　❹ hire ～を雇う ready 準備のできた　register 登録する　keynote address 基調講演　scheduled 予定された session セッション、集まり　❺ agree to do ～することに同意する　speak 講演をする　interesting 興味深い create ～を創設する　roaster 焙煎機　build ～ into … ～を…に築き上げる　profitable 利益を上げる ❻ be pleased to do 喜んで～する、～できることをうれしく思う　food-related 食品関連の

174 What does Ms. Kang ask about?

    (A) The broadcasting details
    (B) The registration forms
    (C) The Web site
    (D) The hiring process

Kangさんは何について尋ねていますか。

    (A) 配信の詳細情報
    (B) 登録フォーム
    (C) ウェブサイト
    (D) 雇用の過程

> 正解 **A** ❷で、協議会をインターネット上で生配信する予定であると伝えるMiyashiroさんに対し、Kangさんは❸で、Is that completely arranged—camera operators, software, viewer access, and so on?「それは完全に手配済みか——撮影スタッフ、ソフトウエア、視聴者の参加方法なども」と、配信に関する詳しい情報を尋ねているので、(A)が正解。details「詳細情報」。
> (B) ❹で、インターネットによる視聴者の登録に言及はあるが、Kangさんはフォームについて尋ねてはいない。form「フォーム、書式」。
> (C) ❸で、Kangさんが尋ねているのはインターネット視聴者の参加方法などの手配の完了について。ウェブサイトについてではない。
> (D) ❹で、撮影スタッフ全員を雇ったことが述べられているが、Kangさんはその過程について尋ねてはいない。process「過程」。

175 At 9:23 A.M., what does Ms. Blum mean when she writes, "He is pleased to do it"?

    (A) Mr. Akana is glad to go out for coffee.

    (B) Mr. Akana is happy to give a speech.
    (C) Mr. Akana is satisfied with the live-streaming arrangements.
    (D) Mr. Akana is delighted with the work arrangements.

午前9時23分に、Blumさんは "He is pleased to do it" という発言で、何を意味していますか。

    (A) Akana氏は、コーヒーを飲みに外出できることをうれしく思っている。
    (B) Akana氏は講演することをうれしく思っている。
    (C) Akana氏はライブストリーミングの手配に満足している。
    (D) Akana氏は仕事の手配に喜んでいる。

> 正解 **B** Lontocさんが❺で、Tom Akana氏が講演に応じてくれたのは素晴らしいことであり、彼の起業の体験談は興味深いだろうと講演への期待を述べている。それに対し、Blumさんは❻の下線部の発言を書き、直後に講演者のAkana氏も講演がレストランや食品関連事業の立ち上げを望む人々の助けになるだろうと考えていることを伝えている。よって、この発言のdo itは講演することを指し、Akana氏本人も講演に前向きであることを伝えているのだと判断できる。give a speech「講演する」。
> (C) be satisfied with ～「～に満足している」、live-streaming「ライブストリーミングの」、arrangement「手配」。
> (D) be delighted with ～「～に喜んでいる」。

Expressions

make certain (that) ～ 「必ず～であるようにする、～であることを確かめる」(❶)

We will make certain those packages arrive on schedule.
当社はそれらの小包が必ず予定通りに到着するよう取り計らいます。

Questions 176-180 refer to the following memo and e-mail.

MEMO

To: All Employees
From: Xinhua Huang, IT Solutions Manager
Date: Wednesday, 18 November
Re: Upcoming Multi-Factor Authentication

❶ Jurong Distribution takes the confidentiality of its communication seriously. This is why we will be implementing multi-factor authentication (MFA). MFA is a two-step process that safeguards corporate information, including data contained in e-mail and other communications.

❷ All Jurong Distribution employees are required to set up MFA for their work e-mail accounts before 1 December. You will receive an e-mail from me tomorrow with instructions.

❸ Once MFA is set up for your company e-mail account, you will be required to enter a six-digit verification code each time you log in to your e-mail account. The code will be sent by text message to your mobile phone. You will have 5 minutes to use it. After this time, the code becomes invalid.

❹ If you still need help or have questions after setting up MFA, please contact it@jurongdistribution.com.sg, and Ms. Laura Smith, an IT specialist, will respond within the next business day. IT support will only be available during the standard business hours of 9 A.M. to 5 P.M.

Thank you,

Xinhua Huang

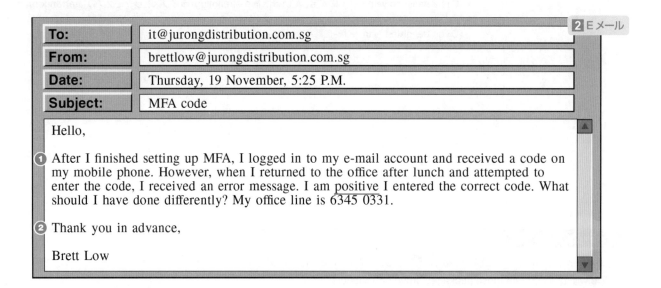

To:	it@jurongdistribution.com.sg
From:	brettlow@jurongdistribution.com.sg
Date:	Thursday, 19 November, 5:25 P.M.
Subject:	MFA code

Hello,

❶ After I finished setting up MFA, I logged in to my e-mail account and received a code on my mobile phone. However, when I returned to the office after lunch and attempted to enter the code, I received an error message. I am positive I entered the correct code. What should I have done differently? My office line is 6345 0331.

❷ Thank you in advance,

Brett Low

問題176-180は次のメモとEメールに関するものです。

メモ

宛先：従業員各位
差出人：Xinhua Huang、ITソリューションマネージャー
日付：11月18日水曜日
件名：近日開始の多要素認証

Jurong流通社は情報の機密性を重要視しています。これが当社が多要素認証（MFA）を実施する理由です。MFAは、Eメールその他の通信手段の中のデータを始めとする企業情報を保護する2段階の手順です。

Jurong流通社の全従業員は12月1日までに業務用Eメールアカウントに MFA を設定するよう義務付けられます。明日、設定手順が書かれた私からのEメールが届きます。

ひとたび業務用Eメールアカウントに MFA が設定されると、ご自身のEメールアカウントにログインするたびに6桁の認証コードを入力するよう求められます。コードは携帯電話にテキストメッセージで送られます。それを使用できるのは5分間です。この時間を過ぎると、コードは無効となります。

MFA を設定した後、なお手助けが必要な場合やご質問がある場合は、it@jurongdistribution.com.sg にご連絡ください。IT スペシャリストのLaura Smithさんが翌営業日以内にお返事します。IT サポートは午前9時から午後5時の通常の営業時間のみ利用できます。

よろしくお願いします。

Xinhua Huang

受信者：it@jurongdistribution.com.sg
送信者：brettlow@jurongdistribution.com.sg
日付：11月19日木曜日、午後5時25分
件名：MFAコード

こんにちは

MFA を設定し終えた後、私は自分のEメールアカウントにログインして携帯電話にコードを受け取りました。しかしながら、昼食後オフィスに戻ってコードを入力しようとしたら、エラーメッセージが出ました。私は正しいコードを入力したと確信しています。何か別のやり方をすべきだったのでしょうか。私のオフィスの電話は6345-0331です。

よろしくお願いいたします。

Brett Low

176 Why did Ms. Huang send the memo?

    (A) To request contact information

    (B) To announce a new company policy

    (C) To welcome new employees

    (D) To apologize for broken equipment

Huangさんはなぜメモを送りましたか。

    (A) 連絡先を求めるため

    (B) 会社の新しい方針を告知するため

    (C) 新しい従業員を歓迎するため

    (D) 故障した設備のことで謝罪するため

正解 B ❶のメモは宛先と件名より、Huangさんが全従業員宛てに「近日開始の多要素認証」について知らせるもの。冒頭でJurong流通社が情報の機密性を重要視していることに言及した後、同❶2～3行目で、This is why we will be implementing multi-factor authentication (MFA).「これが当社が多要素認証（MFA）を実施する理由だ」と述べている。以降で、MFAの詳細や設定の手順について説明していることから、Huangさんは機密保持のための多要素認証導入という会社の新方針を告知するためにメモを送ったと考えられる。announce「～を告知する」、policy「方針」。
(A) request「～を求める」、contact information「連絡先」。
(D) apologize for ～「～のことで謝罪する」、equipment「設備」。

177 According to the memo, how can employees get additional help?

    (A) By calling Ms. Huang directly

    (B) By speaking with their supervisor

    (C) By contacting the IT department

    (D) By attending an instructional session

メモによると、従業員はどのようにして、さらなる手助けを得られますか。

    (A) 直接Huangさんに電話することによって

    (B) 自分の上司と話すことによって

    (C) IT部門に連絡することによって

    (D) 講習会に参加することによって

正解 C ❶の❸で、新しい認証システム設定後の認証コードの扱いについて述べられている。続けて、同❹1～3行目に「MFAを設定した後、なお手助けが必要な場合や質問がある場合は、it@jurongdistribution.com.sgに連絡してください。ITスペシャリストのLaura Smithさんが翌営業日以内に返事をする」とある。つまり、手助けが必要な場合はIT部門にEメールを送ればよいと分かるので、(C)が正解。department「部門」。
(B) speak with ～「～と話す」、supervisor「上司」。
(D) attend「～に出席する」、instructional session「講習会」。

178 Why was Mr. Low unable to log in to his e-mail account?

    (A) He lost his mobile phone.

    (B) He used an incorrect password.

    (C) He did not enter the verification code in time.

    (D) He did not use a valid e-mail address.

Lowさんはなぜ自分のEメールアカウントにログインできなかったのですか。

    (A) 彼は携帯電話をなくした。

    (B) 彼は誤ったパスワードを使った。

    (C) 彼は時間内に認証コードを入力しなかった。

    (D) 彼は有効なEメールアドレスを使わなかった。

正解 C Lowさんはit@jurongdistribution.com.sgに宛てたEメールである❷の❶2～3行目で、認証コードを取得した後の状況について、「昼食後オフィスに戻ってコードを入力しようとしたら、エラーメッセージが出た」と書いている。❶の❸3～4行目に、認証コードが携帯電話に送信された後の注意として、「それを使用できるのは5分間である。この時間を過ぎると、コードは無効となる」とあることから、Lowさんはコード取得後の5分以内にログインしなかったためにエラーが出たと分かる。よって、(C)が正解。be unable to do「～することができない」。in time「時間内に」。
(B) ❶の❸1～3行目より、ログインに必要なのは認証コードであり、パスワードではないので不適切。incorrect「不正確な」。
(D) ❷の❶1～2行目で、Lowさんは自身のEメールアカウントにログインし、認証コードを受け取ったと述べているので不適切。valid「有効な」。

179 When most likely will Ms. Smith contact Mr. Low?

    (A) On November 19
    (B) On November 20
    (C) On November 25
    (D) On December 1

Smithさんはいつ Low さんと連絡を取ると考えられますか。

    (A) 11月19日
    (B) 11月20日
    (C) 11月25日
    (D) 12月1日

| 正解 B | Low さんが it@jurongdistribution.com.sg に宛てたEメールである **2** の日付欄に「11月19日木曜日、午後5時25分」とある。**1** の **❹** 1～3行目で、MFA を設定後に手助けが必要な場合、IT サポートに連絡をすれば、Laura Smith さんが翌営業日以内に返事をすると述べられている。また、同3～4行目に「IT サポートは午前9時から午後5時の通常の営業時間のみ利用できる」とあるので、IT サポートを要望する **2** のEメールを通常の営業時間を過ぎた後に送信した Low さんは、その日のうちには IT スペシャリストの Smith さんから返事がもらえないことになる。よって、Low さんがEメールを送信した日の翌営業日である(B)が正解。 |

180 In the e-mail, the word "positive" in paragraph 1, line 3, is closest in meaning to

    (A) certain
    (B) optimistic
    (C) active
    (D) helpful

Eメールの第1段落・3行目にある "positive" に最も意味が近いのは

    (A) 確信して
    (B) 楽観的で
    (C) 積極的で
    (D) 助けになって

| 正解 A | **2** のEメールの **❶** 1～3行目で、Low さんは MFA を設定してコードを受け取ったものの、昼食に行き、オフィスに戻った後にコードを入力しようとしたところ、エラーメッセージが出たと書いている。同3行目の該当の語を含む文は、「私は正しいコードを入力したと-------いる」という意味。続く同3～4行目で What should I have done differently?「何か別のやり方をすべきだったのだろうか」と述べていることから、Low さんは自分が手順通り正しいコードを入力したと確信していると判断できる。よって、(A)が正解。 |

Words & Phrases

1 メモ

employee 従業員　　IT 情報技術　★information technology の略　　solution 解決、ソリューション
upcoming 近く公開の、近く起こる　　multi-factor 多要素の　　authentication 認証　　**❶** distribution 流通
confidentiality 機密保持　　communication 情報、通信手段　　seriously 真剣に　　implement ～を実施する
two-step 2段階の　　process 手順、過程　　safeguard ～を保護する　　corporate 企業の
including ～を含めて　　contain ～を含む　　**❷** be required to *do* ～するように要求される
set up ～ ～を設定する　　account アカウント　　instructions 説明書　　**❸** once いったん～すると
enter ～を入力する　　-digit ～桁の　　verification 認証、検証　　code コード
log in to ～ ～にログインする　　text message テキストメッセージ　　invalid 無効の
❹ contact ～に連絡する　　specialist 専門家　　respond 返事をする　　business day 営業日
support 支援　　available 利用できる　　standard 通常の、標準の

2 Eメール

❶ attempt to *do* ～しようと試みる　　error message エラーメッセージ　　correct 正しい
differently 異なって　　line 電話番号、電話回線　　**❷** in advance 前もって

Expressions

This is why ～　「これが～の理由だ」（**1** の **❶** 2～3行目）

Mr. Sato will be transferred to our Shanghai branch next year. This is why he has to study Chinese hard.
Sato さんは来年上海支店に異動になります。ですから、彼は中国語を一生懸命に勉強しなければなりません。

TEST1 PART 7

85

Questions 181-185 refer to the following letter and advertisement.

Kenfar Packaging
3 Adavale Road
Blue Earth, MN 56013

June 18

❶ Industrial-Tech Farmers Magazine
324 North Valley Road
Phoenixville, PA 19460

Dear Editor,

❷ Mr. Oseed's letter to the editor last month urged that reusable packaging be made available for bulk agricultural products. I am pleased to report that such a product does exist.

❸ My company, Kenfar Packaging, offers high-quality packaging that meets the industry's needs: not only can our products be reused numerous times, but they are made from nearly 50 percent recycled materials as well. This year alone, we project that our company's packaging solutions will prevent over one million kilos of plastics from ending up in landfills.

❹ We offer a wide variety of bag styles, and every one of them effectively secures goods from pests and spillage, both while in transit and while in storage. Kenfar Packaging proudly offers our environmentally friendly products to the farming community.

Sincerely,

Sally Heffentrager
Sally Heffentrager

KENFAR PACKAGING
Environmentally friendly bulk-sized bags

BAG TYPES	SPECIAL FEATURES
Type 1: Large Produce	Wide-mesh fabric for ventilation; suitable for potatoes, onions, and citrus fruits
Type 2: Grains and Seeds	Impermeable liner blocks moisture and prevents product leakage
Type 3: Beans and Nuts	Stackable for efficient use of storage space; suitable for coffee beans and peanuts
Type 4: Animal Feed Pellets	Innovative opening in top of bag allows for rapid filling

Bags can be customized with your logo and information.
See our Web site for further information, quantities, and prices.
www.kenfarpackaging.com

問題181-185は次の手紙と広告に関するものです。

Kenfar包装材社
アダベール通り3番地
ブルーアース、MN 56013

6月18日

農産業技術雑誌社
ノースバレー通り324番地
フェニックスビル、PA 19460

編集者様

先月のOseedさんの投書は、再利用可能な包装材を大量の農産物用に活用できるようにすべきだと力説するものでした。私はそのような製品が実際にあることを喜んでお知らせします。

弊社Kenfar包装材社は業界のニーズを満たす高品質の包装材を提供しています。弊社製品は何回も再利用可能なだけでなく同時に、ほぼ50パーセント再生材料から作られています。弊社の包装材製品により、今年だけで、100万キロを超えるプラスチックが埋め立て地のごみになるのを防ぐだろうと見込んでおります。

弊社は多種の袋を提供しており、その全てが輸送中でも保管中でも、品物を害虫・害獣や漏出から効果的に守ります。Kenfar包装材社は誇りを持って、環境に優しい製品を農業界に提供しております。

敬具

Sally Heffentrager（署名）
Sally Heffentrager

KENFAR包装材社
環境に優しい大型の袋

袋のタイプ	特徴
タイプ1： 大きめの農産物	通気性の良い粗い網目の生地。ジャガイモ、タマネギ、かんきつ類に適しています
タイプ2： 穀物や種	水分を通さない裏地が湿気を防ぎ、生産物が漏出するのを防ぎます
タイプ3： 豆や木の実	貯蔵スペースを効率的に使用できるよう積み重ねが可能。コーヒー豆やピーナッツに適しています
タイプ4： 動物の飼料用ペレット	袋の上部に革新的な開口部があるので、短時間で袋詰め可能です

袋は貴社のロゴと情報をご要望に応じて入れることができます。
詳しい情報、数量と価格については、当社のウェブサイトをご覧ください。
www.kenfarpackaging.com

181 What is the purpose of the letter?

(A) To review a popular product
(B) To describe a new storage facility
(C) To respond to a recently published letter
(D) To disagree with a policy change

手紙の目的は何ですか。

(A) 人気のある製品を評価すること
(B) 新しい保管施設の特徴を述べること
(C) 最近掲載された投書に反応すること
(D) 方針転換に反対すること

正解 C ❶の手紙は❶の宛先より、農産業技術雑誌社に宛てられたもの。同❷ 1～2行目に Mr. Oseed's letter to the editor last month urged that reusable packaging be made available for bulk agricultural products.「先月のOseedさんの投書は、再利用可能な包装材を大量の農産物用に活用できるようにすべきだと力説するものだった」とある。また、同2～3行目に「私はそのような製品が実際にあることを喜んでお知らせする」と続いているので、この手紙は前月雑誌に掲載されたOseedさんの投書に反応するために送られたと分かる。publish「～(投書、記事)を掲載する」。
(A) review「～を評価する」。
(B) describe「～の特徴を述べる」、storage facility「保管施設」。
(D) disagree with ～「～に反対する」、policy change「方針転換」。

182 Who most likely is Ms. Heffentrager?

(A) A farmworker
(B) A food-safety expert
(C) A farm-magazine journalist
(D) A packaging-company employee

Heffentragerさんとは誰だと考えられますか。

(A) 農業労働者
(B) 食品安全の専門家
(C) 農業雑誌の記者
(D) 包装材会社の従業員

正解 D Heffentragerさんは❶の署名より、手紙の差出人。同❸ 1～2行目で My company, Kenfar Packaging, offers high-quality packaging that meets the industry's needs「弊社 Kenfar包装材社は業界のニーズを満たす高品質の包装材を提供している」と自社について述べている。以降もwe「私たちは」という語を用いて、Kenfar包装材社の製品について詳しく説明しているので、(D)が正解。
(B) food-safety「食品安全の」、expert「専門家」。
(C)❶の❶1行目より、手紙の宛先が農産業技術雑誌社なのであって、Heffentragerさんが雑誌社に所属しているとは述べられていない。journalist「記者」。

183 In the letter, the word "project" in paragraph 2, line 3, is closest in meaning to

(A) assign
(B) extend
(C) arrange
(D) estimate

手紙の第2段落・3行目にある "project"に最も意味が近いのは

(A) ～を割り当てる
(B) ～を拡張する
(C) ～を取り決める
(D) ～と見積もる

正解 D ❶の❸1～3行目で、Kenfar包装材社の製品は何回も再利用可能で、ほぼ50パーセント再生材料から作られていると説明されている。同3～5行目の該当の語を含む文は、「弊社の包装材製品により、今年だけで、100万キロを超えるプラスチックが埋め立て地のごみになるのを防ぐだろう-------」という意味。同社の製品を活用することによる、今年のごみ減量の見込みについて述べている。よって、(D) estimate「～と見積もる、～と推定する」が正解。

184 What is true about the products listed in the advertisement?

(A) They are less expensive than competitors' products.

(B) They are made from plant-based cloth.

(C) They are manufactured using some recycled materials.

(D) They are recent additions to Kenfar Packaging's product line.

広告に記載されている製品について正しいことは何ですか。

(A) それらは競合会社の製品よりも安価である。

(B) それらは植物由来の布からできている。

(C) それらは再生材料を使って製造されている。

(D) それらはKenfar包装材社の製品ラインに最近加わったものである。

> **正解 C** ②の広告には、Kenfar包装材社のEnvironmentally friendly「環境に優しい」と書かれた4つのタイプの袋が示されている。同社の製品の特徴として、①の❸2～3行目で「弊社製品は何回も再利用可能なだけでなく同時に、ほぼ50パーセント再生材料から作られている」と述べられていることから、(C)が正解。manufacture「～を製造する」。
> (A) competitor「競合会社、競争相手」。
> (B) plant-based「植物由来の」、cloth「布」。
> (D) recent「最近の」、addition「加わったもの」、product line「製品ライン」。

185 What product would likely work best for holding oranges?

(A) Type 1
(B) Type 2
(C) Type 3
(D) Type 4

どの製品がオレンジを入れるのに最も適していると考えられますか。

(A) タイプ1
(B) タイプ2
(C) タイプ3
(D) タイプ4

> **正解 A** ②の広告に記載されたタイプ1の製品の特徴にWide-mesh fabric for ventilation; suitable for potatoes, onions, and citrus fruits「通気性の良い粗い網目の生地。ジャガイモ、タマネギ、かんきつ類に適している」とある。よって、かんきつ類であるオレンジを入れるのに適しているのは(A)。work「うまくいく」、hold「～を入れることができる」。

Words & Phrases

①手紙 packaging 包装　❶ industrial 産業の　editor 編集者　❷ letter to the editor 投書　urge that ~ ～ということを力説する　reusable 再利用できる　available 利用できる　bulk 大量(の)　agricultural product 農産物　exist 存在する　❸ high-quality 高品質の　meet ～を満たす、～に合う　industry 産業　needs ニーズ、要求　reuse ～を再利用する　numerous 多数の　nearly ほぼ、もう少しで　recycled 再利用された　material 材料　alone ただ～だけ　solutions 製品、サービス　prevent ~ from doing ～が…することを防ぐ　kilo キログラム　★kilogramの略　plastic プラスチック　end up in ~ 最後には～になる　landfill 埋め立てごみ、埋め立て地　❹ offer ～を提供する　a wide variety of ~ 多種多様な～　style 型　effectively 効果的に　secure ~ from … …から～を守る　goods 品物　pest 有害な小動物、害虫　spillage こぼれ、流出　transit 輸送　storage 保管、貯蔵　proudly 誇りを持って　environmentally friendly 環境に優しい　farming 農業、農場経営　community 社会、～界

②広告 bulk-sized 大型の　❶ features 特徴　produce 農産物、青果物　wide-mesh 粗い網目の　fabric 生地　ventilation 通気、風通し　(be) suitable for ~ ～に適して(いる)　citrus fruit かんきつ類の果物　grain 穀物　seed 種　impermeable 不浸透性の　liner 裏地　block ～を妨げる　moisture 湿気　leakage 漏れ　bean 豆　nut 木の実　stackable 積み重ねられる　efficient 効率的な　feed 飼料　pellet ペレット　★小さく球形に固めたもの　innovative 革新的な　opening 開口部　allow for ~ ～を可能にする　rapid 迅速な　filling 満たすこと　❷ customize ～を注文に合わせて作る　further さらなる　quantity 数量

Expressions

not only ~ but … as well 「～だけでなく…もまた」(①の❸2～3行目)

Not only are these products sold in Japan, but they are exported to many foreign countries as well.
これらの製品は日本で売られているだけでなく、海外の多くの国に輸出もされています。

Questions 186-190 refer to the following advertisement, flyer, and review.

Meet Helpful Hanna, a New Addition to the Modern Home

❶ Helpful Hanna, the Talking Refrigerator, can revolutionize your home. Designed to help organize your life, Hanna uses apps and voice recognition to connect your refrigerator to your phone and to your lifestyle. Available in six stylish colors.

❷ You can ask Hanna to:

- Create a shopping list
- Help plan your meals
- Provide recipes
- Fill your water pitcher
- Display your calendar
  And so much more!

Yohan's Appliances
41 North Franklin Street
Clendenin, West Virginia 25045
(304) 555-0199

❶ **Frigation 100**
[Model FG-100]

- Base model
- 22 cubic feet
- Excellent reliability and energy ratings
- 3 colors in stock
- $1,000

❷ **Coolbry 500**
[Model CB-500]

- Family, digital hub zone, voice activated
- 26 cubic feet
- Hot- and cold-water dispenser
- Many apps available at additional charge
- $2,000 (on sale for $1,800)

❸ **Helpful Hanna**
[Model HRX-276]

- Digital interactive center
- 27 cubic feet
- Extra-large ice capacity
- 2 colors in stock
- $3,100

❹ **Coolbry 700**
[Model CB-700]

- Digital interactive center
- 28 cubic feet
- Translator that recognizes and speaks 6 languages
- Multilevel lighting
- $3,000

Review of Coolbry 500 Refrigerator
May 30

❶ I just returned home from spending two weeks at my daughter's house while she and her husband were away on a business trip. She recently purchased her first smart fridge because she thought it would be helpful to her young family. She likes the novelty of being able to talk to her refrigerator, and I can see that her kids like touching the digital screen. However, I found that the refrigerator doesn't seem to make life easier. It just makes it noisier. Just because the technology exists doesn't mean we need it. For me, a plain old refrigerator that keeps my food cold is more than enough. As long as my refrigerator is reliable, energy saving, and comparatively inexpensive, I'm satisfied. When I buy a new refrigerator in the fall, it will be a simple, old-fashioned model that does not talk back to me. My kitchen is already noisy enough!

—Gertrude Caputo

問題186-190は次の広告、チラシ、レビューに関するものです。

現代の家庭向けの新製品 Helpful Hannaをご覧になってください

しゃべる冷蔵庫、Helpful Hannaはあなたの家を劇的に変化させることができます。あなたの生活を整理するのに役立つように設計されており、Hannaはアプリと音声認識を駆使して、冷蔵庫を携帯電話、そして生活スタイルと連携させます。6つのおしゃれな色をそろえています。

あなたがHannaに頼めるのは：
  ・買い物リストを作ること
  ・食事の計画を手助けすること
  ・レシピを提供すること
  ・水差しを満たすこと
  ・予定表を表示すること
まだまだ他にもあります！

Yohan's 電化製品店
ノースフランクリン通り41番地
クレンデニン、ウェストバージニア 25045
(304) 555-0199

Frigation 100 [FG-100モデル]	**Coolbry 500** [CB-500モデル]
・基本モデル ・22立方フィート ・信頼性とエネルギーの高い評価 ・3色の在庫 ・1,000ドル	・家族向け、デジタルハブ領域、音声起動 ・26立方フィート ・熱湯と冷水のディスペンサー ・多くのアプリを追加料金で利用可能 ・2,000ドル（1,800ドルで特価販売中）
Helpful Hanna [HRX-276モデル]	**Coolbry 700** [CB-700モデル]
・インタラクティブなデジタルセンター ・27立方フィート ・特大容量の製氷室 ・2色の在庫 ・3,100ドル	・インタラクティブなデジタルセンター ・28立方フィート ・6カ国語を認識し発話する翻訳機能 ・レベル調整可能な照明 ・3,000ドル

Coolbry 500冷蔵庫のレビュー
5月30日

私は娘とその夫が出張で留守にしている間、彼女の家で2週間を過ごして自宅に戻ってきたところです。彼女は最近、小さい子どもがいる家庭に役立つだろうと考えたので、初めてのスマート冷蔵庫を買いました。彼女は冷蔵庫と話すことができるという目新しさが気に入っており、子どもたちはデジタルスクリーンに触れるのが好きな様子です。しかしながら、その冷蔵庫は生活を楽にしているようには思えないと気付きました。ただ生活を騒々しくしているだけです。技術が存在しているからといって、私たちがそれを必要としているとは限りません。私にとっては、食べ物を冷やしておいてくれるありふれた昔ながらの冷蔵庫で十分過ぎるほどです。冷蔵庫が信頼できて、省エネで、比較的低価格でありさえすれば、私は満足です。私が秋に新しい冷蔵庫を買うときは、私に言い返さない単純な旧式モデルにするでしょう。私の台所はすでに十分騒々しいのですから！

——Gertrude Caputo

186 According to the advertisement, what is a feature of Helpful Hanna?

(A) A built-in coffee maker
(B) A hot-water dispenser
(C) A language translator
(D) A meal planner

広告によると、Helpful Hannaの一つの機能は何ですか。

(A) 内蔵のコーヒーメーカー
(B) 給湯器
(C) 言語翻訳機能
(D) 食事プランナー

> **正解 D**　❶の広告の❶1～2行目より、Helpful Hannaとは発話機能付き冷蔵庫の商品名。同❷1行目のYou can ask Hanna to:「あなたがHannaに頼めるのは」に続けて、この冷蔵庫の機能が列挙されている。同3行目に、Help plan your meals「食事の計画を手助けすること」と書かれているので、(D)が正解。feature「機能、特徴」。planner「管理ツール」。
> (A) built-in「内蔵の」。
> (B) ❶の❷5行目にFill your water pitcher「水差しを満たす」とあり、給水機能は搭載しているが、給湯機能については書かれていない。

187 What is suggested about Yohan's Appliances?

(A) It recently opened a store in Clendenin.
(B) It does not have all colors of Helpful Hanna available.
(C) It has multiple locations.
(D) It does not offer discounts on its appliances.

Yohan's 電化製品店について何が分かりますか。

(A) 同店は最近クレンデニンに店を開いた。
(B) 同店は Helpful Hanna 全色の在庫があるわけではない。
(C) 同店は複数の店舗を持つ。
(D) 同店は電化製品に対する割引を行っていない。

> **正解 B**　Yohan's 電化製品店のチラシである❷の❸のHelpful Hannaの欄に、2 colors in stock「2色の在庫」と書かれている。一方、Helpful Hannaの広告である❶の❶4行目には、Available in six stylish colors.「6つのおしゃれな色をそろえている」とある。つまり、Yohan's 電化製品店にあるのはHelpful Hanna全6色の製品ラインのうちの2色のみなので、(B)が正解。
> (A) ❷の同店の住所にクレンデニンとあるが、最近開店したとは書かれていない。
> (C) 同店が複数店舗を持っているという記載はない。multiple「複数の」、location「店舗」。
> (D) ❷の❷のCoolbry 500の欄に、「2,000ドル（1,800ドルで特価販売中）」とあり、同店は割引を行っている。

188 How does the Coolbry 700 refrigerator differ from the other refrigerators?

(A) It is more energy efficient.
(B) It offers more apps.
(C) It is larger.
(D) It costs more.

Coolbry 700 冷蔵庫は他の冷蔵庫とどのように異なりますか。

(A) 同製品はエネルギー効率がより良い。
(B) 同製品はより多くのアプリを提供している。
(C) 同製品はより大型である。
(D) 同製品はより価格が高い。

> **正解 C**　❷のYohan's 電化製品店のチラシに説明のある4種の冷蔵庫の大きさを比較すると、❹のCoolbry 700は28 cubic feet「28立方フィート」と最も大型。よって、(C)が正解。differ from ～「～と異なる」。
> (A) ❷の❶のFrigation 100の欄に、「信頼性とエネルギーの高い評価」とあるが、❹のCoolbry 700の欄にエネルギー効率の記載はない。energy efficient「エネルギー効率が良い」。
> (B) ❷の❷のCoolbry 500の欄に、「多くのアプリを追加料金で利用可能」とあるが、❹のCoolbry 700の欄にアプリに関する記載はない。
> (D) ❷の価格を見ると、❹のCoolbry 700が3,000ドルであるのに対し、❸のHelpful Hannaは3,100ドルなので、Coolbry 700は他製品より高価とは言えない。

189 What does the review suggest about Ms. Caputo?

    (A) She lives with her daughter.
    (B) She took a business trip recently.
    (C) She was away from home in May.
    (D) She has young children.

レビューはCaputoさんについて何を示唆していますか。

    (A) 娘と住んでいる。
    (B) 最近出張をした。
    (C) 5月に家を留守にしていた。
    (D) 幼い子どもがいる。

> **正解 C** Caputoさんのレビューである**3**の**①**1〜2行目に、I just returned home from spending two weeks at my daughter's house while she and her husband were away on a business trip.「私は娘とその夫が出張で留守にしている間、彼女の家で2週間を過ごして自宅に戻ってきたところだ」と述べられている。このレビューの日付は「5月30日」なので、(C)が正解。
> (A) **3**の**①**1〜2行目より、Caputoさんは娘が出張の間に娘の家にいたが、娘と同居はしていない。
> (B) **3**の**①**1〜2行目より、出張したのはCaputoさんの娘とその夫。
> (D) **3**の**①**2〜5行目より、幼い子どもがいるのはCaputoさんの娘。

190 What model refrigerator would Ms. Caputo most likely buy?

    (A) FG-100
    (B) CB-500
    (C) HRX-276
    (D) CB-700

Caputoさんはどのモデルの冷蔵庫を買うと考えられますか。

    (A) FG-100
    (B) CB-500
    (C) HRX-276
    (D) CB-700

> **正解 A** **3**のレビューの**①**7〜9行目で、Caputoさんは「私にとっては、食べ物を冷やしておいてくれるありふれた昔ながらの冷蔵庫で十分過ぎるほどだ。冷蔵庫が信頼できて、省エネで、比較的低価格でありさえすれば、私は満足だ」と述べている。さらに同9〜11行目で、「私が秋に新しい冷蔵庫を買うときは、私に言い返さない単純な旧式モデルにする」と続けている。**2**のチラシの**①**で、「基本モデル」、「信頼性とエネルギーの高い評価」と説明されている(A) FG-100はコンピューター機能搭載という記載はなく、価格も1,000ドルと最も安価であり、Caputoさんの希望に合うと考えられる。

Words & Phrases

1 広告
flyer　チラシ
addition　加えられたもの　　modern　現代の　　**①** refrigerator　冷蔵庫　　revolutionize　〜を革命的に変化させる
(be) designed to *do*　〜するように設計されて(いる)　　help *do*　〜する助けとなる　　organize　〜を整理する
app　アプリ　★applicationの略　　voice recognition　音声認識　　connect 〜 to …　〜を…につなぐ
lifestyle　生活スタイル　　available　入手できる　　stylish　おしゃれな　　**②** ask 〜 to *do*　〜に…するよう頼む
meal　食事　　provide　〜を提供する　　fill　〜を満たす　　pitcher　水差し　　display　〜を表示する

2 チラシ
appliance　電化製品　　**①** base　基本(の)　　〜 cubic feet　〜立方フィート　★体積の単位　　excellent　優れた
reliability　信頼性　　rating　評価　　in stock　在庫があって　　**②** hub　中心　　zone　区域
activate　〜を起動する　　dispenser　ディスペンサー　★食品や商品などを一定数量だけ引き出せるようにした機器
additional　追加の　　charge　料金　　on sale　特価で　　**③** interactive　双方向の　　extra-large　特大の
capacity　容量　　**④** translator　翻訳機　　recognize　〜を認識する　　multilevel　さまざまなレベルの、多層の
lighting　照明

3 レビュー
① business trip　出張　　recently　最近　　purchase　〜を購入する　　smart　コンピューター制御の
fridge　冷蔵庫　★refrigeratorの短縮語　　novelty　目新しさ　　touch　〜に触れる
Just because 〜 does not mean …　〜だからといって…というわけではない　　technology　科学技術
exist　存在する　　plain　平凡な、普通の　　old　昔なじみの　　more than enough　必要以上
reliable　信頼できる　　energy saving　省エネの　　comparatively　比較的　　inexpensive　低価格の
satisfied　満足して　　old-fashioned　旧式の　　talk back　応答する、言い返す

Expressions

as long as 〜　「〜さえすれば、〜である限りは」(**3**の**①**8〜9行目)

I will lend you this book as long as you return it by the end of this month.
今月末までに返してくれさえすれば、あなたにこの本をお貸しします。

Questions 191-195 refer to the following e-mails and form.

1 1通目のEメール

To:	Bess Sound Systems staff
From:	Hans Loffler
Date:	August 1
Subject:	Bulldogs Basketball Tickets
Attachment:	Group Ticket Form

Get out your Barbosa Bulldogs jerseys! As we have done in recent years, we are planning to coordinate a group ticket purchase for basketball games at Centerway Arena. Once again, the Bulldogs' schedule includes games against teams from around the region, and many games are already sold out. Group tickets are discounted based on the size of the group.

Group Ticket Pricing

8–20 tickets	$20 each
21–50 tickets	$18 each
51–100 tickets	$15 each
101+ tickets	$12 each

Interested employees should complete the attached form by indicating the number of tickets you would like to order. Completed forms must be returned to me by August 10. I will contact the Bulldogs' ticket office by August 15 to reserve tickets for the games. Once we confirm that we can get enough tickets for those games, full payment will be due within two weeks.

Please e-mail me directly if you have any questions.

Hans Loffler

2 申し込みフォーム

Barbosa Bulldogs Group Tickets

Employee Name: _____

Date	Opponent	Number of Tickets
September 18	Branchfield Parrots	SOLD OUT
September 27	Middletown Rush	
October 1	Tigg Lake Bears	SOLD OUT
October 13	Clarkton Giants	SOLD OUT
November 8	Drake City Comets	

3 2通目のEメール

To:	hloffler@besssound.com
From:	jdodson@barbosabulldogs.org
Date:	August 19
Subject:	Re: Barbosa Bulldogs

Dear Mr. Loffler:

Thank you for your inquiry about Barbosa Bulldogs group tickets. I am pleased to hear that the Bess Sound Systems staff is so enthusiastic about our team! To answer your question, yes, we can reserve a block of 120 seats for the Middletown Rush game and 105 for the game against the Drake City Comets. The seats will be in the upper level of the arena. Once you confirm that this plan is acceptable, we can make arrangements for payment and delivery of the tickets.

Regards,

Jorge Dodson

問題191-195は次の2通のEメールと申し込みフォームに関するものです。

受信者：Bess音響システム社のスタッフ各位
送信者：Hans Loffler
日付：8月1日
件名：Bulldogsバスケットボールチケット
添付ファイル：団体チケット申し込みフォーム

お持ちのBarbosa Bulldogsのユニホームを取り出してください！ ここ数年やってきたように、Centerway競技場でのバスケットボールの試合の団体チケット購入の取りまとめを計画中です。繰り返しになりますが、Bulldogsのスケジュールには地域中のチームとの試合が入っていて、多くの試合がすでに売り切れています。団体チケットは団体の規模に基づいて割引があります。

団体チケット価格設定

8〜20枚	1枚20ドル
21〜50枚	1枚18ドル
51〜100枚	1枚15ドル
101枚以上	1枚12ドル

興味のある従業員は注文したいチケットの数を示して添付のフォームに記入してください。記入済みのフォームは8月10日までに私宛てに返送していただく必要があります。私は試合のチケットを予約するため、8月15日までにBulldogsのチケットオフィスに連絡します。十分な数の試合のチケットを入手できることを確認したら、2週間以内に全額の支払いをする予定です。

もしご質問があれば私に直接Eメールを送ってください。

Hans Loffler

Barbosa Bulldogs 団体チケット

従業員氏名：＿＿＿＿＿＿＿＿＿＿＿＿＿

日付	対戦相手	チケット数
9月18日	Branchfield Parrots	売り切れ
9月27日	Middletown Rush	
10月1日	Tigg Lake Bears	売り切れ
10月13日	Clarkton Giants	売り切れ
11月8日	Drake City Comets	

受信者：hloffler@besssound.com
送信者：jdodson@barbosabulldogs.org
日付：8月19日
件名：Re：Barbosa Bulldogs

Loffler様

Barbosa Bulldogsの団体チケットに関してお問い合わせいただきありがとうございます。Bess音響システム社の皆さんが当チームを熱烈に応援してくれていると聞きうれしく思います。ご質問にお答えしますと、はい、Middletown Rushとの試合に120席の1区画とDrake City Cometsとの試合に105席の1区画を確保することができます。座席は競技場の上階です。この案で進めてよいとご確認いただければすぐに、チケットのお支払いと配送を手配することができます。

敬具

Jorge Dodson

191 In the first e-mail, what does Mr. Loffler suggest about the Barbosa Bulldogs?

(A) Their season begins on August 1.
(B) Their games are popular with fans.
(C) They have moved to a new arena.
(D) They will play fewer games this year.

1通目のEメールで、LofflerさんはBarbosa Bulldogsについて何を示唆していますか。

(A) シーズンは8月1日に始まる。
(B) 試合はファンに人気がある。
(C) 新しい競技場に移った。
(D) 今年は試合が少ない。

> **正解 B** 1通目のEメールである**1**は、LofflerさんがBess音響システム社のスタッフ宛てに送信したもの。同**①**3〜4行目にthe Bulldogs' schedule includes games against teams from around the region, and many games are already sold out「Bulldogsのスケジュールには地域中のチームとの試合が入っていて、多くの試合がすでに売り切れている」と述べられている。よって、Barbosa Bulldogsの試合はファンに人気があると考えられる。
> (A) **1**のEメールの送信日が「8月1日」。

---

192 According to the first e-mail, what is true about group tickets?

(A) They are available for groups of eight or more.
(B) They have not been offered in previous years.
(C) They are cheaper before the season begins.
(D) They must be purchased online.

1通目のEメールによると、団体チケットについて正しいことは何ですか。

(A) 8人以上のグループに利用可能である。
(B) 以前には提供されなかった。
(C) シーズンが始まる前はより安価である。
(D) オンラインで購入しなければならない。

> **正解 A** 1通目のEメールである**1**の**①**のGroup Ticket Pricing「団体チケット価格設定」の表に、「8〜20枚」から「101枚以上」までの4段階の価格帯が設定されている。つまり、団体チケットは8人以上のグループに利用可能だと分かるので、(A)が正解。available「利用できる」。
> (B) **1**の**①**1〜3行目で団体チケットの購入について「ここ数年やってきたように」と前置きして説明しており、過去にも団体チケットが販売されていたことが分かる。previous「前の」。
> (D) purchase「〜を購入する」。

---

193 In the second e-mail, what does Mr. Dodson tell Mr. Loffler about?

(A) Game times
(B) Ticket prices
(C) Seat locations
(D) A special promotion

2通目のEメールで、DodsonさんはLofflerさんに何について述べていますか。

(A) 試合時間
(B) チケットの値段
(C) 座席の位置
(D) 特別な販売促進

> **正解 C** 2通目のEメールである**3**は、DodsonさんがLoffler さん宛てに送信したもの。同**①**1行目でDodsonさんは試合の団体チケットに関する問い合わせにお礼を述べてから、同2〜4行目でTo answer your question「質問に答えると」と、購入可能なチケットに関するLofflerさんからの質問に答えている。予約可能な試合と座席数を提示した後、同4〜5行目で、The seats will be in the upper level of the arena.「座席は競技場の上階だ」と伝えている。よって、(C)が正解。
> (D) promotion「販売促進」。

Expressions

be pleased to *do* 「〜してうれしい」(**3**の**①**1行目)
We are pleased to hear that you were promoted to section chief.
私たちはあなたが課長に昇進したと聞いてうれしいです。

194 How much will Bess Sound Systems employees most likely pay for each ticket?

    (A) $20
    (B) $18
    (C) $15
    (D) $12

Bess音響システム社の従業員はそれぞれのチケットに幾ら払うと考えられますか。

    (A) 20ドル
    (B) 18ドル
    (C) 15ドル
    (D) 12ドル

| 正解 D | 🖸の❶ 3～4行目にwe can reserve a block of 120 seats for the Middletown Rush game and 105 for the game against the Drake City Comets「Middletown Rushとの試合に120席の1区画とDrake City Cometsとの試合に105席の1区画を確保することができる」と2つの試合で希望する座席数の購入が可能なことが述べられている。🖸の❶の「団体チケット価格設定」の表では、チケット105枚と120枚はどちらも一番下の行の「101枚以上──1枚12ドル」に該当する。つまり、Middletown Rushとの試合とDrake City Cometsとの試合のいずれも、価格は1枚当たり12ドルなので、(D)が正解。 |

195 When will Bess Sound Systems employees most likely attend a game?

    (A) On September 18
    (B) On October 1
    (C) On October 13
    (D) On November 8

Bess音響システム社の従業員はいつ試合を観戦すると考えられますか。

    (A) 9月18日
    (B) 10月1日
    (C) 10月13日
    (D) 11月8日

| 正解 D | 🖸の❶ 3～4行目に「Middletown Rushとの試合に120席の1区画とDrake City Cometsとの試合に105席の1区画を確保することができる」と述べられているので、Bess音響システム社の従業員が観戦するのは、このいずれかと考えられる。申し込みフォーム②の❶の表では、Middletown Rushとの試合は「9月27日」だが、(A)～(D)の選択肢の中にはなく、Drake City Cometsとの試合の「11月8日」は(D)の日付と一致する。よって、(D)が正解。attend a game「試合を観戦する」。(A) (B) (C) ②の❶の表から、それぞれBranchfield Parrots、Tigg Lake Bears、Clarkton Giantsとの試合日。いずれもSOLD OUT「売り切れ」とある。 |

Words & Phrases

🞐 1 Eメール	sound system 音響システム ❶ get out ~ ~を取り出す jersey ジャージー ★運動選手が着るシャツ recent 最近の coordinate ~をまとめる、~を調整する purchase 購入 arena 競技場 once again 繰り返し言いますが、もう一度 include ~を含む region 地域 be sold out 売り切れている discount ~を割引して売る based on ~ ~に基づいて pricing 価格設定 ❷ interested 興味のある complete ~に全て記入する attached 添付の indicate ~を示す the number of ~ ~の数 contact ~に連絡する reserve ~を予約する、~を取っておく once ~するとすぐに confirm that ~ ~ということを確認する full payment 全額支払い due 支払われるべき within ~以内に ❸ e-mail ~にEメールを送る directly 直接に
🞐 2 フォーム	❶ opponent 対戦相手
🞐 3 Eメール	❶ inquiry 問い合わせ enthusiastic 熱狂的な a block of ~ ~の1区画 upper 上の level 階 acceptable 受け入れられる、満足できる make arrangements for ~ ~の手配をする delivery 配送、配達

Questions 196-200 refer to the following online post, e-mail, and Web page.

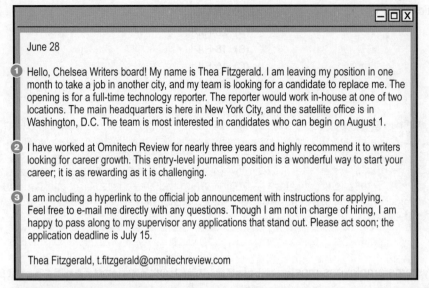

June 28

① Hello, Chelsea Writers board! My name is Thea Fitzgerald. I am leaving my position in one month to take a job in another city, and my team is looking for a candidate to replace me. The opening is for a full-time technology reporter. The reporter would work in-house at one of two locations. The main headquarters is here in New York City, and the satellite office is in Washington, D.C. The team is most interested in candidates who can begin on August 1.

② I have worked at Omnitech Review for nearly three years and highly recommend it to writers looking for career growth. This entry-level journalism position is a wonderful way to start your career; it is as rewarding as it is challenging.

③ I am including a hyperlink to the official job announcement with instructions for applying. Feel free to e-mail me directly with any questions. Though I am not in charge of hiring, I am happy to pass along to my supervisor any applications that stand out. Please act soon; the application deadline is July 15.

Thea Fitzgerald, t.fitzgerald@omnitechreview.com

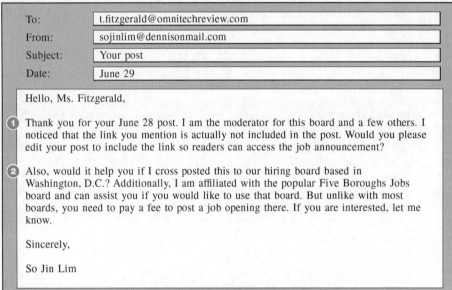

To:	t.fitzgerald@omnitechreview.com
From:	sojinlim@dennisonmail.com
Subject:	Your post
Date:	June 29

Hello, Ms. Fitzgerald,

① Thank you for your June 28 post. I am the moderator for this board and a few others. I noticed that the link you mention is actually not included in the post. Would you please edit your post to include the link so readers can access the job announcement?

② Also, would it help you if I cross posted this to our hiring board based in Washington, D.C.? Additionally, I am affiliated with the popular Five Boroughs Jobs board and can assist you if you would like to use that board. But unlike with most boards, you need to pay a fee to post a job opening there. If you are interested, let me know.

Sincerely,

So Jin Lim

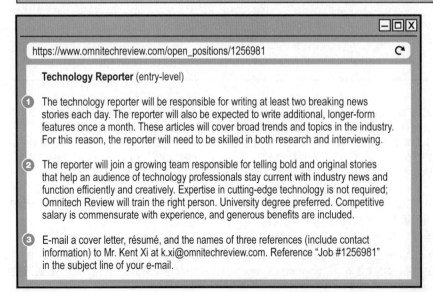

https://www.omnitechreview.com/open_positions/1256981

Technology Reporter (entry-level)

① The technology reporter will be responsible for writing at least two breaking news stories each day. The reporter will also be expected to write additional, longer-form features once a month. These articles will cover broad trends and topics in the industry. For this reason, the reporter will need to be skilled in both research and interviewing.

② The reporter will join a growing team responsible for telling bold and original stories that help an audience of technology professionals stay current with industry news and function efficiently and creatively. Expertise in cutting-edge technology is not required; Omnitech Review will train the right person. University degree preferred. Competitive salary is commensurate with experience, and generous benefits are included.

③ E-mail a cover letter, résumé, and the names of three references (include contact information) to Mr. Kent Xi at k.xi@omnitechreview.com. Reference "Job #1256981" in the subject line of your e-mail.

問題196-200は次のオンラインの投稿、Eメール、ウェブページに関するものです。

6月28日

Chelsea地区のライター向け掲示板をご覧の皆さん、こんにちは！私の名前はThea Fitzgeraldです。私は別の市で仕事に就くため1カ月後に離職することになっています。そこでチームは私の後任の志願者を探しています。空席が出たのは常勤の科学技術記者です。記者は2つの所在地のうちの1つで社内勤務をすることになるでしょう。本社はここニューヨーク市にあり、出張所はワシントンD.C.にあります。チームは8月1日に仕事を始められる志願者に非常に関心を持っています。

私は3年近くOmnitech Review社で働いており、当社をキャリアの向上を求めるライターに大いにお薦めします。この初心者レベルのジャーナリズム職はキャリアをスタートさせるのに素晴らしい方法です。厳しいですが、やりがいもあります。

応募方法が記載された公式の求人告知へのハイパーリンクをここに含めています。ご質問があれば、遠慮なく私に直接Eメールを送ってください。私は採用の担当ではありませんが、喜んで優れた応募書類を上司に渡します。すぐに行動してください。応募締め切りは7月15日です。

Thea Fitzgerald、t.fitzgerald@omnitechreview.com

受信者：t.fitzgerald@omnitechreview.com
送信者：sojinlim@dennisonmail.com
件名：あなたの投稿
日付：6月29日

Fitzgerald様

6月28日の投稿、ありがとうございます。私は当板とその他幾つかの掲示板の管理者です。あなたがおっしゃっているリンクが実際には投稿に含まれていないことに気付きました。読者が求人のお知らせにアクセスできるように、リンクを入れて投稿を修正していただけますか。

また、もし私がこれをワシントンD.C.を本拠としている私どもの雇用掲示板にも重ねて掲示するとお役に立つことができるでしょうか。さらに私は人気のあるFive Boroughs Jobs掲示板にも所属しており、もしその掲示板の利用をご希望でしたらお手伝いできます。しかし大多数の掲示板とは異なり、そこで求人を投稿するには料金を払う必要があります。もし興味がおありなら、私にお知らせください。

敬具

So Jin Lim

---

https://www.omnitechreview.com/open_positions/1256981

科学技術記者（初心者レベル）

科学技術記者は毎日最新ニュース記事を少なくとも2つ書く責任があります。記者はまた1カ月に1度、より掘り下げた内容の特集記事を追加で書くことを求められます。これらの記事はこの業界の幅広い動向や話題を扱います。そのため、記者は調査とインタビューの両方に堪能である必要があります。

記者は、大胆で独創的な記事の執筆を担当する成長途上のチームに加わることになります。それらの記事は、科学技術の専門家である読者が業界の最新ニュースを把握し、能率的かつ創造的に職務を果たす助けとなるものです。最先端の科学技術に関する専門知識は求められていません。Omnitech Review社が適任者を養成します。大学学位があればなお可。給与は経験に応じて優遇し、手厚い福利厚生が含まれます。

カバーレター、履歴書、3人の照会先の名前（連絡先情報を含めて）をk.xi@omnitechreview.comのKent Xiさん宛てにEメールで送ってください。Eメールの件名には、「Job #1256981」と記載してください。

196 What does Ms. Fitzgerald state about herself?

    (A) She is moving soon to Washington, D.C.

    (B) She was recently promoted to a supervisory position.

    (C) She is leaving her job at Omnitech Review in one month.

    (D) She has worked at Omnitech Review for four years.

Fitzgeraldさんは自分自身について何を述べていますか。

    (A) 彼女は間もなくワシントンD.C.に引っ越す。

    (B) 彼女は最近監督的な地位に昇進した。

    (C) 彼女は1カ月後にOmnitech Review社の仕事を辞める。

    (D) 彼女は4年間Omnitech Review社で働いている。

> **正解 C** ❶はFitzgeraldさんによるChelsea地区のライター向け掲示板へのオンラインの投稿。同❶
> 1〜2行目で「私は別の市で仕事に就くため1カ月後に離職する」と述べられている。また同❷
> 1行目に、FitzgeraldさんはOmnitech Review社に3年近く勤務しているとある。よって、Fitzgerald
> さんは1カ月後にOmnitech Review社を辞めると分かるので、(C)が正解。state「〜を述べる」。
> (B) be promoted to 〜「〜に昇進する」、supervisory「監督の」。
> (D) ❶の❷1行目より、Fitzgeraldさんが同社で働いたのは「3年近く」であり、4年間ではない。

197 What is most likely true about the Chelsea Writers board?

    (A) Posts expire within one week.

    (B) Posts are free of charge.

    (C) Posts are always revised by a moderator.

    (D) Posts often contain conflicting information.

Chelsea地区のライター向け掲示板について正しいと考えられることは何ですか。

    (A) 投稿は1週間以内に期限切れとなる。

    (B) 投稿は無料である。

    (C) 投稿はたいてい管理者によって修正される。

    (D) 投稿はよく矛盾する情報を含む。

> **正解 B** Chelsea地区のライター向け掲示板とは、❶の冒頭部分から、6月28日にFitzgeraldさん
> がお知らせを投稿した掲示板。❷のEメール❶1行目で、送信者のLimさんは❶の投稿にお
> 礼を述べ、自分がこの掲示板の管理者だと書いている。同❷2〜4行目で、Limさんは別に自分が関わる
> Five Boroughs Jobs掲示板に触れ、「大多数の掲示板とは異なり、そこで求人を投稿するには料金を払う
> 必要がある」と説明している。例外として言及したFive Boroughs Jobs掲示板とは違い、Chelsea地区
> のライター向け掲示板はmost boards「大多数の掲示板」の1つに当たるので、投稿は無料と考えられる。
> free of charge「無料で」。
> (A) expire「期限切れとなる」。(C) revise「〜を修正する」。
> (D) contain「〜を含む」、conflicting「矛盾する」。

198 What do Ms. Fitzgerald's official work responsibilities at Omnitech Review probably include?

    (A) Writing two articles each day

    (B) Posting job openings

    (C) Conducting training for technology professionals

    (D) Corresponding with editors around the world

FitzgeraldさんのOmnitech Review社での正式な職責はおそらく何を含みますか。

    (A) 毎日2つの記事を書くこと

    (B) 求人広告を投稿すること

    (C) 科学技術の専門家に研修を実施すること

    (D) 世界中の編集者に連絡すること

> **正解 A** ❸のウェブページは科学技術記者（初心者レベル）に関するもの。❶の❶1〜3行目で、
> Fitzgeraldさんは自分が離職した後に欠員となるのは科学技術記者の職であること、また同
> ❷2行目で、This entry-level journalism position「この初心者レベルのジャーナリズム職」に言及してい
> るので、❸のウェブページは、Omnitech Review社がFitzgeraldさんの後任を募集する求人情報と分か
> る。❸の❶1〜2行目に、「科学技術記者は毎日最新ニュース記事を少なくとも2つ書く責任がある」とあり、
> これがFitzgeraldさんの正式な職務内容を記載したものと考えられる。official「正式の」、responsibility
> 「責務」。
> (C) conduct「〜を実施する」。(D) correspond with 〜「〜に連絡する」。

199 In the e-mail, what does Ms. Lim ask Ms. Fitzgerald to do?

(A) Pay an overdue bill as soon as possible

(B) Add some missing information to her online post

(C) Move her online post to a different board

(D) Decide whether she will become a board moderator

Eメールで、LimさんはFitzgeraldさんに何をするように頼んでいますか。

(A) できるだけ早く支払期限の過ぎた請求を支払う

(B) 欠けている情報をオンラインの投稿に加える

(C) オンラインの投稿を別の掲示板に移す

(D) 掲示板の管理者になるかどうか決める

正解 B Limさんが Fitzgeraldさん宛てに送信した**2**のEメール❶1～3行目で、I noticed that the link you mention is actually not included in the post. Would you please edit your post to include the link「あなたが言及しているリンクが実際には投稿に含まれていないことに気付いた。リ ンクを入れて投稿を修正してもらえるか」と述べている。「あなたが言及しているリンク」とは**1**の❸1行目でFitzgeraldさんが投稿に含めていると書いていた「求人告知へのハイパーリンク」を指しているので、(B)が正解。missing「欠けている」。
(A) overdue「支払期限の過ぎた」、bill「請求額、請求書」。

200 According to the Web page, what is a requirement of the technology reporter position?

(A) Attending annual technology conferences

(B) An expert-level understanding of technology issues

(C) An advanced university degree in journalism

(D) The ability to conduct research as needed

ウェブページによると、科学技術記者の職の一つの必要条件は何ですか。

(A) 年1回の科学技術会議に出席すること

(B) 科学技術問題についての専門家レベルの理解

(C) ジャーナリズムにおける大学の上級学位

(D) 必要に応じて調査を行う能力

正解 D Omnitech Review社の求人広告であるウェブページ**3**の❶1～3行目で、記者に採用された場合に書くことになる最新ニュースや特集記事について説明している。同4行目で、これらの記事を書くためにthe reporter will need to be skilled in both research and interviewing「記者は調査とインタビューの両方に堪能である必要がある」と述べられている。よって、(D)が正解。requirement「必要条件」。ability「能力」、as needed「必要に応じて」。
(A) attend「～に出席する」、annual「年1回の」。
(B) **3**の❷3～4行目に「最先端の科学技術に関する専門知識は求められていない」とある。issue「問題」。
(C) **3**の❷4行目に「大学学位があればなお可」とあるが、ジャーナリズムの上級学位とは書かれていない。

Words & Phrases

post 〈名詞で〉投稿、掲示、〈動詞で〉～を投稿する、～を掲示する

1 投稿 ❶ board 掲示板　position 職、勤め口　candidate 志願者　replace ～の後を継ぐ　opening 空き、欠員　full-time 常勤の　in-house 社内で　headquarters 本社　satellite office 出張所　❷ career growth キャリアの向上　entry-level 初心者レベルの　rewarding やりがいのある　challenging 困難な　❸ include ～を含める　apply 応募する　feel free to do 遠慮なく～する　in charge of ～ ～を担当して　hiring 採用、雇用　pass along ～ ～を渡す　supervisor 上司　application 応募書類　stand out 目立つ

2 Eメール ❶ moderator （インターネット掲示板などの）管理者　notice that ～ ～ということに気付く　mention ～に言及する　so (that) ～ can … ～が…するために　❷ cross post ～をクロスポストする　★複数の掲示板に同じ内容の投稿をすること　(be) based in ～ ～を本拠として（いる）　additionally その上　be affiliated with ～ ～に所属している　unlike ～とは異なって　fee 料金

3 ウェブページ ❶ be responsible for ～ ～に責任がある　at least 少なくとも　breaking news 最新ニュース　be expected to do ～することを求められている　long-form 長文の、（記事などが）深く掘り下げた　feature 特集記事　cover ～を扱う　broad 幅広い　trend 動向　industry 業界　skilled 熟練した　❷ growing 大きくなる　bold 大胆な　original 独創的な　audience 読者　stay current with ～ ～の最新情報に精通している　function 職分を果たす　efficiently 能率的に　creatively 創造的に　expertise 専門知識　cutting-edge 最先端の　degree 学位　prefer ～をより好む　competitive 競争力の高い　salary 給与　be commensurate with ～ ～に相応する、～にふさわしい　generous 寛大な、気前のよい　benefits 給付金　❸ cover letter 送付状　résumé 履歴書　reference 〈名詞で〉照会先、身元保証人、〈動詞で〉～に言及する

TEST 2 の正解一覧

リスニングセクション

問題番号	正解
Part 1	
1	C
2	C
3	D
4	C
5	B
6	B
Part 2	
7	A
8	B
9	B
10	C
11	C
12	B
13	B
14	A
15	C
16	C
17	A
18	C
19	B
20	A
21	B
22	B
23	B
24	A
25	B
26	B
27	A
28	C
29	C
30	A
31	A
Part 3	
32	D
33	B
34	C
35	A
36	B
37	A
38	D
39	A
40	C
41	C
42	B
43	A
44	D
45	B
46	A
47	D
48	C
49	A
50	A

問題番号	正解
51	C
52	C
53	A
54	C
55	B
56	A
57	C
58	D
59	B
60	C
61	D
62	C
63	B
64	D
65	C
66	D
67	A
68	A
69	B
70	C
Part 4	
71	A
72	D
73	C
74	A
75	D
76	B
77	B
78	A
79	C
80	C
81	A
82	D
83	B
84	D
85	A
86	C
87	D
88	A
89	C
90	A
91	A
92	A
93	C
94	D
95	C
96	B
97	D
98	B
99	C
100	A

リーディングセクション

問題番号	正解
Part 5	
101	C
102	C
103	C
104	D
105	C
106	C
107	B
108	C
109	B
110	D
111	D
112	D
113	A
114	C
115	D
116	A
117	C
118	D
119	B
120	A
121	D
122	A
123	B
124	A
125	D
126	C
127	A
128	B
129	B
130	A
Part 6	
131	D
132	C
133	A
134	B
135	C
136	A
137	B
138	D
139	C
140	B
141	B
142	A
143	A
144	D
145	C
146	D
Part 7	
147	C
148	A
149	B
150	A

問題番号	正解
151	D
152	B
153	C
154	D
155	C
156	D
157	B
158	B
159	D
160	C
161	A
162	C
163	B
164	B
165	D
166	D
167	B
168	B
169	D
170	A
171	B
172	A
173	C
174	C
175	D
176	C
177	B
178	D
179	A
180	D
181	C
182	D
183	B
184	A
185	A
186	A
187	D
188	B
189	B
190	C
191	D
192	B
193	B
194	C
195	B
196	A
197	B
198	D
199	A
200	B

1

2

3

---

1 🇺🇸 W

(A) He's looking through some window shades.
(B) He's dusting a shelf.
(C) He's using a printer.
(D) He's plugging in some equipment.

(A) 彼はブラインドから外を見ている。
(B) 彼は棚のほこりを払っている。
(C) 彼はプリンターを使用している。
(D) 彼は機器を電源につないでいるところである。

> **正解 C** 男性はプリンターを使っているところである。printer「プリンター」。
> (A) look through ～「～を通して見る」、window shade「ブラインド、日よけ」。
> (B) dust「～のほこりを払う」、shelf「棚」。
> (D) equipment「機器」は写っているが、男性はそれを電源につないでいるところではない。plug in ～「～を電源につなぐ」。

---

2 🇨🇦 M

(A) The people are cleaning a counter.
(B) The people are greeting one another.
(C) One of the women is sipping through a straw.
(D) One of the women is filling up a water bottle.

(A) 人々はカウンターを掃除している。
(B) 人々はお互いにあいさつしている。
(C) 女性の1人はストローで少しずつ飲んでいる。
(D) 女性の1人は水筒を満たしているところである。

> **正解 C** 右側の女性がストローを使って飲み物を飲んでいる。sip「少しずつ飲む」。
> (A) 人々はcounter「カウンター、売り台」の前に立っているが、それを掃除してはいない。
> (B) 人々はお互いに向き合っていない。greet「～にあいさつする」、one another「お互い」。
> (D) 中央の女性が液体を注ごうとしているのは、water bottle「水筒」ではない。fill up ～「～を満たす」。

---

3 🇬🇧 W

(A) He is replacing some tiles.
(B) He is bending over a toolbox.
(C) Some bikes are being repaired.
(D) Some plants are growing in bins.

(A) 彼はタイルを交換している。
(B) 彼は道具箱の上にかがみ込んでいる。
(C) 自転車が修理されているところである。
(D) 植物が大箱の中に生えている。

> **正解 D** 大箱の中に複数の植物が見える。grow「生える」、bin「大箱、容器」。
> (A) replace「～を交換する」、tile「タイル」。
> (B) 男性がかがみ込んでいる位置は大箱の上であり、toolbox「道具箱」の上ではない。bend over ～「～の方向にかがむ」。
> (C) 奥に複数の自転車が写っているが、男性はそれらを修理しているところではない。repair「～を修理する」。

4

5

6

---

4 🇦🇺 M

(A) Promotional posters are being attached to the wall.
(B) One of the shoppers is holding a freezer door open.
(C) Some groceries are being pushed in shopping carts.
(D) The shoppers are walking toward each other.

(A) 販売促進用ポスターが壁に貼り付けられているところである。
(B) 買い物客の1人は冷凍庫の扉を押さえて開けたままにしている。
(C) 食料雑貨品がカートに入れられて押されているところである。
(D) 買い物客たちはお互いに向かって歩いている。

正解 **C** 買い物客たちは複数の食料品の入ったショッピングカートを押している。groceries「食料雑貨品」。
(A) 天井に販売促進用のバナーがつるしてあるが、ポスターが壁に貼り付けられているところではない。promotional「販売促進の」、attach「〜を貼り付ける」。
(B) hold 〜 …「〜を…のままにしておく」、freezer「冷凍庫」。
(D) 買い物客は別々の方向に向かっている。

---

5 🇬🇧 W

(A) One of the women is removing her glasses.
(B) One of the women has her arms extended up.
(C) The women are putting paper into a shredder.
(D) The women are passing through a door.

(A) 女性の1人は眼鏡を外しているところである。
(B) 女性の1人は両腕を上に伸ばしている。
(C) 女性たちは紙をシュレッダーにかけている。
(D) 女性たちはドアを通り抜けているところである。

正解 **B** 右側の女性が両腕を上方に伸ばしている。extend「〜を伸ばす」。
(A) 左側の女性は眼鏡を掛けている状態で、外しているところではない。remove「〜（身に着けている物）を外す、〜を脱ぐ」。
(C) shredder「シュレッダー」。
(D) pass through 〜「〜を通り抜ける」。

---

6 🇨🇦 M

(A) Some bricks are piled on a corner.
(B) Some wires are suspended above a street.
(C) Some cars are parked in a garage.
(D) Some buildings are under construction.

(A) れんがが曲がり角に積み重ねられている。
(B) 電線が通りの上に架かっている。
(C) 車が車庫に駐車されている。
(D) 建物が建設中である。

正解 **B** 複数の電線が道の上方に架かっている。wire「電線」、suspend「〜をつるす」。
(A) 道は brick「れんが」で舗装されているが、それらは積み重ねられてはいない。pile「〜を積み重ねる」、corner「曲がり角」。
(C) 車が駐車されているのは garage「車庫」ではなく路上である。park「〜を駐車する」。
(D) 建設中の建物は写っていない。under construction「建設中で」。

PART 2

7 W What did you order to eat?

M (A) Pasta with meat sauce.
(B) It's a new restaurant.
(C) I'd like the check, please.

あなたは食事に何を注文しましたか。
(A) ミートソースパスタです。
(B) そこは新しいレストランです。
(C) お勘定をお願いします。

正解 A 食事に何を注文したか尋ねているのに対し、具体的な料理名を伝えている(A)が正解。order「～を注文する」。pasta「パスタ」、meat sauce「ミートソース」。
(B) itが何を指すか不明であり、レストランについては尋ねられていない。
(C) check「勘定書」。

8 M Where should I leave the maintenance report?

W (A) No, I haven't left yet.
(B) On my desk.
(C) Every day this month.

保守管理報告書はどこに置いておけばいいですか。
(A) いいえ、私はまだ出発していません。
(B) 私の机の上に。
(C) 今月中は毎日です。

正解 B Where ～?で保守管理報告書をどこに置いておけばいいか尋ねているのに対し、「私の机の上」という具体的な場所を示している(B)が正解。leave「～を置いておく」、maintenance「保守管理」、report「報告書」。
(A) 場所を尋ねられているので、Yes/Noでは応答にならない。
(C) 日や期間は尋ねられていない。

9 W When will my library book be due?

M (A) Yes, I do.
(B) In three weeks.
(C) The reference section.

私の図書館の本はいつが返却期限ですか。
(A) はい、そうします。
(B) 3週間後です。
(C) 参考文献コーナーです。

正解 B When ～?で借りている図書館の本の返却期限がいつか尋ねているのに対し、具体的な期限を伝えている(B)が正解。due「(提出物などの)期限が来て」。
(A) 時を尋ねられているので、Yes/Noでは応答にならない。また、Yesで何を肯定しているか不明。
(C) reference「参考文献、レファレンス」、section「部門」。

10 M Why haven't I been receiving e-mails?

W (A) I'll read the review right now.
(B) Usually a new assignment.
(C) Because you need to update your software.

なぜ私は、ずっとEメールを受信できていないのですか。
(A) 今すぐにそのレビューを読みます。
(B) 通常は新しい業務です。
(C) ソフトウエアを更新する必要があるからです。

正解 C Why ～?で自分がEメールを受信できない状態でいる理由を尋ねている。これに対し、Because ～を用いて、「ソフトウエアを更新する必要があるからだ」と答えている(C)が正解。receive「～を受信する」。update「～を更新する」。
(A) review「レビュー、書評」は話題に上っていない。right now「今すぐに」。
(B) assignment「(割り当てられた)業務」。

11 M Could you please set up the equipment for tomorrow's experiment?

W (A) They had a great experience.
(B) Some important research.
(C) Sure, I'd be happy to.

明日の実験に向けて機器を準備していただけますか。
(A) 彼らは素晴らしい体験をしました。
(B) 重要な研究です。
(C) いいですよ、喜んでやります。

正解 C Could you ～?で明日の実験に向けて機器を準備することを依頼しているのに対し、Sure, I'd be happy to (set it up).と快諾している(C)が正解。set up ～「～を準備する、～を使える状態にする」、equipment「機器」、experiment「実験」。
(A) 質問にあるexperimentと似た音のexperience「体験」に注意。
(B) important「重要な」、research「研究」。

12 🇦🇺 M Who do I ask about getting a visitor badge?

🇺🇸 W (A) It was a long trip.
(B) The security guard will help you.
(C) OK, I'll meet you in the parking area.

訪問者用バッジの入手について誰に尋ねたらいいですか。

(A) それは長旅でした。
(B) 警備員が手助けしてくれるでしょう。
(C) 分かりました、駐車場で会いましょう。

正解 B Who ～?で訪問者用バッジの入手について誰に尋ねたらいいか質問しているのに対し、「警備員が手助けしてくれるだろう」と、尋ねるべき人物を教えている(B)が正解。visitor「訪問者」、badge「バッジ、名札」。security guard「警備員」。
(A) Itが何を指しているか不明。
(C) OKで何を了承しているか不明であり、どこで会うかは尋ねられていない。parking area「駐車場」。

13 🇺🇸 W How many employees will participate in the training session?

🇨🇦 M (A) I'm great, thanks.
(B) Fourteen signed up.
(C) On Wednesday.

研修会には何人の従業員が参加する予定ですか。

(A) とても元気です、ありがとう。
(B) 14人が受講登録しました。
(C) 水曜日です。

正解 B How many ～?で何人の従業員が研修会に参加する予定か尋ねているのに対し、「14人が受講登録した」と登録人数を伝えている(B)が正解。employee「従業員」、participate in ～「～に参加する」、training session「研修会」。sign up「受講登録をする」。
(A) 人数を尋ねられているので、体調を答える内容は応答にならない。
(C) 曜日は尋ねられていない。

14 🇬🇧 W Should we call the contest winner today or tomorrow?

🇨🇦 M (A) Let's call now.
(B) In your inbox.
(C) No, it's the other one.

私たちはコンテストの優勝者に今日電話をかけるべきですか、それとも明日がいいですか。

(A) 今電話をかけましょう。
(B) あなたの受信箱の中です。
(C) いいえ、それはもう一方の人です。

正解 A A or B?の形で、コンテストの優勝者への電話連絡を今日と明日のどちらにすべきか尋ねている。これに対し、「今電話をかけよう」と、すぐに連絡することを提案している(A)が正解。call「～に電話をかける」、contest「コンテスト、大会」、winner「受賞者、受賞作品」。
(B) 場所は尋ねられていない。inbox「受信箱」。
(C) Noで何を否定しているか不明。またoneが優勝者を指すとしても、誰を指すのか不明。

15 🇨🇦 M Excuse me, when will our food be ready?

🇬🇧 W (A) The chef created the menu.
(B) A new microwave.
(C) The kitchen is really busy.

すみません、私たちの料理はいつ用意ができますか。

(A) 料理長がそのメニューを作りました。
(B) 新しい電子レンジです。
(C) 厨房が大変込み合っておりまして。

正解 C Excuse meと呼び掛けて、when ～?で料理の用意がいつできるか尋ねているのに対し、「厨房が込み合っている」と述べ、料理の提供に時間がかかることを示唆している(C)が正解。ready「用意ができて」、kitchen「厨房」。
(A) chef「料理長、シェフ」、create「～を作る」。
(B) foodと関連する名詞microwave「電子レンジ」が含まれるが、応答になっていない。

16 🇦🇺 M How can we stay in budget for these repairs?

🇺🇸 W (A) Around 500 euros.
(B) Sure, I can buy lightbulbs tonight.
(C) We can get estimates from several companies.

どうすればこれらの修理作業を予算内に収めることができるでしょうか。

(A) およそ500ユーロです。
(B) 分かりました、私は今夜、電球を買うことができます。
(C) 複数の会社から見積もりを取ればいいですよ。

正解 C How ～?で、どうすれば修理作業を予算内に収めることができるか、方法を尋ねている。これに対し、複数業者からの見積もり入手を提案している(C)が正解。stay in ～「～にとどまる」、budget「予算」、repairs「修理作業」、estimate「見積もり」、several「複数の」。
(A) 金額は尋ねられていない。euro「ユーロ」。
(B) lightbulb「電球」。

17 W Is there enough seating for the seminar?

M (A) Yes, we added extra chairs in the back.
(B) A biology conference.
(C) Because I sat in economy class.

セミナーのために十分な座席数がありますか。
(A) はい、私たちは後ろの方に追加の椅子を足しました。
(B) 生物学の協議会です。
(C) 私はエコノミークラスの席に座っていたからです。

正解 A　セミナーのために十分な座席数があるか尋ねているのに対し、Yesと肯定してから、「私たちは後ろの方に追加の椅子を足した」と述べ、座席数が十分であることを説明している(A)が正解。seating「座席数」、seminar「セミナー」。add「～を追加する」、extra「余分の」、back「後方」。
(B) 質問にあるseminarと関連するconference「協議会」が含まれるが、応答にならない。biology「生物学」。
(C) economy class「エコノミークラス（旅客機などの価格が低い座席区分）」。

18 W Where do you keep the paper for the printer?

M (A) No, you can throw that away.
(B) A newspaper subscription.
(C) I just reloaded it.

プリンターの用紙をどこに保管していますか。
(A) いいえ、それは処分しても構いませんよ。
(B) 新聞の定期購読です。
(C) 私がちょうど、それに給紙したところです。

正解 C　Where ～?でプリンター用紙の保管場所を尋ねているのに対し、「私がちょうど、それに給紙したところだ」と、プリンターに用紙を補充する必要がないことを示唆している(C)が正解。itは質問にあるthe printerを指す。reload「～に補充する」。
(A) 場所を尋ねられているので、Yes/Noでは応答にならない。throw away ～「～を処分する」。
(B) subscription「定期購読」。

19 W Your boxes are ready to be picked up from the warehouse.

M (A) A detailed description.
(B) Thanks, I'll come for them this afternoon.
(C) The old delivery truck.

あなたの箱は倉庫から受け取れる準備ができています。
(A) 詳細な説明です。
(B) ありがとう、今日の午後にそれらを取りに行きます。
(C) 古い配達用トラックです。

正解 B　「あなたの箱は倉庫から受け取れる準備ができている」と知らせる発言に対し、礼を述べて「今日の午後にそれらを取りに行く」と、受け取りに行く時間帯を伝えている(B)が正解。be ready to do「～する準備ができている」、pick up ～「～を受け取る」、warehouse「倉庫」。
(A) detailed「詳細な」、description「説明」。
(C) 質問にあるpicked upやwarehouseと関連するdelivery truckが含まれるが、応答になっていない。

20 M Isn't the city mayor supposed to give a speech at one P.M.?

W (A) No unfortunately—it's been delayed.
(B) I ordered the gift online.
(C) A meeting invitation.

市長は午後1時にスピーチをすることになっているのではないですか。
(A) いいえ、あいにく——それは遅れています。
(B) 私はオンラインでその贈り物を注文しました。
(C) 会議への招待状です。

正解 A　否定疑問文で、「市長は午後1時にスピーチをすることになっているのではないか」と確認しているのに対し、Noと否定してから、スピーチ開始の遅延を知らせている(A)が正解。be supposed to do「～することになっている」、city mayor「市長」、give a speech「スピーチをする」。unfortunately「あいにく」、delay「～を遅らせる」。
(B) 質問にあるgiveと関連するgift「贈り物」に注意。order「～を注文する」、online「オンラインで」。
(C) invitation「招待状」。

21 W I'd like to schedule my next appointment, please.

M (A) No, thank you, I can wait.
(B) OK, does Monday work for you?
(C) It's next to the calendar.

次の予約を入れたいのですが。
(A) いいえ、結構です、私は待てますよ。
(B) 分かりました、月曜日はご都合はいかがですか。
(C) それはカレンダーの隣です。

正解 B　「次の予約を入れたい」と予約の設定を求めているのに対し、OKと了承した上で、月曜日は都合が良いか聞き返している(B)が正解。schedule「～を予定に入れる」、appointment「予約、会う約束」。work for ～「～に都合が良い」。
(A) No, thank youは申し出を断る表現。
(C) Itが何を指しているか不明であり、応答になっていない。next to ～「～の隣に」、calendar「カレンダー」。

22 🇨🇦 M I lost my bus pass.

🇺🇸 W (A) Did you buy tickets to the game?
(B) Well, the ticket machine is right there.
(C) Sure, tomorrow sounds perfect.

バスの定期券を紛失してしまいました。
(A) あなたはその試合のチケットを買いましたか。
(B) それなら、券売機はすぐそこにありますよ。
(C) いいですね、明日は完璧に思えます。

正解 B 「バスの定期券を紛失した」という発言に対し、Wellと一呼吸置いてから、「券売機はすぐそこにある」と券売機の位置を教え、購入を勧めている(B)が正解。pass「定期券」。ticket machine「券売機」。
(A) 発言にあるbusやpassと関連するticketsが含まれるが、試合については言及されていない。
(C) Sureで何を肯定しているか不明であり、明日についての状況は尋ねられていない。

23 🇦🇺 M Why is Ridderson's Supermarket closing?

🇺🇸 W (A) Milk, yogurt, and orange juice.
(B) Sorry, I don't live around here.
(C) I use plastic bags.

Ridderson'sスーパーマーケットはなぜ閉店するのですか。
(A) 牛乳、ヨーグルト、オレンジジュースです。
(B) すみませんが、私はこの辺りに住んでいないのです。
(C) 私はビニール袋を使います。

正解 B Why ～?でRidderson'sスーパーマーケットが閉店する理由を尋ねている。それに対し、Sorryと謝ってから、「私はこの辺りに住んでいない」と答え、閉店理由を知らないことを示唆している(B)が正解。
(A) 質問にあるSupermarketに関連するMilk、yogurt、orange juiceが含まれるが、商品は尋ねられていない。
(C) plastic bag「ビニール袋」。

24 🇬🇧 W You didn't cancel the flight, did you?

🇺🇸 W (A) No, did you want me to?
(B) About two hours long.
(C) It stops on Fifth Avenue.

あなたはその便をキャンセルしなかったのですよね？
(A) していません、私にそうしてほしかったのですか。
(B) 約2時間の長さです。
(C) それは五番街に止まります。

正解 A 否定文の文末に ～, did you?を付けて「～でしたよね」と、飛行機の便をキャンセルしなかったのか確認している。これに対し、「していない」と伝えて、キャンセルすることが自分に求められていたのか聞き返して確かめている(A)が正解。cancel「～をキャンセルする」、flight「航空機の便、フライト」。
(B) 時間の長さについては尋ねられていない。
(C) avenue「大通り」。

25 🇺🇸 W What's today's meeting about?

🇦🇺 M (A) About an hour away.
(B) The agenda wasn't very clear.
(C) In Conference Room A, I think.

今日の会議は何についてですか。
(A) 約1時間の所にあります。
(B) 議題はあまり明瞭ではありませんでした。
(C) 会議室Aだと思います。

正解 B 今日の会議が何に関するものか尋ねているのに対し、「議題はあまり明瞭ではなかった」と述べ、何に関しての会議なのか自分は十分に把握していないことを示している(B)が正解。agenda「議題」、clear「明瞭な」。
(A) 距離や時間は尋ねられていない。an hour away「1時間で行ける距離」。
(C) 場所は尋ねられていない。conference「会議」。

26 🇬🇧 W Hasn't the redesigned Web site been launched already?

🇨🇦 M (A) That historical site overlooks the mountains.
(B) The client wanted another change.
(C) Maybe some online reviews.

再設計されたウェブサイトはもう立ち上げられているのではないのですか。
(A) あの史跡からは山が見渡せます。
(B) 顧客がもう一点変更を求めたのです。
(C) おそらくオンラインのレビューです。

正解 B 否定疑問文で、「再設計されたウェブサイトはもう立ち上げられているのではないのか」と確認している。それに対し、顧客が新たな変更を求めたことを伝えて、ウェブサイトが開設されていない状況を示唆している(B)が正解。redesign「～を再設計する」、launch「～を立ち上げる」。client「顧客」。
(A) historical site「史跡」、overlook「～を見渡す」。
(C) online「オンラインの」、review「レビュー、批評」。

27 🇨🇦 M Who's receiving the shipment of construction materials today?

🇺🇸 W (A) Please check with Ms. Choi.
(B) A production schedule.
(C) I hope that's OK.

誰が今日、建設資材の積み荷を受け取りますか。
(A) Choiさんに確認してください。
(B) 生産計画表です。
(C) それで大丈夫だと良いのですが。

正解 A Who ～?で誰が今日、建設資材の積み荷を受け取ることになっているか尋ねているのに対し、「Choiさんに確認してください」と、その情報を知っている人物名を挙げて、その人に確認するよう促している(A)が正解。who'sはwho isの短縮形。receive「～を受け取る」、shipment「積み荷」、construction「建設」、material「材料」。check with ～「～に確認する」。
(B) production「生産」、schedule「計画表」。
(C) thatが何を指すか不明。

---

28 🇨🇦 M Would you prefer renting an office in the financial district or the historic district?

🇦🇺 M (A) A rental car agreement.
(B) It wasn't very long.
(C) Both will be expensive.

金融地区に事務所を借りるのをご希望ですか、それとも歴史地区をご希望ですか。
(A) レンタカーの契約です。
(B) それはあまり長くありませんでした。
(C) どちらも費用がかかるでしょうね。

正解 C A or B?の形で、金融地区と歴史地区のどちらに事務所を借りたいか尋ねている。これに対し、「どちらも費用がかかるだろう」と述べ、両方とも好ましくないことを示唆している(C)が正解。prefer doing「～する方を好む」、rent「～を賃借する」、financial「金融の」、district「地区」、historic「歴史上重要な」。expensive「費用がかかる」。
(A) rental car「レンタカー」、agreement「契約、契約書」。

---

29 🇦🇺 M We need to hire another graphic designer to keep up with demand.

🇬🇧 W (A) No, we keep it in the top drawer.
(B) Turn left at the stop sign.
(C) I've already posted a job opening.

私たちは需要についていけるよう、グラフィックデザイナーをもう1人雇用する必要があります。
(A) いいえ、私たちはそれを最上段の引き出しに保管しています。
(B) 一時停止標識の所を左に曲がってください。
(C) 私はすでに求人の掲示をしました。

正解 C 「私たちは需要についていけるよう、グラフィックデザイナーをもう1人雇用する必要がある」という発言に対し、「私はすでに求人の掲示をした」と述べ、すでに募集をかけていることを伝えている(C)が正解。hire「～を雇用する」、keep up with ～「～に遅れずについていく」、demand「需要」。post「～を掲示する」、job opening「求人、職の空き」。
(A) 質問にあるkeepを含むが、itが何を指すか不明。top drawer「最上段の引き出し」。
(B) stop sign「一時停止標識」。

---

30 🇬🇧 W Have you heard the radio advertisement for our company yet?

🇦🇺 M (A) They chose a good voice actor.
(B) Check the supply closet.
(C) A jazz concert.

あなたはもう、当社のラジオ広告を聞きましたか。
(A) 良い声優を選びましたね。
(B) 備品保管室を確認してください。
(C) ジャズのコンサートです。

正解 A 会社のラジオ広告をもう聞いたか尋ねているのに対し、「良い声優を選んだ」と肯定的な感想を述べ、すでに広告を耳にしたことを伝えている(A)が正解。advertisement「広告」。choose「～を選ぶ」、voice actor「声優」。
(B) supply closet「備品保管室」。
(C) 質問にあるheardやradioと関連するjazz「ジャズ」やconcert「コンサート」を含むが、応答になっていない。

---

31 🇺🇸 W The wood cutting machine's being fixed today, isn't it?

🇨🇦 M (A) I just saw a service technician leave.
(B) The human resources department.
(C) Yes, it comes in several colors.

木材切削機は今日、修理されているのですよね？
(A) たった今、修理技術者が去るのを見ました。
(B) 人事部です。
(C) はい、それは数色で販売されています。

正解 A 肯定文の文末に ～, isn't it?を付けて、木材切削機が今日修理されているか確認している。これに対し、「たった今、修理技術者が去るのを見た」と述べ、修理の完了を示唆している(A)が正解。wood cutting machine「木材切削機」、fix「～を修理する」。service technician「修理技術者」。
(B) human resources department「人事部」。
(C) come in ～「(商品などが)～の形で売られる」。

109

Questions 32 through 34 refer to the following conversation.

問題32-34は次の会話に関するものです。

M ❶Thanks for calling Dratson's Musical Instruments. ❷Guitars, drums, or clarinets—we have it all!

Dratson楽器店にお電話いただきありがとうございます。ギター、ドラム、クラリネット——当店は何でも取りそろえています！

W Hi, I'm calling on behalf of Spring Tree Learning. We're a nonprofit educational organization.

こんにちは、私はSpring Tree Learningを代表してお電話しています。私どもは非営利教育団体です。

M Sure, I'm familiar with that name.

もちろん、そのお名前はよく知っています。

W ❸I'm calling to see if your business would be interested in becoming one of our sponsors for an upcoming fund-raising event that we'll be holding.

お電話しているのは、そちらのお店が、私どもが近々開催する資金集めイベントの後援企業の一つになることにご関心がおありかどうかお伺いするためです。

M That sounds interesting, but ❹the owner's out on a family vacation. Can I take your number so that he can return your call?

それは興味深いお話ですが、オーナーが家族休暇中で不在にしています。彼が折り返しお電話差し上げられるよう、そちらの番号を控えさせていただくことはできますか。

32 Where does the man work?

(A) At a theater
(B) At a radio station
(C) At an art gallery
(D) At a musical instrument shop

男性はどこで働いていますか。

(A) 劇場
(B) ラジオ局
(C) 画廊
(D) 楽器店

正解 D 男性は❶で、Dratson楽器店にお電話ありがとう、と応答してから、❷「ギター、ドラム、クラリネット——当店は何でも取りそろえています」と、楽器の品ぞろえの豊富さをアピールしている。よって、男性は楽器店で働いていると判断できる。
(A) theater「劇場」。
(B) station「放送局」。
(C) art gallery「画廊、美術館」。

33 What does the woman ask the business to do?

(A) Post some signs
(B) Sponsor an event
(C) Mentor some students
(D) Change a policy

女性は店に何をするよう求めていますか。

(A) 掲示を貼り出す
(B) イベントを後援する
(C) 学生に助言する
(D) 方針を変更する

正解 B 電話をかけてきた女性は、自分が所属している団体について伝えた後、❸「電話しているのは、あなたの店が、私たちが近々開催する資金集めイベントの後援企業の一つになることに関心があるかどうか確かめるためだ」と電話の目的を述べている。よって、(B)が正解。sponsor「～を後援する」。
(A) post「～（ビラなど）を貼り出す」、sign「掲示」。
(C) mentor「～に助言する」。
(D) policy「方針」。

34 Why is the owner currently unavailable?

(A) He is taking a lunch break.
(B) He is conducting an interview.
(C) He is on vacation.
(D) He is visiting a client.

オーナーはなぜ、現在都合がつかないのですか。

(A) 彼は昼食休憩を取っているから。
(B) 彼は面接を実施しているから。
(C) 彼は休暇中だから。
(D) 彼は顧客を訪問しているから。

正解 C 女性が❸で、店がイベントの後援に関心があるか尋ねているのに対し、男性はそれが興味深い話だと言いつつも、❹「オーナーが家族休暇中で不在だ」と、現在の状況を説明しているので、(C)が正解。currently「現在」、unavailable「都合がつかない」。
(A) break「休憩」。
(B) conduct「～を実施する」、interview「面接」。
(D) client「顧客」。

Words & Phrases

musical instrument 楽器　guitar ギター　drum ドラム　clarinet クラリネット　on behalf of ～ ～を代表して　nonprofit 非営利の　educational 教育の　organization 団体　be familiar with ～ ～をよく知っている　business 店、会社　be interested in ～ ～に関心がある　sponsor 後援者、スポンサー　upcoming 今度の、近づいている　fund-raising 資金集めの　hold ～を開催する　interesting 興味深い　owner オーナー、所有者　out （家や職場などから）外出して、不在の　on vacation 休暇中で　take ～を書き留める　return one's call ～に折り返し電話する

Questions 35 through 37 refer to the following conversation.

M Hello, ❶are you ready to order?

W ❷Can I have a cup of coffee and a slice of lemon cake?

M ❸Certainly. It'll be just a minute.

W Thanks. ❹I just love the cake here—I wish I knew what made it so tasty.

M Actually, ❺we just released a cookbook with some of our signature recipes since so many customers often ask us about them.

W Wonderful! I'll definitely purchase one.

M And you should know, ❻we're having a photo competition. ❼If you bake something from the cookbook and put a photograph of it on our social media page, you could win a gift card.

問題35-37は次の会話に関するものです。

こんにちは、ご注文はお決まりですか。

コーヒーを1杯とレモンケーキを1切れ頂けますか。

かしこまりました。すぐにお持ちします。

ありがとう。私はこちらのケーキがとにかく大好きです――どうすればこんなにおいしくなるのか分かったら良いのですが。

実は、非常にたくさんのお客さまが頻繁にレシピについてお尋ねになるので、私どもはちょうど、当店の代表的なレシピの一部を掲載した料理本を発売したところです。

素晴らしいですね！絶対に1冊買います。

それから、ぜひ知っておいていただきたいのですが、私どもは写真コンテストを開催中です。その料理本から何かを作って、当店のソーシャルメディアのページにその写真を載せていただければ、あなたはギフトカードを勝ち取れるかもしれませんよ。

---

35 Where does the conversation most likely take place?

(A) At a café
(B) At a library
(C) At an electronics shop
(D) At a sports arena

会話はどこで行われていると考えられますか。

(A) カフェ
(B) 図書館
(C) 電子機器店
(D) 運動競技場

正解 A ❶で注文を尋ねる男性に、女性は❷「コーヒーを1杯とレモンケーキを1切れもらえるか」と答えている。注文を受けた男性が❸で、すぐに持ってくると伝えていることからも、会話は飲食物を提供するカフェで行われていると考えられる。take place「行われる」。
(C) electronics「電子機器」。
(D) arena「競技場」。

---

36 According to the man, what did the business recently do?

(A) It opened a second location.
(B) It released a book.
(C) It changed a floor plan.
(D) It finalized a contract.

男性によると、店は最近何をしましたか。

(A) 第2号店を開店した。
(B) 本を発売した。
(C) 間取りを変更した。
(D) 契約を締結した。

正解 B ❹で、この店のケーキがおいしい理由を知りたいと述べる女性に対し、男性は❺で、多くの客からの質問に応えて、最近店のレシピの料理本を発売したと伝えている。recently「最近」。
(A) location「店舗、所在地」。
(C) floor plan「間取図、フロアプラン」。
(D) finalize「～を最終決定する」、contract「契約」。

---

37 How can the woman win a gift card?

(A) By posting a photograph
(B) By completing an online survey
(C) By attending a special event
(D) By commenting on a video

女性はどうすればギフトカードを手に入れることができますか。

(A) 写真を投稿することによって
(B) オンライン調査に全て回答することによって
(C) 特別なイベントに出席することによって
(D) 動画についてコメントをすることによって

正解 A 男性は❻で、店が写真コンテストを開催中であることを知らせた後、❼「その料理本から何かを作って、当店のソーシャルメディアのページにその写真を載せてもらえれば、あなたはギフトカードを勝ち取れるかもしれない」とそのコンテストでギフトカード獲得の可能性があると案内をしている。post「～を投稿する」。
(B) complete「～に全て記入する」、survey「調査」。
(C) attend「～に出席する」。
(D) comment on ～「～についてコメントをする」。

Words & Phrases

be ready to *do* ～する準備ができている　　a cup of ～ 1杯の～　　a slice of ～ 1切れの～
wish (that) ～ ～であれば良いのだが　　tasty おいしい　　release ～を発売する　　cookbook 料理本
signature 代表的な　　recipe レシピ　　definitely 絶対に、断然　　purchase ～を購入する
competition コンテスト、競技会　　bake ～を焼く　　social media ソーシャルメディア　　win ～を獲得する
gift card ギフトカード

TEST 2 PART 3

Questions 38 through 40 refer to the following conversation.

問題38-40は次の会話に関するものです。

W Akira, **❶**I just checked which booth we'll have at the job fair this weekend. **❷**It looks like all the software companies will be located near the entrance.

Akira、私はちょうど、今週末の合同企業説明会で当社がどのブースをもらえるか確認したところです。全てのソフトウエア企業が、入り口近くに配置されるようですよ。

M Great. **❸**I hope we'll find some experienced software engineers there.

良かったです。そこで経験豊かなソフトウエアエンジニアが見つかることを願います。

W So do I. The doors open at eight, so we should leave here by five thirty A.M.

私もです。8時開場なので、私たちはここを午前5時30分までに出発すべきですね。

M OK. **❹**I already reserved a company car. **❺**Let's meet in the parking area at five twenty.

はい。私はすでに社用車を予約しました。5時20分に駐車場で会いましょう。

W Good idea. **❻**We'll need a little extra time to load the boxes with the promotional materials we'll be handing out to the job applicants.

いいですね。求職者に配布予定の宣伝資料が入った箱を積み込むのに、私たちには少し余分な時間が必要でしょうから。

---

38 What field do the speakers most likely work in?

(A) Hospitality
(B) Advertising
(C) Interior design
(D) Software development

話し手たちはどんな分野で働いていると考えられますか。

(A) 接客業
(B) 広告
(C) 室内装飾
(D) ソフトウエア開発

正解 D 女性は❶で、合同企業説明会における自社ブースの位置を確認したと伝えてから、❷「全てのソフトウエア企業が、入り口近くに配置されるようだ」と知らせている。また、男性が❸「そこで経験豊かなソフトウエアエンジニアが見つかることを願う」と述べていることからも、話し手たちはソフトウエア開発の分野で働いていると判断できる。field「分野」。development「開発」。
(A) hospitality「もてなし」。
(B) advertising「広告」。
(C) interior design「室内装飾」。

---

39 What does the man say he did?

(A) He reserved a car.
(B) He updated a schedule.
(C) He created a new logo.
(D) He paid a registration fee.

男性は何をしたと言っていますか。

(A) 彼は車を予約した。
(B) 彼は予定表を更新した。
(C) 彼は新しいロゴを作成した。
(D) 彼は登録料を支払った。

正解 A 説明会当日に出発すべき時刻を伝える女性に対し、男性は同意した後、❹「私はすでに社用車を予約した」と自身が車の予約を済ませたことを知らせている。
(B) update「～を更新する」、schedule「予定表」。
(C) create「～を作成する」、logo「ロゴ」。
(D) registration「登録」、fee「料金」。

---

40 Why will the speakers need extra time?

(A) To stop for some food
(B) To check in at a hotel
(C) To load some boxes
(D) To read some directions

話し手たちにはなぜ余分な時間が必要になるのですか。

(A) 食料を買うのに店に立ち寄るため
(B) ホテルにチェックインするため
(C) 箱を積み込むため
(D) 道順を見て理解するため

正解 C ❺で、説明会当日の集合場所と時刻を提案する男性に対し、女性は了解してから、❻「求職者に配布予定の宣伝資料が入った箱を積み込むのに、私たちには少し余分な時間が必要だろう」と述べている。よって、(C)が正解。
(A) stop「(店などに)立ち寄る」。
(B) check in at ～「～にチェックインする、～で(宿泊や搭乗の)手続きをする」。
(D) directions「道順」。

Words & Phrases

booth ブース　job fair 合同企業説明会　It looks like ～ ～のようである
locate ～を配置する　entrance 入り口　experienced 経験豊かな　reserve ～を予約する　company car 社用車
parking area 駐車場　extra 余分の　load ～を積み込む　promotional 宣伝の、販売促進の　material 資料
hand out ～ ～を配布する　job applicant 求職者

Questions 41 through 43 refer to the following conversation.

W Laurent, ❶did you get the e-mail I sent you about our meeting on Wednesday? ❷I'd like to meet at eleven o'clock instead of one so I can go to the doctor in the afternoon.

M I can't connect to the Internet. ❸But I think eleven o'clock on Wednesday should work fine. Have you been having any issues with the Wi-Fi today?

W No, I was able to connect. ❹Are you using the new password? The IT department changed it this morning—routine security maintenance. ❺I have it written down at my desk. I'll go get it for you.

問題41-43は次の会話に関するものです。

Laurent、水曜日の会議について私が送ったEメールは受け取りましたか。私は午後に医者に行けるよう、1時ではなく11時に集まりたいと思っているのですが。

私はインターネットに接続できないのです。でも、水曜日の11時で都合がつくはずだと思います。あなたの方は、今日Wi-Fiに何か問題が生じていますか。

いいえ、私は接続できましたよ。あなたは新しいパスワードを使っていますか。情報技術部は今朝、それを変更しました――いつものセキュリティー保守管理です。私はそれを書き留めてデスクに置いています。あなたのためにそれを取りに行ってきましょう。

TEST 2 PART 3

41 Why does the woman want to change a meeting time?

(A) She will be training some employees.
(B) She is scheduled to attend a lunch.
(C) She has a doctor's appointment.
(D) She is finishing a report.

女性はなぜ会議の時刻を変更したいと思っているのですか。

(A) 彼女は従業員を研修することになっている。
(B) 彼女は昼食会に出席する予定である。
(C) 彼女には医者の予約がある。
(D) 彼女は報告書を仕上げている。

正解 C 女性は❶で、水曜日の会議について送ったEメールを受け取ったか男性に尋ねた後、❷「私は午後に医者に行けるよう、1時ではなく11時に集まりたい」と、会議の時刻変更を希望していることとその理由を伝えている。appointment「(病院などの)予約」。
(A) train「～を研修する」、employee「従業員」。
(B) be scheduled to do「～する予定である」、attend「～に出席する」。
(D) finish「～を仕上げる」、report「報告書」。

42 What does the man imply when he says, "I can't connect to the Internet"?

(A) A meeting place is unsuitable.
(B) He has not read an e-mail.
(C) A project he is working on is delayed.
(D) He needs to buy a new computer.

男性は "I can't connect to the Internet" という発言で、何を示唆していますか。

(A) 会議の場所が適していない。
(B) 彼はEメールを読んでいない。
(C) 彼が取り組んでいる企画が遅れている。
(D) 彼は新しいコンピューターを買う必要がある。

正解 B 女性は会議時刻変更を依頼するため送信したEメールを受け取ったか、男性に尋ねている。それに対し男性は下線部の発言で「私はインターネットに接続できない」と接続不良を伝えた後、❸「でも、水曜日の11時で都合がつくはずだ」と応じている。よって、下線部の発言は、インターネットにつながらないため、女性のEメールを読んでいないことを示唆していると判断できる。
(A) unsuitable「適していない」。
(C) work on ～「～に取り組む」、delay「～を遅らせる」。

43 What will the woman get for the man?

(A) A password
(B) A calendar
(C) An operator's manual
(D) A manager's signature

女性は男性のために何を取ってきますか。

(A) パスワード
(B) カレンダー
(C) 操作者用マニュアル
(D) 責任者の署名

正解 A 女性は❹で、新しいパスワードを使用しているか男性に尋ね、今朝パスワードが変更されたと教えている。続けて、❺「私はそれを書き留めてデスクに置いている。あなたのためにそれを取りに行く」と申し出ている。itはthe new passwordを指しているので、(A)が正解。
(C) operator「(機械などの)操作者」。
(D) signature「署名」。

Words & Phrases

instead of ～ ～ではなくて connect 接続する work 都合が良い、うまくいく
fine 申し分なく issue 問題、問題点 Wi-Fi ワイファイ ★wireless fidelityの略で、無線LAN接続の規格の一つ
be able to do ～することができる password パスワード IT 情報(通信)技術 ★information technologyの略
routine いつもの、決まった security セキュリティー、安全確保 maintenance 保守管理、メンテナンス
have ～ … ～を…の状態にしておく write down ～ ～を書き留める

Questions 44 through 46 refer to the following conversation.

W Hi, Bernard. ❶How are you doing on developing the marketing strategies for our new line of energy drinks?

M I'm just finishing the presentation slides. ❷I was asked to have them ready for the marketing meeting at the end of the month, right?

W ❸Right. To stay on schedule for a summertime launch.

M ❹I was planning to send you the slides to review tomorrow.

W Great. ❺After I see them, we have to decide who should speak about which slides. I was thinking Salma could handle anything related to social media, but you may have other ideas.

問題44-46は次の会話に関するものです。

こんにちは、Bernard。当社のエネルギー補給飲料の新商品ラインのマーケティング戦略の進み具合はどうですか。

ちょうど、プレゼンテーション用のスライドを仕上げているところです。私はそれを月末のマーケティング会議のために準備するよう頼まれたのでしたよね？

そうです。夏期の売り出しに向けて予定通りに進めるためです。

私は明日、あなたに見直してもらうためにそのスライドを送るつもりでいました。

素晴らしい。それを私が確認した後、私たちは誰がどのスライドについて話すか決める必要があります。私は、Salmaがソーシャルメディア関連のことは何でもうまくこなせるだろうと思っていましたが、あなたには別の考えがあるかもしれませんね。

44 What does the woman ask for?

(A) An explanation of a policy
(B) A suggestion for a new product
(C) A recommendation for an employee
(D) An update on an assignment

女性は何を求めていますか。
(A) 方針の説明
(B) 新商品のための提案
(C) 従業員の推薦
(D) 業務の最新情報

正解 D　女性は❶「当社のエネルギー補給飲料の新商品ラインのマーケティング戦略の進み具合はどうか」と担当業務の進捗状況を男性に尋ねている。ask for ～「～を求める」。update「最新情報」、assignment「割り当てられた仕事」。
(A) explanation「説明」、policy「方針」。
(B) 女性は新商品に言及しているが、そのための提案については触れていない。suggestion「提案」。
(C) recommendation「推薦」。

45 What will take place at the end of the month?

(A) A client visit
(B) A marketing meeting
(C) A social media event
(D) A new hire orientation

月末に何が行われますか。
(A) 顧客訪問
(B) マーケティング会議
(C) ソーシャルメディア上のイベント
(D) 新入社員向けの説明会

正解 B　担当業務の進捗を尋ねられた男性は、プレゼン用のスライドを仕上げている最中だと報告してから、❷で、それを月末のマーケティング会議のために準備するよう頼まれていたことを女性に確認している。女性は❸でそれに同意しているので、(B)が正解。
(C) ソーシャルメディアへの言及はあるが、そこで行われるイベントについては述べられていない。
(D) new hire「新入社員」、orientation「説明会」。

46 What does the woman want to discuss later?

(A) Speakers for a presentation
(B) Locations for a workshop
(C) Upgrades for equipment
(D) Estimates for a budget

女性は後で、何について話し合いたいと思っていますか。
(A) プレゼンテーションの発表者
(B) 講習会の場所
(C) 機器の改良
(D) 予算の見積もり

正解 A　❹で、翌日プレゼン用のスライドを女性に送る予定だったことを知らせる男性に対し、女性は❺「それを私が確認した後、私たちは誰がどのスライドについて話すか決める必要がある」と、スライドの完成後に発表役の分担を相談する必要性を伝えている。よって、(A)が正解。discuss「～について話し合う」。
(B) location「場所」。
(C) upgrade「改良」、equipment「機器」。
(D) estimate「見積もり」、budget「予算」。

Words & Phrases
develop ～を進展させる　marketing マーケティング、市場取引　strategy 戦略　line 商品ライン　energy drink エネルギー補給飲料　presentation プレゼンテーション、発表　slide スライド　ready 準備のできた　stay ～のままでいる　on schedule 予定通りに　summertime 夏期　launch （新製品の）売り出し　plan to do ～するつもりである　review ～を見直す、～を精査する　handle ～をうまく扱う　related to ～ ～に関連した　social media ソーシャルメディア

Questions 47 through 49 refer to the following conversation.

🇨🇦 M Hi, Insook. ❶I have a great story for our *Town Hall* segment on tonight's program.

🇬🇧 W What is it?

🇨🇦 M Well, ❷I think we should open with a report on the renovated Harbor Bridge. You know, the one the Port Authority's been rebuilding?

🇬🇧 W Excellent. ❸That bridge is being renovated to allow larger container ships to easily access the port, right?

🇨🇦 M ❹Yes, the construction will be completed next week.

🇬🇧 W So it's the perfect time to discuss it. ❺Do we have any videos of the construction on file?

🇨🇦 M ❻I'm sure I can find one. I've been covering this story since the project started.

問題47-49は次の会話に関するものです。

こんにちは、Insook。今夜の番組の『市庁舎』コーナー向けに格好のネタがありますよ。

それは何ですか。

ええと、私たちは改修されているHarbor橋に関する報道で始めるべきだと思います。ほら、港湾局が建て直しているものですよ。

いいですね。あの橋は、より大型のコンテナ船が簡単に港に出入りできるように改修されているのですよね？

はい、工事は来週完了する予定です。

では、取り上げるのに完璧なタイミングですね。工事の動画はファイルにありますか。

私がきっと何か見つけられますよ。計画の開始以来、私はこの話を取材し続けていますから。

47 What are the speakers most likely preparing for?

(A) A press conference
(B) An industry convention
(C) A team dinner
(D) A news broadcast

話し手たちは何の準備をしていると考えられますか。

(A) 記者会見
(B) 業界の協議会
(C) チームの夕食会
(D) ニュース放送

正解 D　男性は❶「今夜の番組の『市庁舎』コーナー向けに格好のネタがある」と女性に話し掛けている。そのネタが何か尋ねられた男性は、❷で、改修中のHarbor橋に関する報道で始めることを提案しているので、話し手たちは今夜のニュース放送番組の準備をしているところだと考えられる。prepare for ～「～の準備をする」。
(A) press conference「記者会見」。
(B) industry「業界」、convention「協議会、大会」。

48 According to the speakers, why was a project undertaken?

(A) To increase safety
(B) To reduce costs
(C) To improve access to a port
(D) To repair damage to a highway

話し手たちによると、計画はなぜ着手されたのですか。

(A) 安全性を高めるため
(B) 諸経費を削減するため
(C) 港への出入りを改善するため
(D) 幹線道路に対する損傷を修復するため

正解 C　改修中の橋について、❸「あの橋は、より大型のコンテナ船が簡単に港に出入りできるように改修されているのですよね」と目的を確認する女性に対し、男性は❹でYesと肯定している。easily access the portをimprove access to a portと言い換えている(C)が正解。improve「～を改善する」、access「出入り」。
(A) increase「～を高める」、safety「安全性」。
(B) reduce「～を削減する」、costs「諸経費」。
(D) repair「～を修復する」、damage「損傷」、highway「幹線道路」。

49 What will the man probably do soon?

(A) Locate a video
(B) Give a talk
(C) Set up some equipment
(D) Pick up a guest speaker

男性は間もなく何をすると考えられますか。

(A) 動画を探し当てる
(B) 講演をする
(C) 機器の準備をする
(D) 招待講演者を車で迎えに行く

正解 A　❺で、橋の改修工事の動画があるか尋ねる女性に対し、男性は❻「私がきっと何か見つけられる」と答えている。代名詞oneはvideoを指しているので、男性は間もなくその動画を探すと考えられる。locate「～の位置を探し当てる」。
(B) give a talk「講演をする」。
(C) set up ～「～を準備する」、equipment「機器」。
(D) pick up ～「～を車で迎えに行く」。

> **Words & Phrases**
> story （放送の）ネタ　town hall　市庁舎、町役場　segment　部分　program　番組
> report　報道　renovate　～を改修する　port authority　港湾局　rebuild　～を建て直す
> allow ～ to do　～が…できるようにする　container ship　コンテナ船　access　～を利用する、～に進入する
> construction　工事　complete　～を完了する　discuss　～を取り上げる　on file　ファイルに保管されて、記録されて
> cover　～を取材する　since　～以来

Questions 50 through 52 refer to the following conversation with three speakers.

M Thanks for meeting with us, Ms. Ortiz. ❶Our clothing store has been doing really well, so we'd like to expand next year. ❷In order to do that, we need to apply for a bank loan.

M Yes, ❸so first we need a financial audit completed by a certified public accountant.

W Well, ❹I'm glad to help. I do these all the time.

M Great! So what's the process?

W Well, ❺I'll need to review your store's financial data. Did you bring those documents with you?

M Yes, I have the printouts right here.

問題50-52は3人の話し手による次の会話に関するものです。

我々とお会いいただきありがとうございます、Ortizさん。私たちの衣料品店は非常にうまくいっていますので、来年に拡大したいと思っています。それを実行するために、私たちは銀行の融資を申し込む必要があります。

そうです、それでまず、私たちは財務会計監査を公認会計士の方に済ませていただく必要があるのです。

なるほど、喜んでお手伝いします。私は常々、この類のことを行っていますから。

良かった！それで、どういう手順になりますか。

ええと、そちらのお店の財務データを精査する必要があるでしょう。それらの書類はお持ちになりましたか。

はい、ちょうどここにプリントアウトしたものがあります。

50 What do the men want to do next year?

(A) Expand a business
(B) Host a charity gala
(C) Start an internship program
(D) Attend a trade show

男性たちは来年に何をしたいと思っていますか。

(A) 事業を拡大する
(B) 慈善祭典を主催する
(C) インターンシップ制度を開始する
(D) 見本市に出席する

正解 A 1人目の男性は、❶「私たちの衣料品店は非常に成功しているので、来年に拡大したいと思っている」と事業拡大の展望を伝えている。business「事業」。
(B) host「～を主催する」、charity「慈善」、gala「祭典」。
(C) internship「インターンシップ」。
(D) attend「～に出席する」、trade show「見本市」。

51 What most likely is the woman's job?

(A) Lawyer
(B) Travel agent
(C) Accountant
(D) Computer technician

女性の職業は何だと考えられますか。

(A) 弁護士
(B) 旅行代理店従業員
(C) 会計士
(D) コンピューター技術者

正解 C 1人目の男性が❶・❷で、事業拡大のために銀行の融資を申し込みたいと述べたのに続き、2人目の男性は❸「それでまず、私たちは財務会計監査を公認会計士の方に済ませてもらう必要がある」と補足している。それに対し、女性は❹で、男性たちに力を貸すことと、自分が常日頃からこの類の業務を行っていることを伝えているので、女性は会計士だと考えられる。
(A) lawyer「弁護士」。
(B) travel agent「旅行代理業者」。
(D) technician「技術者」。

52 What does the woman need to see?

(A) Some schedules
(B) Product samples
(C) Some data
(D) Security badges

女性は何を見る必要がありますか。

(A) 予定表
(B) 製品の見本
(C) データ
(D) 保安バッジ

正解 C 1人目の男性に財務会計監査の手順を尋ねられた女性は、❺「あなたたちのお店の財務データを精査する必要があるだろう」と述べている。
(A) schedule「予定表」。
(B) product「製品」、sample「見本」。
(D) security「保安、警備」、badge「バッジ」。

Words & Phrases
meet with ～　～と約束して会う　clothing　衣料品　do well　成功する　expand　拡大する
in order to do　～するために　apply for ～　～を申し込む　loan　融資　financial　財務の　audit　会計監査
complete　～を仕上げる　certified public accountant　公認会計士　be glad to do　喜んで～する　all the time　常に
process　手順、工程　review　～を精査する、～を見直す　document　書類、文書　printout　プリントアウトされたもの

Questions 53 through 55 refer to the following conversation.

M Hi, Mei Ting. ❶How do you like our company's new four-day workweek policy?

W It's great. ❷I'm just as productive at work, and with three days off, I can do more things on weekends. ❸Like last weekend, I went to Tokyo to visit my sister.

M Nice. And it's also a good way for the company to save on energy costs!

W True, but ❹one thing I've noticed is how cold it is in here on Monday mornings now. They turn the heat down in all the offices on the weekend since no one is here.

M Well, a lot of our coworkers bring a sweater to work.

W Hmm, I'll start doing that.

問題53-55は次の会話に関するものです。

こんにちは、Mei Ting。当社の週4日勤務の新方針はどうですか。

素晴らしいです。職場では変わらず生産的でいられますし、3日間休みがあるので、週末にはもっとたくさんのことができます。例えば先週末には、姉を訪ねに東京へ行きました。

いいですね。それはまた会社にとって光熱費を節約する上でも良い方法です。

確かにそうなのですが、私が1点気付いたのは、今の時期、月曜日の午前中にこの場所がいかに寒いかということです。誰もここにいないので、週末には全ての執務室で暖房を弱くしています。

そうですね、多くの同僚は職場にセーターを持って来ていますよ。

なるほど、私もそうすることにします。

53 What are the speakers discussing?

(A) A company policy
(B) A business merger
(C) Some vacation plans
(D) Some training sessions

話し手たちは何について話し合っていますか。

(A) 会社の方針
(B) 企業の合併
(C) 休暇の計画
(D) 研修会

正解 A ❶「当社の週4日勤務の新方針はどうか」と意見を尋ねる男性に対し、女性はそれが素晴らしいと言った後、❷でこの新方針の利点を述べている。以降でも、話し手たちは週4日勤務制について話をしているので、(A)が正解。
(B) business「企業」、merger「合併」。
(C) 女性は先週末の休みの過ごし方について述べているが、休暇の計画には言及していない。
(D) training session「研修会」。

54 What does the woman say she did last weekend?

(A) She took a class.
(B) She packed boxes.
(C) She visited a relative.
(D) She prepared a presentation.

女性は先週末に何をしたと言っていますか。

(A) 彼女は講座を受講した。
(B) 彼女は箱に荷物を詰めた。
(C) 彼女は親類を訪ねた。
(D) 彼女はプレゼンテーションの準備をした。

正解 C 女性は、週4日勤務制の利点を挙げた後、❸「例えば先週末には、姉を訪ねに東京へ行った」と、直近の自分の週末の過ごし方を具体的に述べている。my sisterをa relativeと表している(C)が正解。relative「親類」。
(B) pack「〜に荷物を詰める」。
(D) prepare「〜の準備をする」、presentation「プレゼンテーション」。

55 Why does the man say, "a lot of our coworkers bring a sweater to work"?

(A) To request a favor
(B) To make a suggestion
(C) To disagree with a dress code
(D) To explain a decision

男性はなぜ "a lot of our coworkers bring a sweater to work" と言っていますか。

(A) 頼み事をするため
(B) 提案をするため
(C) 服装規定に異議を唱えるため
(D) 決断について説明するため

正解 B 週4日勤務制が光熱費の節約にもなると言う男性に対し、女性は❹で、週末に暖房を弱めていることによる月曜日午前中の社内の寒さについて述べている。それに対し、男性は下線部の発言で「多くの同僚は職場にセーターを持って来ている」と伝えているので、女性に他の従業員のように寒さ対策としてセーターを持参するよう提案していると考えられる。make a suggestion「提案する」。
(A) request a favor「頼み事をする」。
(C) disagree with 〜「〜に異議を唱える」、dress code「服装規定」。
(D) explain「〜について説明する」、decision「決断」。

Words & Phrases
How do you like 〜　(好き嫌いについて)〜はどうですか　workweek 週労働日数　policy 方針
just as 〜　ちょうど同じくらい〜　productive 生産的な　at work 職場で　off （仕事などを）休んで、休暇で
save on 〜　〜を節約する　energy costs 光熱費　notice 〜に気付く　turn down 〜　〜（温度など）を下げる
heat 暖房　coworker 同僚　sweater セーター　start doing 〜し始める

Questions 56 through 58 refer to the following conversation.

M Hello. ❶You've reached customer service at Aberland Irrigation.

W Hi. ❷I'm calling from Jackson Fields. We purchased an irrigation system from you last month, and we're having a problem.

M What's the issue?

W ❸I was just checking our broccoli and onion crops, and noticed no water was coming out of the irrigation tubes. We're in the middle of the growing season for these crops, so I'm concerned.

M ❹Have you filled out a service request form online?

W Well, ❺I'm not in my office. I'm calling from my mobile phone, out in the field, and I can't access my computer right now. ❻Can you send someone here?

M ❼Absolutely. I'll have one of our technicians out there today.

問題56-58は次の会話に関するものです。

はい。こちらはAberland Irrigation社お客さまサービスです。

もしもし。Jackson農園よりお電話しています。私たちは先月、御社からかんがい装置を購入したのですが、問題がありまして。

どのような問題でしょうか。

先ほど当農園のブロッコリーとタマネギの作物を確認していたところ、かんがい用チューブから水が全く流れてきていないことに気付きました。これらの作物は成長期の真っ最中なので、心配しています。

オンライン上の点検依頼フォームの入力はお済みですか。

ええと、私は事務所にはいないのです。屋外の畑で携帯電話から電話していまして、今はコンピューターにアクセスできません。こちらにどなたか派遣してもらえますか。

もちろんです。本日中に、当社の技術者を1名そちらに向かわせます。

---

56 Where does the woman most likely work?

(A) At a farm
(B) At a supermarket
(C) At a restaurant
(D) At a landscaping company

女性はどこで働いていると考えられますか。

(A) 農場
(B) スーパーマーケット
(C) レストラン
(D) 造園会社

正解 A ❶「こちらはAberland Irrigation社のお客さまサービスです」と電話に応答する男性に対し、女性は❷で、先月購入したかんがい装置に問題が生じていると伝えている。また女性は❸で、自農園の作物を確認した際に、かんがい用チューブから水の放出がないと気付いたこと、作物の成長の真っ最中であるため心配していることを伝えているので、農場で働いていると考えられる。

(D) landscaping「造園」。

57 Why is the woman unable to fill out a form?

(A) She is busy with some customers.
(B) She has lost a vendor's telephone number.
(C) She does not have access to a computer.
(D) She cannot remember a product ID number.

女性はなぜフォームに入力することができないのですか。

(A) 彼女は顧客との対応に忙しい。
(B) 彼女は販売業者の電話番号を紛失した。
(C) 彼女はコンピューターにアクセスできる環境にない。
(D) 彼女は製品識別番号を思い出すことができない。

正解 C ❹で、オンライン上の点検依頼フォームを入力済みか尋ねる男性に対し、女性は❺で、自分が事務所にはいないと伝えた後、「屋外の畑で携帯電話から電話していて、今はコンピューターにアクセスできない」と、依頼フォームの入力ができていない理由を説明している。be unable to do「～することができない」。access「アクセス」。

(B) vendor「販売業者」。
(D) ID number「識別番号」。

58 What does the man agree to do?

(A) Extend a warranty
(B) Provide an access code
(C) Apply a discount
(D) Send a technician

男性は何をすることに同意していますか。

(A) 保証を延長する
(B) アクセスコードを提供する
(C) 割引を適用する
(D) 技術者を派遣する

正解 D 屋外の畑にいるためにコンピューターにアクセスできないと述べた女性は、❻「ここに誰か派遣してもらえるか」と男性に依頼している。それに対し男性は、❼でAbsolutelyと快諾してから、技術者を1名その場に向かわせると伝えている。agree to do「～することに同意する」。

(B) provide「～を提供する」、access code「アクセスコード(利用者識別用に求められる番号など)」。
(C) apply「～を適用する」、discount「割引」。

Words & Phrases

reach ～と連絡を取る　irrigation かんがい、水を引くこと　field 畑　system 装置
issue 問題　crop 作物、収穫物　notice (that)～ ～だと気付く　tube チューブ　in the middle of ～ ～の最中で
growing season (農作物の)成長期　concerned 心配して　fill out ～ ～に記入する　service 点検、修理
access ～にアクセスする　Absolutely 〈返事として〉もちろんです　technician 技術者

Questions 59 through 61 refer to the following conversation with three speakers.

🏴󠁧󠁢W **Thanks for meeting with us, Mr. Samir.** ❶Maria and I are pleased that your city's planning to start using our company's new fare payment system in your train stations.

🇨🇦M **Yes.** ❷My transportation department's eager to introduce the new tap-to-pay technology your company created.

🇺🇸W **Great.** ❸We advise starting off by installing our payment devices in a limited number of stations—maybe target the less-busy stations first.

🇨🇦M **That makes sense.**

🏴󠁧󠁢W ❹Could you provide the latest ridership statistics, so we'll know the number of passengers that use each station?

🇨🇦M **Sure. But** ❺I'm concerned about the project deadline. ❻Can we be sure all stations have it by the end of the year?

問題59-61は3人の話し手による次の会話に関するものです。

我々とお会いいただきありがとうございます、Samirさん。Mariaと私は、御市が鉄道駅で当社の新しい料金支払いシステムの使用を開始する計画であることをうれしく思っています。

はい。当市の運輸局は、御社が考案した新しいタッチ決済技術をぜひ導入したいと思っています。

素晴らしい。限定した数の駅で当社の決済端末を設置することから始めるようお勧めします——まずは比較的利用客の少ない駅を対象にするのが良いかもしれません。

それは理にかなっていますね。

各駅を利用する乗客の数を把握できるよう、乗客数の最新統計を見せていただけますか。

もちろんです。でも、計画の最終期限が心配です。年末までに全駅にそれを設置することが必ずできるでしょうか。

59 What are the speakers mainly discussing?

(A) A security-camera network
(B) A payment system
(C) A billboard advertisement
(D) A pedestrian walkway

話し手たちは主に何について話し合っていますか。

(A) 防犯カメラ網
(B) 支払いシステム
(C) 掲示板の広告
(D) 歩行者用通路

正解 **B** 1人目の女性が、❶「Mariaと私は、市が鉄道駅で当社の新しい料金支払いシステムの使用を開始する計画であることをうれしく思う」と述べ、以降の❷・❸でも、その決済技術や決済端末について話し合われている。
(A) security-camera「防犯カメラの」、network「情報網」。
(C) billboard「掲示板」、advertisement「広告」。
(D) pedestrian「歩行者」、walkway「通路」。

60 What is the man asked to provide?

(A) A city map
(B) Some additional funding
(C) Some passenger statistics
(D) Updated transit schedules

男性は何を提供するよう頼まれていますか。

(A) 市街地図
(B) 追加の資金提供
(C) 乗客の統計
(D) 最新の交通機関の時刻表

正解 **C** 2人目の女性が❸で、利用客の少ない駅から限定的に決済端末を設置するよう提案している。それに肯定的な反応を示す男性に対し、1人目の女性は❹「各駅を利用する乗客の数を把握できるよう、乗客数の最新統計を見せてもらえるか」と男性に統計を提供するよう頼んでいる。
(B) additional「追加の」、funding「資金提供」。
(D) update「～を最新のものにする」、transit「輸送」、schedule「時刻表」。

61 Why is the man concerned?

(A) A project is too expensive.
(B) Some software is unreliable.
(C) A design is unappealing.
(D) A deadline might be missed.

男性はなぜ心配しているのですか。

(A) 計画の費用がかかり過ぎる。
(B) ソフトウエアが信頼できない。
(C) デザインが魅力的ではない。
(D) 最終期限に間に合わないかもしれない。

正解 **D** 男性は❺「計画の最終期限が心配だ」と懸念を述べ、❻で、確実に年末までに全駅に新支払いシステムを設置できるか尋ねている。よって、男性は最終期限に遅れる可能性を懸念していると判断できる。miss「～に間に合わない」。
(A) expensive「費用のかかる」。
(B) unreliable「信頼できない」。
(C) unappealing「魅力のない」。

Words & Phrases

fare （交通機関の）運賃　transportation department　運輸局
be eager to *do*　～することを熱望する　introduce　～を導入する　tap-to-pay　タッチ決済　create　～を考案する
advise *doing*　～することを勧める　start off by *doing*　～することから始める　limited　限定された
less-busy　比較的利用客の少ない　make sense　道理にかなう　latest　最新の　ridership　（公共交通機関の）乗客数
statistics　統計　be concerned about ～　～を心配している　deadline　最終期限　be sure (that) ～　必ず～する

Questions 62 through 64 refer to the following conversation and logos.

問題62-64は次の会話とロゴに関するものです。

W ❶Korkmaz Department Stores just agreed to carry our line of perfumes!

Korkmaz百貨店はたった今、当社の香水製品ラインを取り扱うことに同意してくれました!

M Wow! That means our perfumes are going to be in a lot of new markets.

わあ! ということはつまり、当社の香水の販路が広がることになるのですね。

W ❷This is the perfect time to order shopping bags with our new company logo. ❸That way Korkmaz will have them to use when they start carrying our perfumes.

これは、当社の新しいロゴ入りの買い物袋を発注するのに完璧なタイミングですね。そうすれば、Korkmazは当社の香水の取り扱いを始めた際にそれを使用してくれるでしょう。

M ❹Here are the logo designs I'm working on. Take a look.

ここに、私が取り組んでいるロゴのデザインがあります。見てみてください。

W ❺The one with the ribbon is perfect! It looks like a little gift box.

リボンが描かれたものはぴったりですね! ちょっとした贈答用の箱のようです。

62 What news does the woman share with the man?

    (A) Annual revenue has increased.

    (B) An item will be temporarily unavailable.

    (C) A department store will sell their product.

    (D) A factory has sent some packaging samples.

女性は男性にどんな知らせを伝えていますか。

    (A) 年間収益が増えた。

    (B) ある商品が一時的に購入できなくなる。

    (C) ある百貨店が彼らの製品を販売する予定である。

    (D) ある工場が包装の見本を送ってきた。

正解 C	女性は❶「Korkmaz百貨店はたった今、当社の香水製品ラインを取り扱うことに同意してくれた」と男性に朗報を伝えている。carry our line of perfumes を sell と product を用いて言い換えている(C)が正解。share ～ with …「…に～を話す、～を…と共有する」。

(A) annual「年間の」、revenue「収益」。

(B) item「商品」、temporarily「一時的に」、unavailable「購入できない」。

(D) packaging「包装」、sample「見本」。

---

63 What does the woman suggest doing?

    (A) Filming some commercials

    (B) Ordering shopping bags

    (C) Conducting a survey

    (D) Updating a Web site

女性は何をすることを提案していますか。

    (A) コマーシャルを撮影すること

    (B) 買い物袋を発注すること

    (C) 調査を行うこと

    (D) ウェブサイトを更新すること

正解 B	Korkmaz百貨店が香水製品の取り扱いを開始してくれるという朗報に、販路が拡大すると喜ぶ男性に対し、女性は❷「これは、当社の新しいロゴ入りの買い物袋を発注するのに完璧なタイミングだ」と言っている。女性は続けて、❸「そうすれば、Korkmazは当社の香水の取り扱いを始めた際にそれを使用してくれるだろう」と、今のタイミングで買い物袋を発注することによって得られる利点を説明している。

(A) film「～を撮影する」、commercial「コマーシャル」。

(C) conduct「～を行う」、survey「調査」。

(D) update「～を更新する」。

---

64 Look at the graphic. Which logo does the woman prefer?

    (A) Design 1

    (B) Design 2

    (C) Design 3

    (D) Design 4

図を見てください。女性はどのロゴを好んでいますか。

    (A) デザイン1

    (B) デザイン2

    (C) デザイン3

    (D) デザイン4

正解 D	会社の新しいロゴ入りの買い物袋の発注を提案する女性に対し、男性は❹で、ロゴのデザイン候補を見せている。それを確認した女性は、❺「リボンが描かれたものはぴったりだ。ちょっとした贈答用の箱のようだ」と述べている。図を見ると、リボンが描かれており、かつ贈答用の箱のように見えるものはデザイン4。よって、(D)が正解。prefer「～の方を好む」。

Words & Phrases

logo ロゴ   department store 百貨店   agree to *do* ～することに同意する   carry ～(商品)を取り扱う

line 製品ライン   perfume 香水   market 販路、市場   order ～を発注する   shopping bag 買い物袋

start *doing* ～し始める   design デザイン、設計   work on ～ ～に取り組む   take a look 見る   ribbon リボン

Questions 65 through 67 refer to the following conversation and map.

🇬🇧 w Hi, Robert. I'm Noriko with Osman Realty. ❶I understand you're interested in renting commercial space at the new shopping center.

🇨🇦 M That's right. ❷I'm planning to open a pottery studio.

🇬🇧 w Excellent. ❸As you can see on this map, there are still four spaces available.

🇨🇦 M Hmm, ❹the units on either side of the grocery store are too small. I need space to hold pottery classes.

🇬🇧 w Well, ❺the end units are larger.

🇨🇦 M OK. ❻I like the unit next to the ice cream shop.

🇬🇧 w Wonderful. ❼In that case, I'll write up a contract. We can meet next week to go over the terms.

問題65-67は次の会話と地図に関するものです。

こんにちは、Robert。Osman不動産のNorikoです。あなたは新しいショッピングセンターの商業用スペースの賃借にご関心をお持ちだと伺っています。

その通りです。私は陶芸工房を開くことを計画しています。

素晴らしい。この区画図でご覧いただけますように、まだ4つのスペースが空いています。

うーん、食料雑貨店の横の区画はどちらも狭過ぎますね。私には陶芸講座を開くためのスペースが必要です。

なるほど、両端の区画はもっと広いですよ。

そうですね。アイスクリーム店の隣の区画にしたいです。

良かったです。それでしたら、私がご契約書を作成いたします。来週お会いして一緒にその条件を見返すことができますね。

Grocery Store	105	Ice Cream Shop	107
103			
Fitness Center		Parking Area	
101			

食料雑貨店	105	アイスクリーム店	107
103			
フィットネスセンター		駐車場	
101			

65

What kind of business is the man going to open?

(A) A bakery
(B) A bookstore
(C) A pottery studio
(D) An antique store

男性はどのような事業所を開くつもりですか。

(A) パン屋
(B) 書店
(C) 陶芸工房
(D) 骨董品店

正解 C　女性は、Osman不動産という勤め先と自分の名前を伝えてから、❶で、男性がショッピングセンター内の商業用スペースの賃借に関心を持っていることを確認している。それに対し、男性は肯定した後、❷「私は陶芸工房を開くことを計画している」と賃貸物件の利用用途を知らせている。business「事業所、会社」。

(A) bakery「パン屋」。
(D) antique「骨董品」。

66

Look at the graphic. Which unit does the man choose?

(A) Unit 101
(B) Unit 103
(C) Unit 105
(D) Unit 107

図を見てください。男性はどの区画を選んでいますか。

(A) 101区画
(B) 103区画
(C) 105区画
(D) 107区画

正解 D　❸で、区画図を見せながら4区画が空いていることを示す女性に対し、男性は❹「食料雑貨店の横の区画はどちらも狭過ぎる」と、そのうちの2区画を選択肢から除外している。それを受け、女性は❺でより広い両端の区画を薦め、男性は❻「アイスクリーム店の隣の区画にしたい」と希望を伝えている。図を見ると、アイスクリーム店の隣のうち、端にあり、食料雑貨店に接していないのは107区画なので、(D)が正解。choose「～を選ぶ」。

(A) 端の区画ではあるものの、アイスクリーム店の隣に位置していないので不適切。
(B) (C) 食料雑貨店の両隣の区画なので不適切。

67

What will the speakers do next week?

(A) Discuss a contract
(B) Take some pictures
(C) Create a company logo
(D) Meet with an interior decorator

話し手たちは来週に何をしますか。

(A) 契約について話し合う
(B) 写真を撮る
(C) 会社のロゴを作成する
(D) 室内装飾家と会う

正解 A　希望の区画を伝える男性に対し、女性は❼「そうであれば、私が契約書を作成する。来週会って一緒にその条件を見返すことができる」と伝えている。

(B) take a picture「写真を撮る」。
(C) create「～を作成する」。
(D) interior decorator「室内装飾家」。

TEST 2　PART 3

Words & Phrases

with　～で勤務して　　realty　不動産　　be interested in doing　～することに関心を持っている　　rent　～を賃借する

commercial　商業用の　　space　スペース、空間　　plan to do　～することを計画している　　pottery　陶芸　　studio　工房

excellent　素晴らしい　　available　利用可能な　　unit　1戸　　either　〈sideなど2つで1対の語と共に〉両方の　　side　側

grocery store　食料雑貨店　　hold　～を開催する　　class　講座　　end　端　　next to ～　～の隣に

in that case　もしもそうであれば、その場合　　write up ～　～を書き上げる、～をきちんと書く　　contract　契約書、契約

go over ～　～を見返す、～を詳しく検討する　　terms　（契約などの）条件、条項

地図　fitness center　フィットネスセンター　　parking area　駐車場

Questions 68 through 70 refer to the following conversation and bar graph.

問題68-70は次の会話と棒グラフに関するものです。

🇺🇸 w Hi, Jae-Min. ❶I know you missed the meeting yesterday to tour the new factory, but there was a presentation on the quarterly report. ❷Did you have a chance to review it?

こんにちは、Jae-Min。あなたが新工場の視察のために昨日の会議に出られなかったことは知っていますが、四半期報告書に関する発表がありました。それを詳しく見る機会はありましたか。

🇨🇦 M Yes, I did! It was a great report!

はい、ありました！それは素晴らしい報告書でしたね！

🇺🇸 w I agree. ❸We're producing more automobiles than ever before.

その通りです。当社はこれまでにないほど多くの自動車を生産しています。

🇨🇦 M ❹I'm especially happy that we hit a peak of 387,000 units.

特に、当社が38万7千台という最高値に達したことをうれしく思います。

🇺🇸 w Yes, that was the highlight of the presentation. ❺I was also encouraged because production costs should fall significantly next year. ❻Our raw material suppliers are lowering prices.

はい、それが発表の目玉でした。それに、生産コストが来年には著しく下がるはずなので、私は心強く思いました。当社の原材料の納入業者が価格を下げてくれるのです。

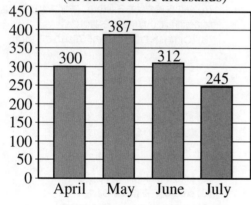

Units Produced per Month
(in hundreds of thousands)

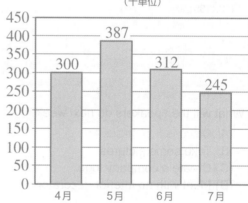

月ごとの生産台数
（千単位）

68 What does the woman ask the man about?

(A) A quarterly report
(B) A production schedule
(C) An expense statement
(D) A factory location

女性は男性に何について尋ねていますか。

(A) 四半期報告書
(B) 生産計画
(C) 経費明細書
(D) 工場の場所

正解 A 女性は❶で、男性が欠席した会議で四半期報告書に関する発表があったことに言及した後、❷「それを詳しく見る機会はあったか」と男性に尋ねている。it は the quarterly report を指しているので、(A)が正解。
(B) 女性は自動車の生産に言及しているが、その計画については尋ねていない。production「生産」。
(C) expense「経費、費用」、statement「明細書」。
(D) 女性は男性が工場視察に行ったことに言及しているが、その場所は尋ねていない。location「場所」。

69 Look at the graphic. What month is the man referring to?

(A) April
(B) May
(C) June
(D) July

図を見てください。男性はどの月に言及していますか。

(A) 4月
(B) 5月
(C) 6月
(D) 7月

正解 B 四半期報告書が素晴らしいものだったと言う男性に、女性は同意してから、❸「当社はこれまでにないほど多くの自動車を生産している」と述べている。それに対し、男性は❹「特に、当社が38万7千台という最高値に達したことをうれしく思う」と感想を伝えている。図を見ると、5月の生産台数が最も多く、38万7千台という最大値に達しているので、(B)が正解。refer to ～「～に言及する」。
(A) (C) (D) いずれの月も生産台数が最大値に達してはいない。

70 Why is the woman optimistic about next year?

(A) A new factory will open.
(B) Demand is expected to increase.
(C) Raw material costs will fall.
(D) A new product will be available.

女性はなぜ来年について楽観的なのですか。

(A) 新工場が開設する予定である。
(B) 需要が増える見込みである。
(C) 原材料費が下がる予定である。
(D) 新製品が購入可能になる予定である。

正解 C 会議での発表について、女性は❺「それに、生産コストが来年には著しく下がるはずなので、私は心強く思った」と自分が楽観視していることとその理由を伝えた後、❻「当社の原材料の納入業者が価格を下げてくれる」と補足している。optimistic「楽観的な」。
(A) 男性が視察に訪れた新工場への言及はあるが、工場が来年開設するとは述べられていない。
(B) demand「需要」、be expected to *do*「～する見込みである」、increase「増加する」。
(D) available「購入できる」。

Words & Phrases

bar graph 棒グラフ　　miss ～を欠席する　　tour ～の見学をする　　presentation 発表　　quarterly 四半期の

chance 機会　　review ～を精査する、～を見直す　　agree 同意する　　produce ～を生産する　　automobile 自動車

than ever before これまでになく　　especially 特に　　hit ～に達する ★過去形・過去分詞も同形　　peak 最大値

unit (製品の)1単位　　highlight 目玉　　encourage ～に自信を与える、～を励ます　　costs コスト、経費　　fall 下がる

significantly 著しく　　raw material 原材料　　supplier 供給会社　　lower ～を下げる

棒グラフ　per month　月ごとの

Questions 71 through 73 refer to the following broadcast.

🇬🇧 w

❶We'd like to remind our listeners about this weekend's art fair. **Many local artists will be showing their work.** ❷One of the feature artists is Emiko Ito, who is known for her modern furniture designs. ❸What makes her artwork special is that she recycles materials, such as rubber and plastic, to create her furniture pieces. **This is great for the environment!** ❹I invited Ms. Ito here for an interview. ❺After this short commercial break, Ms. Ito will be discussing her creative process.

問題71-73は次の放送に関するものです。

今週末のアートフェアについて、当番組のリスナーの皆さんに改めてお知らせしたいと思います。多数の地元芸術家が作品を展示する予定です。その目玉となる芸術家の1人はEmiko Itoで、彼女は現代的な家具デザインで知られています。彼女の芸術作品を特別なものにしているのは、家具作品を創作するのに、ゴムやプラスチックといった材料を再生利用しているという点です。これは環境にとても優しいです! インタビューのためにItoさんをこちらにお招きしました。これから流れる短いコマーシャル時間の後、Itoさんが彼女の創造的な制作方法についてお話しくださいます。

---

71 What event will take place on the weekend?

(A) An art fair
(B) A product launch
(C) An award ceremony
(D) An art gallery opening

どんなイベントが週末に開かれますか。

(A) アートフェア
(B) 新製品の売り出し
(C) 授賞式
(D) 画廊の開館行事

正解 **A** 話し手は❶「今週末のアートフェアについて、当番組のリスナーの皆さんに改めてお知らせしたいと思う」と話を切り出し、以降ではイベント概要と、その目玉である地元芸術家の1人について紹介している。よって、(A)が正解。
(B) product launch「新製品の売り出し」。
(C) award「賞」、ceremony「式典」。
(D) art gallery「画廊、美術館」、opening「開店行事、オープニングセレモニー」。

---

72 According to the speaker, what is special about Emiko Ito's creations?

(A) They are signed by Ms. Ito.
(B) They are sold entirely online.
(C) They are distributed worldwide.
(D) They are made with recycled materials.

話し手によると、Emiko Itoの創作品について何が特別ですか。

(A) それらにはItoさんの署名が入っている。
(B) それらは全面的にオンラインで販売されている。
(C) それらは世界中に販売されている。
(D) それらはリサイクル材料で作られている。

正解 **D** 話し手は❷で、Emiko Itoの名に言及した後、❸「彼女の芸術作品を特別なものにしているのは、家具作品を創作するのに、ゴムやプラスチックといった材料を再生利用しているという点だ」と、特徴を伝えている。そのことを表している(D)が正解。creation「創作品」。
(A) sign「～に署名する」。
(B) sell「～を販売する」、entirely「もっぱら、完全に」。
(C) distribute「～を販売する、～を供給する」、worldwide「世界中に」。

---

73 What will the speaker most likely do next?

(A) Lead a guided tour
(B) Give a demonstration
(C) Conduct an interview
(D) Announce a prize winner

話し手は次に何をすると考えられますか。

(A) ガイド付きツアーを先導する
(B) 製品の実演をする
(C) インタビューを行う
(D) 賞の受賞者を発表する

正解 **C** 話し手は、地元芸術家であるItoさんについて紹介してから、❹「インタビューのためにItoさんをこちらに招いた」と述べ、❺で、CMの後に彼女に自身の創造的な制作方法について語ってもらう、と番組の段取りを説明している。よって、話し手は次にItoさんにインタビューすると考えられる。conduct「～を行う」。
(A) lead「～を先導する、～を統率する」、guided「ガイド付きの」。
(B) demonstration「製品の実演」。
(D) announce「～を発表する」、prize「賞」、winner「受賞者」。

Words & Phrases

broadcast 放送　　remind ～ about … …について～に念押しする　　fair フェア、見本市
local 地元の　　show ～を展示する　　work 作品　　feature 目玉　　be known for ～ ～で知られている
modern 現代的な　　design デザイン　　artwork 芸術品　　special 特別な　　recycle ～を再生利用する
material 材料　　such as ～ ～のような　　rubber ゴム　　plastic プラスチック　　create ～を創作する　　piece 作品
environment 環境　　invite ～を招く　　interview インタビュー、会談　　commercial break コマーシャルのための番組中断
discuss ～を論じる、～を説明する　　creative 創造的な　　process 過程、プロセス

Questions 74 through 76 refer to the following excerpt from a meeting.

🇦🇺 M

To end this meeting, ❶I'd like to thank you all for filling out the survey about the company cafeteria that was distributed a few months ago. ❷There were many comments about the amount of food from the prepackaged meals that was being thrown away. ❸We've almost eliminated that problem by adding a new self-serve area in the cafeteria. **Now, before you leave,** ❹our executive chef has created some new recipes that she'd like us to try. ❺Please take some samples on your way out of the room.

問題74-76は次の会議の抜粋に関するものです。

この会議を終えるに当たって、数カ月前に配布された社員食堂に関する調査票に記入していただき、皆さんにお礼を申し上げます。パック入りにしたことが元で廃棄されていた食品の量について、たくさんのご意見がありました。当社は、食堂内にセルフサービスの新コーナーを増設することで、その問題をほぼなくしました。さて、ご退出の前に、総料理長が新しいレシピを開発して、私たちにそれを試食してもらいたいと望んでいます。部屋から出る途中で幾つかの試食品をお取りください。

---

74 Why was a change made in the company cafeteria?

(A) To reduce food waste
(B) To decrease waiting time
(C) To save energy
(D) To comply with new regulations

なぜ、社員食堂で変更がなされたのですか。

(A) 食品廃棄物を削減するため
(B) 待ち時間を減らすため
(C) エネルギーを節約するため
(D) 新しい規定に従うため

正解 A 話し手は❶で、社員食堂に関する調査票の回答に対して聞き手に礼を述べてから、❷「パック入りにしたことが元で廃棄されていた食品の量について、たくさんの意見があった」と言っている。続く❸では、食堂内に新コーナーを増設することによりその問題を解決できたと説明しているので、食品廃棄物を削減するために変更がなされたと判断できる。make a change「変更する、変化をもたらす」。
(B) decrease「～を減らす」。
(C) save「～を節約する」。
(D) comply with ~「～に従う」、regulations「規定」。

---

75 What action was taken?

(A) Cash registers were upgraded.
(B) Plastic trays were replaced.
(C) Healthier food was made available.
(D) A self-serve area was added.

どのような措置が取られましたか。

(A) レジをより性能の高いものに替えた。
(B) プラスチック製のトレーが取り換えられた。
(C) より健康的な料理が購入可能になった。
(D) セルフサービスのコーナーが増設された。

正解 D 話し手は、多数の従業員に指摘されていた食品廃棄問題について、❸「当社は、食堂内にセルフサービスの新コーナーを増設することで、その問題をほぼなくした」と、新コーナーの増設により概ね問題解決に至った現状を報告しているので、(D)が正解。take an action「措置を取る」。
(A) cash register「レジ」、upgrade「～を改良する」。
(B) plastic「プラスチック製の」、tray「トレー、盆」、replace「～を取り換える」。
(C) healthy「健康的な」、available「購入できる」。

---

76 What are the listeners encouraged to do next?

(A) Place an order
(B) Taste some food
(C) Vote on a proposal
(D) Clean up a room

聞き手は次に何をするよう勧められていますか。

(A) 注文をする
(B) 食べ物を試食する
(C) 提案に関して投票する
(D) 部屋をきれいにする

正解 B 話し手は❹で、総料理長が新しいレシピを開発し、それを聞き手に試食してほしいと望んでいることを知らせ、❺「部屋から出る途中で幾つかの試食品を取ってください」と試食を勧めている。encourage ~ to do「～に…するよう勧める」。taste「～を試食する」。
(A) place an order「注文する」。
(C) vote on ~「～に関して投票する」、proposal「提案」。
(D) clean up ~「～をきれいにする」。

Words & Phrases

end ～を終える　fill out ~ ～に必要事項を記入する　survey 調査票、調査　cafeteria 食堂　distribute ～を配布する　comment 意見　amount 量　prepackaged パック入りの、包装済みの　meal 1食分、1回分の食事　throw away ~ ～を捨てる　eliminate ～を排除する　add ～を加える　self-serve セルフサービスの　executive chef 総料理長　sample 試食品　on one's way out of ~ ～から出る途中で

TEST 2 PART 4

Questions 77 through 79 refer to the following telephone message.

🇦🇺 M

Hi, Susan. This is Thomas from the New York office. ❶The company leadership just received the headphone prototype your team developed. ❷They're very impressed with the audio quality, but some of them felt the padding was uncomfortable. ❸They want your team to use softer cushioning around the ears. ❹If you'd like a different materials supplier to correct the problem, I can send you the contact info for Custom Fiber. They worked with us on last year's products. Please call me back so we can talk about this more.

問題77-79は次の電話のメッセージに関するものです。

こんにちは、Susan。こちらはニューヨーク・オフィスのThomasです。会社の上層部は先ほど、あなたのチームが開発したヘッドホンの試作品を受け取りました。彼らはその音質に感心していますが、中にはパッドの付け心地が良くないと感じる人もいました。彼らは、あなたのチームが両耳周りにもっと柔らかいクッション材を使用することを望んでいます。もし別の材料供給会社に問題を是正してもらうことをご希望であれば、私はCustom Fiber社の連絡先をあなたに送ることができます。同社は昨年の製品で私たちに協力してくれました。これについてさらに話し合えるよう、私に折り返し電話してください。

77 What type of product is the speaker discussing?

(A) Automobiles
(B) Headphones
(C) Shoes
(D) Cameras

話し手はどんな種類の製品について話していますか。

(A) 自動車
(B) ヘッドホン
(C) 靴
(D) カメラ

正解 B 話し手は、自分の名前と所属するオフィスを伝えてから、❶「会社の上層部は先ほど、あなたのチームが開発したヘッドホンの試作品を受け取った」と知らせている。続く❷以降でも、そのヘッドホンについて話を進めているので、(B)が正解。
(A) automobile「自動車」。

78 What issue does the speaker mention?

(A) Some padding is uncomfortable.
(B) A budget is limited.
(C) Sound quality needs to be improved.
(D) A shipment has been delayed.

話し手はどんな問題について述べていますか。

(A) パッドが心地よくない。
(B) 予算が限られている。
(C) 音質が改善される必要がある。
(D) 出荷物が遅れている。

正解 A 話し手は、聞き手のチームが開発したヘッドホンの試作品を上層部が受け取ったと知らせた後、❷「彼らはその音質に感心しているが、中にはパッドの付け心地が良くないと感じる人もいた」と問題点を伝え、❸「彼らは、あなたのチームが両耳周りにもっと柔らかいクッション材を使用することを望んでいる」と言っている。issue「問題」。
(B) budget「予算」、limited「限られた」。
(C) improve「～を改善する」。

79 Why does the speaker say, "They worked with us on last year's products"?

(A) To request a meeting
(B) To warn the listener
(C) To recommend a supplier
(D) To criticize a decision

話し手はなぜ "They worked with us on last year's products" と言っていますか。

(A) 会議を要請するため
(B) 聞き手に注意喚起するため
(C) 供給会社を推薦するため
(D) 決断を批判するため

正解 C 試作品のヘッドホンのクッション材に関する問題点を伝え、材料交換の必要性に言及した話し手は、❹「もし別の材料供給会社に問題を是正してもらうことを希望するなら、私はCustom Fiber社の連絡先をあなたに送ることができる」と述べている。その直後に下線部の発言で、過去に同社と提携した実績があることを伝えているので、話し手はCustom Fiber社を推薦するためにこの発言をしていると判断できる。recommend「～を推薦する」。
(B) warn「～に注意喚起する」。
(D) criticize「～を批判する」、decision「決断」。

Words & Phrases
office 営業所、会社　leadership 上層部　headphone ヘッドホン　prototype 試作品　develop ～を開発する　be impressed with ～ ～に感心している　audio quality 音質　padding パッド、当て物　uncomfortable 心地よくない　cushioning クッション材、緩衝材　different 別の　material 材料　supplier 供給会社　correct ～を正す　contact 連絡先　info 情報 ★informationの略　call ～ back ～に折り返し電話する

Questions 80 through 82 refer to the following excerpt from a meeting.

問題80-82は次の会議の抜粋に関するものです。

🇺🇸 W

❶Remember that our annual building inspection will take place this Friday. ❷Before you leave on Thursday, please make sure all documents are locked in your desk drawers to help protect our client-related information. **Speaking of clients,** ❸several clients have requested that we be on call to answer questions in the evenings. ❹We'll be implementing that for select clients next month. ❺Evening work hours will be discussed at next week's meeting.

今週の金曜日に、年に1度の建物の点検が行われることを覚えておいてください。木曜日の退社前には、当社の顧客関連情報を保護できるよう、必ず全書類を自分の机の引き出しに入れて施錠してください。顧客といえば、複数の顧客が、夜間の問い合わせへの即時対応を当社に要請しています。私たちは来月、特定の顧客向けにそれを実施する予定です。夜間の勤務時間については、来週の会議で話し合われます。

---

80 What will take place on Friday?

(A) A town meeting
(B) A product release
(C) A building inspection
(D) A software update

金曜日に何が行われますか。

(A) 市民集会
(B) 製品の発売
(C) 建物の点検
(D) ソフトウエアの更新

正解 C 話し手は❶「今週の金曜日に、年に1度の建物の点検が行われることを覚えておいてください」と聞き手に念押しし、❷で、点検日前日にすべきことを伝えている。
(A) town meeting「市民集会」。
(B) product「製品」、release「発売」。
(D) update「更新」。

---

81 What should the listeners do on Thursday?

(A) Put documents away
(B) Shut down computers
(C) Meet with a supervisor
(D) Sign up for training

聞き手は木曜日に何をすべきですか。

(A) 書類を片付ける
(B) コンピューターの電源を切る
(C) 上司と会談する
(D) 研修に登録する

正解 A 話し手は、金曜日に建物の点検が実施されることを念押しした後、❷「木曜日の退社前には、当社の顧客関連情報を保護できるよう、必ず全書類を自分の机の引き出しに入れて施錠してください」と、点検日前日である木曜日に聞き手がすべきことを伝えている。put away ～「～を片付ける」。
(B) shut down ～「～（コンピューター）の電源を切る」。
(C) meet with ～「～と会談する」、supervisor「上司」。
(D) sign up for ～「～に登録する」、training「研修」。

---

82 What will be discussed next week?

(A) Volunteer opportunities
(B) Project expenses
(C) Overseas travel arrangements
(D) Employee schedules

来週に何が話し合われますか。

(A) ボランティアの機会
(B) プロジェクトの経費
(C) 海外出張の手配
(D) 従業員の予定

正解 D 話し手は❸で、聞き手である従業員に対し、一部の顧客が夜間の問い合わせへの即時対応を要請していることを伝えてから、❹で、来月からその対応を実施する予定だと知らせている。その直後に、❺「夜間の勤務時間については、来週の会議で話し合われる」と述べているので、来週に従業員の勤務予定が話し合われると判断できる。
(A) volunteer「ボランティア、志願者」、opportunity「機会」。
(B) expenses「経費」。
(C) overseas「海外への」、arrangement「手配」。

Words & Phrases

annual 年に1度の　　inspection 点検　　take place 行われる
make sure (that) ～ 必ず～であるようにする　　document 書類　　lock ～を(鍵を掛けて)保管する　　drawer 引き出し
protect ～を保護する　　client 顧客　　-related ～関連の　　speaking of ～ ～といえば　　several 複数の
request (that) ～ ～であることを要請する　　be on call 呼び出しにいつでも応じられる　　evening 夜
implement ～を実施する　　select 選ばれた　　discuss ～について話し合う

Questions 83 through 85 refer to the following speech.

🇨🇦 M

Thank you for attending our product launch event. ❶Did you know that it's never too early for children to start learning science—and that there's an exciting way to do it? ❷Kids all around the country love Lex, the chemistry board game that's as much fun as it is educational. ❸What's special about Lex is that it's been endorsed by the National Teachers' Association. And now ❹we're offering Lex with free shipping! Keep in mind, this product will be very popular. ❺Visit our online store at www.lexgames.com to order now.

問題83-85は次のスピーチに関するものです。

当社の製品発売イベントにご出席いただきありがとうございます。子どもが科学学習を始めるのに決して早過ぎることはないということ——そして、それをするための刺激的な方法があるということはご存じでしたか。国中の子どもが、ためになると同時に楽しい化学ボードゲームのLexが大好きです。Lexの特別な点は、全国教員協会から推奨されていることです。さて、当社は現在、送料無料でLexをご提供しています！ご留意ください、この製品は大変な人気になるでしょう。今すぐ注文するために、www.lexgames.comまで当社のオンラインストアにアクセスしてください。

83 What subject does the game focus on?

(A) Reading
(B) Science
(C) Math
(D) History

ゲームはどんな学科に焦点を当てていますか。

(A) 読解
(B) 科学
(C) 数学
(D) 歴史

正解 B 話し手は製品発売イベントへの出席に対し、聞き手に謝意を伝えてから、❶で、子どもが科学を学ぶのに早過ぎることはないと述べている。そして、❷「国中の子どもが、ためになると同時に楽しい化学ボードゲームのLexが大好きだ」と化学のボードゲームを紹介しているので、このゲームが焦点を当てている学科は科学だと判断できる。subject「学科」、focus on ～「～に焦点を当てる」。

84 What does the speaker say is special about the game?

(A) It is appropriate for families.
(B) It was designed by teachers.
(C) It can be played outdoors.
(D) It is recognized by an educational organization.

話し手はゲームについて何が特別だと言っていますか。

(A) それは家族向けだ。
(B) それは教員によって設計された。
(C) それは屋外ですることができる。
(D) それは教育組織から評価されている。

正解 D 話し手は、Lexという化学ボードゲームについて、❸「Lexの特別な点は、全国教員協会から推奨されていることだ」と説明している。endorsedをrecognizedと、the National Teachers' Associationをan educational organizationとそれぞれ表している(D)が正解。recognize「～を認める」、organization「組織」。
(A) appropriate「ふさわしい」。
(B) design「～を設計する」。
(C) outdoors「屋外で」。

85 What does the speaker mean when he says, "this product will be very popular"?

(A) The listeners should act quickly.
(B) A marketing strategy has been successful.
(C) Sales projections were incorrect.
(D) A product line should be expanded.

話し手は "this product will be very popular" という発言で、何を意味していますか。

(A) 聞き手は素早く行動すべきである。
(B) マーケティング戦略は成功している。
(C) 販売予測は不正確だった。
(D) 製品ラインは拡大されるべきである。

正解 A 話し手は❹で、新製品であるLexを現在、送料無料で提供していると知らせた後、下線部を含む発言で、製品が大人気となる見込みであることを念押ししている。その直後に❺で、注文のためのオンラインサイトを案内しているので、話し手は製品発売イベントの出席者である聞き手に、製品が売り切れてしまう前に迅速に注文するよう促していると考えられる。act「行動する」、quickly「素早く」。
(B) marketing「マーケティング」、strategy「戦略」、successful「成功した」。
(C) projection「予測」、incorrect「不正確な」。
(D) line「製品ライン」、expand「～を拡大する」。

Words & Phrases

attend ～に出席する   product launch 新製品の発売   science 自然科学、科学
exciting 刺激的な   kid 子ども   chemistry 化学   board game ボードゲーム   as much ～ as … …と同じくらい～
educational 教育的な、有益な   endorse ～を推奨する   national 全国的な   association 協会
free shipping 送料無料   keep in mind (that) ～ ～ということを心に留めておく

Questions 86 through 88 refer to the following speech.

🇬🇧 w

❶Thank you all for coming to the grand opening of the Gerhard Vogel exhibit here at the International Music Museum. ❷Our museum curators worked hard to create this permanent exhibit. As you know, Mr. Vogel is a world-renowned violinist. ❸All the items in the collection were kindly donated by Mr. Vogel last year. His legacy will continue for many years to come through this priceless collection. ❹To commemorate the exhibit opening, we are selling signed posters featuring Mr. Vogel with his violin. ❺These are available in our gift shop.

問題86-88は次のスピーチに関するものです。

ここ国際音楽博物館のGerhard Vogel展の大オープン記念イベントにお越しいただき、ありがとうございます。当館学芸員たちが、この常設展を実現するために尽力しました。ご存じの通り、Vogelさんは世界的に有名なバイオリン奏者です。所蔵品の全点が、昨年Vogelさんのご厚意により寄贈されました。後世に残る彼の業績は、この大変貴重な所蔵品を通じて末長く継続することでしょう。展覧会の開幕を記念し、当館はバイオリンを抱えたVogelさんを収めたサイン入りポスターを販売いたします。これらは当館のギフトショップでご購入いただけます。

86 Where is the speech being given?

(A) At a library
(B) At a theater
(C) At a museum
(D) At a convention center

スピーチはどこで行われていますか。

(A) 図書館
(B) 劇場
(C) 博物館
(D) コンベンションセンター

正解 C 話し手は❶「ここ国際音楽博物館のGerhard Vogel展の大オープン記念イベントに来てくれて、ありがとう」と聞き手に謝意を伝えた後、❷で、同博物館の学芸員たちの貢献をたたえている。よって、スピーチは博物館で行われていると判断できる。
(D) convention center「コンベンションセンター、会議場」。

87 What did Gerhard Vogel do last year?

(A) He spoke at a conference.
(B) He wrote an autobiography.
(C) He gave a final performance.
(D) He donated some items.

Gerhard Vogelは昨年、何をしましたか。

(A) 彼は会議で講演をした。
(B) 彼は自叙伝を著した。
(C) 彼は最後の公演を行った。
(D) 彼は幾つかの物品を寄贈した。

正解 D 話し手は、博物館のGerhard Vogel展が常設展であること、そしてVogelさんが世界的なバイオリン奏者であることに言及してから、❸「所蔵品の全点が、昨年Vogelさんの厚意により寄贈された」と伝えている。(D)が正解。
(A) conference「会議」。
(B) autobiography「自叙伝」。
(C) final「最後の」、performance「公演」。

88 What does the speaker say are available for purchase?

(A) Posters
(B) Books
(C) Tickets
(D) Musical instruments

話し手は何が購入可能であると言っていますか。

(A) ポスター
(B) 本
(C) チケット
(D) 楽器

正解 A 話し手は❹で、博物館でVogelさんのサイン入りポスターを販売することを知らせた後、❺「これらは当館のギフトショップで購入できる」とポスターの購入可能な場所を伝えている。purchase「購入」。
(D) 購入可能だと言及しているのは、バイオリンを抱えたVogelさんを収めたポスターであり、楽器ではない。musical instrument「楽器」。

Words & Phrases

grand opening オープン記念イベント　exhibit 展覧会　international 国際的な　curator 学芸員　permanent exhibit 常設展　world-renowned 世界的に有名な　violinist バイオリン奏者　item 品物　collection 所蔵品、コレクション　kindly 親切にも　donate ～を寄贈する　legacy 後世に残る業績、遺産　continue 続く　for many years to come 末長く、これから先何年も　through ～を通じて　priceless 非常に貴重な　commemorate ～を記念する　signed サイン入りの　poster ポスター　feature ～を目玉とする　violin バイオリン　available 購入できる、入手できる

Questions 89 through 91 refer to the following telephone message.

🇦🇺 M

❶I'm calling from Dr. Garcia's office to confirm an appointment tomorrow for Zeyneb Rashad. ❷You're scheduled to see the doctor at one P.M. for a tooth cleaning and then… I see you've also scheduled a whitening procedure. That'll be conducted by one of our assistants. ❸The whitening process is different for each patient. I hope the rest of your afternoon is free. Oh, and ❹I see that we've already received payment for all the work tomorrow, so there won't be any need for you to pay at the end.

問題89-91は次の電話のメッセージに関するものです。

Garcia医院から、Zeyneb Rashad様の明日のご予約を確認させていただくためにお電話しています。あなたは歯のクリーニングのため、午後1時に当医師の診察を受けるご予定で、それから…ホワイトニングの処置もご予定に入れておられますね。そちらは当院の助手の1人によって行われます。ホワイトニングの方法は患者さまごとに異なります。午後の残りのお時間が空いているとよいのですが。ああ、それから、当院は明日の全処置に対するお支払いをすでに受領しておりますので、終了時にお支払いいただく必要は一切ございません。

---

89 Where does the speaker most likely work?

(A) At a bank
(B) At a pharmacy
(C) At a dental clinic
(D) At an auto repair shop

話し手はどこで働いていると考えられますか。

(A) 銀行
(B) 薬局
(C) 歯科医院
(D) 自動車修理店

正解 C 話し手は❶「Garcia医院から、Zeyneb Rashadさんの明日の予約を確認するために電話している」と電話の目的を伝えた後、❷で、聞き手が受ける予定の処置について確認している。よって、聞き手はZeyneb Rashadという名の患者であり、話し手は歯科医院で働いていると考えられる。dental「歯の」、clinic「診療所」。
(B) pharmacy「薬局」。
(D) auto「自動車（automobileの略）」、repair「修理」。

---

90 What does the speaker mean when he says, "I hope the rest of your afternoon is free"?

(A) He needs some assistance with a project.
(B) His office is very busy.
(C) A later appointment time would be better.
(D) A procedure might take a long time.

話し手は "I hope the rest of your afternoon is free" という発言で、何を意味していますか。

(A) 彼には計画に対する支援が必要である。
(B) 彼の医院は非常に忙しい。
(C) もっと後の予約時間の方が望ましいだろう。
(D) 処置には長い時間がかかるかもしれない。

正解 D 話し手は、聞き手が明日受ける予定の処置であるホワイトニングについて、❸「ホワイトニングの方法は患者ごとに異なる」と述べてから、「午後のあなたの残りの時間が空いているとよいのだが」という下線部の発言を続けている。よって、話し手はこの発言で、患者ごとにホワイトニングの方法が違うため、処置には長時間かかる可能性もあることを事前に知らせているのだと考えられる。
(A) assistance「支援」。

---

91 What does the speaker say has happened?

(A) A payment has been submitted.
(B) Paperwork has been signed.
(C) Transportation has been scheduled.
(D) Supplies have been ordered.

話し手は何があったと述べていますか。

(A) 支払いは済んでいる。
(B) 必要書類は署名済みである。
(C) 移動手段は予定済みである。
(D) 備品は注文済みである。

正解 A 話し手は❹「当院は明日の全処置に対する支払いをすでに受領したので、あなたは終了時に支払う必要はない」と聞き手に伝えている。submit「～を提出する」。
(B) paperwork「必要書類」、sign「～に署名する」。
(C) 話し手は歯のクリーニングとホワイトニングの処置の予定を伝えているが、移動手段の予定には言及していない。transportation「交通手段」。
(D) supplies「備品」、order「～を注文する」。

Words & Phrases

doctor's office 医院　confirm ～を確認する　appointment （医者などの）予約
be scheduled to do ～する予定である　see the doctor 医者の診察を受ける　tooth 歯　cleaning クリーニング
schedule ～を予定に入れる　whitening ホワイトニング　★歯を白くすること　procedure 処置　conduct ～を行う
assistant 助手　process 方法、手順　patient 患者　rest 残り　free 空いている　receive ～を受け取る
payment 支払金　pay 支払う　at the end 終わりに

Questions 92 through 94 refer to the following talk.

問題92-94は次の話に関するものです。

 W

Good morning. ❶As you know, we pledge timely delivery to all our customers. ❷Since you deliver packages by bike in the city every day, we want your feedback on a new cargo bike. ❸It has a storage unit attached that will allow you to carry many more packages than usual. We're currently borrowing a few from the manufacturer to test out before we purchase them. So today you'll be using them on your regular routes. ❹Just a reminder: please lock up the bikes while making a stop to keep them safe. ❺There's a lock and key attached to each one.

おはようございます。ご存じの通り、当社は全顧客に適時の配達を約束しています。皆さんは毎日市内で自転車で荷物を配達しているので、私たちは新しいカーゴバイクについての皆さんの意見をもらいたいと思っています。それには、通常よりも多くの荷物の運搬を可能にする収容スペースが取り付けられています。当社は現在、購入する前に試すため、メーカーから数台を借り受けています。そこで今日は、皆さんには自分の通常の配達区域でそれらを使用していただきます。ただ、1点ご注意ください。立ち寄り先では、自転車を安全に管理するために施錠しておいてください。1台ごとに錠前と鍵が取り付けられています。

92 Who are the listeners?
(A) Delivery workers
(B) Automotive mechanics
(C) Professional cyclists
(D) Factory workers

聞き手は誰ですか。
(A) 配達作業員
(B) 自動車整備士
(C) プロの自転車競技選手
(D) 工場労働者

正解 A 話し手は❶で、聞き手に対し、全顧客に適時の配達を約束しているという自社の方針を再確認してから、❷「皆さんは毎日市内で自転車で荷物を配達しているので、私たちは新しいカーゴバイクについての皆さんの意見をもらいたいと思っている」と述べている。よって、聞き手は荷物の配達作業員だと判断できる。
(B) automotive「自動車の」、mechanic「整備士」。
(C) professional「プロの、職業的な」、cyclist「自転車競技選手」。

93 What advantage does the speaker mention?
(A) Faster product assembly
(B) Improved workplace safety
(C) Additional storage capacity
(D) Efficient payment processing

話し手はどんな長所について述べていますか。
(A) より速い製品組み立て
(B) 改善された職場の安全性
(C) 追加の収納容量
(D) 効率的な支払い処理

正解 C 話し手は、新しいカーゴバイクへの意見を集めたいと述べた後、❸「それには、通常よりも多くの荷物の運搬を可能にする収容スペースが取り付けられている」と、その特長を述べている。そのことをadditional storage capacityと表している(C)が正解。advantage「長所」。additional「追加の」、capacity「容量、収容能力」。
(A) product「製品」、assembly「組み立て」。
(B) improved「改善された」、workplace「職場」。
(D) efficient「効率的な」、processing「処理」。

94 What does the speaker remind the listeners to do?
(A) Wear their helmets
(B) Submit their time sheets
(C) Collect customer feedback
(D) Use a lock

話し手は聞き手に何をするよう念を押していますか。
(A) ヘルメットをかぶる
(B) タイムシートを提出する
(C) 顧客の意見を収集する
(D) 鍵を使用する

正解 D 話し手は、聞き手に今日、新しいカーゴバイクに試乗してもらうと言ってから、❹「ただ、1点注意してください。立ち寄り先では、自転車を安全に管理するために施錠してください」と念を押し、❺で、各車に錠前と鍵が取り付けられていると補足している。remind ~ to do「~に…するよう念を押す」。
(A) helmet「ヘルメット」。
(B) submit「~を提出する」、time sheet「タイムシート(勤務時間などを記録するもの)」。
(C) collect「~を収集する」。

Words & Phrases
pledge ~ to … ~を…に誓う　timely 適時の、タイミングのよい　package 荷物、小包
cargo bike カーゴバイク ★荷物運搬用の自転車　storage unit 収容部分　attach ~を取り付ける
allow ~ to do ~が…するのを可能にする　carry ~を運搬する　than usual 通常よりも　currently 現在
borrow ~を借りる　manufacturer メーカー、製造業者　test out ~ ~を試してみる　reminder 注意、思い出させるもの
lock up ~ ~の鍵を全部掛ける　make a stop 立ち寄る　safe 安全な　lock 錠前

Questions 95 through 97 refer to the following announcement and airport departure board.

🇬🇧 w

❶Attention passengers taking flight JB2508 to San Francisco. **Passengers are now permitted to board.** ❷Please note that once you're seated on the plane, there will be a slight departure delay. ❸The baggage handlers for this flight need some extra time to finish loading luggage onto the plane. ❹If you need any assistance during your flight, I encourage you to approach the flight attendants. ❺They'll be happy to assist you. **Have a great flight.**

問題95-97は次のお知らせと空港の出発便案内板に関するものです。

サンフランシスコ行きJB2508便にご搭乗の乗客の皆さまにお知らせします。乗客の皆さまは、これよりご搭乗いただけます。機内でご着席の後に少々出発の遅延がありますのでご注意ください。本便の手荷物係員が、機内に荷物を積み終えるのに追加の時間を必要としています。飛行中に何かお手伝いが必要の際には、客室乗務員にお声掛けください。彼らは喜んで皆さまの手助けをいたします。素晴らしい空の旅を。

Flight	Destination	Gate
DA3049	Sacramento	1
AA1637	Philadelphia	2
JB2508	San Francisco	3
SW6421	Washington, D.C.	4

Airport Departure Board

便名	行き先	搭乗口
DA3049	サクラメント	1
AA1637	フィラデルフィア	2
JB2508	サンフランシスコ	3
SW6421	ワシントンD.C.	4

本空港の出発便案内板

95 Look at the graphic. Which gate are the listeners waiting at?

(A) Gate 1
(B) Gate 2
(C) Gate 3
(D) Gate 4

図を見てください。聞き手はどの搭乗口で待機していますか。

(A) 1番搭乗口
(B) 2番搭乗口
(C) 3番搭乗口
(D) 4番搭乗口

正解 C 話し手は❶で、サンフランシスコ行き JB2508便の乗客向けにお知らせがあると述べ、以降ではその詳細を聞き手に伝えている。図を見ると、サンフランシスコ行きのJB2508便の搭乗口は3番だと分かるので、(C)が正解。

---

96 What is the reason for a delay?

(A) The weather is too windy for takeoff.
(B) Luggage is still being loaded.
(C) The ground crew is fueling the plane.
(D) Repairs are being made.

何が遅延の原因ですか。

(A) 離陸には風が強過ぎる天候である。
(B) 手荷物がまだ積み込まれているところである。
(C) 地上整備員が飛行機に燃料を補給しているところである。
(D) 修理作業が行われているところである。

正解 B 話し手はJB2508便の乗客向けに、今から搭乗可能であることを知らせてから、❷で、機内で着席の後に少し出発の遅延があることに留意するよう伝えている。そして、❸「本便の手荷物係員が、機内に荷物を積み終えるのに追加の時間を必要としている」と、遅延の原因について説明している。そのことをluggageを主語にして、受動態で表している(B)が正解。
(A) windy「風の強い」、takeoff「(飛行機などの)離陸」。
(C) ground crew「(飛行機の)地上整備員」、fuel「〜に燃料を補給する」。
(D) repairs「修理作業」。

---

97 What does the speaker encourage the listeners to do?

(A) Fasten seat belts
(B) Look at a snack menu
(C) Watch in-flight movies
(D) Ask staff for assistance

話し手は聞き手に何をするよう勧めていますか。

(A) シートベルトを締める
(B) 軽食のメニューを見る
(C) 機内映画を見る
(D) スタッフに手助けを求める

正解 D 話し手は❹で、飛行中に何か手伝いが必要の際には客室乗務員に声を掛けることを聞き手に勧め、❺「彼らは喜んで皆さんの手助けをする」と補足している。❹のapproach the flight attendantsを、ask staffと表している(D)が正解。ask 〜 for …「〜に…を求める」、staff「スタッフ」。
(A) fasten「〜を留める」、seat belt「シートベルト」。
(B) snack「軽食」。
(C) in-flight「機内の、飛行中の」。

Words & Phrases

departure board　出発便案内板　　Attention 〜　〜にお知らせします　★空港などのアナウンスで使われる表現

passenger　乗客　　flight　飛行機の便、フライト　　permit 〜 to do　〜に…することを許可する　　board　(乗り物に)乗り込む

note that 〜　〜であることに留意する　　once　いったん〜すると　　be seated　座る　　slight　少しの

departure　出発(の)　　delay　遅延　　baggage handler　(空港などの)手荷物係員　　extra　追加の、余分な

finish doing　〜し終える　　load 〜 onto …　〜を…に積む　　luggage　手荷物　　assistance　手助け、支援

encourage 〜 to do　〜に…するよう勧める　　approach　〜に話を持ち掛ける、〜に接触する　　flight attendant　客室乗務員

be happy to do　喜んで〜する　　assist　〜を手伝う

出発便案内板　destination　行き先、目的地　　gate　搭乗口

Questions 98 through 100 refer to the following telephone message and table.

🇨🇦 M

Hi, Mr. Nakamura. It's Takumi Sato. ❶I received your request for a solar panel consultation. ❷Thanks for e-mailing me your home energy bills, since that helps me create a proposal that's tailored to your needs. But, um, ❸I'm puzzled because the July usage seems low. ❹Our data shows that houses typically use a lot more energy during that month. Could you call me back? I need reliable figures so I can determine how many solar panels to recommend. ❺I'd also like to set up an in-person meeting for later this week, so that I can go through the proposal with you and answer questions about the project.

問題98-100は次の電話のメッセージと表に関するものです。

こんにちは、Nakamuraさん。Takumi Satoです。ソーラーパネルに関する相談のご依頼をお受けしました。ご自宅の光熱費情報を私にEメールで送っていただきありがとうございます。それは私がご要望に合わせた案を作成するのに役立つからです。ですが、ええと、7月の使用量が少ないようなので困惑しています。私どものデータでは、一般家庭は概してその月に、はるかに多くの電力を使用するということが示されています。私に折り返し電話していただけますか。何台のソーラーパネルをお勧めすべきか割り出せるよう、信頼できる数値が必要です。また、今週後半に対面の打ち合わせを設けたいと考えています。そうすればあなたと一緒に案を詳しく検討して計画に関するご質問にお答えできます。

Energy Usage	
May	850 kWh
June	900 kWh
July	1,000 kWh
August	1,200 kWh

消費電力量	
5月	850 キロワット時
6月	900 キロワット時
7月	1,000 キロワット時
8月	1,200 キロワット時

98 Who most likely is the speaker?

(A) A building inspector
(B) A sales consultant
(C) An apartment landlord
(D) A utility company executive

話し手は誰だと考えられますか。

(A) 建物の検査官
(B) 販売コンサルタント
(C) アパートの家主
(D) 公益事業会社の重役

正解 **B** 話し手は名前を名乗った後、❶「ソーラーパネルに関するあなたの相談の依頼を受けた」と述べている。続けて❷で、聞き手の自宅の光熱費情報を送ってくれたことに謝意を伝えた上で、その情報は自分が要望に合わせた案を作成するのに役立つと述べている。よって、話し手はソーラーパネル設置を望む顧客向けの販売コンサルタントだと考えられる。
(A) inspector「検査官」。
(C) apartment「アパート」、landlord「家主」。
(D) utility「(電気・ガス・水道などの)公益事業」、executive「重役」。

99 Look at the graphic. Which number is the speaker confused about?

(A) 850 kWh
(B) 900 kWh
(C) 1,000 kWh
(D) 1,200 kWh

図を見てください。話し手はどの数値に困惑していますか。

(A) 850 キロワット時
(B) 900 キロワット時
(C) 1,000 キロワット時
(D) 1,200 キロワット時

正解 **C** 話し手は❸「7 月の使用量が少ないようなので困惑している」と、聞き手の自宅の消費電力量に疑問を抱いていることを述べた後、❹「私たちのデータでは、一般家庭は概してその月に、はるかに多くの電力を使用するということが示されている」と、困惑の理由を説明している。図を見ると、7 月の消費電力量は 1,000 キロワット時なので、(C)が正解。be confused about ～「～に困惑している、～に混乱している」。

100 What does the speaker say he wants to do later this week?

(A) Meet with the listener
(B) Announce a rate change
(C) Repair some equipment
(D) Document some damage

話し手は今週後半に何をしたいと言っていますか。

(A) 聞き手と会う
(B) 規定料金の変更を知らせる
(C) 機器を修理する
(D) 損害の詳細を記録する

正解 **A** 話し手は、聞き手に折り返し電話するよう依頼した後、❺「また、今週後半に対面の打ち合わせを設けたいと考えている。そうすればあなたと一緒に案を詳しく検討して計画に関する質問に答えられる」と伝えている。set up an in-person meeting を meet with ～「～と約束して会う、～と会談する」を用いて表している(A)が正解。
(B) announce「～を知らせる」、rate「規定料金」。
(C) repair「～を修理する」、equipment「機器」。
(D) document「～の詳細を記録する」、damage「損害」。

TEST 2 PART 4

Words & Phrases

table 表　　solar panel ソーラーパネル、太陽電池板　　consultation 相談　　e-mail ～ … ～に…をEメールで送る

energy bill 光熱費　　help ～ *do* ～が…するのに役立つ　　create ～を作成する　　proposal 提案、計画

tailored to ～ ～(要求や条件など)に合わせた　　needs ニーズ、要求　　puzzled 困惑した　　usage 使用量、使用

house 一般家庭、所帯　　typically 概して　　call ～ back ～に折り返し電話する　　reliable 信頼できる　　figure 数値

determine ～を決定する　　recommend ～を推奨する　　set up ～ ～を設ける、～の手はずを整える

in-person 対面の、直接の　　go through ～ ～を詳しく検討する

表　kWh キロワット時　★kilowatt-hour(s)の略で、1 時間当たりの消費電力量を示す単位

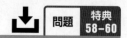

101 It is advisable to assign new tasks ------- to interns during the first month of training.

(A) slow
(B) slowest
(C) slowly
(D) slows

研修の最初の1カ月間は、インターンの人たちに新しい仕事を徐々に割り当てていくのが望ましいです。

(A) 遅い
(B) 最も遅い
(C) 徐々に
(D) 遅くなる

正解 C It is advisable to do「～するのが望ましい」を使って新しい仕事の割り当て方についての勧めを述べている。assign ～ to …「…に～を割り当てる」の形の後ろは、interns「インターンの人たち」と続いている。空所にassignを修飾する副詞の(C) slowly「徐々に、ゆっくりと」を入れると、「インターンの人たちに対して仕事を徐々に割り当てるのが良い」となり、適した文意になる。advisable「望ましい、賢明な」、task「仕事」、intern「インターン、研修生」、training「研修」。
(A) 形容詞の原級。(B) 形容詞の最上級。
(D) 動詞slowの三人称単数現在形。

102 Mr. Barton and his team provide services ranging ------- fund-raising to coordinating events.

(A) like
(B) for
(C) from
(D) through

Bartonさんと彼のチームは、資金集めからイベントのコーディネートにわたるサービスを提供します。

(A) ～のような
(B) ～のための
(C) ～から
(D) ～を通して

正解 C 選択肢は全て前置詞の働きを持つ語。文の主語はMr. Barton and his teamで、述語動詞はprovide。range from A to B「AからBに及ぶ」の形になる(C) fromを入れると、ranging from fund-raising to coordinating events「資金集めからイベントのコーディネートにわたる」が、直前の名詞servicesを修飾する形になり、適切。provide「～を提供する」、fund-raising「資金集め」、coordinate「～をコーディネートする、～の調整を行う」。

103 Customers who sign up for Garrett Tea Company's mailing list will receive free shipping on ------- next online order.

(A) theirs
(B) them
(C) their
(D) themselves

Garrett紅茶社のメーリングリストに登録されるお客さまは、次回のオンライン注文の際、配送料が無料になります。

(A) 彼らのもの
(B) 彼らを
(C) 彼らの
(D) 彼ら自身

正解 C 選択肢は全て三人称複数の人称代名詞。空所の前に前置詞onがあり、後ろにはnext online order「次回のオンライン注文」が続いているので、空所には名詞句を修飾する語が入る。所有格の(C) theirが適切。their next online orderで「彼ら(メーリングリストに登録する顧客)の次回のオンライン注文」という適した意味になる。sign up for ～「～に登録する」、mailing list「メーリングリスト」、free「無料の」、shipping「配送」、online order「オンライン注文」。
(A) 所有代名詞。(B) 目的格。(D) 再帰代名詞。

104 Mr. Iwata likes to be prepared, so he ------- arrives fifteen minutes early to meetings.

    (A) very
    (B) once
    (C) quite
    (D) always

Iwataさんは準備のできた状態でいたいので、会議にはいつも15分早く着きます。

    (A) 非常に
    (B) 一度
    (C) かなり
    (D) いつも

正解 D 選択肢は全て副詞の働きを持つ語。文頭からsoまでの部分で、「Iwataさんは準備のできた状態でいたいので」という理由を表している。(D) always「いつも」を入れると、he以降が「彼（Iwataさん）はいつも会議に15分早く着く」となり、意味が通る。like to do「〜したい」、prepared「準備のできた」。
(A) (B) (C) いずれも意味が通らない。

105 Ms. Fache is heading a committee that will explore ways to make the province more ------- for small businesses.

    (A) afford
    (B) affording
    (C) affordable
    (D) afforded

Facheさんは、その州を小企業にとって、より金銭的に手頃な場所にするための方法を模索する委員会を率いています。

    (A) 余裕がある
    (B) 与えている
    (C) 手頃な
    (D) 与えられた

正解 C make 〜 …は「〜を…にする」の意味でwaysを修飾するto不定詞句を作っている。explore ways to make the province more ------- for small businessesは「その州を小企業にとってより-------にするための方法を模索する」となる。moreと共に比較級を作る形容詞(C) affordable「（金銭的に）手頃な」を入れると、小企業の金銭的な負担を軽減する方法を模索するということになり、意味が通る。head「〜を率いる」、committee「委員会」、explore「〜を探求する」、province「州」、small business「小企業」。

106 The repair estimate ------- all costs for labor and parts.

    (A) prefers
    (B) accepts
    (C) includes
    (D) surrounds

その修理見積もりは、全ての工賃と部品代を含んでいます。

    (A) 〜をより好む
    (B) 〜を引き受ける
    (C) 〜を含む
    (D) 〜を取り囲む

正解 C 最も自然な文になる動詞を選ぶ。主語はThe repair estimate「修理見積もり」で、all costs for labor and parts「労働と部品のための全てのコスト」が、空所に入る他動詞の目的語になる。(C) includes「〜を含む」が適切。repair「修理」、estimate「見積もり（書）」、labor「（修理請求書での）技術料、労働」、part「部品、パーツ」。
(A) (B) (D) いずれも適した文意にならない。

107 The Destven Institute contact is a key ------- of information on energy-related matters.

(A) sourced
(B) source
(C) sources
(D) sourcing

そのDestven研究所の知人は、エネルギー関連事情についての重要な情報源です。

(A) 出どころの明らかにされた
(B) 出どころ
(C) 出どころ
(D) 調達

正解 B 主語はThe Destven Institute contact。contactには、「(情報などが得られる)知人、関係筋」という意味がある。空所の後ろのof以降の部分「エネルギー関連事情についての情報の」が、直前のa key -------を修飾していると考えられる。名詞句a key source「重要な出どころ」となる(B) source「出どころ」を入れると、意味が通る。institute「研究所、協会」、key「重要な」、energy-related「エネルギー関連の」、matters「事情、状況」。
(C) 空所の前に冠詞のaが付いているので、複数形は不適切。

108 East Highlands Adventures now offers guided hikes along several trails that the state ------- opened.

(A) especially
(B) rigidly
(C) recently
(D) intensely

East Highlandsアドベンチャー社は現在、州が最近開設した幾つかの山道に沿って歩く、ガイド付き徒歩ツアーを提供しています。

(A) 特に
(B) 厳しく
(C) 最近
(D) 激しく

正解 C 選択肢は全て副詞。that the state ------- openedは「州が-------開設した」の意味で、直前のtrails「山道」を修飾する関係代名詞節になっている。空所に(C) recentlyを入れると、州が最近開設した山道でのツアーを案内する文になり、適切。adventure「アドベンチャー、冒険」、offer「〜を提供する」、guided「ガイド付きの」、hike「徒歩ツアー、ハイキング」、state「州」、open「〜(道など)を開通させる」。

109 Customer complaints that cannot be resolved ------- a call-center representative should be referred to a supervisor.

(A) out
(B) by
(C) and
(D) or

顧客からの苦情で、コールセンターのオペレーターでは解決できないものは、監督者に委ねられるべきです。

(A) 外へ
(B) 〜によって
(C) 〜と
(D) 〜または

正解 B 文頭からrepresentativeまでがこの文の主語に当たり、should be referredが述語動詞。主語の中のthat節はCustomer complaintsを修飾し、受動態の形になっている。空所に行為者を表す(B) by「〜によって」を入れると、Customer complaints that cannot be resolved by a call-center representativeが「顧客からの苦情で、コールセンターのオペレーターでは解決できないもの」という長い主語になり、意味が通る。complaint「苦情」、resolve「〜を解決する」、call-center representative「コールセンターのオペレーター、電話受付係」、refer 〜 to …「〜(問題解決など)を…に委ねる、〜を…に照会する」、supervisor「監督者、管理者」。

110 ------- filling out the online form, applicants must also upload a résumé.

　(A) Furthermore
　(B) Except for
　(C) As far as
　(D) In addition to

オンラインの申し込みフォームに記入するのに加えて、応募者は履歴書のアップロードもしなければなりません。

　(A) さらに
　(B) 〜を除いて
　(C) 〜である限り
　(D) 〜に加えて

> **正解 D** also「〜もまた」があり、カンマの後ろは、「応募者は履歴書のアップロードもしなければならない」という意味なので、カンマの前にも応募者がしなければならないことが述べられていると考えられる。filling out the online form「オンラインの申し込みフォームに記入すること」が名詞句なので、空所には前置詞（句）が入る。前置詞句の(D) In addition to「〜に加えて」が意味からも適切。fill out 〜「〜に記入する」、form「申し込みフォーム」、applicant「応募者」、upload「〜をアップロードする」、résumé「履歴書」。
> (A) 副詞。(B) 前置詞句だが、整合性のある文にならない。(C) 接続詞句。

111 Allentown Paint Supply relocated ------- downtown office to Trenton Street.

　(A) they
　(B) ours
　(C) yours
　(D) its

Allentown塗料用品社は、同社の中心街のオフィスをトレントン通りに移しました。

　(A) 彼らは
　(B) 私たちのもの
　(C) あなたのもの
　(D) その

> **正解 D** 選択肢は全て代名詞。主語はAllentown Paint Supply。述語動詞relocatedの目的語となるdowntown officeを修飾する所有格の代名詞(D) itsが適切。its downtown officeで「その（Allentown塗料用品社の）中心街にあるオフィス」という意味になる。relocate「〜を移転させる」、downtown「中心街の、繁華街の」。
> (A) 主格。(B) (C) 所有代名詞。

112 The merchandise will be placed in a storage facility ------- the warehouse roof repairs are completed.

　(A) over
　(B) past
　(C) with
　(D) until

倉庫の屋根の修理作業が完了するまで、商品は保管施設に置いておかれます。

　(A) 〜の上に
　(B) 〜を通り過ぎて
　(C) 〜と
　(D) 〜まで

> **正解 D** 空所の前後は共に〈主語＋動詞〉という節の形なので、空所には2つの節をつなぐ接続詞が入る。選択肢の中で唯一接続詞として使える(D) until「〜まで」が適切。untilは、前置詞としても接続詞としても使うことができる。merchandise「商品」、place「〜を置く」、storage「保管」、facility「施設」、warehouse「倉庫」、repairs「修理作業」、complete「〜を完了させる」。
> (A) (B) (C) 前置詞。

113 The Hartsfield Hotel offers ------- contemporary comforts for a building that was constructed a century ago.

(A) impressive
(B) impression
(C) impressed
(D) to impress

Hartsfieldホテルは、100年前に建設された建物としては、素晴らしい現代的設備を提供しています。

(A) 素晴らしい
(B) 印象
(C) 感心した
(D) 感心させること

正解 **A** 主語はThe Hartsfield Hotelで、offers「～を提供する」が述語動詞。空所に形容詞の(A) impressive「素晴らしい、印象的な」を入れると、impressive contemporary comforts「素晴らしい現代的設備」が他動詞offersの目的語となって意味が通る。contemporary「現代的な」、comforts「生活を快適にするもの、便利な設備」、for「～としては」、construct「～を建設する」、century「100年間」。
(D) offer to do は「～することを申し出る」の意味だが、適した文意にならない。

114 ------- Mr. Assink placed the order early, it still arrived late.

(A) Equally
(B) Besides
(C) Although
(D) Likewise

Assinkさんはその注文を早く出しましたが、それでもやはり、それは遅れて届きました。

(A) 同様に
(B) その上
(C) ～だが
(D) 同じく

正解 **C** カンマの前の「Assinkさんはその注文を早く出した」に対し、後ろはit still arrived late「それでもやはり、それは遅れて届いた」と反対の内容が続くので、空所には2つの節を逆接でつなぐ接続詞が入る。選択肢の中で唯一の接続詞である(C) Although「～だが」が、文意からも適切。place an order「注文を出す」、still「それでも（やはり）」。
(A) (D) 副詞。(B) 副詞または前置詞。

115 Due to the lack of -------, the president of Murtha Industries was not informed of the employees' concerns.

(A) communicate
(B) communicative
(C) communicated
(D) communication

コミュニケーションの欠如のため、Murtha産業社の社長は従業員たちの懸念について知らされませんでした。

(A) ～を伝達する
(B) 伝達の
(C) 伝えられた
(D) コミュニケーション

正解 **D** 選択肢は動詞communicate「～を伝達する」と、その変化形や派生語。空所の前には前置詞ofがあり、直後にはカンマがあるので、空所には前置詞の目的語となる名詞が入る。名詞の(D) communicationを入れると「コミュニケーションの欠如」となり、意味が通る。due to ～「～のため、～のせいで」、lack「欠如、不足」、president「社長」、industry「産業」、inform ～ of …「～に…について知らせる」、employee「従業員」、concern「懸念、心配事」。
(A) 動詞の原形。(B) 形容詞。(C) 過去分詞。

116 The board of directors came to the ------- that it was necessary to hire a new CEO.

(A) conclusion
(B) distinction
(C) requirement
(D) statement

取締役会は、新しいCEOを雇う必要があるという結論に達しました。

(A) 結論
(B) 区別
(C) 必要条件
(D) 陳述

正解 A 選択肢は全て名詞。that以降の部分は、接続詞thatに導かれる節で、空所に入る名詞と同格の関係になると考えられる。(A) conclusion「結論」を入れると、「新しいCEOを雇う必要があるという結論」という意味になり、最も自然。come to the conclusion that ~ で「~という結論に達する」という成句。board of directors「取締役会、重役会」、hire「~を雇う」、CEO「最高経営責任者（chief executive officerの略）」。

117 Claudine Dumay has been Neelon's head of purchasing ------- it opened for business.

(A) ever
(B) before
(C) since
(D) nonetheless

Claudine Dumayは、Neelon社の購買責任者を同社が開業して以来ずっとしています。

(A) かつて
(B) ～する前に
(C) ～以来
(D) それでもなお

正解 C 空所の前後は共に節の形なので、空所には2つをつなぐ接続詞が入る。空所の後ろが過去時制、空所の前が現在完了時制になっているので、(C) since「～以来」を入れると、空所以降が「それ（Neelon社)が開業して以来ずっと」を表し、適した意味になる。head「責任者、部局などの長」、purchasing「購買、仕入れ」、open for business「開業する、営業を開始する」。
(A) (D) 副詞。
(B) 接続詞の働きがあるが、整合性のある文にならない。

118 Amaford Stationery Store customers are asked to ------- a customer satisfaction survey after shopping.

(A) delegate
(B) rehearse
(C) accompany
(D) complete

Amaford文具店の顧客は買い物の後、顧客満足度調査票に記入するよう依頼されます。

(A) ～を委任する
(B) ～のリハーサルをする
(C) ～に同行する
(D) ～に記入する

正解 D 主語は文頭からcustomersまでで、述語動詞であるare askedにto不定詞が続いている。空所には直後のa customer satisfaction survey「顧客満足度調査票」を目的語とする他動詞が入る。店の顧客が買い物後に、顧客満足度調査票について依頼されることとして適切なのは、(D) complete「～（アンケートなど）に記入する」。stationery「文房具」、customer「顧客」、ask ~ to do「～に…することを依頼する」。

119 Argorot Ltd. is working to create a steady supply chain ------- many challenges.

(A) former
(B) despite
(C) about
(D) otherwise

Argorot社は多数の難題にもかかわらず、安定した供給経路を構築しようと尽力しています。

(A) 前の
(B) 〜にもかかわらず
(C) 〜について
(D) さもなければ

正解 B 空所の前が文として成立しているので、空所以降は文全体を修飾する語句と考えられる。前置詞の(B) despite「〜にもかかわらず」を入れると、despite many challengesが「多数の難題にもかかわらず」という副詞句となり、意味からも適切。work to do「〜しようと努力する」、create「〜を作り出す」、steady「安定した」、supply chain「供給経路、サプライチェーン」、challenge「難題」。
(A) 形容詞。(C) 前置詞だが、適した文意にならない。
(D) 副詞。接続詞的に用いられるので不適切。

120 The director of North Ridge Library states that giving young children easy ------- to books promotes a love of reading.

(A) access
(B) path
(C) key
(D) way

North Ridge図書館の館長は、幼い子どもたちが本に触れやすくすることは読書への愛好心を促進する、と述べています。

(A) 利用する機会
(B) 道
(C) 鍵
(D) 道

正解 A state that 〜は「〜と述べる」の意味で、that以降の部分が述べている内容になる。that節内の述語動詞はpromotes「〜を促進する」で、giving young children easy ------- to booksが主語。空所に(A) access「利用する機会、近づく手段」を入れると、主語が「幼い子どもたちが本に触れやすくすること」となって、意味が通る。director「館長、責任者」、give 〜 easy access to …「〜が…を簡単に利用できるようにする」、love of 〜「〜に対する愛着」。

121 The city council president said that getting the road-improvement bill passed was a significant -------.

(A) achieve
(B) achieves
(C) achieving
(D) achievement

市議会議長は、道路改善法案を可決させたことは大きな成果であると述べました。

(A) 〜を達成する
(B) 〜を達成する
(C) 達成すること
(D) 成果

正解 D that節内の主語は、getting the road-improvement bill passed「道路改善法案を可決させること」で、wasが述語動詞。空所の前に不定冠詞aと形容詞significant「重大な、重要な」があるので、空所には名詞の単数形が入る。(D) achievement「成果、業績」を入れると、適した文意になる。council「議会、評議会」、president「議長」、get 〜 done「〜を…させる」、improvement「改善」、bill「法案」、pass「〜を可決する、〜を通す」。
(C) 動詞achieve「〜を達成する」を動名詞にする場合は通常、前に不定冠詞を付けない。また、意味の上でも不適切。

144

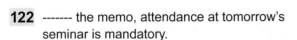

122 ------- the memo, attendance at tomorrow's seminar is mandatory.

(A) According to
(B) Ahead of
(C) Along with
(D) Away from

その連絡文書によると、明日のセミナーへの出席は義務だということです。

(A) 〜によると
(B) 〜に先立って
(C) 〜と共に
(D) 〜から離れて

正解 **A** カンマ以降の部分は、「明日のセミナーへの出席は義務である」という意味。memoには「社内の業務連絡用の短い文書」という意味があり、空所に(A) According to「〜によると」を入れると「その連絡文書によると」となり、適切。attendance at 〜「〜への出席」、seminar「セミナー、講習会」、mandatory「義務的な、必須の」。memoはmemorandumの略。

123 Mr. Park ------- missed his flight because of the severe traffic congestion this morning.

(A) near
(B) nearly
(C) nearing
(D) nearest

Parkさんは今朝の激しい交通渋滞のために、危うく飛行機に乗り遅れるところでした。

(A) 近い
(B) 危うく〜するところで
(C) 近づきつつある
(D) 最も近い

正解 **B** 空所に何も入れなくても文として成立するので、空所には修飾語が入る。動詞missed「乗り遅れた」を修飾する副詞の(B) nearly「危うく〜するところで」を入れると、交通渋滞のためにもう少しで飛行機に乗り遅れるところだった、となり意味が通る。flight「飛行機の便」、because of 〜「〜のために、〜のせいで」、severe「激しい、厳しい」、traffic congestion「交通渋滞」。
(C) 動詞near「〜に近づく」のing形。

124 ------- breakfast is served daily for our club members from 6:00 A.M. to 9:30 A.M.

(A) Complimentary
(B) Appreciative
(C) Favorable
(D) Courteous

当クラブの会員には、毎日午前6時から午前9時30分まで、無料の朝食が出されます。

(A) 無料の
(B) 感謝している
(C) 好都合な
(D) 礼儀正しい

正解 **A** 選択肢は全て形容詞。空所の後ろの名詞breakfastを修飾するのに適切なのは、(A) Complimentary「無料の」。無料の朝食が毎日午前6時から9時半までクラブの会員に出される、という内容の文になり、意味が通る。serve「〜(食べ物など)を出す、〜を給仕する」、daily「毎日」。
(C) 意見などが「好意的な」、状況などが「有望な」といった意味で使い、breakfastを修飾するには不適切。

125 The study looks at major competitors in the marketplace and how they ------- themselves.

    (A) different
    (B) difference
    (C) differently
    (D) differentiate

その研究は、市場の主要な競合企業と、それらの企業がどのように自社を差別化しているかに注目しています。

    (A) 異なる
    (B) 違い
    (C) 異なって
    (D) ～を差別化する

正解 D 選択肢はdifferent「異なる」とその派生語。how以降の部分は疑問詞howに導かれる節を作り、major competitors in the marketplaceと並んでlook atの目的語になると考えられる。how以降を節にするためには動詞が必要なので、動詞の (D) differentiate「～を差別化する、～を区別する」が適切。study「研究」、look at ～「～に注目する、～を見る」、major「主要な」、competitor「競合企業」、marketplace「市場、マーケット」。
(A) 形容詞。(B) 名詞。(C) 副詞。

---

126 Because Mr. Takata will be at the trade show, other marketing team members will ------- be there as well.

    (A) sharply
    (B) longer
    (C) probably
    (D) almost

Takataさんがその展示会に行く予定なので、マーケティング部の他のメンバーたちも、おそらくそこに行くことになるでしょう。

    (A) 鋭く
    (B) より長く
    (C) おそらく
    (D) ほとんど

正解 C 選択肢は全て副詞の働きを持つ語。接続詞Becauseからカンマまでの従属節は、「Takataさんがその展示会に行く予定なので」という意味。空所に (C) probably「おそらく」を入れると、カンマまでの従属節が、マーケティング部の他のメンバーたちもおそらく展示会の会場に行くことになるだろうと予想する根拠となり、自然。trade show「展示会、見本市」、marketing team「マーケティング部、マーケティング担当チーム」、as well「その上」。

---

127 Inxspace Corporation is the region's largest company, employing ------- 4,000 people.

    (A) approximately
    (B) approximate
    (C) approximation
    (D) approximated

Inxspace社はその地域最大の企業で、おおよそ4,000人を雇用しています。

    (A) おおよそ
    (B) おおよその
    (C) 概算
    (D) 概算された

正解 A カンマの前までで文として成立するので、employing以降は現在分詞で、副詞的に働いて付帯状況を表していると考えられる。4,000という数量形容詞を修飾できる副詞の (A) approximately「おおよそ」を入れると、approximately 4,000 peopleがemployingの目的語になり、意味が通る。region「地域、地方」、employ「～を雇用する」。
(B) 形容詞。(C) 名詞。(D) 過去分詞。

128 Rojo Kitchen Products is following its ------- expansion plans by purchasing the Vernick Square Group.

(A) retired
(B) ambitious
(C) hesitant
(D) automatic

Rojoキッチン用品社は、Vernick Squareグループを買収することによって、同社の野心的な拡大計画を推し進めています。

(A) 引退した
(B) 野心的な
(C) 気乗りしない
(D) 自動的な

正解 B　空所の前には所有格のits、後ろには名詞句のexpansion plans「拡大計画」があるので、空所にはexpansion plansを修飾して適した意味になる形容詞が入ると考えられる。byの前は、「Rojoキッチン用品社は、拡大計画を推し進めている」という意味で、by以降は、「Vernick Squareグループを買収することによって」と方法を表している。(B) ambitious「野心的な」を入れると、Rojoキッチン用品社が他の企業グループの買収という手段で自社の野心的な拡大計画を推し進めていることになり、意味が通る。follow「～(道など)をたどる、～に従う」、expansion「拡大」、purchase「～を買収する、～を購入する」。

129 Horsham Engineering's accountant Kae Jung-Ho ------- the average yearly cost of company operations.

(A) determine
(B) determined
(C) determining
(D) determination

Horshamエンジニアリング社の会計士であるKae Jung-Hoは、会社運営の平均年間コストを割り出しました。

(A) ～を定める
(B) ～を定めた
(C) 決定的な
(D) 決定

正解 B　この文には述語動詞がないので、空所には動詞が入る。主語はHorsham Engineering's accountant Kae Jung-Ho「Horshamエンジニアリング社の会計士であるKae Jung-Ho」。この三人称単数を主語にできる動詞の形は、過去形の(B) determined。この場合のdetermineは「(計算などをして)～を定める、～を決定する」の意味。accountant「会計士、会計係」、average「平均の」、yearly「年間の」、cost「コスト、費用」、operation「運営、経営、オペレーション」。
(A) 動詞の原形。主語が三人称単数なので、不適切。

130 Making digital copies of files is a smart way to deal with an ------- of important documents.

(A) abundance
(B) extension
(C) accordance
(D) instance

ファイルのデジタルコピーを作ることは、大量の重要書類に対処するための賢明な方法です。

(A) 大量
(B) 拡張
(C) 一致
(D) 実例

正解 A　Making digital copies of files is a smart wayは、「ファイルのデジタルコピーを作ることは賢明な方法である」の意味。to deal with以降はa smart wayを修飾して、どのような方法かを述べている。an abundance of ～で「大量の～」の意味になる、(A) abundance「大量」が適切。digital copy「デジタルコピー」、smart「賢明な、賢い」、way「方法、やり方」、deal with ～「～に対処する」、document「書類」。

TEST 2 PART 5

Questions 131-134 refer to the following e-mail.

To: Troy Diallo <diallo.t@bushwickcompany.com>
From: Margery Petersen <petersen.m@bushwickcompany.com>
Date: September 27
Subject: Springford Marketer

Dear Mr. Diallo,

❶ Per your request, I ------- my evaluation of the Springford Marketer application. In my opinion,
131.
this would be a ------- purchase for the marketing department. It centralizes all aspects of the
132.
production process in one online location. This enables the marketing team leader to
------- the team's workflow on a day-to-day basis. I was particularly impressed by the fact that
133.
Springford Marketer can be used on phones as well as laptops. -------. However, I am confident
134.
that the program would ultimately save us time and prove to be cost-effective.

Margery Petersen

問題131-134は次のEメールに関するものです。

受信者：Troy Diallo <diallo.t@bushwickcompany.com>
送信者：Margery Petersen <petersen.m@bushwickcompany.com>
日付：9月27日
件名：Springford Marketer

Dialloさん

ご要望にお応えして、私はSpringford Marketerアプリの評価を終えたところです。私の見解では、これはマーケティング部にとって有用な買い物になるでしょう。このアプリは、生産プロセスの全ての局面をオンライン上の1カ所に集めます。これにより、マーケティング・チームのリーダーはチームの仕事の流れを日々調整することができます。私が特に感心したのは、Springford Marketerはノートパソコンだけでなく携帯電話でも使用可能である点です。*コストは多少高いかもしれません。しかしながら、このプログラムは最終的には私たちの時間を節約してくれ、費用対効果が大きいことが分かるだろうと、私は確信しています。

Margery Petersen

*問題134の挿入文の訳

Words & Phrases

❶ (as) per *one's* request　～からの要望により　　evaluation　評価　　application　アプリ、コンピューターのソフトウエア
in *one's* opinion　～の意見では　　purchase　買い物、購入　　marketing　マーケティング　　department　部、課
centralize　～を一カ所に集中させる、～を中心に集める　　aspect　局面、状況　　production　生産　　process　プロセス、過程
online　オンライン上の、インターネット上の　　enable ～ to do　～が…することを可能にする　　leader　リーダー、主任
workflow　仕事の流れ、ワークフロー　　on a ～ basis　～単位で　　day-to-day　日々の、毎日の　　particularly　特に
impress　～を感心させる　　fact　事実、実際にあったこと　　phone　電話機　★ここでは携帯電話の意味で使われている
～ as well as …　…だけでなく～も　　laptop　ノートパソコン　　be confident that ～　～であると確信している
program　コンピュータープログラム、アプリ　　ultimately　最終的に、結局　　save ～ …　～の…を節約する、～に…を節約させる
cost-effective　費用対効果の高い

131
(A) will complete
(B) completes
(C) completing
(D) have completed

＊選択肢の訳は省略

正解 **D** 動詞complete「〜を終える、〜を完了する」の適切な形を選ぶ。空所を含む文は「あなたの要望に応えて、私はSpringford Marketerアプリの評価を-------」という意味。次の文以降で、このアプリについての自分の見解を述べていることから、すでに評価は完了していると分かるので、現在完了形の(D) have completedが適切。
(A) 未来形。まだ評価が終わっていないことになるので不適切。
(B) 三人称単数現在形。主語が一人称のIなので不適切。
(C) 現在分詞。単独では述語動詞にならない。

132
(A) trivial
(B) portable
(C) useful
(D) memorable

(A) ありふれた
(B) 持ち運べる
(C) 有用な
(D) 忘れられない

正解 **C** 選択肢は全て形容詞の働きを持つ語。空所を含む文のthisは前の文のSpringford Marketer applicationを指し、「私の見解では、これはマーケティング部にとって-------買い物になるだろう」という意味。続く3つの文で、生産プロセスの集中管理が可能であることや、携帯電話でも使用可能なことなど、このアプリの有益な点を挙げていることから、(C) useful「有用な」が適切。
(A) (B) (D) いずれも文脈に合わない。

133
(A) adjust
(B) remind
(C) expel
(D) decline

(A) 〜を調整する
(B) 〜を思い出させる
(C) 〜を排出する
(D) 〜を断る

正解 **A** 選択肢は全て動詞の働きを持つ語。空所を含む文は、「このこと（直前の文で述べられたアプリの機能である、生産プロセスをオンライン上の1カ所に集中させること）により、マーケティング・チームのリーダーはチームの仕事の流れを日々-------ことができる」という意味。the team's workflowは、空所に入る動詞が作るto不定詞の目的語となる。(A) adjust「〜を調整する」を入れると、リーダーは毎日、仕事の流れを調整できるということになり、文脈に合う。
(B) (C) (D) いずれも文脈に合わない。

134
(A) This was our most creative campaign so far.
(B) The cost is perhaps a little high.
(C) The reviews have been uniformly positive.
(D) Our sales increased dramatically afterward.

(A) これは、当社におけるこれまでで最も創造的なキャンペーンでした。
(B) コストは多少高いかもしれません。
(C) レビューは一様に肯定的なものでした。
(D) その後、当社の売り上げは劇的に増加しました。

正解 **B** 空所の直後の文は、反意を表すHoweverで始まり、「しかしながら、このプログラムは最終的には私たちの時間を節約してくれ、費用対効果が大きいことが分かるだろうと、私は確信している」と前文の内容を覆して長所を述べている。よって、空所の文ではSpringford Marketerの否定的な側面に言及していると考えられるので、コスト面の問題を挙げている(B)を入れると、自然な流れになる。cost「コスト、費用」、perhaps「ことによると、ひょっとしたら」。
(A) (C) (D) いずれも肯定的な内容なので、Howeverで始まる次の文に論理的につながらない。
(A) creative「創造的な、独創的な」、campaign「キャンペーン、宣伝活動」、so far「今までのところ」。
(C) review「レビュー、評価」、uniformly「一様に、一律に」、positive「肯定的な」。
(D) sales「売り上げ」、increase「増加する」、dramatically「劇的に」、afterward「その後、後で」。

TEST 2 PART 6

Expressions

prove to be 〜 「〜であることが分かる、〜と判明する」（❶ 6行目）
Mary's statement last week has proved to be true.
Maryが先週話したことは、真実だと分かりました。

Questions 135-138 refer to the following notice.

❶ Scherwin-Lloyd Ltd. employees are advised that building maintenance will be conducted starting on 11 July. It is expected to ------- on 14 July. The work will take place only on the second and **135.** third floors of the building and may cause disruptions to staff in the proximity. -------. Workers **136.** with offices on the fourth floor and higher could be ------- affected by the process but should still **137.** plan for possible minor interruptions to their schedules. Please also note that staff will not have basement access ------- this maintenance process, since that space will be used for storage of **138.** materials.

❷ Please contact the building supervisor at 0149 5285 with any questions or concerns.

問題135-138は次のお知らせに関するものです。

Scherwin-Lloyd社の従業員の方へ、ビルの補修作業が7月11日から行われることをお知らせします。7月14日に終了する予定です。作業は建物の2階と3階のみで行われる予定で、その近辺にいるスタッフの方には仕事の妨げになるかもしれません。*これらの階に執務室がある方は、一時的な執務室の移動を願い出ることができます。4階とそれより上の階に執務室がある職員は、この作業工程によって受ける影響は最小限でしょうが、それでも仕事の予定に多少の支障を来す可能性に備えておく必要があります。また、地階は資材の保管場所として使用されるため、職員はこの補修作業期間中、地階には出入りできないことにもご注意ください。

もしご質問やご懸念がありましたら、0149-5285番まで、ビル管理責任者にご連絡ください。

*問題136の挿入文の訳

Words & Phrases

notice お知らせ、告知 ❶ employee 従業員 advise ~ that … ~に…と知らせる maintenance 補修工事、整備 conduct ~を行う be expected to do ~する予定である work 作業 take place 行われる floor 階、フロア cause ~を引き起こす disruption （進行などを妨げる）障害、混乱 proximity 近いこと、近辺 affect ~に影響を与える process 工程、プロセス still それでも possible 可能性がある、あり得る minor 重大でない、小さな interruption 妨害、じゃま schedule スケジュール、予定 note that ~ ~ということに注意する have access 出入りできる、アクセス可能である basement 地階 since ~だから、~なので space 場所、空間 storage 保管 material 資材 ❷ contact ~と連絡を取る supervisor 管理責任者、監督者 concern 懸念、心配

135

(A) return
(B) arrive
(C) conclude
(D) increase

(A) 戻る
(B) 到着する
(C) 終了する
(D) 増加する

正解 C お知らせの冒頭では、ビルの補修作業が7月11日に始まる旨が述べられている。それに続く空所を含む文のItはビルの補修作業を指し、「7月14日に------- 予定だ」という意味。開始から3日後の予定について述べているので、冒頭の2文で補修作業の期間を説明していると考えられる。(C) conclude「終了する」を入れると、7月11日に始まる補修作業は、7月14日に終了するということになり、文脈に合う。
(A) (B) (D) いずれも文脈に合わない。

136

(A) Those with offices on these floors may request temporary office relocation.
(B) The maintenance crews will work only after all offices close for the day.
(C) The dates of this project have not yet been decided upon.
(D) Disruptions, including noise and dust, have already caused delays.

(A) これらの階に執務室がある方は、一時的な執務室の移動を願い出ることができます。
(B) 補修作業員は、全ての執務室がその日の業務を終了した後でしか作業をしません。
(C) この作業計画の日程は、まだ決まっていません。
(D) 騒音やほこりをはじめとする障害によって、すでに遅延が生じています。

正解 A 空所の直前の文では、補修作業が行われるのは2階と3階のみであると述べられ、空所の直後の文では、4階以上のフロアへの影響について言及されている。影響を受ける階に執務室がある人への対応を述べた (A) を入れると、these floors が2階と3階を指し、自然な流れになる。those「(~という) 人々」、office「執務室、仕事部屋」、temporary「一時的な」、relocation「移動」。
(B) 仕事の妨げになるかもしれないという記述に合わないので不適切。crew「作業員、クルー」、close for the day「その日の業務を終える」。
(C) 日程は案内されているので不適切。dates「日程」、decide upon ~「~に決める」。
(D) 作業はまだ始まっていないので不適切。noise「騒音」、dust「ほこり、粉じん」、delay「遅延、遅れ」。

137

(A) minimum
(B) minimally
(C) minimalize
(D) minimal

(A) 最小限
(B) 最小限に
(C) 最小限にする
(D) 最小限の

正解 B 選択肢は全て、名詞 minimum「最小限」とその派生語。❶ 3~4行目のWorkers ...... could be ------- affected by the process は、「職員は、この作業工程によって ------- 影響を受けるかもしれない」という意味。空所に何も入れなくても文が成立するので、修飾語が入る。be affected を修飾する副詞の (B) minimally「最小限に」を入れると、be minimally affected で「最小限に影響を受ける」を表すことになり、適切。
(A) 名詞。(C) 動詞。(D) 形容詞。

138

(A) toward
(B) between
(C) inside
(D) during

(A) ~の方へ
(B) ~ (2つの物) の間に
(C) ~の中で
(D) ~の間中ずっと

正解 D 選択肢は全て前置詞の働きをする語。❶ 1~2行目で補修作業の期間が、同2~5行目で職員への注意事項が述べられている。空所を含む文も、Please also note that ~「また、~ということにも注意してください」で始まっているので、補修作業期間中に職員が注意すべきことが追加で述べられていると考えられる。(D) during「~の間中ずっと」を入れると、during this maintenance process で「この補修作業期間中」を表し、文脈に合う。

TEST 2 PART 6

Expressions

plan for ~ 「~に備える、~の計画を立てる」(❶ 5行目)

Dr. Johnson's team is planning for the next experiment.
Johnson博士のチームは、次の実験の計画を立てています。

Questions 139-142 refer to the following article.

① Whether for business or relaxation, traveling can ------- you all over the globe. While this can be
139.
exciting, long flights, for example from New York City to Beijing, can often result in a

phenomenon ------- as jet lag. That is, you may feel extremely tired, due to both the duration of
140.
the flight and the fact that you crossed multiple time zones.

② There are a few ways to fight jet lag so that you can enjoy your trip. First, drink plenty of water.

Hydration is key to feeling good. ------- , skip naps. Napping during the day makes it even more
141.
difficult to fall asleep at the correct time of night. Finally, get some physical exercise, preferably

outdoors. ------- .
142.

問題139-142は次の記事に関するものです。

ビジネスのためであれ、余暇のためであれ、旅はあなたを世界中へ連れて行ってくれる。これはわくわくするようなことであり得る一方、例えばニューヨークから北京までのような長距離フライトはしばしば、時差ぼけとして知られる現象を引き起こす可能性がある。つまり、フライト時間の長さと、複数のタイムゾーンを越えたという事実の両方から、あなたが極度の疲れを感じるかもしれないということだ。

旅行を楽しめるように、時差ぼけを克服する幾つかの方法がある。まず、水をたくさん飲むこと。水分補給は気分を良くする秘訣だ。また、昼寝はしないこと。日中に昼寝をすると、夜、適切な時間に眠りに落ちるのがより一層難しくなる。最後に、できるなら屋外で少し運動をすること。*それによって、あなたは新しい環境により素早く順応することができる。

*問題142の挿入文の訳

Words & Phrases

❶ whether 〜 or … 〜であれ…であれ relaxation くつろぎ、気晴らし all over the globe 世界中に
exciting 刺激的な flight フライト、飛行、飛行距離 Beijing 北京 result in 〜 〜を引き起こす、〜という結果になる
phenomenon 現象 jet lag 時差ぼけ that is つまり、換言すると extremely 極度に
due to 〜 〜の理由から、〜のせいで both 〜 and … 〜と…の両方 duration 持続期間 cross 〜を越える
multiple 複数の time zone タイムゾーン、時間帯 ❷ way 方法 fight 〜を克服するために戦う
plenty of 〜 たくさんの〜 hydration 水分補給 key to doing 〜 〜するのに重要な skip 〜を抜かす、〜を省く
nap 〈名詞で〉昼寝、〈動詞で〉昼寝をする even 〈比較級を強調して〉さらに、一層 fall asleep 眠りに落ちる、寝入る
correct 適切な physical exercise 運動 preferably できれば outdoors 屋外で

Expressions

the fact that 〜 「〜という事実」（❶4行目）
My team and I are aware of the fact that we're running out of time before the deadline.
私のチームと私は、締め切りまでの時間がなくなりつつあるという事実に気付いています。

139
(A) teach
(B) change
(C) take
(D) help

(A) 〜を教える
(B) 〜を変える
(C) 〜を連れて行く
(D) 〜を助ける

正解 **C** 選択肢は全て動詞の働きを持つ語。空所を含む文は、「ビジネスのためであれ、余暇のためであれ、旅はあなたを世界中へ------ことができる」という意味。(C) take「〜を連れて行く」を入れると、「旅はあなたを世界中へ連れて行くことができる」、つまり「旅をすることで、あなたは世界中へ行くことができる」という意味となり、文脈に合う。
(A) (B) (D) いずれも文脈に合わない。

140
(A) knows
(B) known
(C) knowing
(D) knowingly

(A) 〜を知っている
(B) 知られた
(C) 知っている
(D) 訳知り顔で

正解 **B** 選択肢は全て動詞know「〜を知っている」の変化した形と派生語。空所の直後に as jet lag があるので、be known as 〜「〜として知られている」の形が使われていると考えられる。(B) が適切。ここでは known as jet lagという句が、直前のphenomenonを後ろから修飾しており、「時差ぼけとして知られている現象」を表す。
(A) 三人称単数現在形。
(C) 現在分詞。前の名詞phenomenonが動作主、現在分詞がその動作という能動の意味を表すので、文脈に合わない。
(D) 副詞。

141
(A) Lastly
(B) Also
(C) Instead
(D) Therefore

(A) 最後に
(B) また
(C) その代わりに
(D) それゆえ

正解 **B** ❷の1文目で「旅行を楽しめるように、時差ぼけを克服する幾つかの方法がある」と述べた後、2〜7文目でその「幾つかの方法」を具体的に3種類挙げて説明している。2文目はFirst「最初に、まず」、空所の後ろにある6文目はFinally「最後に」で文が始まっている。空所はその間にあるので、(B) Also「また、それから」を入れると、自然な流れになる。
(A) (C) (D) いずれも文脈に合わない。

142
(A) It allows you to adjust more quickly to your new environment.
(B) It increases your ability to be innovative and productive.
(C) It will improve the health and well-being of your staff.
(D) It enables you to manage your travel reservations.

(A) それによって、あなたは新しい環境により素早く順応することができる。
(B) それによって、あなたは革新的かつ生産的になる能力が高まる。
(C) それによって、あなたのスタッフの健康と幸福度は向上するだろう。
(D) それによって、あなたは旅行の予約を管理できるようになる。

正解 **A** ❷では「時差ぼけを克服する方法」が3つ挙げられており、3文目は1つ目の方法「水をたくさん飲む」がなぜ有効かの補足説明、5文目は2つ目の方法「昼寝をしない」の補足説明になっている。7文目である空所に(A)を入れると、3つ目の方法「少し運動をする」の補足説明として、環境に順応しやすくなるという効果を述べることになり、流れとして自然。挿入文のItは前文の「運動すること」を指している。allow 〜 to do「〜が…できるようにする」、adjust to 〜「〜に順応する」、environment「環境」。
(B) increase「〜を高める、〜を増加させる」、ability「能力」、innovative「革新的な」、productive「生産的な」。
(C) improve「〜を向上させる」、well-being「幸福、満足のいく状態」。
(D) enable 〜 to do「〜が…することを可能にする」、manage「〜を管理する」、reservation「予約」。

Questions 143-146 refer to the following e-mail.

To: All Tenants
From: Maintenance Team
Date: April 18
Subject: Parking

To all 1520 Elm Street tenants:

❶ We are excited to inform you that next month will see the beginning of ------- updates to the
    143.
shared areas of our apartment complex. A complete schedule of updates was posted last month
and is available on the community Web site.

❷ The parking garage ------- for repairs May 15 to 17. -------. If your car is not removed from the
                      144.   **145.**
garage by 8:00 A.M. on May 15, it will be towed at your expense. Temporary ------- are available
                                                                          146.
at the 1500 Elm Street apartment complex or at the municipal parking lot down the street. The
1520 garage will reopen on May 18. We thank you in advance for your cooperation and
patience.

Sincerely,

Angela Connetti
1520 Elm Street Maintenance Supervisor

問題143-146は次のEメールに関するものです。

受信者：居住者の皆さま
送信者：管理チーム
日付：4月18日
件名：駐車について

エルム街1520の居住者の皆さまへ

当マンション共用部の改修工事計画が来月開始される運びとなりましたことをお知らせでき、うれしく思います。改修工事の全日程表は、居住者用ウェブサイトに先月掲載されており、閲覧することができます。

立体駐車場は5月15日から17日まで、修繕作業のため閉鎖される予定です。*この期間中、エルム街1520の駐車場には、車両は一切駐車できません。5月15日午前8時までに車を移動しなかった場合、所有者負担でレッカー移動されます。エルム街1500のマンション施設、もしくは、通りの先の市営駐車場において、臨時の駐車スペースが利用できます。1520用の駐車場は、5月18日に再開の予定です。皆さまのご協力とご辛抱に、前もってお礼を申し上げます。

敬具

Angela Connetti
エルム街1520管理責任者

*問題145の挿入文の訳

Expressions

at *one's* expense　「～の費用で、～の負担で」（❷2行目）

In case you are not satisfied with the product, it can be returned at our expense.
もし商品にご満足いただけない場合は、当社負担でご返送いただけます。

143
(A) planned
(B) contested
(C) mixed
(D) satisfied

(A) 計画された
(B) 異議を唱えられた
(C) 混ざり合った
(D) 満足した

正解 A　空所を含む文は、「当マンション共用部の-------改修工事が来月開始される運びとなったと知らせることができてうれしく思う」という意味。空所にはupdates「改修工事」を修飾して意味が通る形容詞が入る。(A) planned「計画された」が適切。

144
(A) has been closed
(B) to close
(C) did close
(D) will be closed

＊選択肢の訳は省略

正解 D　動詞close「～を閉める」の適切な形を選ぶ。空所を含む文は、「立体駐車場は5月15日から17日まで、修繕作業のため-------」という意味。メールが送信された日付は4月18日で、❶1～2行目に工事が始まるのは翌月である旨が書かれていることから、この5月15日から17日は、過去でなく未来のことだと判断できる。よって、未来形の受動態の(D) will be closedが適切。
(A) 受動態の現在完了形。
(B) to不定詞。
(C) 過去形closedを強調する言い方。

145
(A) The next project involves the installation of new digital locks on the front doors.
(B) Community members are invited to the reopening ceremony next weekend.
(C) No vehicles may be parked in the 1520 Elm Street garage during this time.
(D) There will be more noise outside than usual due to ongoing work.

(A) 次のプロジェクトには、正面玄関への新しいデジタル式ロックの設置が含まれます。
(B) 居住者の方々は、次の週末の再開セレモニーにお越しください。
(C) この期間中、エルム街1520の駐車場には、車両は一切駐車できません。
(D) 進行中の工事のため、外では騒音が通常より大きくなるでしょう。

正解 C　空所直前の文では、5月15日から17日に駐車場の修繕作業が行われる旨が、直後の文では、15日の朝までに車を駐車場から出しておかないとレッカー移動される旨が述べられている。よって空所でも、この駐車場の工事に言及していると考えられる。駐車場への駐車禁止の指示である(C)を入れると、前後のつながりが良く、流れとして自然。vehicle「車両」。
(A) involve「～を含む」、installation「設置」、lock「ロック、鍵」、front door「正面玄関」。
(B) ceremony「セレモニー、式典」。
(D) outside「外で」、due to ～「～のため、～のせいで」、ongoing「進行中の」、work「工事、作業」。

146
(A) adjustments
(B) guides
(C) points
(D) spaces

(A) 調整
(B) ガイド
(C) 点
(D) スペース

正解 D　空所を含む文は、「エルム街1500のマンション施設、もしくは、通りの先の市営駐車場において、臨時の-------が利用できる」という意味。❷1～2行目では、5月15日から17日の修繕作業の間は駐車場に車を置いておけないことが説明されている。空所に(D) spaces「スペース」を入れると、Temporary spacesが「臨時の(車を置いておける)スペース」を表すことになり、工事期間中の代替の駐車場所を案内する文となるので、適切。このspacesは区切られた、車1台用のスペースが複数あることを示しているため、複数形になっている。

TEST 2 PART 6

Words & Phrases

tenant　居住者、テナント　　maintenance　保守管理、メンテナンス
❶ be excited to *do*　～することをうれしく思う、喜んで～する　　inform ～ that …　…ということを～に知らせる
see　(時代などが)～を(出来事)を目撃する　　update　改装(工事)、最新化　　shared　共用の、共有の
apartment　マンション、アパート　　complex　複合施設　　complete　完全な　　post　～を掲示する
available　利用できる、入手可能な　　community　共同体、コミュニティー　　❷ parking garage　立体駐車場
repairs　修繕作業、修理作業　　remove　～を移す、～を移動させる　　tow　～をレッカー車で移動する、～を撤去する
temporary　臨時の、一時的な　　municipal　市営の、町営の、地方自治の　　parking lot　駐車場
down the street　通りの先の、この先の　　reopen　再開する、再び開く　　in advance　前もって　　cooperation　協力
patience　辛抱、我慢

PART 7

Questions 147-148 refer to the following advertisement.

For Rent

❶ Spacious suite available starting next month in a small office building in Glasgow. Approximately 140 square metres, with ample storage space and several large windows to brighten your work space. Employee break room with a kitchen shared by three units on the same floor. Monthly rent covers electricity, water, Internet access, alarm system, and after-hours monitoring. Tenants are responsible for their own telephone and janitorial services. Call 0141 496 0199 for more information.

問題147-148は次の広告に関するものです。

入居者募集

来月より、グラスゴーの小規模オフィスビル内の広々とした続き部屋がご利用可能になります。約140平方メートルの広さで、豊富な収納スペースと、作業スペースを明るくする幾つかの大窓が備わっています。同じ階に3戸で共用のキッチン付き従業員休憩室もあります。毎月の賃料には、電気、水道、インターネット接続、警報装置、営業時間外の監視の代金が含まれます。電話代と清掃管理費はご入居者のご負担になります。詳しい情報については、0141-496-0199までお電話ください。

Words & Phrases	

advertisement 広告　　For Rent 貸室あり　★広告や掲示で使う　❶ spacious 広々とした　　suite 一続きの部屋
available 利用できる　　office building オフィスビル　　approximately 約、およそ
〜 square metre 〜平方メートル　★米国表記は square meter　　ample 豊富な　　storage 収納、保管
space スペース、場所　　several 幾つかの　　brighten 〜を明るくする　　employee 従業員　　break room 休憩室
share 〜を共同で利用する　　unit 1戸　　floor 階　　monthly 毎月の　　rent 賃料　　cover 〜を賄う
electricity 電気　　Internet access インターネット接続　　alarm system 警報装置　　after-hours 営業時間外の
monitoring 監視、モニターサービス　　tenant 借家人、テナント　　own 自身の　　janitorial service 清掃管理業務
information 情報

147 What is suggested about the suite?

 (A) It can be rented immediately.
 (B) It includes a private kitchen.
 (C) It has a lot of natural light.
 (D) It is in a large office building.

続き部屋について何が分かりますか。

 (A) 即座に借りられる。
 (B) 専用のキッチンを備えている。
 (C) 自然光がたくさん入る。
 (D) 大規模オフィスビル内にある。

正解 C 見出しと❶1行目より、テナント募集の広告だと分かる。来月に利用可能になる部屋の特徴について、同2～3行目に、Approximately 140 square metres, with ample storage space and several large windows to brighten your work space.「約140平方メートルの広さで、豊富な収納スペースと、作業スペースを明るくする幾つかの大窓が備わっている」とある。よって、テナント募集中のこの部屋には太陽の光がたくさん入ると考えられるので、(C)が正解。natural light「自然光」。
(A) ❶1行目より、部屋を借りることができるのは来月から。rent「～を賃借する」、immediately「即座に」。
(B) ❶3～4行目より、この続き部屋の入居者が利用できるキッチンは同じ階を借りている別の区画との共用。private「特定の一個人・一グループ用の」。
(D) ❶1行目より、続き部屋自体は広々としているが、部屋が入っているオフィスビルは大規模ではなく小規模。

---

148 What is NOT included in the suite's cost of rent?

 (A) Cleaning
 (B) Electricity
 (C) Security service
 (D) Internet service

続き部屋の賃料に含まれていないものは何ですか。

 (A) 清掃
 (B) 電気
 (C) 警備サービス
 (D) インターネットサービス

正解 A ❶4～5行目に、毎月の賃料で賄われるものについての記述があり、続く同5～6行目に、Tenants are responsible for their own telephone and janitorial services.「電話代と清掃管理費は入居者の負担になる」と明記されているので、(A)の清掃は賃料に含まれていないと分かる。よって、(A)が正解。include「～を含む」、cost「費用」。
(B) ❶4～5行目より、毎月の賃料で賄われるものに含まれている。
(C) ❶4～5行目のalarm systemとafter-hours monitoringに当たる。
(D) ❶4～5行目のInternet accessに当たる。

Expressions

be responsible for ～ 「～に責任がある」(❶5～6行目)
 Ms. Murray is responsible for the PR Department.
 Murrayさんが広報部の責任者です。

Questions 149-150 refer to the following e-mail.

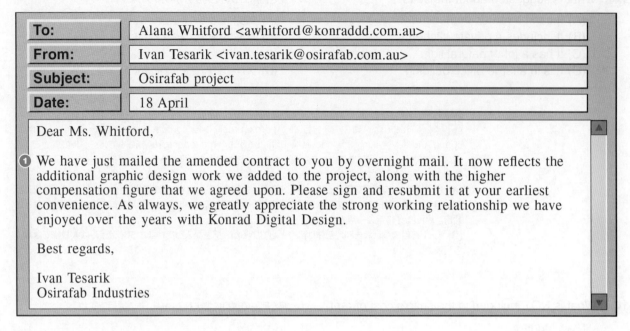

To:	Alana Whitford <awhitford@konraddd.com.au>
From:	Ivan Tesarik <ivan.tesarik@osirafab.com.au>
Subject:	Osirafab project
Date:	18 April

Dear Ms. Whitford,

We have just mailed the amended contract to you by overnight mail. It now reflects the additional graphic design work we added to the project, along with the higher compensation figure that we agreed upon. Please sign and resubmit it at your earliest convenience. As always, we greatly appreciate the strong working relationship we have enjoyed over the years with Konrad Digital Design.

Best regards,

Ivan Tesarik
Osirafab Industries

問題149-150は次のＥメールに関するものです。

受信者：Alana Whitford <awhitford@konraddd.com.au>
送信者：Ivan Tesarik <ivan.tesarik@osirafab.com.au>
件名：Osirafab プロジェクト
日付：4月18日

Whitford 様

私どもは先ほど、修正した契約書を翌日配達郵便で貴社にお送りしたところです。それには、双方が合意済みのより高い報酬額に加え、プロジェクトに組み込まれた追加のグラフィックデザイン業務が反映されています。ご署名の上、なるべく早く再提出してください。私どもは常々、長年にわたり享受している Konrad デジタルデザイン社との強固な取引関係に大変感謝しております。

敬具

Ivan Tesarik
Osirafab Industries 社

149 What does Mr. Tesarik indicate in his e-mail?

(A) A new staff member was hired.
(B) An agreement was revised.
(C) A deadline was missed.
(D) Some company policies were updated.

Tesarikさんは E メールで何を示していますか。

(A) 新しい従業員が雇用された。
(B) 契約書が修正された。
(C) 締め切りが守られなかった。
(D) 会社の方針が更新された。

正解 B	Tesarikさんは❶1行目で、We have just mailed the amended contract to you by overnight mail.「私たちは先ほど、修正した契約書を翌日配達郵便で貴社に送ったところだ」と述べ、続く同1〜3行目で、新しい契約書に反映されている変更内容について説明している。よって、そのことを言い換えた(B)が正解。agreement「契約書、合意」、revise「〜を修正する」。

(A) hire「〜を雇用する」。
(C) deadline「締め切り」、miss「〜に間に合わない、〜を逃す」。
(D) policy「方針」、update「〜を更新する」。

---

150 What does Mr. Tesarik ask Ms. Whitford to do?

(A) Return a document
(B) Schedule a meeting
(C) Submit a proposal
(D) Change a design

Tesarikさんは Whitford さんに何をするよう求めていますか。

(A) 文書を返送する
(B) 会議の予定を立てる
(C) 提案書を提出する
(D) デザインを変更する

正解 A	Tesarikさんは、修正版の契約書の送付および内容について説明した後、❶3〜4行目で、Please sign and resubmit it at your earliest convenience.「署名の上、なるべく早く再提出してください」と Whitford さんに依頼している。it は同1行目の the amended contract を指しているので、修正した契約書に署名して返送するよう求めていると分かる。よって、(A)が正解。return「〜を返送する」。

(B) schedule「〜の予定を立てる」。
(C) Tesarikさんが Whitford さんに求めているのは、提案書を提出することではなく契約書を再提出すること。submit「〜を提出する」、proposal「提案書」。

Words & Phrases

project プロジェクト、計画 ❶ mail 〜を郵送する amend 〜を修正する contract 契約書
overnight mail 翌日配達郵便 reflect 〜を反映する additional 追加の
graphic design work グラフィックデザイン業務 add 〜 to … 〜を…に加える along with 〜 〜に加え、〜と一緒に
compensation 報酬、補償 figure 額 agree upon 〜 〜について意見が一致する sign 〜に署名する
resubmit 〜を再提出する as always いつものように greatly 大いに appreciate 〜をありがたく思う
strong 強固な relationship 関係 digital デジタルの industry 産業、工業

Expressions

at *one's* earliest convenience 「なるべく早く、〜の都合がつき次第」(❶3〜4行目)

Could you call me back at your earliest convenience?
ご都合がつき次第、折り返し私にお電話いただけますか。

文書 | 特典 94

Questions 151-152 refer to the following instructions.

---

❶ **Operating the D343L Drill**

The following tips will help you get started using the D343L successfully.

❷ • If necessary, secure the material to be drilled with clamps or a vise.

• Carefully and firmly place the tip of the drill bit exactly on the desired location of the hole to be drilled.

• Start at a slow speed to prevent the drill bit from slipping off the starting point. Begin drilling by lightly pressing the trigger switch.

• Intensify pressure on the trigger to increase to the desired speed once the bit begins to penetrate the material being drilled.

❸ Be careful not to exert too much pressure on the material when using the D343L drill. Doing so may cause the motor of the device to overheat. Overheating the drill's motor may cause premature wear and eventually lead to the failure of the device.

問題 151-152 は次の説明書に関するものです。

D343L ドリルの操作

以下のヒントは、D343L を上手に使い始めるのに役立ちます。
・必要であれば、締め具や万力で、穴を開ける素材をしっかり固定してください。
・ドリル刃の先端を、穴を開けたい位置ぴったりに、注意深くかつ動かないように当ててください。
・ドリル刃が開始地点からずれてしまうのを防ぐために、低速で始めます。トリガー式スイッチを軽く押しながら穴を開け始めてください。
・刃が穴を開ける素材を貫通し始めたら、トリガーを押す力を強めて、お望みの速度まで上げてください。

D343L ドリルをご使用の際には、素材に力を加え過ぎないようご注意ください。そのような行為は、機器のモーターをオーバーヒートさせる恐れがあります。ドリルのモーターのオーバーヒートは摩耗を早め、結果的に機器の故障を引き起こす可能性があります。

Words & Phrases

instructions 説明書 ❶ operate ～を操作する drill 〈名詞で〉ドリル、〈動詞で〉～に穴を開ける following 以下の
tip ヒント、秘訣、先端 help ～ do ～が…するのに役立つ get started 始める successfully うまく
❷ if necessary 必要なら secure ～をしっかり固定する material 素材 clamp 締め具
vise 万力 ★工作物を固定する工具 carefully 注意深く firmly しっかりと place ～ on … ～を…に置く
bit ビット、刃 ★ドリルなどの先端に取り付ける刃 exactly 正確に desired 望ましい location 位置、場所
hole 穴 prevent ～ from doing ～が…するのを防ぐ slip off ～ ～からするっと外れる starting point 開始地点
lightly 軽く press ～を押す trigger switch トリガー式スイッチ ★レバーを握ったときのみ運転するスイッチ
intensify ～を強める pressure 圧力 increase to ～ ～まで増す once ～するとすぐに penetrate ～を貫通する
❸ be careful not to do ～しないよう気を付ける exert ～ on … ～（圧力など）を…に加える
cause ～ to do ～に…させる（原因となる） device 機器 overheat オーバーヒートする、～をオーバーヒートさせる
cause ～を引き起こす premature 早過ぎる wear 摩耗、消耗 eventually 結局、最終的に failure 故障

---

151 What is suggested about the D343L drill?

    (A) It is expensive.
    (B) It is covered under a warranty.
    (C) It is a new model.
    (D) It operates at different speeds.

D343L ドリルについて何が分かりますか。

    (A) それは高価である。
    (B) それは保証の対象である。
    (C) それは新しいモデルである。
    (D) それはさまざまな速度で作動する。

正解 D ❶の1～3行目より、この文書はD343L ドリルという製品の取扱説明書だと分かる。その使用法を箇条書きで示している❷の3項目目に、Start at a slow speed to prevent the drill bit from slipping off the starting point.「ドリル刃が開始地点からずれてしまうのを防ぐために、低速で始める」とあり、4項目目にIntensify pressure on the trigger to increase to the desired speed once the bit begins to penetrate the material being drilled.「刃が穴を開ける素材を貫通し始めたら、トリガーを押す力を強めて、望む速度まで上げる」とある。よって、このドリルは速度調整が可能だと分かるので、(D)が正解。operate「(機械などが)作動する」、different「さまざまな」。
(A) expensive「高価な」。
(B) cover「～を賄う、～を補償する」、warranty「保証、保証書」。
(C) model「モデル、型」。

---

152 According to the instructions, what might cause the drill to stop working?

    (A) Pressing its trigger too hard when beginning to drill
    (B) Pushing it too hard against a surface being drilled
    (C) Holding it too loosely in place while drilling
    (D) Running it continuously for too long

説明書によると、何がドリルの作動を停止させる可能性がありますか。

    (A) 穴を開け始める際に、そのトリガーを強く押し過ぎること
    (B) 穴を開ける面に、それを強く押し付け過ぎること
    (C) 穴を開けているときに、それを所定の位置に当てて持つのが弱過ぎること
    (D) あまりにも長時間、それを続けて操作すること

正解 B ❸1～2行目に、「D343L ドリルを使用の際には、素材に力を加え過ぎないよう注意してください」と注意喚起があり、続く同2～3行目で、それがモーターのオーバーヒートの原因となり得ると述べられている。そして、同4～5行目で、Overheating the drill's motor may cause premature wear and eventually lead to the failure of the device.「ドリルのモーターのオーバーヒートは摩耗を早め、結果的に機器の故障を引き起こす可能性がある」と説明されているので、素材、つまり穴を開ける面にドリルを強く押し付け過ぎると、モーターがオーバーヒートし、ひいてはドリルが故障する恐れがあると分かる。よって、(B)が正解。stop working「作動を停止する」。push ～ against … 「～を…に押し付ける」、surface「面」。
(C) loosely「緩く」、in place「適切な位置で」。
(D) run「～(機械)を動かす」、continuously「途切れなく」。

Expressions

lead to ～ 「～を引き起こす、～につながる」(❸ 5行目)
  Ms. Bailey's commitment to the team led to outstanding sales results.
  Baileyさんのチームへの献身が、傑出した販売実績につながりました。

Questions 153-154 refer to the following text-message chain.

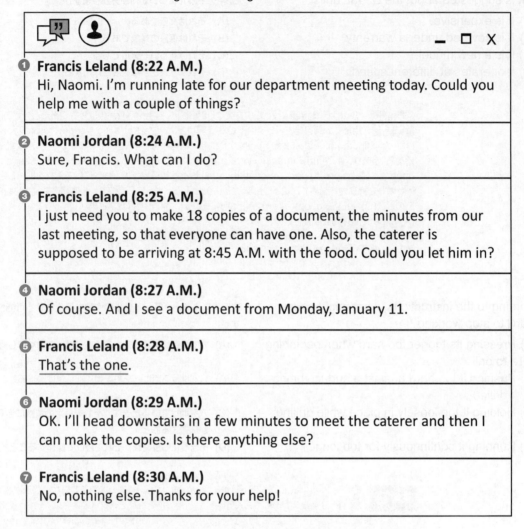

❶ Francis Leland (8:22 A.M.)
Hi, Naomi. I'm running late for our department meeting today. Could you help me with a couple of things?

❷ Naomi Jordan (8:24 A.M.)
Sure, Francis. What can I do?

❸ Francis Leland (8:25 A.M.)
I just need you to make 18 copies of a document, the minutes from our last meeting, so that everyone can have one. Also, the caterer is supposed to be arriving at 8:45 A.M. with the food. Could you let him in?

❹ Naomi Jordan (8:27 A.M.)
Of course. And I see a document from Monday, January 11.

❺ Francis Leland (8:28 A.M.)
That's the one.

❻ Naomi Jordan (8:29 A.M.)
OK. I'll head downstairs in a few minutes to meet the caterer and then I can make the copies. Is there anything else?

❼ Francis Leland (8:30 A.M.)
No, nothing else. Thanks for your help!

問題153-154は次のテキストメッセージのやりとりに関するものです。

Francis Leland（午前8時22分）
こんにちは、Naomi。私は今日の部署会議に遅れそうです。幾つか手伝っていただけますか。

Naomi Jordan（午前8時24分）
いいですよ、Francis。何をすればいいですか。

Francis Leland（午前8時25分）
全員に1部ずつ行き渡るよう、書類、つまり前回の会議の議事録のコピーを18部取ってほしいのです。それから、ケータリング業者が、午前8時45分に料理を持って到着することになっています。彼を中に入れていただけますか。

Naomi Jordan（午前8時27分）
もちろんです。ええと、1月11日月曜日の書類がありますね。

Francis Leland（午前8時28分）
まさにそれです。

Naomi Jordan（午前8時29分）
分かりました。すぐに下に行ってケータリング業者を出迎えてから、コピーを取ります。他に何かありますか。

Francis Leland（午前8時30分）
いいえ、他にはありません。手助けをありがとう！

153 At 8:28 A.M., what does Mr. Leland mean when he writes, "That's the one"?

    (A) He approves of the menu selected for the meeting.

    (B) The meeting location has not changed.

    (C) Ms. Jordan found the right meeting minutes.

    (D) Ms. Jordan should hire the same caterer.

午前8時28分に、Lelandさんは "That's the one" という発言で、何を意味していますか。

    (A) 彼は会議向けに選択されたメニューに賛成している。

    (B) 会議の場所は変更されていない。

    (C) Jordanさんは正しい会議議事録を見つけた。

    (D) Jordanさんはいつものケータリング業者を雇うべきだ。

> **正解 C** ❶で、部署会議に遅れそうだと伝えたLelandさんは❸で、前回の会議議事録の書類のコピーを18部取るようJordanさんに頼んでいる。それに対し、Jordanさんは❹で快諾した後、I see a document from Monday, January 11「1月11日月曜日の書類がある」と特定の書類を確認したことを知らせている。下線部の発言はそれに対する応答なので、Lelandさんは、Jordanさんが見つけたものがまさにコピーすべき会議議事録の書類であるということを伝えていると判断できる。(C)が正解。下線部のoneはdocumentを表している。
>
> (A) approve of ～「～に賛成する、～を良いと思う」、menu「メニュー」、select「～を選ぶ」。
> (B) location「場所」。
> (D) hire「～を雇う」。

154 What will Ms. Jordan most likely do next?

    (A) Revise a document

    (B) Begin a meeting

    (C) Contact a coworker

    (D) Let the caterer in

Jordanさんは次に何をすると考えられますか。

    (A) 文書を修正する

    (B) 会議を始める

    (C) 同僚に連絡する

    (D) ケータリング業者を中に入れる

> **正解 D** ❸で、午前8時45分に到着予定のケータリング業者を中に入れるよう頼むLelandさんに対し、Jordanさんは❹で快諾している。その後、Jordanさんはコピーすべき書類を特定した後、❻で、I'll head downstairs in a few minutes to meet the caterer and then I can make the copies.「私はすぐに下に行ってケータリング業者を出迎えてから、コピーを取る」と、これから自分が行うことを順に伝えているので、(D)が正解。
>
> (A) revise「～を修正する」。
> (C) coworker「同僚」。

Words & Phrases

❶ be running late 遅れている　　department 部署　　help ～ with … …に関して～を手伝う
a couple of ～ 幾つかの～、2つの～　　❸ make ～ copies of … …のコピーを～部取る　★～には数が入る　　document 書類
minutes 議事録　　caterer ケータリング業者　　arrive 到着する　　let ～ in ～を中に入れる　　❻ head 向かう
downstairs 階下へ　　in a few minutes すぐに、数分後に　　else 他に

Expressions

be supposed to *do*　「～することになっている、～するはずである」(❸)

The newer model of this water dispenser was supposed to be released later this week.
このウォーターサーバーの新型モデルは、今週後半に発売される予定でした。

Questions 155-157 refer to the following e-mail.

From:	Laura Batista
To:	All Library Staff
Date:	October 3
Subject:	Next year's budget

Hello, everyone,

❶ Last night, the library's board of trustees met to determine the budget for our next fiscal year. Unfortunately, the board did not approve the level of funding I requested. Consequently, I am planning to make a couple of adjustments over the next few months. First, we will not fill the positions left vacant when two employees resigned in August. I am currently analyzing their <u>duties</u> and thinking of ways to cover the work with our current staff. Second, I will evaluate our subscriptions to various periodicals and discontinue those for which patron interest is the lowest. We will discuss these and further measures in more detail at our next staff meeting.

Regards,

Laura Batista
Director, Abrams City Library

問題155-157は次のEメールに関するものです。

送信者：Laura Batista
受信者：図書館職員各位
日付：10月3日
件名：次年度予算

こんにちは、皆さん

昨夜、次の会計年度の予算を決定するため当図書館の評議員会が開かれました。残念ながら、私が要請した資金水準を評議員会は承認しませんでした。従って、今後数カ月間で2つの調整を行うつもりです。第1に、職員2名が8月に退職してから欠員となったままの職には人員を補充しません。私は現在、彼らの職務を分析し、現行の職員でその業務を穴埋めする方法を考えているところです。第2に、私はさまざまな定期刊行物の定期購読の状況を評価し、利用者の関心が最も低いものを打ち切る予定です。私たちはこれらのことと、さらなる措置について、次回の職員会議でもっと詳しく話し合います。

よろしくお願いします。

Laura Batista
エイブラムス市立図書館館長

Words & Phrases

budget 予算　❶ board of trustees 評議員会　meet （会が）開かれる　determine ～を決定する
fiscal year 会計年度　unfortunately 残念ながら、あいにく　board 評議員会　approve ～を承認する　level 水準
funding 資金　consequently 従って、その結果　adjustment 調整　fill ～を埋める　position 職
vacant （職などが）欠員になっている　resign 退職する、辞職する　currently 現在　analyze ～を分析する
think of ～ ～を考える　cover ～を穴埋めする　current 現在の、現行の　evaluate ～を評価する、～の重要性を判断する
subscription 定期購読　various さまざまな　periodical 定期刊行物
discontinue ～（予約購読など）を途中で打ち切る、～を中止する　patron （図書館などの）利用者　interest 関心
discuss ～について話し合う　further さらなる　measures 措置　director 館長

Expressions

in detail 「詳しく」（❶8行目）

This brochure explains in detail how to enter the DIY contest.
このパンフレットは、DIYコンテストへの参加方法を詳しく説明しています。

155 According to the e-mail, what happened earlier in the year?

(A) New board members were chosen.
(B) A building was vacated.
(C) Some employees left their jobs.
(D) Some job requirements changed.

Eメールによると、今年これまでに何が起きましたか。

(A) 新しい評議員が選ばれた。
(B) 建物が空室になった。
(C) 複数の職員が退職した。
(D) 幾つかの職務要件が変更された。

> **正解 C** このEメールは一番下の署名と宛先より、図書館館長から全職員に宛てたもの。送信日より、10月3日に送信されたと分かる。❶ 4行目に、we will not fill the positions left vacant when two employees resigned in August「職員2名が8月に退職してから欠員となったままの職には人員を補充しない」とあるので、今年これまでに、複数の職員が退職したと判断できる。よって(C)が正解。leave *one's* job「退職する、仕事を辞める」。
> (B) vacate「～を空にする、～(建物など)を引き払う」。
> (D) requirements「要件」。

156 The word "duties" in paragraph 1, line 5, is closest in meaning to

(A) taxes
(B) habits
(C) allowances
(D) responsibilities

第1段落・5行目にある "duties" に最も意味が近いのは

(A) 税金
(B) 習慣
(C) 手当て
(D) 職責

> **正解 D** ❶ 1～3行目では、次年度の予算決めで館長が要請していた資金水準が承認されなかったため、調整を行う旨が述べられている。同4行目に「職員2名が8月に退職してから欠員となったままの職には人員を補充しない」とあり、続く該当の語を含む文では、「私は現在、彼らの-------を分析し、現行の職員でその業務を穴埋めする方法を考えているところだ」と述べられている。空所の前の「彼ら」が指すのは退職した2名なので、館長は現在、この2名が担当していた業務を穴埋めできるよう、職務内容を調べていると考えられる。よって、(D) responsibilities「職責」が正解。
> (A) tax「税金」の複数形。
> (B) habit「習慣」の複数形。
> (C) allowance「手当て」の複数形。

157 What is suggested about the staff meeting?

(A) It may need to be rescheduled for next month.
(B) It will include a discussion of changes to the budget.
(C) It may be attended by members of the board of trustees.
(D) It will be held in a different location than in the past.

職員会議について何が分かりますか。

(A) それは来月に予定を変更する必要があるかもしれない。
(B) それは予算の変更についての話し合いを含む予定である。
(C) それには評議員会の評議員が出席するかもしれない。
(D) それは従来とは異なる場所で開かれる予定である。

> **正解 B** 館長は、要請した資金水準が承認されなかったことを受けて、❶ 3～7行目で今後数カ月間で行う予定の2つの調整を説明している。同7～8行目で、We will discuss these and further measures in more detail at our next staff meeting.「私たちはこれらのことと、さらなる措置について、次回の職員会議でもっと詳しく話し合う」と伝えているので、次回の職員会議では予算の変更について話し合われる予定だと判断できる。(B)が正解。include「～を含む」、discussion「話し合い」。
> (A) reschedule「～の予定を変更する」。
> (C) attend「～に出席する」。
> (D) hold「～を開く」、location「場所」、in the past「従来、過去に」。

Questions 158-160 refer to the following e-mail.

From:	Mitch Dyson <mdyson@skelmonco.com.au>
To:	All Employees <employees@skelmonco.com.au>
Date:	Monday, 30 April
Subject:	Inspection

Dear staff,

❶ The Auditing Department has informed me that it will begin auditing the company's inventory of computer equipment on Monday, 7 May. Please leave all computers, laptops, and monitors on your desks so that the bar codes can be scanned by the auditors. The department hopes to complete its inspection by Friday, 11 May.

❷ If you are missing a piece of equipment or have disposed of it, please <u>fill out</u> a Missing Equipment form no later than Friday, 4 May. To obtain the form or for help in filling it out, please stop by my office any day this week before 4:00 P.M.

Thank you,

Mitch Dyson
Administrative Assistant
Skelmon Corporation

問題158-160は次のEメールに関するものです。

送信者：Mitch Dyson <mdyson@skelmonco.com.au>
受信者：従業員各位 <employees@skelmonco.com.au>
日付：4月30日月曜日
件名：監査

従業員各位

監査部から、当社のコンピューター機器類の財産目録の監査を5月7日月曜日に開始する予定だと連絡がありました。監査員がバーコードを読み取ることができるよう、コンピューター、ノートパソコン、モニター類は全て、各自の机の上に置いたままにしておいてください。同部署は5月11日金曜日までにその監査を完了することを望んでいます。

機器を紛失もしくは処分した場合は5月4日金曜日までに、機器紛失届に記入してください。届け出フォームの入手、もしくはその記入に際して手助けが必要な場合は、午後4時までなら今週どの日でも、私の執務室に立ち寄ってください。

よろしくお願いいたします。

Mitch Dyson
管理補佐
Skelmon社

Words & Phrases

inspection 監査、点検　❶ auditing 監査　inform ~ that … ~に…であることを知らせる　audit ~を監査する
inventory 財産目録、在庫　equipment 機器　laptop ノートパソコン　monitor モニター　bar code バーコード
scan ~を読み取る　auditor 監査員　hope to do ~することを望む　complete ~を完了する
❷ miss ~の不在に気付く　a piece of ~ 〈数えられない名詞と共に〉1つの~　dispose of ~ ~を処分する
form フォーム、書式　obtain ~を入手する、~を取得する　stop by ~ ~に立ち寄る　administrative assistant 管理補佐
corporation 企業、株式会社

Expressions

no later than ~　「遅くとも~までに、~より遅くなることなく」（❷2行目）

I'd appreciate it if you could inform me of the product details no later than Thursday.
木曜日までに、製品詳細について私に知らせていただけると助かります。

166

158 What is the purpose of the inspection?

    (A) To confirm that all computers are using updated software

    (B) To verify the accuracy of the company's inventory list

    (C) To determine whether there are any equipment safety violations

    (D) To check that employees are using equipment properly

監査の目的は何ですか。

    (A) 全てのコンピューターが最新のソフトウエアを使用しているか確認すること

    (B) 会社の財産目録の正確性を確認すること

    (C) 機器の安全基準違反があるかどうかを突き止めること

    (D) 従業員が機器を適切に使用しているか確認すること

> **正解 B** ❶1〜2行目に、The Auditing Department has informed me that it will begin auditing the company's inventory of computer equipment on Monday, 7 May.「監査部から、当社のコンピューター機器類の財産目録の監査を5月7日月曜日に開始する予定だと連絡があった」とある。よって、監査の目的は、会社の財産目録が正しいかどうかを確かめることだと分かるので、(B)が正解。verify「〜を確認する、〜を証明する」、accuracy「正確性」、list「目録」。
> (A) confirm that 〜「〜ということを確認する」、update「〜を最新の状態にする」、software「ソフトウエア」。
> (C) determine whether 〜「〜かどうかを突き止める」、safety「安全性」、violation「違反」。
> (D) check that 〜「〜であることを確認する」、properly「適切に」。

159 When is the inspection expected to end?

    (A) On April 30

    (B) On May 4

    (C) On May 7

    (D) On May 11

監査はいつ終了する見込みですか。

    (A) 4月30日

    (B) 5月4日

    (C) 5月7日

    (D) 5月11日

> **正解 D** ❶3〜4行目で、監査部によって行われるコンピューター機器類の財産目録の監査について、The department hopes to complete its inspection by Friday, 11 May.「同部署は、5月11日金曜日までにその監査を完了することを望んでいる」と述べられている。よって、監査は5月11日に終了する見通しであると分かるので、(D)が正解。be expected to do「〜する見込みである」、end「終了する」。
> (A) 日付の欄より、このEメールの送信日。
> (B) ❷1〜2行目より、機器紛失届の提出期限日。
> (C) ❶1〜2行目より、監査の開始予定日。

160 The phrase "fill out" in paragraph 2, line 1, is closest in meaning to

    (A) expand

    (B) integrate

    (C) complete

    (D) exchange

第2段落・1行目にある "fill out" に最も意味が近いのは

    (A) 〜を拡大する

    (B) 〜を統合する

    (C) 〜に全て記入する

    (D) 〜を交換する

> **正解 C** 該当の語を含む文は、「機器を紛失もしくは処分した場合は5月4日金曜日までに、機器紛失届------してください」という意味の丁寧な命令文。fill outの目的語はa Missing Equipment form「機器紛失届」なので、機器を紛失したか処分した場合には、財産目録の監査前にその届け出フォームに記入するよう従業員に求めている文だと考えられる。よって、(C) complete「〜に全て記入する」が適切。

Questions 161-163 refer to the following brochure.

Eleanor's Professional Cleaning

❶ Eleanor's has been Forton County's leading professional cleaning service for over 25 years. — [1] —. We customize our services to meet your residential and commercial cleaning needs. For most customers, this includes dusting and polishing furniture, sweeping and vacuuming floors, washing windows, and sanitizing all surfaces. — [2] —.

❷ Our excellent communication and years of experience set Eleanor's Professional Cleaning apart from the rest. — [3] —. In addition, we are proud of our commitment to using only gentle, all-natural products that are free of harsh chemicals and dyes. — [4] —. Call us today at 713-555-0177 to schedule an appointment. Our first visit is free.

問題161-163は次のパンフレットに関するものです。

Eleanor's 清掃専門社

Eleanor's社は25年以上にわたり、フォートン郡内随一の清掃サービス専門業者であり続けています。当社は、皆さまの住宅向けおよび事業所向け清掃のニーズにお応えすべく、ご要望に応じたサービスを提供しています。ほとんどのお客さまにとって、これには家具のほこり掃除や艶出し、床の掃き掃除や掃除機掛け、窓の洗浄、あらゆる表面の消毒が含まれます。＊また、当社は特別契約で徹底清掃も行っています。

卓越したお客さま対応と長年の経験により、Eleanor's清掃専門社は他社から際立っています。それに加えて当社は、刺激の強過ぎる化学物質や染料を含まない、低刺激性の全天然素材製品のみを使用するという自社の取り組みを誇りに思っています。今すぐ713-555-0177まで当社にお電話いただき、ご予約を入れてください。初回訪問は無料です。

＊問題163の挿入文の訳

Words & Phrases

brochure パンフレット　professional 専門職の、プロフェッショナルな　cleaning 清掃　❶ county 郡　leading 一流の、トップの　service サービス業　customize ～を注文に応じて作る、～を好みに合わせて変える　meet ～を満たす　residential 住宅の　commercial 商業上の　needs ニーズ、要求　customer 顧客　include ～を含む　dust ～のほこりを拭き取る　polish ～の艶を出す、～を磨く　furniture 家具　sweep ～を掃く　vacuum ～を電気掃除機で掃除する　floor 床　wash ～を洗う　sanitize ～を衛生的にする　surface 表面　❷ excellent 非常に優れた　communication 意思疎通　experience 経験　set ～ apart from … ～を…から際立たせる　the rest 残り　in addition その上　be proud of ～ ～を誇りに思う　commitment to *doing* ～するという取り組み・献身　gentle （薬などが）強くない　all-natural 100パーセント天然の　product 製品　harsh （洗剤などが）きつ過ぎる　chemical 化学物質　dye 染料　schedule ～を予定に入れる　appointment 予約、会う約束　visit 訪問　free 無料の

Expressions

be free of ～ 「～（望ましくないもの）がない」（❷3行目）
　All of the pastries in the showcase are free of gluten.
　ショーケース内のパン菓子は全て、グルテンフリーです。

161 What is stated about Eleanor's Professional Cleaning?

(A) It serves clients in homes and offices.
(B) It uses products supplied by customers.
(C) It provides cost estimates for a small fee.
(D) Its rates are competitive.

Eleanor's清掃専門社について何が述べられていますか。

(A) 同社は、住宅およびオフィスの顧客にサービスを提供する。
(B) 同社は、顧客によって提供される製品を使用する。
(C) 同社は、少額の料金で費用見積もりを用意する。
(D) 同社の規定料金は格安である。

正解 A　❶2～3行目に、Eleanor's清掃専門社が提供している業務の内容について、We customize our services to meet your residential and commercial cleaning needs.「当社は、あなたの住宅向けおよび事業所向け清掃のニーズに応えるべく、要望に応じたサービスを提供している」とある。よって、同社の対象顧客は一般家庭および事業者だと分かるので、(A)が正解。serve「～のために働く、～の役に立つ」。
(B) supply「～を提供する」。
(C) provide「～を用意する、～を提供する」、estimate「見積もり」、fee「料金」。
(D) ❷1～2行目より、同社が他社から際立っているとされるのは料金面においてではなく、顧客対応や長年の経験において。rate「規定料金」、competitive「格安の、優位性のある」。

---

162 What does the business NOT typically clean?

(A) Floors
(B) Windows
(C) Dishes
(D) Furniture

この会社が通常では清掃を行っていないものは何ですか。

(A) 床
(B) 窓
(C) 食器類
(D) 家具

正解 C　❶3～4行目に、Eleanor's清掃専門社が大半の顧客に提供しているサービスとして、this includes dusting and polishing furniture, sweeping and vacuuming floors, washing windows, and sanitizing all surfaces「これには家具のほこり掃除や艶出し、床の掃き掃除や掃除機掛け、窓の洗浄、あらゆる表面の消毒が含まれる」と書かれており、(A)の床、(B)の窓、(D)の家具は同社が普段清掃しているものだと分かる。(C)の食器類についての言及はないので、正解は(C)。business「会社」、typically「通常」。

---

163 In which of the positions marked [1], [2], [3], and [4] does the following sentence best belong?

"We also do in-depth cleaning by special arrangement."

(A) [1]
(B) [2]
(C) [3]
(D) [4]

[1]、[2]、[3]、[4]と記載された箇所のうち、次の文が入るのに最もふさわしいのはどれですか。

「また、当社は特別契約で徹底清掃も行っています」

正解 B　挿入文は特別契約で請け負う清掃業務内容を説明するもので、追加を表すalsoを含んでいる。❶2～4行目で、Eleanor's清掃専門社が顧客に通常提供している清掃業務の内容が具体的に紹介されている。この直後の(B)[2]に挿入文を入れると、同社がその通常清掃業務に加え、特別な取り決めで徹底清掃も行うことを伝える文が続くことになり、流れとして適切。in-depth「徹底した、徹底的な」、arrangement「取り決め」。

Questions 164-167 refer to the following online chat discussion.

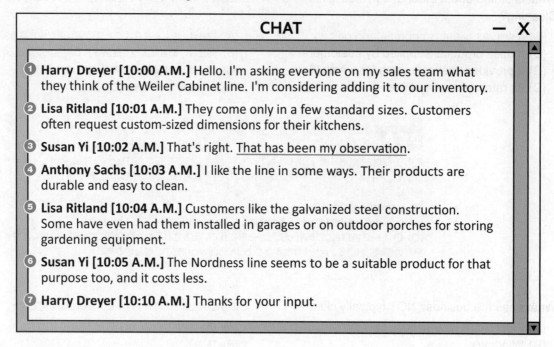

CHAT — X

① **Harry Dreyer [10:00 A.M.]** Hello. I'm asking everyone on my sales team what they think of the Weiler Cabinet line. I'm considering adding it to our inventory.

② **Lisa Ritland [10:01 A.M.]** They come only in a few standard sizes. Customers often request custom-sized dimensions for their kitchens.

③ **Susan Yi [10:02 A.M.]** That's right. That has been my observation.

④ **Anthony Sachs [10:03 A.M.]** I like the line in some ways. Their products are durable and easy to clean.

⑤ **Lisa Ritland [10:04 A.M.]** Customers like the galvanized steel construction. Some have even had them installed in garages or on outdoor porches for storing gardening equipment.

⑥ **Susan Yi [10:05 A.M.]** The Nordness line seems to be a suitable product for that purpose too, and it costs less.

⑦ **Harry Dreyer [10:10 A.M.]** Thanks for your input.

問題164-167は次のオンラインチャットの話し合いに関するものです。

チャット

Harry Dreyer [午前10時]	こんにちは。うちの販売チームの皆さんに、Weiler Cabinet社の製品ラインについてどう思うか尋ねたいと思います。それを当店の在庫に加えることを検討しているところです。
Lisa Ritland [午前10時1分]	それらは数種類の標準サイズでしか入手できません。顧客はよく、自宅の台所用にオーダーメードサイズの寸法を求めます。
Susan Yi [午前10時2分]	その通りです。それが私の所見でもあります。
Anthony Sachs [午前10時3分]	私は幾つかの点で同製品ラインは良いと思います。同社の製品は耐久性があり、掃除もしやすいです。
Lisa Ritland [午前10時4分]	顧客は、その亜鉛めっきのスチール製品を気に入っています。園芸用具の収納用に、それらをガレージや屋外ポーチに設置している人もいるくらいです。
Susan Yi [午前10時5分]	Nordness社の製品ラインもそういった用途に向いた製品であるようですし、あれの方が安価です。
Harry Dreyer [午前10時10分]	ご意見をありがとうございます。

Words & Phrases

① think of ～ ～について思う　　cabinet キャビネット、収納棚　　line 製品ライン　　consider *doing* ～することを検討する　　add ～ to … ～を…に加える　　inventory 在庫　　② come in ～ ～で手に入る　　standard 標準の　　request ～を頼む　　custom-sized オーダーメードサイズの　　dimension 寸法、大きさ　　③ observation 所見、観察　　④ in some ways 幾つかの点で　　durable 耐久性のある　　clean ～を掃除する　　⑤ galvanized 亜鉛めっきした　　steel スチール、鋼鉄　　construction 構造物、建造物　　install ～を設置する　　garage ガレージ、車庫　　outdoor 屋外の　　porch ポーチ、車寄せ　　store ～を収納する　　gardening 園芸　　equipment 用具　　⑥ suitable 向いている、適した　　purpose 用途、目的　　cost ～(費用)がかかる　　⑦ input 意見提供

Expressions

seem to be ～ 「～のようだ」(⑥)

One of the 3-D printers we ordered seems to be defective.
注文した3Dプリンターのうち1台に欠陥があるようです。

164 Who most likely is Mr. Dreyer?

(A) A furniture manufacturer
(B) A sales manager
(C) A cabinet designer
(D) A consumer news reporter

Dreyerさんとは誰だと考えられますか。

(A) 家具の製作者
(B) 販売部の責任者
(C) キャビネットの設計者
(D) 消費者情報の報道記者

正解 B Dreyerさんは❶で、I'm asking everyone on my sales team what they think of the Weiler Cabinet line.「うちの販売チームの皆さんに、Weiler Cabinet社の製品ラインについてどう思うか尋ねたい」と、自分のチームメンバーに意見提供を求めた後、同社製品を在庫に加えることを検討中だと伝えている。それを受け、❷～❻で意見提供をした3名に対し、

Dreyerさんは❼で、Thanks for your input.「意見をありがとう」とお礼を述べている。よって、Dreyerさんはこの3名が所属する販売チームの責任者だと考えられるので、(B)が正解。manager「責任者、管理者」。
(A) manufacturer「製作者、製造業者」。
(D) consumer「消費者」、reporter「記者」。

165 At 10:02 A.M., what does Ms. Yi most likely mean when she writes, "That has been my observation"?

(A) She has noticed that many customers have large kitchens.
(B) She feels she is well qualified for her current position.
(C) She has had similar experiences at a previous workplace.
(D) She has found that customers prefer a variety of cabinet sizes.

午前10時2分に、Yiさんは "That has been my observation" という発言で、何を意味していると考えられますか。

(A) 彼女は、多数の顧客が広い台所を持っているということに気付いている。
(B) 彼女は、自分が現在の職務に適任だと思っている。
(C) 彼女は、以前の職場でも似たような体験をしたことがある。
(D) 彼女は、顧客がいろいろなキャビネットのサイズがある方を好むことが分かっている。

正解 D ❶で、Weiler Cabinet社の製品ラインについての意見を求めるDreyerさんに対し、Ritlandさんは❷で、「それらは数種類の標準サイズでしか入手できない。顧客はよく、自宅の台所用にオーダーメードサイズの寸法を求める」と伝えている。それに対し、Yiさんは❸で、その通りだと同意した後に下線部の発言を続けているので、顧客が多様なサイズのキャビ

ネットを求めるという所見を伝えていると考えられる。prefer「～の方を好む」、a variety of ～「さまざまな～」。
(A) notice that ～「～ということに気付く」。
(B) be qualified for ～「～にふさわしい」、current「現在の」。
(C) similar「類似した」、previous「以前の」、workplace「職場」。

166 What is indicated about products in the Nordness line?

(A) They are expensive.
(B) They are easy to assemble.
(C) They are available in only one color.
(D) They are appropriate for use outdoors.

Nordness社の製品ラインについて何が示されていますか。

(A) それらは高価である。
(B) それらは組み立てやすい。
(C) それらは1色でしか手に入らない。
(D) それらは屋外での使用に適している。

正解 D Ritlandさんが❺で、Weiler Cabinet社製品について、「園芸用具の収納用に、それらをガレージや屋外ポーチに設置している人もいるくらいだ」と述べた後、Yiさんは❻で、The Nordness line seems to be a suitable product for that purpose too「Nordness社の製品ラインもそういった用途に向いた製品であるようだ」と述べている。よって、

Nordness社製品は屋外での使用に適していると考えられるので、(D)が正解。appropriate「適した」、outdoors「屋外で」。
(A) ❻に、Nordness社製品はWeiler Cabinet社製品よりも安価とある。expensive「高価な」。
(B) assemble「～を組み立てる」。
(C) available「購入できる」。

167 Which writer mentions the Weiler Cabinet line's construction material?

(A) Mr. Dreyer
(B) Ms. Ritland
(C) Ms. Yi
(D) Mr. Sachs

どの発言者が、Weiler Cabinet社の製品ラインの構造素材について述べていますか。

(A) Dreyerさん
(B) Ritlandさん
(C) Yiさん
(D) Sachsさん

正解 B ❷～❹で交わされた、Weiler Cabinet社の製品ラインについての意見を受けて、Ritlandさんは❺で、Customers like the galvanized steel construction.「顧客は、

その亜鉛めっきのスチール製品を気に入っている」と、同社製品の構造素材に言及している。よって、(B)が正解。material「素材、材料」。

171

Questions 168-171 refer to the following e-mail.

To:	Elaine Cho <e_cho@lukachinc.com>
From:	Khalon Brown <k_brown@lukachinc.com>
Date:	March 7
Subject:	Workshop registration

Hello Elaine,

① You are receiving this e-mail because you enrolled in the financial literacy workshop led by Anita Golden on March 9. — [1] —. Due to insufficient registration, that workshop will no longer take place.

② If you would still like to participate in a financial literacy workshop, you may enroll online in another session we are offering. It is a workshop on March 13, and it will cover the same topics as the one on March 9. — [2] —.

③ To register for this workshop or to view a full list of upcoming workshops, visit www.lukachinc.com/stafftraining. — [3] —. You can also check your registration for other upcoming workshops on the same Web site.

④ — [4] —. Please let me know if you have any questions.

Best,

Khalon Brown

問題168-171は次のEメールに関するものです。

受信者：Elaine Cho <e_cho@lukachinc.com>
送信者：Khalon Brown <k_brown@lukachinc.com>
日付：3月7日
件名：講習会への登録

Elaineさん

あなたはAnita Goldenが指導する3月9日の金融リテラシー講習会に参加登録したため、このEメールを受け取っています。登録者数の不足のため、この講習会はもはや開催されません。

金融リテラシー講習会への参加を引き続き希望する場合は、当社が設けている別の講習会へのオンライン参加登録が可能です。それは3月13日の講習会で、3月9日のものと同じ主題を扱う予定です。＊それは午後1時から午後2時まで、403号室にて開催されます。

この講習会に登録、もしくは近日中に開催される講習会の全リストを閲覧するには、www.lukachinc.com/stafftrainingにアクセスしてください。また、同ウェブサイト上では、今後予定されている他の講習会に関してご自分の登録状況を確認することもできます。

ご質問があれば、私にお知らせください。

よろしくお願いいたします。

Khalon Brown

＊問題171の挿入文の訳

168 What does the e-mail indicate about the workshop on March 9?

(A) Its location has changed.
(B) It has been canceled.
(C) It is fully booked.
(D) Its content has been updated.

Eメールは、3月9日の講習会について何を示していますか。

(A) 会場が変更になった。
(B) 中止された。
(C) 予約がいっぱいである。
(D) 内容が更新された。

正解 B ❶1〜2行目で、3月9日の講習会に言及した後、同2〜3行目で、Due to insufficient registration, that workshop will no longer take place.「登録者数の不足のため、この講習会はもはや開催されない」と、同講習会の中止を知らせている。よって、(B)が正解。cancel「〜を中止する」。
(A) location「場所」。
(C) ❶2〜3行目より、3月9日の講習会への登録者数は不足していたと分かる。be fully booked「予約がいっぱいである」。
(D) content「内容」、update「〜を更新する」。

---

169 What is suggested about Ms. Cho?

(A) She is unable to attend an event on March 13.
(B) She has previously led a workshop.
(C) She works in the same department as Ms. Golden.
(D) She is interested in learning about finance.

Choさんについて何が分かりますか。

(A) 彼女は3月13日の催しに出席することができない。
(B) 彼女は以前、講習会で指導をしたことがある。
(C) 彼女はGoldenさんと同じ部署に勤務している。
(D) 彼女は金融について学ぶことに関心がある。

正解 D Choさんとは、このEメールの受信者。❶1〜2行目で、Eメールの受信理由について、You are receiving this e-mail because you enrolled in the financial literacy workshop「あなたは金融リテラシー講習会に参加登録したため、このEメールを受け取っている」と述べられているので、Choさんは金融について学ぶことに関心があると分かる。(D)が正解。be interested in *doing*「〜することに関心がある」、finance「金融」。
(A) be unable to *do*「〜することができない」、attend「〜に出席する」、event「催し」。
(B) previously「以前に」。
(C) department「部署」。

Words & Phrases

workshop 講習会　　registration 登録、登録者数　　❶ receive 〜を受け取る　　enroll in 〜 〜に登録する
financial 金融の、財政上の　　literacy リテラシー、(特定分野の)知識　　lead 〜を主導する、〜を取り仕切る
due to 〜 〜のために　　insufficient 不十分な　　take place 開催される　　❷ participate in 〜 〜に参加する
session 集まり　　offer 〜を提供する　　cover 〜を扱う　　topic 主題　　❸ register for 〜 〜に登録する
view 〜を見る　　full 完全な、無削除の　　list リスト　　upcoming 近づいている、間近に迫る

170 According to Mr. Brown, what can Ms. Cho do on the Web site?

(A) Make sure she is enrolled in a workshop
(B) Update her contact information
(C) Suggest topics for future workshops
(D) View a list of courses offered in the past

Brownさんによると、Choさんはウェブサイト上で何をすることができますか。

(A) 自分が講習会に登録していることを確かめる
(B) 自分の連絡先情報を更新する
(C) 今後の講習会のための主題を提案する
(D) これまでに提供された講座のリストを閲覧する

正解 A Choさん宛てのこのEメールの送信者であるBrownさんは、❸1～2行目でウェブサイトに言及した後、同2～3行目で、You can also check your registration for other upcoming workshops on the same Web site. 「また、同ウェブサイト上では、今後予定されている他の講習会に関して自分の登録状況を確認することもできる」と知らせている。よって、(A)が正解。make sure (that) ～「～ということを確かめる、必ず～であるようにする」。
(B) contact information「連絡先情報」。
(C) suggest「～を提案する」、future「今後の」。
(D) ❸1～2行目より、ウェブサイト上で確認可能なのは、過去に提供された講座のリストではなく、これから開催される講習会のリスト。course「講座」、in the past「これまでに」。

---

171 In which of the positions marked [1], [2], [3], and [4] does the following sentence best belong?

"It will be held in room 403 from 1:00 P.M. to 2:00 P.M."

(A) [1]
(B) [2]
(C) [3]
(D) [4]

[1]、[2]、[3]、[4]と記載された箇所のうち、次の文が入るのに最もふさわしいのはどれですか。

「それは午後1時から午後2時まで、403号室にて開催されます」

正解 B 挿入文は開催時間と開催場所の予定を知らせるもの。❶で、3月9日に予定されていた講習会の中止が知らされ、❷1～2行目で、別の講習会へのオンライン参加登録が可能であることが述べられている。続く同2～3行目では、It is a workshop on March 13, and it will cover the same topics as the one on March 9. 「それは3月13日の講習会で、3月9日のものと同じ主題を扱う予定だ」とその別の講習会の日程と内容が案内されている。この直後の(B)[2]に挿入文を入れると、Itが3月13日の講習会を指し、その時間と場所を補足する文が続くことになり、適切。hold「～を開催する」。

Expressions

no longer ～ 「もはや～ない」（❶3行目）
I am afraid your discount coupon is no longer valid.
恐れ入りますが、お客さまの割引クーポンはもはや有効ではありません。

Questions 172-175 refer to the following advertisement.

Vivanti Uniform Rentals

❶ Having employees in uniforms enhances professionalism and increases a company's brand recognition. In fact, uniforms are a relatively inexpensive yet effective form of advertising. They can convey the impression that a company is well established and that it cares for its workers. When customers observe your uniformed employees, it gives them confidence in doing business with your company.

❷ Our rental system serves businesses that seek a completely managed uniform program. We provide clean and fresh uniforms for your entire staff weekly. We take care of everything, including laundering, making repairs or replacements, and ensuring appropriate sizing.

❸ Contact us to discuss your industry and apparel needs. We offer custom designs and materials for many sectors, including health care, food processing, hospitality, trades, and manufacturing. Let us know the number of uniforms you need. We extend discounts for organizations outfitting 50 or more employees.

❹ Contact a Vivanti Uniform Rentals representative today and receive a quote within two days!

問題172-175は次の広告に関するものです。

Vivanti制服レンタル社

従業員に制服を着用させることはプロ意識を高め、企業のブランド認知度を上げます。実際、制服は比較的安価ながらも効果的な広告形態です。それらは、企業が定評を得ており、自社の従業員を大事にしているという印象を伝えることができます。顧客が制服を着用した貴社の従業員を目にすれば、貴社との取引における信頼感につながります。

当社のレンタル制度は、完全管理の制服プログラムをお探しの企業のお役に立つものです。当社は毎週、貴社の全従業員に清潔で洗いたての制服をご提供します。当社は洗濯、修繕、交換、寸法合わせの保証を含め、万事責任を持ってお引き受けします。

当社にご連絡いただき、貴社の業界ニーズと衣服ニーズについてご相談ください。当社は医療、食品加工、接客、貿易、製造などの多様な分野向けに特注のデザインと素材をご提供しています。ご入り用の制服の数量を当社にお知らせください。当社は、50名以上の従業員に制服支給を行う組織様に対して割引をご提供しています。

今すぐVivanti制服レンタル社の担当者にご連絡いただき、2日以内に見積書をお受け取りください!

Words & Phrases

uniform 制服　rental レンタル、賃貸　❶ have ~ … ~を…の状態にしておく　~ in … …を着用した~　enhance ~を高める　professionalism プロ意識　increase ~を増やす　brand ブランド　recognition 認知、認識　in fact 実際　relatively 比較的　inexpensive 安価な　effective 効果的な　form 形態　advertising 広告、宣伝　impression 印象　well established 定評のある、確立した　care for ~ ~を大事にする　worker 従業員、労働者　observe ~に気付く、~を観察する　uniformed 制服を着用した　confidence 信頼　do business with ~ ~と取引する　❷ system 制度　serve ~の役に立つ　seek ~を探す　completely 完全に、徹底的に　manage ~を管理する　clean 清潔な　fresh 新しい、出来たばかりの　entire 全部の　weekly 週に1度　take care of ~ 責任を持って~を引き受ける　including ~を含めて　laundering 洗濯　make repairs 修繕する　make a replacement 交換する　ensure ~を保証する　appropriate 適切な　sizing 寸法合わせ　❸ contact ~に連絡する　discuss ~について話し合う　industry 業界　apparel 衣服　needs ニーズ、要求　offer ~を提供する　custom 特注の　material 素材　sector 分野、部門　health care 医療　processing 加工　hospitality 接客、もてなし　trade 貿易、商取引　manufacturing 製造　extend ~を供与する　organization 組織　outfit ~に(着るものなどを)支給する　❹ representative 担当者　receive ~を受け取る　quote 見積書

Expressions

provide ~ for … 「…に~を提供する」(❷2行目)
Refreshments will be provided for workshop attendees.
講習会出席者には軽食が提供されます。

172 What is NOT mentioned as a benefit of having uniformed employees?

(A) It makes employees feel loyal to a company.
(B) It is an inexpensive marketing method.
(C) It raises customers' confidence in a business.
(D) It builds a company's brand recognition.

制服を着用した従業員を抱えることの利点として述べられていないものは何ですか。

(A) それは従業員に企業への忠誠心を持たせる。
(B) それは安価なマーケティング手法である。
(C) それは企業に対する顧客の信頼感を高める。
(D) それは企業のブランド認知を確立する。

正解 A 従業員に制服を着用させることで得られるメリットについては、❶に説明がある。(D)の企業のブランド認知の確立については、同1～2行目に「従業員に制服を着用させることは企業のブランド認知度を上げる」とある。(B)の安価なマーケティング手法であることについては、同2～3行目に「制服は比較的安価ながらも効果的な広告形態だ」とある。(C)の企業に対する顧客の信頼の向上については、同4～5行目に「顧客が制

服を着用した貴社の従業員を目にすれば、貴社との取引における信頼感につながる」とある。(A)の従業員の企業への忠誠心には言及がないので、(A)が正解。benefit「利点」。loyal「忠誠心のある」。
(B) marketing「マーケティング」、method「手法」。
(C) raise「～を高める」。
(D) build「～を高める、～を増強する」。

---

173 The word "convey" in paragraph 1, line 3, is closest in meaning to

(A) transport
(B) personalize
(C) communicate
(D) resemble

第1段落・3行目にある "convey" に最も意味が近いのは

(A) ～を輸送する
(B) ～を個人のニーズに合わせる
(C) ～を伝達する
(D) ～に似ている

正解 C ❶では、従業員に制服を着用させることで企業が得られる利点について述べられている。該当の語を含む文は、「それらは、企業が定評を得ており、自社の従業員を大事にしているという印象-------ことができる」という意味。この文の

主語であるTheyは直前の文にあるuniformsを指しているので、制服が与える企業の好印象について説明している文だと考えられる。よって、(C) communicate「～を伝達する」が正解。

---

174 How frequently does Vivanti Uniform Rentals deliver items to its clients?

(A) Once a day
(B) Twice a day
(C) Once a week
(D) Once a month

Vivanti制服レンタル社は、どのくらいの頻度で顧客に品物を届けますか。

(A) 1日に1度
(B) 1日に2度
(C) 1週間に1度
(D) 1カ月に1度

正解 C 見出しより、Vivanti制服レンタル社とはこの広告の広告主と分かる。❷2行目に、We provide clean and fresh uniforms for your entire staff weekly.「当社は毎週、

貴社の全従業員に清潔で洗いたての制服を提供する」とあるので、(C)が正解。設問文のitemsはuniformsを指す。frequently「頻繁に」、item「品物」。

---

175 According to the advertisement, how can a business receive a discounted rate?

(A) By using a special promotional code
(B) By identifying itself as a manufacturer
(C) By signing a new contract within two days
(D) By ordering a certain number of uniforms

広告によると、企業はどのようにすると割引料金を受けることができますか。

(A) 特別な販促用コードを使用することによって
(B) 自社が製造業者であると伝えることによって
(C) 2日以内に新しい契約書に署名することによって
(D) 特定の数の制服を注文することによって

正解 D ❸3～4行目に、We extend discounts for organizations outfitting 50 or more employees.「当社は、50名以上の従業員に制服支給を行う組織に対して割引を提供する」とあるので、Vivanti制服レンタル社を利用する企業は、50人分以上の注文で割引料金を受けることができると分かる。50人分以上をa certain number「特定の数」と表している(D)が正解。discounted「割引された」、rate「料金」。certain「特

定の」。
(B) identify ～ as … 「～を…と特定する」、manufacturer「製造業者」。
(C) ❹より、2日以内という期間は、Vivanti制服レンタル社担当者への連絡から見積書受領までの期間。sign「～に署名する」、contract「契約書」。

TEST 2 PART 7

Questions 176-180 refer to the following invoice and e-mail.

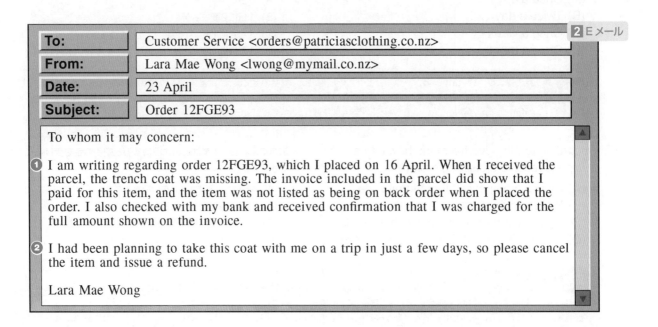

請求書

Patricia's Clothing

Order number: 12FGE93   **Date of purchase:** 16 April

Quantity	Size	Item No.	Description	Price
1	M	SD2391	Women's trench coat, tan	$100.00
1	M	SS2131	Men's striped sweater, red/white	$70.00
1	L	DS231	Women's crew socks, black 3-pack	$15.00
1	M	LSP23109	Women's long-sleeved blouse, blue	$65.00
1	M	SST210	Men's short-sleeved T-shirt, white	$25.00

	Subtotal	$275.00
	Tax	$41.25
Paid with bank card	Shipping	$0.00
XXXX XXXX XXXX 3457	**Total**	**$316.25**

If you have questions about your order, please contact us at orders@patriciasclothing.co.nz.

Items may be returned within 60 days of purchase by postal mail or at any Patricia's Clothing location in New Zealand. To locate a store, visit www.patriciasclothing.co.nz.

E メール

To:	Customer Service <orders@patriciasclothing.co.nz>
From:	Lara Mae Wong <lwong@mymail.co.nz>
Date:	23 April
Subject:	Order 12FGE93

To whom it may concern:

I am writing regarding order 12FGE93, which I placed on 16 April. When I received the parcel, the trench coat was missing. The invoice included in the parcel did show that I paid for this item, and the item was not listed as being on back order when I placed the order. I also checked with my bank and received confirmation that I was charged for the full amount shown on the invoice.

I had been planning to take this coat with me on a trip in just a few days, so please cancel the item and issue a refund.

Lara Mae Wong

Patricia's衣料品店

ご注文番号：12FGE93　　　　　　　　　　　　　　　　　　　ご購入日：4月16日

数量	サイズ	商品番号	品目	価格
1	M	SD2391	女性用トレンチコート、黄褐色	100.00ドル
1	M	SS2131	男性用ストライプセーター、赤・白色	70.00ドル
1	L	DS231	女性用クルーソックス、黒色の3足組	15.00ドル
1	M	LSP23109	女性用長袖ブラウス、青色	65.00ドル
1	M	SST210	男性用半袖Tシャツ、白色	25.00ドル

	小計	275.00ドル
	税	41.25ドル
クレジットカードにてお支払い済み	送料	0.00ドル
XXXX XXXX XXXX 3457	合計	**316.25ドル**

もしご注文にご質問がありましたら、orders@patriciasclothing.co.nzまでご連絡ください。
商品は購入後60日以内に、郵送またはPatricia's衣料品店のニュージーランド全店舗で返品が可能です。店舗を探すには www.patriciasclothing.co.nzにアクセスしてください。

受信者：顧客サービス <orders@patriciasclothing.co.nz>
送信者：Lara Mae Wong<lwong@mymail.co.nz>
日付：4月23日
件名：注文番号12FGE93

担当者様

4月16日に注文した注文番号12FGE93に関してメールを書いています。私が小包を受け取ったとき、トレンチコートが見当たりませんでした。小包に同梱されていた請求書には私がこの商品の支払いをしたことが書かれており、私が注文したときには、この商品が入荷待ち状態だとは記載されていませんでした。また、私は銀行に問い合わせて、請求書にある全額を請求されたという確認を取りました。

私は、このコートをほんの数日後の旅行に持って行く計画を立てていました。ですので、商品のキャンセルと返金をお願いします。

Lara Mae Wong

176 What information is given on the invoice?

(A) A phone number for customer service
(B) A customer's shipping address
(C) A store's return policy
(D) A list of store locations

請求書には何の情報がありますか。

(A) 顧客サービスの電話番号
(B) 顧客の配送先住所
(C) 店の返品条件
(D) 店舗所在地のリスト

> **正解 C** Patricia's衣料品店の請求書である**1**の**❸**1〜2行目に、Items may be returned within 60 days of purchase by postal mail or at any Patricia's Clothing location in New Zealand.「商品は購入後60日以内に、郵送またはPatricia's衣料品店のニュージーランド全店舗で返品が可能」と、同店の返品条件が書かれているので、(C)が正解。
> (B) shipping address「配送先住所」。
> (D) **1**の**❸**2〜3行目に、「店舗を探すにはwww.patriciasclothing.co.nzにアクセスしてください」とあり、請求書に店舗所在地のリストは載っていない。

177 What does the invoice indicate about Ms. Wong's order?

(A) It included a discounted item.
(B) It was shipped free of charge.
(C) It arrived in two separate boxes.
(D) It consisted of children's clothing.

請求書はWongさんの注文について何を示していますか。

(A) 割引商品を含んでいた。
(B) 無料で配送された。
(C) 2つの別個の箱で届いた。
(D) 内容は子ども服だった。

> **正解 B** 請求書**1**のShipping「送料」欄に「0.00ドル」とあり、配送費用は発生していない。(B)が正解。ship「〜を配送する」、free of charge「無料で」。
> (A) 割引に関する記載はない。
> (C) **2**の**❶**1〜2行目に、When I received the parcel「私が小包を受け取ったとき」とparcelが単数形で使われている。また請求書に2つの箱で発送したという記載はない。separate「別個の」。
> (D) **1**のDescription「品目」欄にはいずれもWomen's「(成人)女性用」、またはMen's「(成人)男性用」とあり、子ども服ではない。consist of 〜「〜から成る」。

178 What is the price of the item that Ms. Wong did not receive?

(A) $25.00
(B) $65.00
(C) $70.00
(D) $100.00

Wongさんが受け取らなかった品物の価格は幾らですか。

(A) 25.00ドル
(B) 65.00ドル
(C) 70.00ドル
(D) 100.00ドル

> **正解 D** WongさんがPatricia's衣料品店の顧客サービスに宛てたEメールである**2**の**❶**1〜2行目で、When I received the parcel, the trench coat was missing.「私が小包を受け取ったとき、トレンチコートが見当たらなかった」と述べられている。それにもかかわらず、同2〜5行目に、請求書にはトレンチコートの記載があり、請求書上の全額が請求されたことが書かれている。**1**の請求書を見ると、商品の最初の行に「女性用トレンチコート、黄褐色——100.00ドル」とあるので、(D)が正解。

179 What did Ms. Wong do before e-mailing customer service?

(A) She contacted her bank.
(B) She visited a nearby store location.
(C) She sent a damaged item back.
(D) She reordered the missing item.

Wongさんは顧客サービスにEメールを送る前に何をしましたか。

(A) 彼女は銀行に連絡した。
(B) 彼女は近くの店舗を訪れた。
(C) 彼女は破損商品を送り返した。
(D) 彼女は不足している商品を再注文した。

> **正解 A** Wongさんは顧客サービスに宛てたEメールである**2**の**❶** 4～5行目で、I also checked with my bank and received confirmation that I was charged for the full amount shown on the invoice.「また、私は銀行に問い合わせて、請求書にある全額を請求されたという確認を取った」と述べている。よって、(A)が正解。
> (B) nearby「すぐ近くの」。
> (C) damaged item「破損商品」。
> (D) **2**の**❷** 1～2行目に、不足していたトレンチコートについて「商品のキャンセルと返金をお願いします」とある。reorder「～を再注文する」。

180 What does the e-mail indicate about Ms. Wong?

(A) She frequently places orders with Patricia's Clothing.
(B) She is waiting to receive a new credit card.
(C) She recently changed her e-mail address.
(D) She will be traveling out of town soon.

Eメールは Wong さんについて何を示していますか。

(A) 彼女は頻繁にPatricia's衣料品店に注文している。
(B) 彼女は新しいクレジットカードを受け取るのを待っている。
(C) 彼女は最近Eメールアドレスを変えた。
(D) 彼女は間もなく町から離れて旅行する予定である。

> **正解 D** Wongさんは**2**のEメール**❷** 1～2行目で、I had been planning to take this coat with me on a trip in just a few days「私は、このコートをほんの数日後の旅行に持って行く計画を立てていた」と述べている。よって、(D)が正解。
> (A) frequently「頻繁に、たびたび」。

Words & Phrases

invoice 請求書

1 請求書 clothing 衣料品　purchase 購入　**❶** quantity 数量　item 商品　description 品目
trench coat トレンチコート　tan 黄褐色　striped しま模様の　sweater セーター
crew socks クルーソックス　★厚手の短い靴下　-pack ～個入りパック　long-sleeved 長袖の
blouse ブラウス　short-sleeved 半袖の　subtotal 小計　tax 税　shipping 送料
bank card （銀行発行の）クレジットカード、キャッシュカード　**❷** contact ～に連絡する
❸ return ～を返品する　within ～以内に　postal mail 郵便　location 所在地、位置
locate ～（の場所）を見つける

2 Eメール customer service 顧客サービス　to whom it may concern 担当者の方へ　**❶** regarding ～に関して
place an order 注文する　parcel 小包　missing 見当たらない　include ～を含む
list ～を（カタログなどに）載せる　be on back order （商品が）入荷待ちの状態である　confirmation 確認
be charged for ～ ～を請求されている　full amount 全額　**❷** in a few days 数日後に
cancel ～をキャンセルする　issue a refund 返金する

Expressions

check with ～ 「～に確認する、～に問い合わせる」（**2**の**❶** 4行目）

I will check with the Personnel Department again and get back to you.
もう一度人事部に確認して、あなたにお返事します。

TEST 2 PART 7

Questions 181-185 refer to the following e-mails.

To:	Carlos Redondo
From:	Meg Finley
Date:	March 6
Subject:	Inventory update

1通目のEメール

Hi Carlos,

Jim Herndon has sent me a list of a number of paperbacks that are selling poorly. Here is what I propose we do to sell some of them.

Memories of a Roadie by Teri Gerrity: It's an insider's perspective on the life of the support team that travels with musicians. Hardesty House Publishing (HHP) will be releasing Ms. Gerrity's new work in October. If we can put displays of *Memories of a Roadie* in the store windows at the same time, we could sell out our stock of 8,439 copies.

African Foundations by James Okuma: We have about 11,000 copies of this book left. It deals with the origins of political thought on the African continent. Given that several African countries will be having presidential elections this year, I suggest we feature Mr. Okuma's book in store displays on world events.

A Considered Point of View by Culp Dillon: This is a biography of the famous economist Judith Dartwell. With a new documentary about her groundbreaking work in economics now available on a popular streaming service, it may be possible to sell half of the 12,850 copies we have in stock.

Meg

To:	Meg Finley
From:	Carlos Redondo
Date:	March 7
Subject:	RE: Inventory update

2通目のEメール

Hi Meg,

Please give me tip sheets for the three titles. Our sales staff can promote all three when they next call stores. Regarding the displays for *Memories of a Roadie*, I will ask our team to link the release of *She Who Lived* to the timing of HHP's display. I've set a sales target of 10,000 copies; I am hopeful we will sell at least 7,500. Also, I just saw Jim Herndon in the hallway, and he mentioned three other titles with lagging sales: *Pitch Fast*, *Conditional Approval*, and *Middle of Center*. What are your thoughts about those?

Carlos

問題181-185は次の2通のEメールに関するものです。

受信者：Carlos Redondo
送信者：Meg Finley
日付：3月6日
件名：在庫の最新情報

Carlosさん

Jim Herndonが私に、売れ行きが悪い幾つものペーパーバックをリスト化したものを送ってきました。以下が、そのうちの一部を売るために私たちが何をすべきかの提案です。

Teri Gerrity著『ロックコンサートスタッフの思い出』：これはミュージシャンと共に旅をするサポートチームの生活を内部関係者の視点で描いたものです。Hardesty House出版社（HHP）は10月にGerrity氏の新作を発売する予定です。もし私たちが同時期にショーウインドーに『ロックコンサートスタッフの思い出』を展示することができれば、8,439部の在庫を売り切ることができるかもしれません。

James Okuma著『アフリカの根底』：この本は約11,000部残っています。これはアフリカ大陸における政治思想の起源を扱った本です。アフリカの数カ国で今年大統領選挙を行う予定であることを考慮に入れ、世界事情関連の店内陳列でOkuma氏の本を大きく取り上げることを提案します。

Culp Dillon著『熟慮された観点』：これは有名な経済学者Judith Dartwellの伝記です。経済学における彼女の革新的な活動に関する新しいドキュメンタリーが、人気のストリーミングサービスで現在視聴できますから、在庫の12,850部の半分を売ることが可能かもしれません。

Meg

受信者：Meg Finley
送信者：Carlos Redondo
日付：3月7日
件名：RE：在庫の最新情報

Megさん

私にその3点の本の情報シートを下さい。当社の営業スタッフが次に店舗に電話するときに、3点全部を宣伝することができます。『ロックコンサートスタッフの思い出』の展示に関しては、HHPの展示のタイミングを『彼女の軌跡』の発売と合わせるように当社のチームに頼んでみます。私は10,000部の販売目標を立てました。少なくとも7,500部を売ることを期待しています。また、廊下でJim Herndonにちょうど会いました。彼は売り上げが低迷する他の3点の本についても触れました。『速球投げ』、『条件付き承認』、『中道の真ん中』です。それらについてあなたはどうお考えですか。

Carlos

181 What is the purpose of the first e-mail?

    (A) To recommend an employee for a salary increase

    (B) To suggest that a company publish some new books

    (C) To give details about some books that need to be sold

    (D) To explain the benefits of a partnership with HHP

1通目のEメールの目的は何ですか。

    (A) 昇給にふさわしい従業員を推薦すること

    (B) 会社が新しい本を出版するよう提案すること

    (C) 売れるようにすべき本について詳細を述べること

    (D) HHPとの提携の利点を説明すること

> **正解 C** Meg FinleyさんがCarlos Redondoさん宛てに送信した1通目のEメールである**1**の❶1～2行目に、「Jim Herndonが私に、売れ行きが悪い幾つものペーパーバックをリスト化したものを送ってきた。以下が、そのうちの一部を売るために私たちが何をすべきかの提案だ」と述べられている。同❷～❹で、その提案の詳細が続くので、Megさんは売れるよう何らかの対処が必要な本について詳細を述べるためにEメールを書いたと判断できる。details「詳細」。
> (A) recommend ～ for …「～を…に適していると推薦する」、salary increase「昇給」。
> (D) explain「～を説明する」、benefit「利点」、partnership「提携、協力」。

182 What most likely is Mr. Herndon's role in the company?

    (A) He is the founder of the company.

    (B) He is a new member of the sales staff.

    (C) He heads the marketing department.

    (D) He keeps track of sales and inventory.

Herndonさんの会社での役割は何だと考えられますか。

    (A) 彼は会社の創立者である。

    (B) 彼は営業スタッフの新たな一員である。

    (C) 彼はマーケティング部の長である。

    (D) 彼は販売と在庫を記録している。

> **正解 D** Herndonさんについて、Megさんは1通目のEメールである**1**の❶1行目で、売れ行きが悪い本のリストを送ってきたと書いている。続けてMegさんは、同❷～❹でそのうちの3点の本の売り方について、詳細な在庫部数を提示しながら提案している。Carlosさんによる2通目のEメール**2**の❶4～5行目には、I just saw Jim Herndon in the hallway, and he mentioned three other titles with lagging sales「廊下でJim Herndonにちょうど会った。彼は売り上げが低迷する他の3点の本についても触れた」とある。これらから、Herndonさんの会社での役割は本の販売と在庫を把握することだと考えられる。keep track of ～「～を記録する、～の動静を把握している」。
> (A) founder「創立者」。
> (C) head「～の長である」、marketing department「マーケティング部」。

183 In the second e-mail, the word "promote" in paragraph 1, line 1, is closest in meaning to

    (A) raise the rank of

    (B) give publicity to

    (C) make an argument for

    (D) increase the amount of

2通目のEメールの第1段落・1行目にある"promote"に最も意味が近いのは

    (A) ～の位を上げる

    (B) ～の宣伝をする

    (C) ～を支持する論説を行う

    (D) ～の量を増やす

> **正解 B** Carlosさんは、Megさん宛てに送信した2通目のEメールである**2**の❶1行目で、売れ行きが悪い3点の本について、Please give me tip sheets for the three titles.「私にその3点の本の情報シートを下さい」と書いている。同1～2行目の該当の語を含む文は、「当社の営業スタッフが次に店舗に電話するときに、3点全部------ことができる」という意味。Carlosさんは、営業スタッフが店舗に対し販促活動を行う際に情報シートがあれば、これら3点の本を宣伝できる、と言っていると判断できる。

184 In the second e-mail, what is suggested about Mr. Redondo?

(A) He works for the same company as Mr. Herndon.
(B) He will reschedule a meeting with Ms. Finley.
(C) He will be visiting several bookstores.
(D) He is hiring additional salespeople.

2通目のEメールで、Redondoさんについて何が分かりますか。

(A) 彼はHerndonさんと同じ会社で働いている。
(B) 彼はFinleyさんとの会合の日時を変更する。
(C) 彼は幾つかの書店を訪れる予定である。
(D) 彼は追加の販売員を雇う。

正解 A Redondoさんとは2通目のEメールの送信者のこと。Carlos Redondoさんは**2**の**❶**1〜4行目で、Meg Finleyさんから伝えられた本の販売戦略の対応について述べている。さらに同**❶**4〜6行目で、「廊下でJim Herndonにちょうど会った。彼は売り上げが低迷する他の3点の本についても触れた」と書いている。廊下で出くわして仕事の話をしていることから、RedondoさんはHerndonさんと同じ会社で働いていると分かる。
(B) reschedule「〜の日時を変更する」。
(D) hire「〜を雇う」、additional「追加の」、salespeople「販売員」。

185 What is the title of Ms. Gerrity's new book?

(A) *She Who Lived*
(B) *Pitch Fast*
(C) *Conditional Approval*
(D) *Middle of Center*

Gerrity氏の新しい本のタイトルは何ですか。

(A) 『彼女の軌跡』
(B) 『速球投げ』
(C) 『条件付き承認』
(D) 『中道の真ん中』

正解 A Gerrity氏とは、1通目のEメールである**1**の**❷**より、*Memories of a Roadie*『ロックコンサートスタッフの思い出』という本の著者。同2〜3行目に、「Hardesty House出版社（HHP）は10月にGerrity氏の新作を発売する予定だ」と同著者の刊行の発売予定が述べられている。また、2通目のEメールである**2**の**❶**2〜3行目に『ロックコンサートスタッフの思い出』の展示に関して、I will ask our team to link the release of *She Who Lived* to the timing of HHP's display「HHPの展示のタイミングを『彼女の軌跡』の発売と合わせるように当社のチームに頼んでみる」とある。つまり、10月にHHPから発売されるGerrity氏の新しい本の書名は『彼女の軌跡』だと判断できるので、正解は(A)。
(B) (C) (D) **2**の**❶**5〜6行目より、「売り上げが低迷する他の3点の本」。

Words & Phrases

1 Eメール inventory 在庫　update 最新情報　**❶** a number of 〜 多くの〜、幾つかの〜　paperback ペーパーバック
sell poorly 売れ行きが悪い　propose (that) 〜 〜と提案する　**❷** roadie ロックコンサートの設営スタッフ
insider 内部の人、消息通　perspective 視点、考え方　publishing 出版業
release 〈動詞で〉〜を発売する、〈名詞で〉発売　work 作品　display 展示、陳列　at the same time 同時に
sell out 〜 〜を売り切る　stock 在庫　copy 部、冊　**❸** foundation 基礎、基盤　deal with 〜 〜を扱う
origin 起源　political thought 政治思想　continent 大陸　given that 〜 〜を考慮に入れると
presidential election 大統領選挙　feature 〜を大きく取り上げる　**❹** considered 熟考された
point of view 観点　biography 伝記　economist 経済学者　groundbreaking 革新的な
economics 経済学、経済的側面　available 利用可能で　streaming ストリーミング　possible 可能な
in stock 在庫があって

2 Eメール **❶** tip sheet 情報シート　★商品の特長や最新情報などが記載された内部資料　title （本などの）作品、タイトル
regarding 〜に関して　ask 〜 to *do* 〜に…するように頼む　link 〜 to … 〜を…につなぐ　timing タイミング
sales target 販売目標　be hopeful (that) 〜 〜を期待している　at least 少なくとも　hallway 廊下
mention 〜に言及する　lagging のろい、ぐずぐずした　pitch 投球する　conditional 条件付きの
approval 承認　middle 中間

Expressions

What are your thoughts about 〜? 「あなたは〜についてどう思いますか」（**2**の**❶**6行目）

What are your thoughts about **this new product**?
あなたはこの新商品についてどうお考えですか。

Questions 186-190 refer to the following notice, Web page, and online form.

Ooltewah Broadcasting Network

❶ The Ooltewah Broadcasting Network (OBN) is proud to be a leader in public programming for the local community. From informative documentaries and investigative local news to high school sports and children's programming, OBN makes it our mission to keep you informed.

❷ We could not do this without the generous support of viewers such as yourself! Here is just some of the quality programming that we are able to offer thanks to the contributions of viewers like you:

- *Greg Travels the World*—Follow our favorite foodie, Greg Romero, as he tries the delicacies of the world in countries like Peru, Morocco, and Japan.
- *Coaching the Game*—Get an inside view of how coaches train and motivate their teams.
- *Mysterious Earth*—Learn about wildlife from diverse climates around the world, such as the elephants that roam the Serengeti and the narwhals that swim in the Arctic waters.
- *The Wonderful Outdoors*—Child-development expert Mary Tisdale takes children on a journey in exploring the nature in their own backyards and parks.

❸ If you have enjoyed our programming, please consider joining our community of supporters. Contributing to OBN has never been easier! Simply visit our Web site at ooltewahbroadcastingnet.org/support for more information.

http://www.ooltewahbroadcastingnet.org/support

Support the Ooltewah Broadcasting Network

❶ Becoming a monthly donor of the Ooltewah Broadcasting Network is the best way to show your support for all the great programming OBN has to offer. Make monthly monetary contributions using your checking account or credit card. Donations can be paid automatically each month on the day of your choice.

❷ As a token of our appreciation for your generosity, OBN is proud to offer gifts to all supporters who pledge $20 or more per month. This year's gift is a smartphone case. Gifts change every year, so our supporters will always enjoy something new.

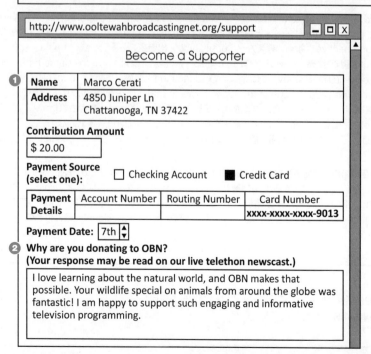

http://www.ooltewahbroadcastingnet.org/support

Become a Supporter

Name	Marco Cerati
Address	4850 Juniper Ln Chattanooga, TN 37422

Contribution Amount

$ 20.00

Payment Source (select one): ☐ Checking Account ■ Credit Card

Payment Details	Account Number	Routing Number	Card Number
			xxxx-xxxx-xxxx-9013

Payment Date: 7th ▲▼

❷ **Why are you donating to OBN?**
(Your response may be read on our live telethon newscast.)

I love learning about the natural world, and OBN makes that possible. Your wildlife special on animals from around the globe was fantastic! I am happy to support such engaging and informative television programming.

問題186-190は次のお知らせ、ウェブページ、オンラインのフォームに関するものです。

<u>Ooltewah放送ネットワーク社</u>

当Ooltewah放送ネットワーク社（OBN）は地域社会向け公共番組におけるトップ企業であることを誇りにしています。有益なドキュメンタリーや調査に基づく地域ニュースから高校生スポーツや子ども番組まで、OBNは皆さんに情報を提供し続けることを使命としております。

当社はあなたのような視聴者の方々の寛大なご支援なしに、これを成し遂げることはできません！以下はあなたのような視聴者の方々のご寄付のおかげで、当社が提供することのできる上質な番組のほんの数例です。
・『Gregの世界旅行』——ペルー、モロッコ、日本といった国々で、世界のごちそうを試す人気美食家Greg Romeroを追い掛けましょう。
・『競技をコーチする』——どのようにしてコーチがチームを教えたりやる気にさせたりするのか、その内情を見ることができます。
・『神秘的な地球』——世界中の多様な気候における野生生物について学ぶことができます。例えばセレンゲティ国立公園を歩き回るゾウや北極の海を泳ぐイッカクなど。
・『素晴らしい屋外』——児童発達の専門家Mary Tisdaleが、子どもたちを家の裏庭や公園での自然探検の旅に導きます。

当社の番組をお楽しみいただいていましたら、どうぞ支援者の輪に加わることをご検討ください。OBNへのご寄付はこれまでになく簡単になりました！詳しい情報を知るには、当社ウェブサイトooltewahbroadcastingnet.org/supportにアクセスするだけです。

---

http://www.ooltewahbroadcastingnet.org/support

Ooltewah放送ネットワーク社をご支援ください

Ooltewah放送ネットワーク社の月額寄付者になることは、OBNが提供する全ての素晴らしい番組への支援を示す最善の方法です。当座預金口座かクレジットカードをご利用になり、毎月定期的な寄付金をお願いします。寄付金はご自身で選んだ日に毎月自動的に払うことが可能です。

寛大なご寄付に対する感謝の印として、OBNは月ごとに20ドル以上の寄付を約束してくださる全支援者にギフトを贈呈します。今年のギフトはスマートフォンケースです。ギフトは毎年変わりますので、支援者の方々は常に新しいものを楽しむことができるでしょう。

---

http://www.ooltewahbroadcastingnet.org/support

支援者になってください

氏名	Marco Cerati
住所	ジュニパー通り4850番地 チャタヌーガ、TN 37422

寄付額

20.00ドル

支払い方法
（1つ選択）: □ 当座預金口座　■ クレジットカード

支払い詳細	口座番号	銀行支店コード	カード番号
			xxxx-xxxx-xxxx-9013

支払日： 7日

なぜOBNに寄付をなさるのですか。
（あなたの回答は当社の長時間ニュース生放送番組で読まれる可能性があります。）

私は自然界について学ぶことが大好きで、OBNはそれを可能にしてくれます。世界中の野生生物に関する御社の特別番組は素晴らしかったです！私はこのような魅力的で有益なテレビ番組を喜んで支援します。

186 According to the notice, what is true about Mr. Romero?

(A) He has traveled to many countries.
(B) He coaches a sports team.
(C) He is a nature photographer.
(D) He works with Ms. Tisdale.

お知らせによると、Romeroさんについて正しいことは何ですか。

(A) 彼は多くの国を旅している。
(B) 彼はスポーツチームをコーチしている。
(C) 彼は自然写真家である。
(D) 彼はTisdaleさんと働いている。

正解 A Ooltewah放送ネットワーク社のお知らせ**1**の**❷**に、同社の番組の一部が紹介されている。同4～6行目に*Greg Travels the World*—Follow our favorite foodie, Greg Romero, as he tries the delicacies of the world in countries like Peru, Morocco, and Japan. 「『Gregの世界旅行』――ペルー、モロッコ、日本といった国々で、世界のごちそうを試す人気美食家Greg Romeroを追い掛けよう」とある。Romeroさんは番組のために世界中を旅している美食家だと分かるので、(A)が正解。
(C) nature「自然」、photographer「写真家」。
(D) **1**の**❷** 12～14行目に『素晴らしい屋外』という児童発達の専門家Mary Tisdale出演の番組説明があるが、Romeroさんと一緒に働いているという記述はない。

187 What does the notice encourage the reader to do?

(A) Contact a news program
(B) Plan an overseas trip
(C) Attend a local event
(D) Go to a Web site

お知らせは読み手に何をするように勧めていますか。

(A) ニュース番組に連絡する
(B) 海外旅行を計画する
(C) 地元のイベントに参加する
(D) ウェブサイトにアクセスする

正解 D お知らせ**1**の**❸** 1～2行目では、視聴者にOBN支援者の輪に加わるよう呼び掛け、寄付を募っている。続けて、同3～4行目でSimply visit our Web site ...... for more information. 「詳しい情報を知るには、当社ウェブサイトにアクセスするだけだ」と同社のウェブサイトにアクセスするよう勧めているので、(D)が正解。encourage ～ to *do*「～に…するように勧める」。
(A) contact「～に連絡する」。
(B) overseas「海外の」。
(C) attend「～に参加する」、local「地元の」。

188 What does the Web page indicate about donations?

(A) They can be made in cash.
(B) They can be made automatically each month.
(C) They can be canceled at any time.
(D) They can be set up by sending an e-mail.

ウェブページは寄付について何を示していますか。

(A) 現金ですることが可能である。
(B) 毎月自動的にすることが可能である。
(C) いつでも中止することが可能である。
(D) Eメールの送信によって始めることが可能である。

正解 B Ooltewah放送ネットワーク社のウェブページ**2**の**❶** 1～2行目で、同社への月額寄付者になるよう呼び掛けており、同2～3行目で「当座預金口座かクレジットカードを利用して、毎月定期的な寄付金をお願いします」と寄付金の支払い方法を伝えている。続けて同3～4行目に、Donations can be paid automatically each month on the day of your choice. 「寄付金は自分で選んだ日に毎月自動的に払うことが可能だ」と書かれているので、(B)が正解。
(A) **2**の**❶** 2～3行目に、寄付の方法として案内があるのは当座預金口座かクレジットカードの2種のみ。in cash「現金で」。
(C) 寄付の中止方法については書かれていない。cancel「～を中止する」、at any time「いつでも」。
(D) **3**は、寄付を行うためのオンラインフォームだが、**2**にEメールによる申し込みについての言及はない。set up ～「～を始める、～を設定する」。

189 What is most likely true about Mr. Cerati?

    (A) He recently moved to Chattanooga.

    (B) He will receive a smartphone case.

    (C) He has made donations to OBN for several years.

    (D) He was featured on a live television program.

Ceratiさんについて正しいと考えられることは何ですか。

    (A) 彼は最近チャタヌーガに引っ越した。

    (B) 彼はスマートフォンケースを受け取る。

    (C) 彼はOBNに数年間寄付をしている。

    (D) 彼はテレビ生番組で大きく取り上げられた。

> **正解 B** Ceratiさんとは、**3**Ooltewah放送ネットワーク社への寄付申し込みオンラインフォームの**❶**の「氏名」欄にある名前で、「寄付額」の欄には「20.00ドル」とある。一方、ウェブページ**2**の**❷**1～2行目に寄付への感謝の印として、「OBNは月ごとに20ドル以上の寄付を約束してくれる全支援者にギフトを贈呈する。今年のギフトはスマートフォンケースだ」と書かれている。よって、20ドルの寄付を申し出たCeratiさんはスマートフォンケースを受け取ると考えられる。
> (D) **3**の**❷**2行目に、回答はニュース番組で読まれる可能性がある、と注意書きがあるが、Ceratiさんが実際に番組で取り上げられたとは述べられていない。feature「～を大きく取り上げる」。

190 What television program did Mr. Cerati enjoy?

    (A) *Greg Travels the World*

    (B) *Coaching the Game*

    (C) *Mysterious Earth*

    (D) *The Wonderful Outdoors*

Ceratiさんはどのテレビ番組を楽しみましたか。

    (A) 『Gregの世界旅行』

    (B) 『競技をコーチする』

    (C) 『神秘的な地球』

    (D) 『素晴らしい屋外』

> **正解 C** オンラインフォーム**3**の**❷**1行目の「なぜOBNに寄付をするのですか」という質問の記述欄に「私は自然界について学ぶことが大好きで、OBNはそれを可能にしてくれる。世界中の野生生物に関する御社の特別番組は素晴らしかった」とCeratiさんは書いている。お知らせ**1**の**❷**9～11行目を見ると、*Mysterious Earth*『神秘的な地球』がゾウやイッカクなどの野生生物を取り上げた番組であることが分かるので、Ceratiさんが楽しんだテレビ番組は(C) *Mysterious Earth*。

Words & Phrases

1 お知らせ   broadcasting 放送   **❶** be proud to *do* ～することを誇りに思う   leader トップ企業、リーダー
public programming 公共番組   local community 地域社会   informative 有益な、情報に富む
investigative 調査に基づく   mission 使命   informed 情報に通じた   **❷** generous 寛大な
viewer 視聴者   quality 上質な   thanks to ～ ～のおかげで   contribution 寄付
follow ～について行く   foodie 美食家   delicacy 美味、きめ細かさ   coach ～をコーチする
inside 内側の、内情に通じた   view 見方   motivate ～に動機を与える   mysterious 神秘的な
earth 地球   wildlife 野生生物   diverse 多様な   climate 気候   roam ～を歩き回る
the Serengeti セレンゲティ国立公園   narwhal イッカク   Arctic 北極の   outdoors 屋外
development 発達   expert 専門家   journey 旅   explore ～を探検する   backyard 裏庭
❸ consider *doing* ～することを検討する   supporter 支援者   contribute to ～ ～に寄付する
simply ただ～のみ

2 ウェブページ   **❶** monthly 毎月の   donor 寄付者   monetary 金銭的な   checking account 当座預金口座
credit card クレジットカード   donation 寄付、寄付金   automatically 自動的に
of *one's* choice 自分で選んだ   **❷** token 印   appreciation 感謝   generosity 寛大さ
pledge ～(寄付など)を約束する   per ～につき

3 フォーム   **❶** ～ Ln ～通り ★Laneの略   amount 額   payment 支払い   source 源、供給源   select ～を選ぶ
details 詳細   account number 口座番号   routing number 銀行支店コード
❷ donate to ～ ～に寄付する   response 返答   live 生の
telethon 長時間テレビ放送 ★慈善の寄付などを呼び掛ける番組   newscast ニュース放送
natural world 自然界   possible 可能な   special 特別番組   around the globe 世界中の
fantastic 素晴らしい   engaging 魅力がある

Expressions

such as ～ 「～のような」（**1**の**❷**1～2行目、同10～11行目）

Social networking sites, such as Smileface and Birdie, have become popular places to interact with other people.
SmilefaceやBirdieのようなソーシャルネットワーキングサイトは、他者と交流する人気の場所になっています。

Questions 191-195 refer to the following advertisement, Web page, and e-mail.

YOUTH ARTS FESTIVAL

The annual Leyton Youth Arts Festival features the work of promising artists aged 14 to 24. A panel of experts will critique entries, and the public is invited to exhibitions and live demonstrations at Leyton Town Hall.

Highlights will include the following:

- *Painting Showcase*—April 2 to 4. View original contemporary paintings by young artists.
- *Textile Art*—April 6 to 8. Witness artists create tapestries and more using a variety of weaving techniques. Artists will welcome your questions about their looms and the materials that they use.
- *Sculpture Garden*—April 10 to 12. Walk outside in the town hall's gardens to see classical and modern creations by young sculptors.
- *Furniture Design*—April 14 to 16. See the future of practical household items handcrafted by young designers.
- *Art in an Hour*—April 17. Observe artists as they race to complete a detailed sketch of a model in only 60 minutes. Ask the artists questions as they work—but not too many since they will be very busy!

To see the full brochure, visit our Web site at www.lyafestival.org.

http:// www.lyafestival.org/meet_the_judges ▶

Esme Bacanu writes:

"As a child, there was nothing more fascinating to me than the feel, weight, and color of cloth. Making one's living as an artist is difficult. Having completed almost 100 tapestries in response to commissions from patrons of the art form, I hope I can offer advice and support in my capacity as a judge and mentor to the talented young people who might follow in my footsteps."

To:	publicity@lyafestival.org
From:	sphillips@phillipsfootwear.com
Date:	January 12
Subject:	Brochure

Dear Ms. Marwick,

I would like to place an advertisement for my business on the Web site for this year's youth arts festival. I submitted the online form for a half-page advertisement today but am currently awaiting the finalized image from the ad company. Could you tell me when the final deadline is to submit the finished artwork? Also, I would like to place posters in my shop window to advertise the festival. Do you have any to share?

The Phillips family has supported the arts for generations. My wife and I have been volunteering in arts programs in local schools for years. In addition, we are fans of Esme Bacanu, and so we are very excited to hear that she will be involved with the festival this year!

Kind regards,

Stanley Phillips
Owner, Phillips Footwear

問題191-195は次の広告、ウェブページ、Eメールに関するものです。

ユース・アート・フェスティバル

毎年恒例のLeytonユース・アート・フェスティバルは14歳から24歳の前途有望な芸術家の作品を取り上げます。専門家による審査員団が出品作品を批評します。そして、一般の方々がLeyton市役所での展示会や生での実演に招かれます。

見どころは以下のものを含む予定です：
・『絵画ショーケース』――4月2日から4日まで。若い芸術家たちによる独創的な現代絵画をご覧ください。
・『織物アート』――4月6日から8日まで。芸術家たちがさまざまな製織技術を使ってタペストリーとその他の作品を作り出すのをご覧ください。芸術家は自分たちの使う織機や素材についての皆さんからの質問を歓迎します。
・『彫刻ガーデン』――4月10日から12日まで。若い彫刻家たちによる古典的な作品や現代的な作品を見るために、市役所の屋外庭園を散策してください。
・『家具デザイン』――4月14日から16日まで。若いデザイナーたちによって手作りされた実用的な生活用品の未来の姿をご覧ください。
・『1時間のアート』――4月17日。芸術家たちがたった60分でモデルの詳細なスケッチを完成させようと競い合う様子をご覧ください。芸術家たちが作業する傍らで、質問をすることができます――しかし彼らはとても忙しいでしょうから、あまりたくさんにならないように！

完全版パンフレットをご覧になるには、当フェスティバルのウェブサイトwww.lyafestival.orgにアクセスしてください。

---

http://www.lyafestival.org/meet_the_judges

Esme Bacanuは次のように書いています：

「子どもの頃、私にとって布の感触、重さ、色は何よりも魅力的なものでした。芸術家として生計を立てるのは難しいことです。私はこの芸術分野の後援者からの依頼を受けて、これまでに100近くものタペストリーを完成させてきましたので、審査員兼指導者という立場で、私の後に続くかもしれない才能ある若者に助言や支援をしたいと考えています」

受信者：publicity@lyafestival.org
送信者：sphillips@phillipsfootwear.com
日付：1月12日
件名：パンフレット

Marwick様

今年のユース・アート・フェスティバルのウェブサイトに当店の広告を出したいと思っております。本日、半ページの広告のためオンラインフォームを提出しましたが、現在広告会社からの最終画像を待っているところです。完成図版を提出する最終期限はいつか教えていただけますか。また、当店のショーウインドーにこのフェスティバルを宣伝するポスターを貼りたいと思っております。何枚か分けていただくものはありますか。

Phillips家は何世代にもわたって芸術を支援してきました。妻と私は何年もの間、地元の学校の芸術プログラムでボランティアをしています。さらに、私たちはEsme Bacanuのファンであり、彼女が今年フェスティバルに関わると聞いて大変興奮しております！

敬具

Stanley Phillips
Phillips履物店オーナー

191 What does the advertisement indicate about the youth arts festival?

    (A) It will take place at an art studio.
    (B) It is being held for the first time.
    (C) It will take place every day in April.
    (D) It includes reviews by arts specialists.

広告はユース・アート・フェスティバルについて何を示していますか。

    (A) それはアトリエで開催される予定である。
    (B) それは初めて開催される。
    (C) それは4月に毎日開催される予定である。
    (D) それは芸術の専門家による批評を含む。

正解 D ユース・アート・フェスティバルの広告 1 の❶ 1～2行目に、有望な若い芸術家たちの作品が取り上げられることが述べられ、同2行目にA panel of experts will critique entries「専門家による審査員団が出品作品を批評する」と書かれている。このexpertsは芸術作品を批評することができる専門家たちと分かるので、(D)が正解。review「批評」、specialist「専門家」。
(A) take place「開催される」、art studio「アトリエ」。
(B) 1 の❶ 1行目に「毎年恒例の」とあるので、初開催ではない。be held「開催される」、for the first time「初めて」。

---

192 What is the public asked to do during the event of April 17?

    (A) Leave the exhibition area after an hour
    (B) Limit their interaction with the artists
    (C) Vote for their favorite creation
    (D) Purchase works of the artists

4月17日のイベントの間、一般の人は何をするように求められていますか。

    (A) 1時間後に展示エリアを去る
    (B) 芸術家との交流を制限する
    (C) お気に入りの作品に投票する
    (D) 芸術家の作品を購入する

正解 B 「4月17日のイベント」とは、広告 1 の❷の最後に書かれているArt in an Hour「1時間のアート」のこと。その内容説明に「芸術家たちがたった60分でモデルの詳細なスケッチを完成させようと競い合う様子を見てください。芸術家たちが作業する傍らで、質問をすることができる──しかし彼らはとても忙しいだろうから、あまりたくさんにならないように」と芸術家に質問をする際はその数を制限するよう求めている。芸術家に質問することを芸術家との交流と言い換えている(B)が正解。limit「～を制限する」、interaction「交流」。
(A) 1 の❷の最後のイベント『1時間のアート』にある1時間とはスケッチの完成時間であり、一般の人の滞在時間を制限してはいない。leave「～を去る、～を離れる」。
(C) vote for ～「～に投票する」。

---

193 On what dates will Ms. Bacanu most likely work at the festival?

    (A) April 2 to April 4
    (B) April 6 to April 8
    (C) April 10 to April 12
    (D) April 14 to April 16

Bacanuさんはどの期間にフェスティバルで仕事をすると考えられますか。

    (A) 4月2日から4月4日まで
    (B) 4月6日から4月8日まで
    (C) 4月10日から4月12日まで
    (D) 4月14日から4月16日まで

正解 B Bacanuさんは、ウェブページ 2 の❶ 1～2行目で、子どもの頃から布が好きだったと述べ、続けて同2～5行目で「この芸術分野の後援者からの依頼を受けて、これまでに100近くものタペストリーを完成させてきたので、審査員兼指導者という立場で、私の後に続くかもしれない才能ある若者に助言や支援をしたい」と書いている。広告 1 を確認すると❷の2つ目のイベントにTextile Art ─ April 6 to 8.「織物アート」──4月6日から8日まで」とあり、タペストリーの制作が行われると説明されている。よって、Bacanuさんは自らの専門分野である織物の実演などが行われる4月6日から4月8日まで仕事をすると考えられる。

Expressions

in addition 「さらに、その上」(3 の❷2行目)

It will cost a lot of money to carry out the plan. In addition, there are many technical problems to be solved.
その計画を実行するには多くのお金がかかるでしょう。さらに、解決すべき多くの技術的な問題があります。

194 Why is Mr. Phillips concerned about a deadline?

    (A) He has not been informed about a volunteer position.

    (B) He wants more time to print posters.

    (C) His advertisement is not finished yet.

    (D) He needs to leave town for a business trip.

Phillipsさんはなぜ締め切りについて心配していますか。

    (A) 彼はボランティアの職務について知らされていない。

    (B) 彼はポスターを印刷する時間がもっとほしい。

    (C) 彼の広告はまだ仕上がっていない。

    (D) 彼は出張で町を出る必要がある。

正解 C Phillipsさんとは **3** の署名から、このEメールの送信者。履物店オーナーのPhillipsさんは、同 **①** 2行目で、ユース・アート・フェスティバルに店の広告を出すためのフォームを提出したと述べている。同2〜4行目で I ...... am currently awaiting the finalized image from the ad company. Could you tell me when the final deadline is to submit the finished artwork?「現在広告会社からの最終画像を待っているところだ。完成図版を提出する最終期限はいつか教えてもらえるか」と尋ねている。つまり、Phillipsさんはまだ図版が入手できず広告が仕上がっていないため締め切りを心配していることが分かる。(C)が正解。
(A) inform「〜に知らせる」。

195 What is true about both Ms. Bacanu and Mr. Phillips?

    (A) They work in related lines of business.

    (B) They want to support young people in the arts.

    (C) They attended Leyton High School together.

    (D) They think careers in the arts can be difficult.

BacanuさんとPhillipsさんについて正しいことは何ですか。

    (A) 彼らは関連した業種で働いている。

    (B) 彼らは芸術の分野で若者を支援したい。

    (C) 彼らは一緒にLeyton高校に通っていた。

    (D) 彼らは芸術の仕事は困難であり得ると考えている。

正解 B タペストリー作家のBacanuさんは、ウェブページ **2** の **①** 3〜5行目に「私の後に続くかもしれない才能ある若者に助言や支援をしたい」と書いている。一方、PhillipsさんはEメール **3** の **②** 1行目でPhillips家が代々芸術を支援してきたことに言及し、同1〜2行目で、「妻と私は何年もの間、地元の学校の芸術プログラムでボランティアをしている」と述べている。よって、BacanuさんとPhillipsさんは芸術分野で若者を支援したいと考えていると判断できる。
(A) related「関連した」、line of business「業種」。
(D) Bacanuさんは、**2** の **①** 2行目に「芸術家として生計を立てるのは難しい」と書いているが、Phillipsさんはそのようなことを述べていない。

Words & Phrases

1 広告
youth 若者、青年 **①** annual 毎年恒例の feature 〜を大きく取り上げる promising 前途有望な
aged 〜歳の panel 審査員団 expert 専門家 critique 〜を批評する entry 出品作品
the public 一般の人々 exhibition 展示会 live 生の demonstration 実演 town hall 市役所
② highlight 呼び物、見どころ include 〜を含む the following 次のもの showcase 展示の場
view 〜を見る original 独創的な contemporary 現代の textile 織物 witness 〜を目撃する
create 〜を作り出す tapestry タペストリー a variety of 〜 さまざまな〜 weave 織物を織る
technique 技術 loom 織機 material 素材 sculpture 彫刻 classical 古典的な
modern 現代的な creation 作品 sculptor 彫刻家 practical 実用的な household item 生活用品
handcraft 〜を手作りする observe 〜を観察する race 競争する complete 〜を完成させる
detailed 詳細な sketch スケッチ **③** full 完全な brochure パンフレット

2 ウェブページ
① fascinating 魅力的な feel 感触 weight 重さ cloth 布
make one's living as 〜 〜として生計を立てる in response to 〜 〜に応えて commission 委託、注文
patron 後援者 art form 芸術形式 in one's capacity as 〜 〜という立場で、〜の資格で judge 審査員
mentor 指導者 talented 才能のある follow in one's footsteps 〜の例に倣う

3 Eメール
① place 〜(広告など)を出す submit 〜を提出する、〜を送信する half-page 半ページの
currently 現在 await 〜を待つ finalize 〜を仕上げる image 画像
ad 広告 ★advertisementの略 final deadline 最終期限 finished 完成した artwork 図版、挿絵
advertise 〜を宣伝する share 〜を分ける **②** for generations 何世代にもわたって
volunteer ボランティアをする local 地元の be excited to do 〜して興奮している
be involved with 〜 〜に関わっている

Questions 196-200 refer to the following Web pages and e-mail.

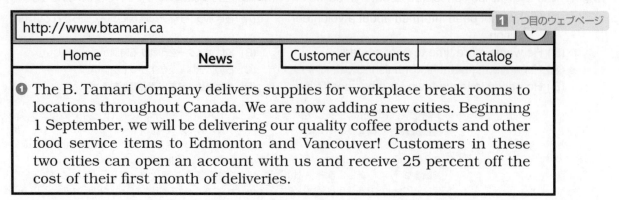

http://www.btamari.ca

1 つ目のウェブページ

| Home | **News** | Customer Accounts | Catalog |

❶ The B. Tamari Company delivers supplies for workplace break rooms to locations throughout Canada. We are now adding new cities. Beginning 1 September, we will be delivering our quality coffee products and other food service items to Edmonton and Vancouver! Customers in these two cities can open an account with us and receive 25 percent off the cost of their first month of deliveries.

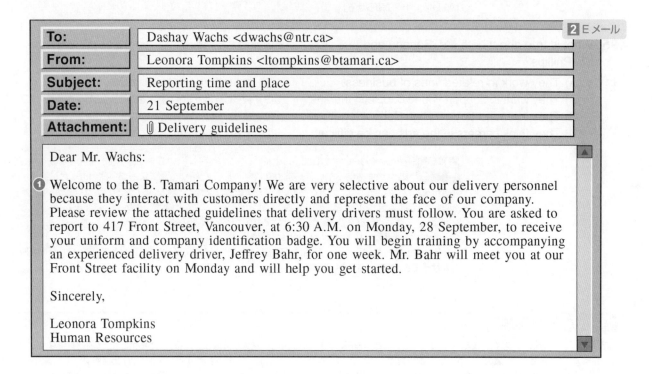

2 E メール

To:	Dashay Wachs <dwachs@ntr.ca>
From:	Leonora Tompkins <ltompkins@btamari.ca>
Subject:	Reporting time and place
Date:	21 September
Attachment:	🔗 Delivery guidelines

Dear Mr. Wachs:

❶ Welcome to the B. Tamari Company! We are very selective about our delivery personnel because they interact with customers directly and represent the face of our company. Please review the attached guidelines that delivery drivers must follow. You are asked to report to 417 Front Street, Vancouver, at 6:30 A.M. on Monday, 28 September, to receive your uniform and company identification badge. You will begin training by accompanying an experienced delivery driver, Jeffrey Bahr, for one week. Mr. Bahr will meet you at our Front Street facility on Monday and will help you get started.

Sincerely,

Leonora Tompkins
Human Resources

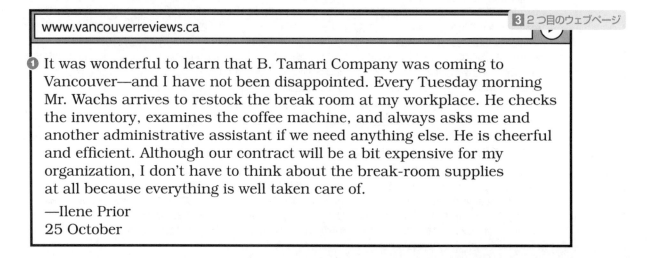

www.vancouverreviews.ca

3 2 つ目のウェブページ

❶ It was wonderful to learn that B. Tamari Company was coming to Vancouver—and I have not been disappointed. Every Tuesday morning Mr. Wachs arrives to restock the break room at my workplace. He checks the inventory, examines the coffee machine, and always asks me and another administrative assistant if we need anything else. He is cheerful and efficient. Although our contract will be a bit expensive for my organization, I don't have to think about the break-room supplies at all because everything is well taken care of.

—Ilene Prior
25 October

問題196-200は次の2つのウェブページとEメールに関するものです。

http://www.btamari.ca

ホーム	**ニュース**	顧客アカウント	カタログ

B. Tamari社は職場の休憩室備品をカナダ中の所在地に配達します。当社は現在新しい市を追加しています。9月1日より、当社の上質なコーヒー製品や他の食品類をエドモントンとバンクーバーにお届けします! この2都市のお客さまは、当社でアカウントを作っていただくと、最初の1カ月のお届け品の代金から25パーセント割引を受けることができます。

受信者：Dashay Wachs <dwachs@ntr.ca>
送信者：Leonora Tompkins <ltompkins@btamari.ca>
件名：出勤時刻と場所
日付：9月21日
添付ファイル：配達ガイドライン

Wachs様

B. Tamari社へようこそ! 当社は配達職員を非常に慎重に選んでいます。お客さまと直接交流して当社の顔となるからです。配達運転手が従わなければならない添付のガイドラインをよく確認してください。制服と社員IDバッジを受け取るため、9月28日月曜日の午前6時30分にバンクーバーのフロント通り417番地に出向いてください。経験豊富な配達運転手Jeffrey Bahrに1週間同行することから訓練を始めていただきます。Bahrさんは月曜日にフロント通りの当社施設であなたと落ち合い、あなたが仕事を始める手助けをしてくれます。

敬具

Leonora Tompkins
人事部

---

www.vancouverreviews.ca

B. Tamari社がバンクーバーにやって来ると知るのは素晴らしいことでした――そしてこれまで期待外れに思ったことはありません。毎週火曜日の朝、Wachsさんは私の職場の休憩室の備品補充に来ます。彼は在庫をチェックし、コーヒーマシンを調べ、いつも私ともう一人の管理補佐に何か他に必要な品がないか尋ねてくれます。彼は快活で有能です。契約はうちの組織にとっては少々高額でしょうが、全てのことがよく管理されているので、私が休憩室の備品について考える必要は全くありません。

――Ilene Prior
10月25日

196 What is the purpose of the first Web page?

 (A) To announce new service areas
 (B) To explain a break-room policy
 (C) To advertise an accounting service
 (D) To describe the history of a company

1つ目のウェブページの目的は何ですか。

 (A) 新しいサービス区域を発表すること
 (B) 休憩室の方針を説明すること
 (C) 会計業務を宣伝すること
 (D) 会社の歴史を述べること

> **正解 A** ❶の❶1〜2行目より、1つ目のウェブページは、休憩室備品をカナダ国内の職場に提供するB. Tamari社のものと分かる。同2〜4行目にWe are now adding new cities.「当社は現在新しい市を追加している」とあり、「9月1日より、当社の上質なコーヒー製品や他の食品類をエドモントンとバンクーバーに届ける」と書かれている。新たにエドモントンとバンクーバーの2都市に、コーヒーなどの配達サービスを開始することを知らせる内容なので、(A)が正解。announce「〜を発表する」。
> (B) explain「〜を説明する」、policy「方針」。
> (C) advertise「〜を宣伝する」、accounting service「会計業務」。
> (D) describe「〜を述べる」。

197 What has been sent with the e-mail?

 (A) A parking permit
 (B) A list of instructions
 (C) A building pass
 (D) A summary of company benefits

Eメールと共に何が送られましたか。

 (A) 駐車許可証
 (B) 指示のリスト
 (C) 建物の通行証
 (D) 会社の給付金の概要

> **正解 B** ❷のEメールは冒頭の歓迎の言葉と最下行にある差出人の所属部署から、B. Tamari社人事部のTompkinsさんがWachsさん宛てに送信したものと分かる。Attachment「添付ファイル」欄にはDelivery guidelines「配達ガイドライン」とある。また、同❶3行目にPlease review the attached guidelines that delivery drivers must follow.「配達運転手が従わなければならない添付のガイドラインをよく確認してください」と述べられているので、(B)が正解。instructions「指示」。
> (A) parking permit「駐車許可証」。
> (C) pass「通行証」。
> (D) summary「概要」、benefits「給付金」。

198 What is suggested about Mr. Wachs?

 (A) He lives in Edmonton.
 (B) He has prior experience as a delivery driver.
 (C) He has just received a job promotion.
 (D) He will be reporting to a newly opened facility.

Wachsさんについて何が分かりますか。

 (A) 彼はエドモントンに住んでいる。
 (B) 彼は配達運転手としての過去の経験がある。
 (C) 彼はちょうど昇進をしたところである。
 (D) 彼は新たに開設した施設に出向く予定である。

> **正解 D** Eメール❷の❶3〜5行目で、Wachsさんは制服と社員IDバッジの受け取りを求められており、You are asked to report to 417 Front Street, Vancouver, at 6:30 A.M. on Monday, 28 September「9月28日月曜日の午前6時30分にバンクーバーのフロント通り417番地に出向いてください」と指示を受けている。1つ目のウェブページ❶の❶3〜4行目に、9月1日から配達を開始する都市として、we will be delivering our quality coffee products and other food service items to Edmonton and Vancouver「当社の上質なコーヒー製品や他の食品類をエドモントンとバンクーバーに届ける」と書かれているので、バンクーバーには新たに開設した配達拠点施設があると判断できる。よって、Wachsさんが出向くのは同社のバンクーバーの新施設ということになるので、(D)が正解。newly「新たに」。
> (B) ❷の❶6行目に「経験豊富な配達運転手」と書かれているのはJeffrey Bahrさん。prior「過去の」。
> (C) job promotion「昇進」。

Expressions

help 〜 do 「〜が…するのを手伝う」（❷の❶7行目）

I would appreciate it if you could help me start my new business.
私が新しいビジネスを始めるのを手伝っていただけるとありがたく思います。

199 What is most likely true about Ms. Prior's workplace?

(A) It benefited from a monthlong service discount.

(B) It requested a change in delivery personnel.

(C) Its break room is not used very frequently.

(D) Its offices have just moved to Front Street.

Prior さんの職場について正しいと考えられることは何ですか。

(A) 1カ月間のサービスの割引で得をした。

(B) 配達職員の変更を要求した。

(C) 休憩室はあまり頻繁には使われていない。

(D) オフィスがちょうどフロント通りに移転したところである。

正解 A　2つ目のウェブページ3は、Prior さんによって書かれたもの。同❶1～2行目に「B. Tamari 社がバンクーバーにやって来ると知るのは素晴らしいことだった――そしてこれまで期待外れだと思ったことはない」とある。続いて休憩室備品の補充に来るWachs さんのことが述べられており、バンクーバーにあるPrior さんの職場がB. Tamari 社を利用していると分かる。1つ目のウェブページ1の❶4～6行目に「この2都市（＝エドモントンとバンクーバー）の顧客は当社でアカウントを作ると、最初の1カ月のお届け品の代金から25パーセント割引を受けることができる」と書かれているので、バンクーバーにあるPrior さんの職場が1カ月間の品代の割引で得をしたと考えられる。benefit from ～「～で得をする、～から恩恵を受ける」、monthlong「1カ月続く」、discount「割引」。
(C) frequently「頻繁に」。

200 What does Ms. Prior indicate in the second Web page?

(A) An order for supplies was incorrect.

(B) Mr. Wachs has made her job easier.

(C) She checks the break-room inventory weekly.

(D) She would prefer a later delivery time.

Prior さんは2つ目のウェブページで何を示していますか。

(A) 備品の注文が間違っていた。

(B) Wachs さんが彼女の仕事を以前より楽にしている。

(C) 彼女は毎週休憩室の在庫を調べる。

(D) 彼女にはもっと遅い配送時間の方が好ましい。

正解 B　Prior さんは、2つ目のウェブページ3の❶2～3行目で、毎週火曜日に職場にやって来る配達員Wachs さんが休憩室備品の補充をしてくれることを述べた後、同3～5行目で、「彼はいつも私ともう一人の管理補佐に何か他に必要な品がないか尋ねてくれる」と書いている。よって、Wachs さんが行う休憩室備品補充の担当者はPrior さんであると判断でき、同❶7～8行目に「全てのことがよく管理されているので、私が休憩室の備品について考える必要は全くない」とあるので、Wachs さんのおかげでPrior さんの仕事が以前より楽になっていると考えられる。
(C) 3の❶7～8行目で、Prior さんが「私が休憩室の備品について考える必要は全くない」と述べているのと矛盾する。休憩室の在庫は毎週Wachs さんが調べている。weekly「毎週」。
(D) prefer「～をより好む」。

Words & Phrases

1 ウェブページ　customer account 顧客アカウント　❶ deliver ～を配達する　supplies 備品、用品　workplace 職場　break room 休憩室　location 所在地　throughout ～中の　add ～を加える　quality 上質な　item 品物　cost 費用　delivery 配達物、配達

2 Eメール　reporting time 出勤時刻　guidelines ガイドライン　❶ selective 入念に選択する　personnel 職員、人員　interact with ～ ～と交流する　represent ～を表す　review ～を見直す　attached 添付の　follow ～に従う　be asked to do ～するように求められている　report to ～ ～に出向く　uniform 制服　identification badge IDバッジ　accompany ～に同行する　experienced 経験豊富な　facility 施設　get started 始める　human resources 人事部

3 ウェブページ　❶ disappointed 失望した　restock ～に補充する　inventory 在庫　examine ～を調べる　administrative 管理の　assistant 補佐　cheerful 快活な　efficient 有能な　contract 契約　a bit 少し　organization 組織　take care of ～ ～の世話をする

CDトラック・特典音声ファイル 一覧表

● CD1

Test	Track No.	Contents
サンプル問題	1	タイトル
	2	Listening Test Directions/ Part 1 Directions
	3	Q1
	4	Part 2 Directions
	5	Q2, Q3
	6	Part 3 Directions
	7	Q4-6
	8	Q7-9
	9	Part 4 Directions
	10	Q10-12
TEST 1	11	Test 1
	12	Listening Test Directions/ Part 1 Directions
	13	Q1
	14	Q2
	15	Q3
	16	Q4
	17	Q5
	18	Q6
	19	Part 2 Directions
	20	Q7
	21	Q8
	22	Q9
	23	Q10
	24	Q11
	25	Q12
	26	Q13
	27	Q14
	28	Q15
	29	Q16
	30	Q17
	31	Q18
	32	Q19
	33	Q20
	34	Q21
	35	Q22
	36	Q23
	37	Q24
	38	Q25
	39	Q26
	40	Q27
	41	Q28
	42	Q29
	43	Q30
	44	Q31
	45	Part 3 Directions

Test	Track No.	Contents
TEST 1	46	Part 3 Q32-34 会話
	47	Q32-34 問題
	48	Q35-37 会話
	49	Q35-37 問題
	50	Q38-40 会話
	51	Q38-40 問題
	52	Q41-43 会話
	53	Q41-43 問題
	54	Q44-46 会話
	55	Q44-46 問題
	56	Q47-49 会話
	57	Q47-49 問題
	58	Q50-52 会話
	59	Q50-52 問題
	60	Q53-55 会話
	61	Q53-55 問題
	62	Q56-58 会話
	63	Q56-58 問題
	64	Q59-61 会話
	65	Q59-61 問題
	66	Q62-64 会話
	67	Q62-64 問題
	68	Q65-67 会話
	69	Q65-67 問題
	70	Q68-70 会話
	71	Q68-70 問題
	72	Part 4 Directions
	73	Q71-73 トーク
	74	Q71-73 問題
	75	Q74-76 トーク
	76	Q74-76 問題
	77	Q77-79 トーク
	78	Q77-79 問題
	79	Q80-82 トーク
	80	Q80-82 問題
	81	Q83-85 トーク
	82	Q83-85 問題
	83	Q86-88 トーク
	84	Q86-88 問題
	85	Q89-91 トーク
	86	Q89-91 問題
	87	Q92-94 トーク
	88	Q92-94 問題
	89	Q95-97 トーク
	90	Q95-97 問題
	91	Q98-100 トーク
	92	Q98-100 問題

● CD2

Test	Track No.	Contents
TEST 2	1	Test 2
	2	Listening Test Directions/ Part 1 Directions
	3	Q1
	4	Q2
	5	Q3
	6	Q4
	7	Q5
	8	Q6
	9	Part 2 Directions
	10	Q7
	11	Q8
	12	Q9
	13	Q10
	14	Q11
	15	Q12
	16	Q13
	17	Q14
	18	Q15
	19	Q16
	20	Q17
	21	Q18
	22	Q19
	23	Q20
	24	Q21
	25	Q22
	26	Q23
	27	Q24
	28	Q25
	29	Q26
	30	Q27
	31	Q28
	32	Q29
	33	Q30
	34	Q31
	35	Part 3 Directions
	36	Q32-34 会話
	37	Q32-34 問題
	38	Q35-37 会話
	39	Q35-37 問題
	40	Q38-40 会話
	41	Q38-40 問題
	42	Q41-43 会話
	43	Q41-43 問題
	44	Q44-46 会話
	45	Q44-46 問題
	46	Q47-49 会話

次ページの「音声を使った学習例の紹介」を参考に、問題に解答した後の学習用教材としてもご活用ください。

音声ダウンロードの手順▶本誌 p.3　音声を使った学習例▶別冊 p.200

Test	Track No.	Contents
TEST 2	47	Part 3 Q47-49 問題
	48	Q50-52 会話
	49	Q50-52 問題
	50	Q53-55 会話
	51	Q53-55 問題
	52	Q56-58 会話
	53	Q56-58 問題
	54	Q59-61 会話
	55	Q59-61 問題
	56	Q62-64 会話
	57	Q62-64 問題
	58	Q65-67 会話
	59	Q65-67 問題
	60	Q68-70 会話
	61	Q68-70 問題
	62	Part 4 Directions
	63	Q71-73 トーク
	64	Q71-73 問題
	65	Q74-76 トーク
	66	Q74-76 問題
	67	Q77-79 トーク
	68	Q77-79 問題
	69	Q80-82 トーク
	70	Q80-82 問題
	71	Q83-85 トーク
	72	Q83-85 問題
	73	Q86-88 トーク
	74	Q86-88 問題
	75	Q89-91 トーク
	76	Q89-91 問題
	77	Q92-94 トーク
	78	Q92-94 問題
	79	Q95-97 トーク
	80	Q95-97 問題
	81	Q98-100 トーク
	82	Q98-100 問題

● 特典（ダウンロード）

Test	File No.	Contents
TEST 1	01	Part 5 Q101 問題
	02	Q102 問題
	03	Q103 問題
	04	Q104 問題
	05	Q105 問題
	06	Q106 問題
	07	Q107 問題
	08	Q108 問題

Test	File No.	Contents
TEST 1	09	Part 5 Q109 問題
	10	Q110 問題
	11	Q111 問題
	12	Q112 問題
	13	Q113 問題
	14	Q114 問題
	15	Q115 問題
	16	Q116 問題
	17	Q117 問題
	18	Q118 問題
	19	Q119 問題
	20	Q120 問題
	21	Q121 問題
	22	Q122 問題
	23	Q123 問題
	24	Q124 問題
	25	Q125 問題
	26	Q126 問題
	27	Q127 問題
	28	Q128 問題
	29	Q129 問題
	30	Q130 問題
	31	Part 6 Q131-134 問題
	32	Q135-138 問題
	33	Q139-142 問題
	34	Q143-146 問題
	35	Part 7 Q147-148 文書
	36	Q149-151 文書
	37	Q152-153 文書
	38	Q154-155 文書
	39	Q156-157 文書
	40	Q158-160 文書
	41	Q161-163 文書
	42	Q164-167 文書
	43	Q168-171 文書
	44	Q172-175 文書
	45-46	Q176-180 文書
	47-48	Q181-185 文書
	49-51	Q186-190 文書
	52-54	Q191-195 文書
	55-57	Q196-200 文書
TEST 2	58	Part 5 Q101 問題
	59	Q102 問題
	60	Q103 問題
	61	Q104 問題
	62	Q105 問題
	63	Q106 問題
	64	Q107 問題

Test	File No.	Contents
TEST 2	65	Part 5 Q108 問題
	66	Q109 問題
	67	Q110 問題
	68	Q111 問題
	69	Q112 問題
	70	Q113 問題
	71	Q114 問題
	72	Q115 問題
	73	Q116 問題
	74	Q117 問題
	75	Q118 問題
	76	Q119 問題
	77	Q120 問題
	78	Q121 問題
	79	Q122 問題
	80	Q123 問題
	81	Q124 問題
	82	Q125 問題
	83	Q126 問題
	84	Q127 問題
	85	Q128 問題
	86	Q129 問題
	87	Q130 問題
	88	Part 6 Q131-134 問題
	89	Q135-138 問題
	90	Q139-142 問題
	91	Q143-146 問題
	92	Part 7 Q147-148 文書
	93	Q149-150 文書
	94	Q151-152 文書
	95	Q153-154 文書
	96	Q155-157 文書
	97	Q158-160 文書
	98	Q161-163 文書
	99	Q164-167 文書
	100	Q168-171 文書
	101	Q172-175 文書
	102-103	Q176-180 文書
	104-105	Q181-185 文書
	106-108	Q186-190 文書
	109-111	Q191-195 文書
	112-114	Q196-200 文書

＊CDに収録の問題音声は全て、TOEIC®公式スピーカーによるものです。

＊特典音声は、CDとは別に収録したもので、標準的な北米発音を採用しています。

音声を使った学習例の紹介

『公式 *TOEIC*® Listening & Reading 問題集 8』は、付属 CD の音声の他、特典として TEST 1、2 のリーディングセクションの一部の音声を、スマートフォンや PC にダウンロードしてお聞きいただけます。以下に音声を使った公式問題集の学習法の一例をご紹介しますので、学習の参考になさってください。

準備するもの：別冊「解答・解説」（本書）、音声をダウンロードしたスマートフォンまたは PC

＊ Part 1 ～ 4 の音声は付属 CD でも聞くことができます。Part 5 ～ 7 の特典音声を含む全ての音声の利用は、abceed への会員登録（無料）とダウンロードが必要です。本誌 p. 3 の「音声ダウンロードの手順」に従ってサイトにアクセスし、『公式 *TOEIC*® Listening & Reading 問題集 8』をダウンロードしてください。リーディングの特典音声のスピードが速くて聞き取りが難しいと感じる方は、abceed のアプリなどのスピード調整機能を利用しましょう。初めのうちは 0.8 ～ 0.9 倍などで聞くことをお勧めします。

Part 1、2

1. 「解答・解説」で正解の英文の意味内容を正しく理解する。
2. 音声を聞き、発音やイントネーションをまねて音読する（リピーティング）。最初はスクリプトを見ながら行い、慣れてきたらスクリプトを見ずに行う。

> Part 1 では写真を見ながら正解の描写文だけを、Part 2 では質問と正解の応答を、音読してみましょう。自分が発話しているつもりで音読すると、表現が定着しやすくなります。

Part 3、4

1. 「解答・解説」でスクリプトの英文と訳を確認。知らない語の意味や英文の内容を把握する。
2. スクリプトを見ながら会話やトークを聞く。発話と同じスピードで英文を目で追い、即座に意味を理解できるようになるまで繰り返す。
3. スクリプトを見ずに会話やトークを聞く。聞き取りづらい箇所や意味が理解できない箇所をスクリプトで確認し、再び音声だけで理解できるか挑戦する。

> Part 3 ではスピーカー同士の関係や会話の目的、Part 4 では場面やトークの趣旨をまず把握し、徐々に理解できる範囲を増やしていくつもりで、細部の情報まで聞き取るようにしましょう。

Part 5、6

1. 「解答・解説」で英文と訳を確認。知らない語の意味や英文の内容を把握する。
2. 本書の TEST 1、2 の該当ページ(p.42-48 と p.84-90)のコピーを取り、音声を聞いて空所の語や文を書き取る。知っている語彙や文法の知識も用いて空所を埋め、書き取ったものと実際の英文を比較する。最後に、もう一度音声を聞く。

> 聞き取れない箇所は、飛ばしたりカタカナで書いたりしても構いません。音声だけに頼らず、語彙力や文法の知識を用いて挑戦してみましょう。Part 5 は短い文なので、ディクテーションするのもよいでしょう。

Part 6、7

1. 「解答・解説」で英文と訳を確認。知らない語の意味や英文の内容を把握する。その際、読み方に迷った箇所に印を付けておく。
2. 音声を聞きながら英文を目で追い（初めはスピードを遅めにしても可）、英語の語順のまま理解できるようになることを目指す。分からなかった箇所は適宜、訳を確認する。
3. 1. で印を付けた、読み方に迷った箇所の言い方を確認する。
   例：数字や記号の言い方（日付、住所、飛行機の便名、価格、URL）など。

> 1 は構文や語彙の学習、2 は速読の学習です。2 では意味のまとまりを意識しながら英文を読み進めていくようにすると、取り組みやすいでしょう。3 は、実際の会話の際にも役立つので積極的に覚えるとよいでしょう。